The Azusa Street Revival and Its Legacy

Edited By
Harold D. Hunter
& Cecil M. Robeck Jr

WIPF & STOCK · Eugene, Oregon

Wipf and Stock Publishers
199 W 8th Ave, Suite 3
Eugene, OR 97401

The Azusa Street Revival and Its Legacy
By Hunter, Harold D., and Robeck, Jr., Cecil M.
Copyright©2006 by Hunter, Harold D., and Robeck, Jr., Cecil M.
ISBN 13: 978-1-60899-154-9
Publication date 10/23/2009
Previously published by Pathway Press, 2006

Dedicated to the memory of
Dr. Robert E. Fisher

Contents

List of Contributors 11

Introduction 13
Harold D. Hunter and Cecil M. Robeck Jr.

Part I: The Azusa Street Revival: 1906-1909 27

1. **Ordinary Prophet: William J. Seymour and the Azusa Street Revival** 29
   Gastón Espinosa

2. **The Role of Women in the Azusa Street Revival** 61
   Estrelda Alexander

3. **Pentecostal Healing at the Mission** 79
   Kimberly Ervin Alexander

4. **Spiritual Hunger "on the Apostolic Faith Line"** 93
   Daniel Woods

5. **From Azusa to Cleveland: The Amazing Journey of G.B. Cashwell and the Spread of Pentecostalism** 111
   David Roebuck

6. **"Networks and Niches": The Worldwide Transmission of the Azusa Street Revival** 127
   David Maxwell

7. **What Good Can Come From Los Angeles? Changing Perceptions of the North American Pentecostal Origins in Early Western European Pentecostal Periodicals** 141
   Cornelis van der Laan

8. Azusa Missionaries in the Context of the Caste System
   in India 161
   Paulson Pulikottil

9. Revivals and the Global Expansion of Pentecostalism
   After Azusa Street 175
   Allan Anderson

10. Constructing Different Memories: Recasting the Azusa
    Street Revival 193
    Anthea Butler

Part II: The Legacy of the Azusa Street Revival 203

11. Signs of Grace in a Graceless World: The Charismatic
    Structure of the Church in Trinitarian Perspective 205
    Frank D. Macchia

12. Encountering the Triune God: Spirituality Since the
    Azusa Street Revival 215
    Simon Chan

13. Pentecostal Eschatology: What Happened When the
    Wave Hit the West End of the Ocean 229
    Wonsuk Ma

14. The Church of God in Christ and the Azusa Street Revival ... 243
    Frederick L. Ware

15. The Blessings of Azusa Street and Doornfontein Revivals and
    Pentecost's Blind Spot 259
    Frank Chikane

16. A Journey Toward Racial Reconciliation: Race Mixing in
    the Church of God of Prophecy 277
    Harold D. Hunter

17. **The "Place" of Women in Pentecostal/Charismatic
    Ministry Since the Azusa Street Revival** 297
    Pamela Holmes

18. **After Azusa Street: Identity and Function of
    Pentecostalisms in the Processes of Social Change** 317
    Bernardo Campos Morante

19. **Pentecostalism and Social Transformation** 335
    Donald E. Miller

20. **The Azusa Street Revival and the Historic Churches** 349
    Thomas P. Rausch, S.J.

Divine Mandates of the Azusa Street Revival 363

List of Contributors

Estrelda Alexander: Associate Professor of Theology, Regent University, Virginia Beach, Virginia, U.S.A.

Kimberly Ervin Alexander: Assistant Professor of Historical Theology, Church of God Theological Seminary, Tennessee, U.S.A.

Allan Anderson: Professor of Global Pentecostal Studies, University of Birmingham, United Kingdom

Anthea Butler: Assistant Professor of Religious Studies, University of Rochester, Rochester, New York, U.S.A.

Bernardo Campos Morante: Director de la Revista Pentecostalidad, Fundador de la Facultad Pentecostal de Teología y de la Red Latinoamericana de Estudios Pentecostales, Peru.

Simon Chan: Earnest Lau Professor of Systematic Theology, Trinity Theological College, Singapore

Frank Chikane: Chairperson of the Council of the AFM International; Honorary Member of the National Leadership Forum of the AFM of South Africa; and Director-General in the Presidency, Government of the Republic of South Africa

Gastón Espinosa: Assistant Professor of Religious Studies, Claremont McKenna College, Claremont, California, U.S.A.

Pamela Holmes: Th.D. Candidate, Wycliffe College, Toronto School of Theology, Toronto, Ontario, Canada

Harold D. Hunter: Director, International Pentecostal Holiness Church Archives & Research Center, Oklahoma City, Oklahoma, U.S.A.

Wonsuk Ma: Vice President for Academic Affairs, Asia Pacific Theological Seminary, Baguio, Philippines

Frank D. Macchia: Professor of Systematic Theology, Vanguard University, Costa Mesa, California, U.S.A.

David Maxwell: Senior Lecturer in History, School of History, Keele University, United Kingdom

Donald E. Miller: Professor of Religion and Director of the Center for Religion and Civic Culture, University of Southern California, Los Angeles, California, U.S.A.

Paulson Pulikottil: Assistant Professor of Biblical Studies, Union Biblical Seminary, Pune, India

Thomas P. Rausch, S.J.: T. Marie Chilton Professor of Catholic Theology, Loyola Marymount University, Los Angeles, California, U.S.A.

Cecil M. Robeck Jr.: Professor of Church History and Ecumenics and Director of the David du Plessis Center for Christian Spirituality, Fuller Theological Seminary, Pasadena, California, U.S.A.

David Roebuck: Director of the Dixon Pentecostal Research Center and Assistant Professor of Religion, Lee University, Cleveland, Tennessee, U.S.A.

Cornelis van der Laan: Professor of Pentecostal Studies, Vrije Universiteit of Amsterdam and President of Azusa Theological Seminary, the Netherlands

Frederick L. Ware: Assistant Professor of Theology, Howard University Divinity School, Washington, D.C., U.S.A.

Daniel Woods: Professor of History, Ferrum University, Ferrum, Virginia, U.S.A.

Introduction

The 20th century witnessed the birth and phenomenal growth of what is known in North America as the Classical Pentecostal Movement. Reaction in the first half of the century was almost unanimously negative from traditional church leaders, theologians, psychologists and sociologists. Many judged Pentecostals to be emotionally disturbed, mentally challenged, sociologically deprived, and concluded that the pneumatic unction claimed by Pentecostals was not genuine. Many still have not abandoned such views, and yet the ecclesiastical landscape was sufficiently rearranged by the rise of Pentecostalism during the 20th century that other traditions reevaluated their opposition to the movement. This change has been due, in no small measure, to the metamorphosis of the movement itself and to the fact that the influence of Pentecostalism is now felt in much of global Christianity. The surprise for many in the 1960s, even many Classical Pentecostals, was that their Pentecostal testimony to life lived in the power of the Holy Spirit came to be embraced by so many in the magisterial Protestant churches and the Roman Catholic Church.

Another reason that the wider Christian community has had to reckon more seriously with Pentecostalism is because of the dramatic increase in the size of the movement. When David Barrett calmly announced in his 1982 *World Christian Encyclopedia* (Oxford) that Classical Pentecostalism then constituted the largest unit within the Protestant family, many scholars and church leaders were stunned. They had no idea this was the case. Besides producing its own Classical Pentecostal denominations, the movement has also contributed to the emergence of[1] Charismatic Renewal in most historic denominations, produced a plethora of independent[2] congregations and networks, served as the forerunner to the so-called Third Wave and New Apostolic churches, and left its substantial mark on many indigenous or independent churches, especially in Africa. The impact of the Pentecostal Movement has subsequently led to claims that together, these groups constitute more than 25 percent of Christians worldwide.

Most impressive during this same period has been the impact of Pentecostalism on theological inquiry. Although the person and work of the Holy Spirit were studied in earlier centuries, particularly in churches of the East, many centuries could be characterized as treating the subject with benign neglect. The Holy Spirit was acknowledged as one person in the Holy Trinity, and was regularly invoked, but it seemed that once the invocation took place, the Holy Spirit was no longer expected to act.

*Scripture references used in this chapter are taken from the *New International Version*.

By way of contrast, during the 20th century the dam that seemed to allow but a trickle of research on the Holy Spirit in previous centuries was demolished by the emergence of the Pentecostal Movement. Once broken, the trickle of research gave way to a veritable torrent of studies. It has been argued that the Holy Spirit was the subject of more studies during the 20th century than in the previous 19 centuries. There are now lengthy bibliographies listing works on the Holy Spirit. The study of Pentecostalism, previously unheard of in non-Pentecostal institutions, is now conducted regularly at places like Harvard University (U.S.A.), the University of Cambridge (England), the Free University of Amsterdam (Netherlands), the University of South Africa (UNISA) and Trinity Theological College (Singapore). It has become increasingly clear that informed theologians, regardless of their tradition, can no longer make the Holy Spirit a mere addendum to their systems.

The April 25-29, 2006, centennial celebration of the legendary 1906-1909 revival at the Azusa Street Mission in Los Angeles, California, may provide a good benchmark for judging the evolution of the Pentecostal tradition, including its successes and its failures. It does not take much imagination to recognize that one of the most significant successes of the movement has occurred on the evangelistic and missionary front. Millions of people worldwide have been brought to faith through their efforts. They have been admonished to live lives of holiness. They have been urged to seek the power of the Holy Spirit in their lives. They have been counseled to expect God to work miracles through them. And they have been charged with discerning what God may have placed upon their lives to engage in evangelism or mission, to serve the church in ministry, or to serve the larger society in which they participate. The explosive growth that the movement has experienced is sufficient evidence of its success in this regard.

On the other hand, there have been failures that all too often have simply been ignored, swept under the proverbial rug. One of these failures involves a commitment that was highly valued and frequently publicized at the Azusa Street Mission.

"The Apostolic Faith Movement stands for the restoration of the faith once delivered unto the saints . . . and Christian Unity everywhere," the Azusa Street Mission proudly proclaimed. Sadly, the divisions that have plagued the Pentecostal Movement since that time have denied the vision for unity that Pastor William J. Seymour and others had for the movement, a vision rooted firmly in Jesus' own prayer life: "May they be brought to complete unity to let the world know that you sent me and have loved them even as you have loved me" (John 17:23).

The fact that there are so many people throughout the world who still do not choose to follow Jesus Christ should come as no surprise if their knowledge of His love for them is conditioned in any way on the unwillingness by Pentecostals to be in "complete unity" with one another, let alone other Christians.

Pentecostals are not alone in this regard, however. Legitimate questions can be raised about the dominant story line that contends that the churches stood in complete unity throughout the first 11 centuries, or that the only schism that emerged before the 16th-century Reformation was one that separated churches in the East from those in the West. The question of Christian unity is a question the whole church must address if it is not to undercut its witness to the saving and reconciling work of Jesus Christ.

Sadly, the division and disunity experienced in the Pentecostal Movement has frequently been excused in the name of independence, individualism and entrepreneurialism, or by appealing to one or another "church growth" theory, or even by claims that the latest sectarian group is the one that best preserves the truth. The tendency for Pentecostals to embrace absolute claims on the one hand and their pragmatism on the other seems all too often to move them toward sectarianism. Still, there is growing evidence that some Pentecostal bodies are beginning to engage in various forms of visible unity, including organic unity, with other Pentecostal and non-Pentecostal groups.

We think that those Pentecostals who are truest to their Azusa Street roots and to Jesus' prayer continue to seek not only spiritual renewal and the restoration of the "Apostolic Faith," but also Christian unity. It might be helpful to consider the Biblical narrative of the journey on the road to Emmaus (Luke 24:13-35), which has become a powerful metaphor for some Pentecostals in this regard.

While many Pentecostal churches are still not at the point of joining an ecumenical organization such as the World Council of Churches, they might still begin to take an "Emmaus walk," a journey of discovery with others who also name the name of Jesus. They may be willing to engage in dialogue, to learn with others, and to come to a place of understanding as Christ becomes present and the will of God, according to the Scriptures, is made manifest in their midst.

The majority of papers included in this volume were presented in an academic track of the Azusa Street Centennial Celebration. Not all invited contributors were able to meet the early deadline required to prepare this volume in time for the centennial. As the editors of this volume, we attempted to include more African-American and Latino voices than we have. We also reached out to the "oneness" community, and to scholars of Pentecostalism in the Orthodox and Protestant communities. For one reason or another, and for reasons beyond our control, they were unable to participate in this venture. Their contributions would have broadened the number of traditions and regions from which we might have heard that have been impacted by the Azusa Street Revival.

Yet clearly, the chapters in this volume have much to say about the Pentecostal and Charismatic movements as envisioned by a diverse body of scholars. The names of some of the best scholars the movement has produced to date may be found in these pages. And we are happy that interested participants joined these speakers in the academic track and this body of scholars attended other major events at the Centennial Celebration.

To help our readers find their way through these studies, we have divided this volume into two main sections. We begin with several chapters that are rooted in the history of the Azusa Street Mission itself. They tell parts of the story of what was.

In the second part, we have included chapters that show how Pentecostalism has developed in subsequent years, that is, they demonstrate something of the mission's legacy. Placement decisions have not all been easy to make. As the editors, we have weighed each contribution and hope that our readers will understand our logic.

The Azusa Street Mission in History

The first three chapters give us a glimpse of the Azusa Street Mission and two of the characteristics that made it famous. Gastón Espinosa leads off with a very helpful overview of the mission and revival that ran from 1906 to 1909. He introduces us to the pastor of the Azusa Street Mission, William J. Seymour, and places him in the contexts of post-Civil War Reconstruction, early 20th-century Progressive politics, and more specifically the ministry of Charles F. Parham, all of which helped to shape him.

Espinosa goes on to demonstrate how Seymour provided an alternative reading of the gospel from that which was so frequently proclaimed in churches around the world at the time. It was a reading of the gospel that demonstrated Seymour's "prophetic social consciousness," a consciousness that led to Seymour's lived emphasis on "racial reconciliation and multicultural, transformative, egalitarian Christianity." The fulfillment of Seymour's radical vision was only partially realized, even at Azusa Street, but its very existence demands that the Pentecostal community rethink and act upon a number of Seymour's overlooked concerns.

Estrelda Alexander has recently published a book on *The Women of Azusa Street* (Pilgrim). In this chapter, she gives us a glimpse of her larger work on women. It is impossible for those of us who are historians of the Pentecostal

Movement to overlook the incredible contribution women have made to the movement. That is doubly true for the Azusa Street Mission. Women were everywhere! They constituted the majority of participants at the mission, they were prominent in all aspects of the mission's worship services (leading music, giving testimonies, providing exhortations, prophesying and preaching sermons), and they led the way in the mission's evangelistic and missionary efforts.

The names of African-American women such as Lucy Farrow, Julia Hutchins, Ruth Asberry, Jennie Evans Moore and Ophelia Wiley; Latinas such as Rosa de López and Suzie Valdez; and Caucasians such as Florence Crawford, Clara Lum and Ivey Campbell, simply cannot be ignored. Had they not been present and played such leading roles at Azusa Street as they did, the revival would have looked much different than it did. We might even wonder whether it would have happened at all.

It has often been acknowledged that the primary message proclaimed by Pastor Seymour at the Azusa Street Mission was composed of five parts—salvation, sanctification, baptism in the Spirit, divine healing and the Second Coming. The mission's teaching on the reality of divine healing and the expectation that miracles could happen today just as they had in the New Testament were clearly cornerstones to a theology that empowered individual believers.

Kimberly Alexander provides an interesting exposition on the place of divine healing within the life of the Azusa Street Mission, reviewing issues of both faith and practice, whether it be through the practice of simple prayer prayed in childlike faith, the laying on of hands, or even the use of such things as blessed handkerchiefs. It should come as no surprise that much of the mission's theology was inherited from the Wesleyan Holiness Movement.

The Holiness group who now made up the majority of people at the Azusa Street Mission linked salvation and healing in what was called a "double cure" for a "double curse." It was rooted in Isaiah 53, and it led to a "healing in the Atonement" theology even in Pentecostal groups, such as the Assemblies of God, that do not see their origins in the Holiness Movement. This position, however, has led Professor Miroslav Volf to observe that Pentecostals have always had a strong commitment to the body, as well as the soul.

As word of the events that flooded the Los Angeles newspapers began to be published across the United States and around the world, people came by the thousands to see for themselves if the claims were true. Among the multitude of inquirers who came to Los Angeles in 1906 was Gaston Barnabas Cashwell. Two chapters are devoted to telling parts of his story because it explains how several "Holiness" denominations came to embrace the "Pentecostal" position.

Daniel Woods leads us to a feast as he paints the story of the spiritual hunger that drove Cashwell to visit the Azusa Street Mission. Upon his arrival in Los Angeles, Cashwell watched, waited and prayed, until his spiritual hunger was met in the spiritual encounter known as baptism in the Spirit. He returned to the southern United States where, beginning in late December 1906, he shared from the bounty of the Azusa Street table with pastors and church leaders alike. Woods emphasizes Cashwell's ministry in North Carolina, Virginia and Georgia, where he convinced Joseph H. King to accept the message of Azusa Street. Their meeting ultimately led to the transformation of two Holiness denominations into one Pentecostal denomination—the Fire-Baptized Holiness Church and the Pentecostal Holiness Church into what is today known as the International Pentecostal Holiness Church.

David Roebuck follows Cashwell's travels in a different direction. He sets the stage by telling about the Holiness preacher, Ambrose J. Tomlinson, and the beginnings of the Church of God (Cleveland, Tennessee). He goes on to explore Cashwell's meetings in Alabama and Tennessee, where people like M.S. Lemon, A.J. Tomlinson and W.W. Simpson were either convinced that the message was true or they came to experience what Cashwell preached.

Tomlinson's invitation of Cashwell to preach at the annual convocation of the Church of God (Cleveland, Tennessee) led the Church of God in 1908 to embrace the Pentecostal position fully. Similarly, W.W. Pinson, who was in fellowship with the Church of God in Christ at that time, helped to develop and lead a "white" section of that group from 1909 to 1914, when the Assemblies of God was formed. Together, these discussions by Woods and Roebuck put considerable meat on the bones of earlier descriptions of this important figure.

The proclamation of the Apostolic Faith did not stay only in the United States, of course. It quickly found its way around the world. Historians of the movement are currently debating various theories of history that might best explain how the Apostolic Faith made its way throughout the world. Some begin the question of Pentecostal origins with claims that it emerged first under Charles F. Parham in Topeka, Kansas, on New Year's Day 1901. Others have argued that the real origin of the Apostolic Faith as a global movement came from the Azusa Street Mission. Still others contend that it is impossible to identify a "Father" of the movement, and they rely upon a theory of "spontaneous origins," that is, they point to the emergence of such things as "glossolalia" in widespread regions of the world that sometimes predate either Parham in Topeka or Seymour in Los Angeles.

Five chapters give us information on some of the variations found in these theories. David Maxwell, a specialist on Pentecostalism throughout Africa, invites us to a study of the ways in which missionaries from the Azusa Street

Mission tapped into preexisting networks. Sometimes these were networks that shared a common teaching or a common expectation. At other times, they were social networks of somewhat like-minded friends. In the end, however, they contributed to the spread of the Pentecostal message by providing space for those who were proclaiming the Apostolic Faith to do so.

Cornelis van der Laan has long been a historian of Pentecostalism in Europe. His chapter introduces a newly identified fault line in European discussion of Pentecostal origins. The earliest story line for Pentecostalism in Europe begins with the conversion of the Norwegian pastor, Thomas Ball Barratt. In 1906, while on a trip to the United States, Barratt picked up a copy of the first issue of Azusa Street Mission's newspaper, *The Apostolic Faith*. After reading testimonies to what was happening at the mission, he wrote and asked for further information. Over a period of six to eight weeks, he made half a dozen inquiries, and the mission staff responded with specific advice and encouragement.

When Barratt learned that workers from the Azusa Street Mission were coming to New York City before departing for the mission field, he waited for their arrival. Among the first to arrive was Lucy Leatherman. Barratt quickly asked her to pray with him, and he was soon baptized in the Spirit. After three weeks, during which the rest of the missionaries arrived in New York City, Barratt worshiped with them in various churches. On December 8, 1906, they boarded the *S.S. Campania* and sailed for Liverpool, England. There, the missionaries traveled south to begin ministry in Liberia and Angola, while Barratt turned north to Norway. A revival began in Christiania (now Oslo) and quickly spread throughout Scandinavia, into the Netherlands, over to Britain where Barratt influenced the Anglican pastor A.A. Boddy, and down into Germany and Switzerland.

What Professor van der Laan has discovered is that while the Scandinavians, the Dutch and the English readily accepted the foundational role of the 1906 Azusa Street Revival in their retelling of the story, the Germans seem to have favored Charles Parham and the events of Topeka, Kansas, in 1901. He offers two reasons for this difference. In England and Scandinavia there were firsthand encounters with a variety of people of the Azusa Street Mission. In Germany, where the Holiness Movement published a document known as the *Berlin Declaration* condemning the Los Angeles origins of Pentecostalism, Pentecostals sought to distance themselves from Los Angeles. They found support in this from the pen of Thomas Atteberry, a Los Angeles pastor who, in reaction to criticisms raised by Parham, sided with Parham's claim that he was the founder of Pentecostalism.

Paulson Pulikottil turns our attention to the subcontinent of India, which played a significant role in the thinking of many at the Azusa Street Mission. Indeed, the first missionaries commissioned by the Azusa Street Mission were A.G. and Lillian Garr, missionaries to India. Pulikottil explores the role played by three types of "Azusa Street" missionaries in India, and notes that glossolalia was already present among Indian believers at the time of the Azusa Street Revival. He recounts the coming of Catholic and Protestant missionaries to India and suggests that the spiritual formation of the earliest Pentecostal missionaries to India led to substantial differences in their success with the Indians, especially among those at the lowest end of the caste system, the Dalits. Their stress on evangelization, racial equality and the baptism of love made them innovators on the field and made it possible for their message to be heard.

Allan Anderson gives us a global perspective once again, when he calls our attention to revivals that emerged in places as diverse as Wales, India and Korea, about the same time as the revival at the Azusa Street Mission appeared. These revivals had many essential things in common. Like Maxwell and Pulikottil, he draws attention to the networks that aided these revivals or emerged from these revivals, and concludes that while the Azusa Street Revival may not have been unique, or even seminal, its contribution to global Pentecostal, Charismatic and independent church life is still undeniable.

Finally, we hear from Anthea Butler. Each of the previous four chapters have raised questions in one way or another about the central role the Azusa Street Mission actually played in the origins of Pentecostalism. Butler brings us back to a discussion that has often been overlooked. In essence, she wonders whether those who raise the question from outside the United States actually understand what that claim means. Are they simply engaged in "American bashing" so that what is indisputably a global movement can be seen as having global origins? Are they simply reacting to the often triumphalistic ways in which American Pentecostals speak about Pentecostalism as their gift to the world might be blunted?

In her chapter, Butler tries to explain how African-Americans, as opposed to white Americans, must view the Azusa Street Revival. If Pastor Seymour's concerns are taken at face value, she maintains, then Azusa Street had a message to the dominant white culture in the United States and an equally radical message for the dominant black-church culture. She explores the details of this radical message and explains that the centrality of Azusa Street for the global Pentecostal Movement is as important as it has ever been.

The Legacy of the Azusa Street Mission

In the second half of this volume, we have gathered together those chapters that seem to speak more centrally to the legacy of the Azusa Street Mission and its three-year revival. In some cases, they tell us how the Pentecostal Movement came to be what it is today. In other cases, they simply reflect on the contemporary situation. Several of these chapters include a historical dimension, but the majority of these chapters, including those that appeal first to history, are largely theological, ethical and practical in their orientation.

The first four chapters in this section deal with theology and spirituality. Frank Macchia begins this section with his claims that a substantial part of the legacy of the Azusa Street Revival was its appeal to the legitimate, ongoing place of God's charismata in the life of the church. Quite pointedly, he has titled his chapter, "Signs of Grace in a Graceless World." He notes that while the world is infused with God's grace, that grace is not always easily recognized. Yet God has given *charismata* (gifts of the Spirit), which are clear manifestations of grace, and through these manifestations, the church is opened up to see God's grace in the world. The inherent relational and interactive character of the charismata contributes substantially to the structure of the church, and bring new meaning to both word and sacrament. In this way, Macchia demonstrates the inherently countercultural and radical vision that Pentecostal spirituality promises through their experience of genuine *koinonia*, fellowship.

Some very interesting theology is currently flowing from the pens of Pentecostal theologians from what most North Americans still look at as missionary fields—Asia, Africa and Latin America. Among these Asian scholars is Simon Chan. Chan has long wrestled with the form and content of what constitutes Pentecostal spirituality. He argues that a genuine Pentecostal spirituality requires a distinctive understanding of the Holy Spirit. He examines the works of another Asian (now American), Amos Yong, as well as the work of C. Peter Wagner. But Chan goes on to argue that Pentecostal spirituality needs to be written as part of a larger traditioning process that takes seriously what has come before, faces the past with a sense of realism rather than romanticism, and points Pentecostals toward a future in which they take the world seriously.

The doctrine of eschatology has played, and continues to play, a significant role in Pentecostal life and spirituality. At the beginning of the movement, eschatology motivated many to engage in evangelistic and missionary activity. If Jesus were coming soon, they contended, they were under a divine mandate to spread around the world and carry the Apostolic Faith message of life and power to those who would otherwise be lost. As time has passed, though, eschatological expectations have changed.

Wonsuk Ma, another Asian and a Biblical scholar, addresses not only the arrival of this primitive understanding of eschatology on the western shores of the Pacific, but what has happened in Asia to the very idea of eschatology since then. It has been transformed from an other-worldly reality to a this-world reality in ways far different than Azusa Street missionaries might have imagined. While this change has produced a number of positive results, Ma notes that it has some weaknesses as well. In this chapter, he educates Western scholars to the nuances in the treatment of this subject in Asian life. He also calls Asian readers to reevaluate their own position, and to do so within a global discussion.

Finally, the Church of God in Christ theologian, Frederick Ware, surveys five theological distinctives he has identified as being present at the Azusa Street Mission. They include the interracial, ecumenical, egalitarian character of its *koinonia*; the ecstatic character of its worship; the theory that views tongues as the Biblical sign of baptism in the Holy Spirit; its understanding of divine healing; and eschatology. He then looks at the Church of God in Christ, the largest Pentecostal group in North America, and shows how the Church of God in Christ has attempted to perpetuate these concerns. Finally, Ware sets forth a series of choices that the denomination must face if it hopes to continue to present a living spirituality to a new generation.

If Pentecostal teaching and spirituality has brought liberation to millions of believers around the world, it has also pointed to places where bondage continues to exist. William J. Seymour was committed to an egalitarian interpretation of the Apostolic Faith. The prophet Joel (2:28-32) had prophesied that God's Spirit would be poured out on *all flesh*—male and female, rich and poor, old and young, slave or free.

The apostle Peter acknowledged (Acts 2:14-21) that the Spirit had been poured out on the Day of Pentecost in direct fulfillment of Joel's prophecy. Like most Pentecostals at the beginning of the 20th century, William J. Seymour preached that what was happening at the Azusa Street Mission was exactly of the same order. The difference between him and many around him was the fact that he actually believed what he preached, and he acted repeatedly to provide space for a completely egalitarian ministry at the Azusa Street Mission.

Seymour attempted to balance the tightrope between fanaticism and wildfire on the one hand, and what he believed to be dead formalism on the other. He also took the Bible quite literally when it came to the empowerment of the Spirit. That meant for him that there would be no discrimination based upon gender, race, class, previous condition of servitude or age. Unfortunately, most Pentecostals around the world are still guilty of submitting to one or another of these artificial and culturally conditioned limitations.

Three chapters draw us into the thick of discussions that look at two such limitations. Frank Chikane is an extremely important voice for Pentecostalism.

Long before he reached his current status as director-general for the office of the presidency in South Africa, he was a minister in the Apostolic Faith Mission of South Africa and a first-rate theologian who spoke out against apartheid on behalf of the oppressed. His commitment to the full equality of the races cost him dearly, with periods of imprisonment and torture. It is not surprising that we asked him to speak of the value of Azusa Street for Pentecostalism in South Africa. Chikane begins his story with the arrival of Azusa Street missionaries John G. Lake and Thomas Hezmalhalch. Together they founded the Apostolic Faith Mission of South Africa. Hezmalhalch was its first president, and after a short term, he returned to the United States and was succeeded by John G. Lake.

One of the sad stories to emerge from South Africa is the strong suggestion that Lake appeared before a committee of the South African parliament and allegedly suggested that South African whites might adopt a policy similar to that of the United States government's policy on Native Americans, that is, that the situation in South Africa might be helped if South African blacks were placed on reservations. The verdict is still out on the full story with respect to Lake's involvement in this discussion, but we do know that he viewed the African blacks as having a status lower than that of American blacks.

In his essay, Chikane points out, at Doornfontein, the Spirit fell on blacks and whites alike, just as the Spirit had fallen at Azusa Street. Equality was part of the initial impact of the falling of the Spirit in both places. In a short time, however, the Apostolic Faith message of racial equality and egalitarianism was ravaged in both places by those who refused to give up their racism. Chikane goes on to challenge the Pentecostal Movement to face the blind spot it seems to possess over this history. He does not stop there, however, but challenges Pentecostals to embrace a new way of looking at the world around them. Instead of being reactive to social problems, as they typically are, Pentecostals are encouraged to live their Pentecostal spirituality, taking contemporary social issues for what they are, and contribute to their resolution. This suggestion is clearly in keeping with one of Seymour's favorite passages of Scripture, Luke 4:18, 19. While many white Pentecostals, especially in North America, have traditionally tended to spiritualize this passage, Pentecostals of color and most Pentecostals outside North America tend to interpret this text in the same way Seymour did: quite literally.

In the second of three essays, the issue of racism is once again addressed, this time by Harold Hunter. While Chikane has written on South African racism in early Pentecostalism and during the time of the former apartheid regime, Hunter addresses the question as it was treated during the Jim Crow era in the United States. If Seymour raised the issue of racial reconciliation during this Jim Crow era, and he provided a practical example at the Azusa Street Mission on how it could work, A.J. Tomlinson also saw the inevitable implications like those about which Seymour preached regarding racial division and how he worked to incorporate African-Americans and Latinos alike, first into the Church of God, and later into the Church of God of Prophecy. Hunter spells out the visionary leadership of Tomlinson who, like Seymour, attempted to provide space for all who had been baptized in the Spirit and called into ministry—regardless of color. The task was not always easy, but his struggle to complete it adds to the success of Seymour's vision of racial equality as Pentecostals in North America continue to work toward the elimination of racism in its midst.

The second limitation that denies the universal character of the outpouring of the Spirit at Pentecost has to do with the role of women in the Pentecostal Movement. We have seen in the first section of this volume the fact that women played a very significant role at the Azusa Street Mission. In this second section, Pamela Holmes surveys the history of how women have functioned, and continue to function, in both Canadian and American Pentecostalism. She carefully introduces the reader to the range of contemporary theological terms (feminist, womanist and *mujerista* [Latino feminist]), and explains how the insights gained from such studies may help Pentecostals strengthen the hand of women that God has undoubtedly graced to lead. Holmes encourages Pentecostals to throw off the yokes that have been placed upon so many of their women—yokes that have been taken on from sources that have never been supportive of any part of the Pentecostal agenda.

The visions as well as the limitations found in Pentecostal spirituality point clearly to the need for Pentecostals to think much more seriously than they have in the past about the socially transformative role Pentecostalism has been called to play in the world today. Two chapters explore the role of Pentecostalism in issues of social transformation. The first of these comes from the Peruvian Pentecostal theologian, Bernardo Campos, who thinks seriously about the place, not only of the Spanish conquerors of the region, but also of the interests of the indigenous peoples.

For two decades, Campos has been a leader in such Pentecostal discussions throughout Latin America. Often provocative, but always thoughtful, like the majority of Latin American Pentecostal theologians in Latin America today, Campos links the success of Pentecostalism in Latin America to its ability to address questions of social change. In his chapter, Campos begins with a survey of the contemporary sociological conversation in the region. He goes on to survey four ways of analyzing the contribution of Pentecostalism to social change.

His final section draws together much of the previous discussion, where he suggests that the trauma the indigenous peoples suffered when their social, cultural, economic, political and religious worlds were violated by the Spanish invasion produced a "memory" that has damaged their psyche, producing what he calls a "collective religious anxiety." Pentecostalism, he argues, is but the latest in a string of potential remedies that has come their way, but it has been a powerful one in the alleviating of the Amerindian religious anxiety.

Donald Miller is a sociologist of religion who has spent considerable time looking at Pentecostal/Charismatic groups over the years. In one of his most recent studies, he found that over 90 percent of the fast-growing, socially active, indigenous, self-sustaining works in the developing world were of a type he has chosen to call "Progressive Pentecostalism." Over a period of four years, he and his colleague, Tetsunao Yamamori, traveled to a number of these churches. Miller's conclusions may surprise many North Americans by their innovation, organization, embrace of technology and success. In light of his findings throughout the developing world, which include the depth of a variety of social, cultural and political crises, he challenges Pentecostals to tap the resources available in the vision of Azusa Street to meet these needs.

Finally, Thomas Rausch, S.J. explores the impact of the Azusa Street Revival and the faithfulness of the Pentecostal testimony through years on the historic churches. In particular, he focuses on the growth of the Catholic Charismatic Renewal, which today claims 100 million participants. This renewal has taken many forms around the world and some of these have become points of light in countries where formal religious practice has become largely a thing of the past.

Rausch takes this opportunity to speak frankly about some of the problems that so frequently torment Pentecostal-Catholic relations, but he also sees them as a source of encouragement. In some cases, the challenges brought by one group have caused the other to change. Clearly, much of the worship accomplished in Catholic churches today is a far cry from what it was before the arrival of the Charismatic Renewal. He also points to the International Catholic-Pentecostal Dialogue, begun in 1972, as a source of hope for the future.

Concluding Observations

This volume was first envisioned by Dr. Robert E. Fisher, executive director of the Center for Spiritual Renewal in Cleveland, Tennessee. He is the grandson of Elmer K. Fisher, pastor of the Upper Room Mission in Los Angeles, friend to William J. Seymour, and frequent preacher at the Azusa Street Mission. With the beginning of the third millennium after the earthly ministry of the Lord, and as the year 2006 loomed on the horizon, Dr. Fisher began to explore the possibility of offering some suitable celebration of the event. He was deeply moved by the testimony of William J. Seymour and equally touched by the realization that much of Seymour's vision—indeed, the vision of the Azusa Street Mission—had, in the end, not been realized. Before his death, October 3, 2005, he began to draw Pentecostal and Charismatic leaders together in gatherings he called simply "Together Again."

Dr. Fisher raised the question of what might provide a suitable celebration that would not be overly triumphalistic in its conception. He wanted it to act as a benchmark for measuring the current state of the 20th-century outpouring of the Spirit and point the resulting movement to some kind of positive, future action *together*. It was out of these discussions that the idea of the "Azusa Street Centennial" event was born. It was scheduled for April 25-29, 2006.

Fisher viewed this centennial as an opportunity to change the way Pentecostals and Charismatics have gone about some things. He had great hope that they might be able to lay down some of their distrust and animosity, their sectarianism. He was strongly motivated to see that racism, in particular, would be addressed and ended within this movement of the Spirit. And he believed that not only church leaders and laity should have something to say at this meeting, but that they should listen to their scholars as they spoke of the Azusa Street Revival and its legacy to the 21st century. To this end, we were asked not only to edit this volume, but to participate with Dr. Fisher in the writing and editing of a number of what he called "Divine Mandates"—statements that we believe best represent what was believed and taught in the Azusa Street Revival. As we did so, we came to see that many of the mandates associated with the original revival can be tied to the verb *liberate*. That arises from the fact that at the Azusa Street Mission, the teaching that the charismatic dimension of the Holy Spirit brought liberation from sin, sickness and divisions based on class, race, gender or age was a fact of daily life. It was demonstrated regularly in the practice of the mission. As we close this introduction, we encourage our readers to look at each one of these mandates, and ask themselves in what way they might be able to contribute to the fulfillment of these mandates.

Harold D. Hunter
Cecil M. Robeck Jr.

Part I
The Azusa Street Revival: 1906-1909

1

Ordinary Prophet

William J. Seymour and the Azusa Street Revival

Gastón Espinosa

"Weird Babel of Tongues" read the headlines of the *Los Angeles Times* on April 18, 1906. The "night is made hideous . . . by the howlings of the worshipers who spend hours swaying back and forth in a nerve-racking attitude of prayer and supplication," the reporter vividly recounted. An "old colored exhorter" with a "stony optic" and "big fist" preached the "wildest theories" and "mad excitement" to his large multiracial crowd for almost an hour.

After his exhortation, he invited people to join in what must have seemed like a never-ending merry-go-round of song, prayer and testimony. Pandemonium broke loose, the reporter claimed, when the "old colored exhorter," named William J. Seymour, urged the "sisters" in the audience to let the "tongues come forth." No sooner had the words left his mouth than tongues burst forth from an "old colored 'mammy' " who began swinging her arms and shouting "You-oo-oo goo-loo-oo boo-loo. . . ."

It was the "strangest harangue . . . and most outrageous jumble of syllables I had ever heard," the reporter squealed. While strange tongues gushed forth from one "sister," another jumped up from her wooden pew and began to unleash a torrent of unintelligible words. This "weird babel of tongues," the participants later claimed, was evidence that the primitive New Testament church was being restored back to its original apostolic purity.

The reporter was shocked by the incessant "howling" and enthusiastic singing he heard blasting out of the Apostolic Faith Mission in an "old tumbled-down shack" at 312 Azusa Street. He had entered into what must have seemed like another world—a place where carnival, anarchy and the supernatural all collided. Flabbergasted by the claims of these "end-times" saints and exhausted by what must have seemed like a roller-coaster ride without brakes, the reporter conceded that although Los Angeles was home to almost numberless creeds, this "new sect of fanatics" surpassed them all.[1]

The Social and Religious Context of the Azusa Street Revival

The newspaper reporter's racialized yellow journalistic reaction to Seymour's "weird babel of tongues" at Azusa Street reflected the sentiment of the age. The Progressive Era (1870-1920) was a period of tremendous social change. The rise of a new middle class and decline of rural island communities created an impersonal society. Industrialization, mechanization, the clock, the Model-T Ford, and the influx of millions of southern Europeans, Asians and Latin American immigrants all created tremendous social upheaval. The middle-class response was a search for order that stressed continuity and regularity, administration and management, functionality and rationality, and the centralization of authority. *Suppression and control* were key ingredients in the psycho-social makeup of the Progressive Era.[2] The revival seemed to challenge these ingredients.

The vast majority of Protestant denominations in the United States embraced the new middle-class values and ethos of the era. The new scientific interpretation of Christianity and the Bible was gaining ground not only in Christian Liberalism but also in Evangelical/Fundamentalist Christianity, with its emphasis on commonsense realism.[3] While Christian Liberalism was outright skeptical of most supernatural truth claims, Evangelicalism/Fundamentalism criticized selected supernatural manifestations such as speaking in tongues

---

[1] "Weird Babel of Tongues," *Los Angeles Times,* April 18, 1906: 1. (*The Apostolic Faith* newspaper, published by William J. Seymour and the Azusa Street Revival, will be referred to as *AF.*)

[2] Robert H. Wiebe, *The Search for Order, 1877-1920* (New York: Hill and Wang, 1967) viii, 56, 76-77, 83.

[3] George M. Marsden, *Fundamentalism and American Culture: The Shaping of Twentieth-Century Evangelicalism, 1870-1925* (New York: Oxford UP, 1980) 15-16, 62, 215-21.

and other ecstatic experiences. This kind of criticism is best exemplified by B.B. Warfield's classic book, *Counterfeit Miracles*.[4] Its interpretation of history and religion tended to denigrate what it considered primitive social arrangements and religious practices, especially those associated with supernatural, miraculous, and ecstatic experiences.[5]

Those in society who were either unready or unwilling to embrace this new ethos found solace and meaning in the growing number of metaphysical, occult, and new religious movements, and in sectarian Protestant traditions advertising their wares in the national religious marketplace. In short, people had choices.[6] Generally, however, their choices lay between a more orderly and rationalistic approach to religion and an intensely personal and supernatural one represented by metaphysical/occult traditions such as Spiritualism.[7]

The birth of Pentecostalism provided a third new alternative that navigated between the polarities of hyperrationality and ecstatic supernaturalism, one that simultaneously offered the trappings of historic Christianity and experiential religion. I argue that Seymour was an ordinary prophet whose prophetic social consciousness and theology of racial reconciliation and multicultural, transformative, egalitarian Christianity created an alternative vision and message that challenged the American church and society to live up to its professed ideals of unity in Christ and liberty and justice for all.

Charles Fox Parham and the Origins of the Pentecostal Movement in the United States

The genealogical roots of Pentecostalism are hotly debated.[8] Although its origins were clearly shaped by 19th-century black–slave religion and black-and-white Holiness, Keswick, dispensational premillennialism, and divine healing movements, it is generally accepted that modern Pentecostalism, now

---

[4] B.B. Warfield, *Counterfeit Miracles* (Carlisle, PA: Banner of Truth, 1918).

[5] Eric Sharpe, *Comparative Religion: A History* (La Salle, IL: Open Court, 1994) 48-49, 54, 56, 94-95, 166.

[6] Sandra Sizer Frankiel, *California's Spiritual Frontiers: Religious Alternatives in Anglo-Protestantism, 1850-1910* (Berkeley, CA: U of California P, 1988).

[7] Ann Braude, *Radical Spirits: Spiritualism and Women's Rights in Nineteenth-Century America* (Boston: Beacon, 1989).

[8] For a discussion of the origins of Pentecostalism, see Walter J. Hollenweger, *The Pentecostals* (Peabody, MA: Hendrickson, 1988) 22-28; Grant Wacker, *Heaven Below: Early Pentecostals and American Culture* (Cambridge, MA: Harvard UP, 2001); Robert M. Anderson, *Vision of the Disinherited: The Making of American Pentecostalism* (Peabody, MA: Hendrickson, 1992) 28-78; Donald W. Dayton, *Theological Roots of Pentecostalism* (Metuchen, NJ: Scarecrow, 1987).

a worldwide movement numbering over 525 million people on six continents, began in the United States in the early 20th century.[9] Many credit the slightly built, eccentric, red-haired evangelist Charles F. Parham (1873-1929) and the black Holiness minister William J. Seymour (1870-1922) as two of its key founders.[10]

Charles Parham was the first person to preach the distinctive Pentecostal doctrine that speaking in unknown tongues is the physical evidence of the baptism with the Holy Spirit. His pre-Pentecostal religious experiences had a tremendous impact on his theology. He was born in Muscatine, Iowa, on June 4, 1873. As a child, he suffered from a virus that stunted his growth and left him looking handsome, but dwarf-like in appearance. Plagued by rheumatic fever, Parham and his mother moved to the wheat fields of Kansas in 1878. Upon his mother's death in 1885, Parham vowed to see her one day in heaven and converted to Protestantism in a Congregational church in town.

As his newfound faith took root, he began wrestling with the idea of becoming a minister. Pushing the idea aside in favor of becoming a medical doctor, Parham entered Southwest Kansas College around 1890. But another severe bout of rheumatic fever made him abandon his "worldly calling." He interpreted the illness as God telling him to give up medicine and become a minister. Dropping out of college in 1893, he assumed the pastorate of two small Methodist churches in Kansas. There he became enamored with the Holiness Movement and its belief in divine healing—something which always seemed to elude him. The Holiness Movement began as a renewal movement primarily in the Methodist church in the 1860s and 1870s. It emphasized complete sanctification and moral perfection in this life and was popularized through the writings of Phoebe Palmer, Charles Finney and Hannah Whitall Smith. After the Methodist church expelled the Holiness Movement from its ranks in 1895, Parham along with 100,000 other Holiness-Methodists left and began their own independent ministries.[11]

---

[9] Dayton, *Theological Roots*. Wacker, *Heaven Below*. Anderson, *Vision of the Disinherited*. Douglas J. Nelson, "For Such a Time as This: The Story of Bishop William J. Seymour and the Azusa Street Revival, A Search for Pentecostal/Charismatic Roots" (Ph.D. diss., U of Birmingham, England, 1981). For the statistical figure, see Wacker, *Heaven Below*, 8.

[10] To date the best book-length biographies on Charles Parham and William Seymour are as follows: James R. Goff Jr., *Fields White Unto Harvest: Charles F. Parham and the Missionary Origins of Pentecostalism* (Fayetteville, AR: The U of Arkansas P, 1988); Nelson, "For Such a Time as This"; and Larry Martin, *The Life and Ministry of William J. Seymour* (Joplin, MO: Christian Life, 1999).

[11] Goff, *Fields White Unto Harvest*, 16, 18-37. James Goff, "Parham, Charles Fox," in *Dictionary of Pentecostal and Charismatic Movements*, ed. Stanley M. Burgess and Gary

In 1896, Parham married Sarah Thistlethwaite, a Quaker. Her grandfather, David, had a profound influence on the 23-year-old Kansan. He persuaded the impressionable Parham to reject the traditional belief in hell, water baptism and mandatory church membership. During this same period, Parham began to crystallize his views on white supremacy and other unorthodox theological positions. Like many Midwestern white Protestants of his day, he embraced the British-Israelite theory, which claimed that the Anglo-Saxon race was the lineal descendant of the 10 lost tribes of Israel who had settled in Britain. His British-Israelite theory gave him a sacred genealogy by which to support Manifest Destiny, Jim Crow segregation, the Ku Klux Klan, and white supremacy. Like many of his contemporaries, Parham saw no major contradiction in mixing racism with Christianity.[12]

The year 1897 was a turning point in Parham's life for two reasons: his first child was born and he claims he was miraculously healed of heart disease. From this time on, he became a faith healer and preached that medicine came from the devil. Not wanting to waste any time before Christ's imminent return to earth, the restless Parham opened up Bethel Healing Home in Topeka, Kansas, and started a Holiness periodical called *The Apostolic Faith*. The year was 1898. Two years later in the summer of 1900, Parham and eight of his students traveled across the country, visiting prominent Holiness centers like Alexander Dowie's Zion City in Illinois, A.B. Simpson's Nyack College in New York, and Frank Sandford's Shiloh commune in Maine. Parham stayed at the Sandford's commune for six weeks.

After soaking up Sandford's Holiness teaching and stories about foreign missionaries speaking in tongues (*xenolalia*, the ability to speak in a human language one has never studied), Parham became convinced that Christ's second coming would not take place until after a worldwide religious revival. Tongues, Parham believed, were the key to world evangelization because they enabled people to preach to "pagans" in their own language without having to waste valuable time studying a foreign language. Energized by his newfound theology, Parham returned to Kansas, where he started Topeka Bible School on October 16, 1900. He opened the school to prepare his followers for the imminent outpouring of the Holy Spirit and Christian missions.[13] Little did he know that they were about to make history.

B. McGee, with Patrick H. Alexander, assoc. ed. (Grand Rapids: Zondervan, 1988), 660-61. Anderson, *Vision of the Disinherited*, 47-52.

[12] Hollenweger, *The Pentecostals*, 22. Goff, *Fields White Unto Harvest*, 107-11, 131-32. Goff, "Parham, Charles Fox," 660-61.

[13] Goff, *Fields White Unto Harvest*, 38-39, 57-59. Goff, "Parham, Charles Fox," 660-61. Anderson, *Vision of the Disinherited*, 52-61.

The Pentecostal Movement began when Parham challenged his students to search the Bible for evidence of the baptism with the Holy Spirit. According to Pentecostal tradition, on New Year's Day 1901, Miss Agnes Ozman (1870-1937), a student of Parham's, received the "gift of tongues" (ecstatic utterances) after he prayed that she might receive the baptism with the Holy Spirit.[14]

Ozman claimed that the Holy Spirit gave her the ability to speak Chinese. Three days later, 12 more students were baptized with the Holy Spirit and allegedly spoke in different languages.[15] From that time on, Parham became convinced that speaking in tongues was the initial, physical evidence of the baptism with the Holy Spirit. Parham also taught that in the New Testament Book of Acts, speaking in tongues accompanied all known instances of the baptism with the Spirit and should thus be a normative experience for all true Christians.[16]

Parham's controversial beliefs and aggressive proselytism attracted sharp criticism from the otherwise mild-mannered Kansans. The local press ridiculed his Bible school, calling it the "Tower of Babel." Some of Parham's own students called him a fake. The storm of controversy that erupted over his newfound beliefs prompted him to flee Topeka in April 1901. With his Bible school disintegrating and his foes attacking him on all sides, Parham retreated from the world he sought to convert—at least for a short while. His ministry was reignited by his powerful revival meetings two years later in Galena, Kansas. The rough and tumble mining region of Galena was ripe for Parham's message of divine healing and spiritual empowerment. Thousands converted to his fledgling Apostolic Faith Movement. Emboldened by his recent campaigns in Kansas, Parham cast his eyes south to Texas. He and his roving bands of tongues speakers invaded Houston, Texas, in 1905. In October, he opened the Houston Bible School. It became a new base of operation and training ground for his Pentecostal "shock troops."[17]

In December 1905, the fledgling Pentecostal Movement took a decisive turn. That month, a 35-year-old, unschooled, black Holiness preacher named William J. Seymour asked Parham if he could attend Houston Bible School. Parham, a white supremacist and strong supporter of Jim Crow segregation, agreed but only on the condition that Seymour take notes outside the classroom in the hallway. Seymour reluctantly agreed to the condition and spent the next

---

[14] For an alternative chronology of events, see Anderson, *Vision of the Disinherited*, 56.

[15] "The Pentecostal Baptism Restored: The Promised Latter Rain Now Being Poured Out on God's Humble People," *AF,* Oct. 1906: 1. Goff, *Fields White Unto Harvest,* 40-41, 44-49, 66-85.

[16] Goff, "Parham, Charles Fox," 660-61.

[17] Anderson, *Vision of the Disinherited,* 57-59. Goff, "Parham, Charles Fox," 660-61.

few weeks listening carefully to Parham's controversial teachings. Although he embraced Parham's view that baptism with the Holy Spirit was evidenced by speaking in tongues, he rejected his belief in white supremacy, Jim Crow segregation and annihilationism. Seymour also rejected Parham's theories that miscegenation caused Noah's flood and that the Anglo-Saxon race was lineally descended from the 10 lost tribes of Israel and therefore God's chosen race.[18]

A classic opportunist and careful propagandist, Parham likely saw the hardworking and mild-mannered Seymour as a way to reach the vast throngs of blacks in Houston and the Deep South. After conducting joint services with Parham among blacks, Seymour recognized that Parham's vision of Pentecostalism differed from his own. Parham's version of Pentecostalism was egalitarian only in the areas of class, education and, in some respects, gender. Seymour, on the other hand, believed that the outpouring of the Holy Spirit and tongues should break down all unbiblical racial, class, educational, social, denominational and gender barriers of the day.[19] His central message was love and born-again transformation, not tongues or eschatology.

In late December, Seymour's opportunity to break out of Parham's sphere of influence came when Mrs. Neely Terry asked Seymour to become a candidate for the pastorate of her home church in Los Angeles. Seymour jumped at the opportunity, even though Parham admonished him to remain in Texas and preach among his "own kind." Seymour insisted that he had to follow God's leading and go to California.

By invoking God, Seymour "pulled rank" on Parham, the only way he could alter the unequal power relationship. Although not entirely happy about Seymour's divine "calling," Parham gave his blessing and even financed part of Seymour's trip after he heard that he would be preaching his message among blacks in Los Angeles. Parham's patronage left Seymour in his debt. Seymour left Texas for California in January 1906.[20] Had Parham known the future, he would have done all he could to have stopped Seymour from going West.

The Birth of an Ordinary Prophet: The Life and Times of William J. Seymour

William J. Seymour was an unlikely prophet and even more unlikely founder of a global religious movement. The son of slaves, the 5-foot-9-inch Seymour

---

[18] H.A. Goss, "Reminiscences of an Eyewitness," *The Weekly Evangel,* Mar. 4, 1916: 4-5. Goff, *Fields White Unto Harvest,* 107-9. Nelson, "For Such a Time as This," 209, 267.

[19] Nelson, "For Such a Time as This," 11-13.

[20] Nelson, 37, 55.

was born to Simon and Phyllis Salabar Seymour in Centerville, Louisiana, on May 2, 1870. Brought up in the Deep South during Reconstruction, Seymour was keenly aware of both his theoretical Fourteenth Amendment "freedom" and the ugly reality of Southern racism. Although little is known about his childhood, we do know that in the early 1890s, like thousands of blacks after him, Seymour left the South and journeyed north to Memphis, Tennessee; St. Louis, Missouri; and then on to Indianapolis, Indiana, around 1900 along the trail of the old Underground Railroad.

There he attended the all-black Simpson Chapel Methodist Episcopal Church, which was part of the larger white Northern Methodist Episcopal denomination. Over the next couple of years he moved on to Chicago and then to Cincinnati, Ohio, in search of a color-blind society. In Cincinnati, he joined Daniel S. Warner's Evening Light Saints (later, Church of God Reformation Movement). This socially progressive, radical Holiness group preached racial equality at the height of Jim Crow segregation and aggressively reached out to blacks. While with the Saints, Seymour received his call from God to go into the ministry and his first vision of a racially egalitarian church.[21]

After resisting the divine call to ministry for a few years, Seymour gave in to what he interpreted as the will of God after suffering a bout with smallpox that almost cost him his life. With his face permanently scarred and now blind in his left eye, Seymour was ordained an evangelist by the Evening Light Saints. A few years later, Seymour traveled to Texas in search of his relatives, with whom his family had lost contact during the days of slavery. In Houston he found not only his lost relatives but also Pentecostalism. While there he joined a Holiness church pastored by a former slave, Lucy Farrow, the niece of Frederick Douglass. After becoming governess of Parham's growing family, Farrow asked Seymour to take over her church until she returned. It was while pastoring Farrow's church that Seymour met Parham and was later invited to Los Angeles.[22]

Traveling in a segregated railroad car to California, Seymour dreamed of a new life and ministry in California. Soon after his arrival at the Holiness mission on Santa Fe Street in Los Angeles, he began preaching Parham's doctrine that baptism with the Holy Spirit must be accompanied by speaking in unknown tongues. Conflict erupted almost immediately when he began preaching that although he had never personally spoken in tongues, speaking in tongues should be practiced by all true Christians of his day. Julia Hutchins was shocked by Seymour's "heretical" claims. Acting as the new interim leader

---

[21] Nelson, 33, 35. Martin, *Life and Ministry of William J. Seymour*, 65-73.

[22] Nelson, "For Such a Time as This," 33, 35.

of the mission, she sought to silence Seymour. On the fifth night of Seymour's candidacy, she padlocked the door and forced Seymour to leave the mission. Penniless and without a place to stay, Seymour turned hat-in-hand to Ed Lee, a black member of Hutchins's congregation. Not having the heart to turn a black man out on the streets of white Los Angeles, Lee agreed to let Seymour stay at his home until Seymour could raise train fare back to Texas. He did so despite his skepticism about Seymour's outlandish claims. Over the course of the next few months, the Lees were struck by Seymour's spirituality, grasp of theology, humility and persuasive abilities. Shortly after this conflict, Richard and Ruth Asbery asked Seymour to conduct a prayer meeting for revival at their home on 214 North Bonnie Brae Street, in the black Temple district of Los Angeles.[23]

Birth and Setting of the Azusa Street Revival

On April 6, 1906, Seymour led the small interracial prayer group on a 10-day fast for spiritual revival. Four days into the fast, on April 9, Pentecostal tradition has it that "the fire came down," meaning that God had poured out the Holy Spirit on the Bonnie Brae participants as on the Day of Pentecost in the Book of Acts. Some eyewitnesses claimed that tongues of fire swirled around the room and above the heads of the band of "prayer warriors." Ed Lee was the first person to speak in tongues. Later, Ms. Jeannie Evans Moore (Seymour's future wife) was also baptized with the Holy Spirit and later allegedly spoke in six languages—Spanish, French, Latin, Greek, Hebrew and Hindustani—none of which she knew prior to that night.[24] This supernatural event attracted a growing host of curious and spiritually hungry washerwomen, cooks, laborers, janitors, ministers and housewives.[25] A fire had been ignited that would spread around the world.

The Bonnie Brae Street prayer meetings began on Monday, April 9, 1906. The growing throngs of parched souls and curious onlookers forced Seymour to move his small interracial flock to the former Stevens African Methodist Episcopal Church at 312 Azusa Street. The first meeting at Azusa Street took place on Saturday, April 14, 1906.

The Stevens African Methodist Episcopal Church was built in 1888 and abandoned in 1903. Seriously damaged by fire, the dilapidated 40-by-60-foot,

---

[23] Charles W. Shumway, "A Critical History of 'The Gift of Tongues' " (A.B. diss., U of Southern California, 1914) 173. "Mother" Emma Cotton, "Inside Story of the Outpouring of the Holy Spirit, Azusa Street, April 1906," *Message of the Apostolic Faith,* April 1939: 1ff. Nelson, "For Such a Time as This," 187-89.

[24] Shumway, "The Gift of Tongues," 174-75.

[25] Nelson, "For Such a Time as This," 57.

two-story whitewashed building had been converted into a horse stable on the first floor and tenement apartments on the second. The low ceilings, sawdust-covered dirt floor, and redwood plank pews gave the services a rustic flavor reminiscent of old Methodist and Holiness camp meetings. The old mission looked and smelled more like a barn than a church. Located on a short dead-end street half a block long, not far from the Los Angeles railroad terminal, the Azusa Mission was surrounded by a lumberyard, a tombstone shop, stockyards, wholesale houses, and less-than-saintly businesses in black Los Angeles. The barn-like atmosphere of the mission was not lost on the participants, who compared it to the manger in Bethlehem where Christ was born 1,900 years earlier.[26] Despite its location and dilapidated state, scores of curious spectators and spiritual vagabonds from all over the city and every walk of life descended on the old church, where "freedom in the Spirit" was the motto and "Spirit-led" spontaneity ruled.

First Supernatural Manifestation and Healing at the Azusa Street Mission

This Spirit-led spontaneity began even before the revival formally began. Although never discussed before, the first supernatural event reportedly took place one day before the revival officially began at the Apostolic Faith Mission on Saturday, April 14, 1906. On Friday, April 13, Arthur G. Osterberg, a key eyewitness and participant in the revival, reported that a Mexican American day worker was reportedly struck by the power of the Holy Spirit after three black women prayed for him. He fell to his knees amidst the clutter and burst into tears. These Mexicans were soon joined by others such as Abundio and Rosa López; Susie, José, and A.C. Valdez; Brigido Pérez; Juan Martínez Navarro; Luís López; probably Genaro and Romanita Carbajal Valenzuela; and many others. In fact, Osterberg reports that "hundreds" of Catholics attended the revival, many of which were Spanish or Mexican.[27] Osterberg stated that this event signaled the first manifestation of the Holy Spirit at the Azusa Mission. He and others also interpreted it as a premonition that something historic was about to happen.[28]

---

[26] Shumway, "The Gift of Tongues," 175. "The Same Old Way," *AF,* Sept. 1906: 3. "Bible Pentecost: Gracious Pentecostal Showers Continue to Fall," *AF,* Nov. 1906: 1. Frank Bartleman, *How Pentecost Came to Los Angeles: As It Was in the Beginning* (Los Angeles: F. Bartleman, 1925) 43.

[27] Arthur G. Osterberg, "Oral History of the Life of Arthur G. Osterberg and the Azusa Street Revival," interview by Jerry Jensen and Jonathan Perkins (transcribed interview, Flower Pentecostal Heritage Center, 1966) 11.

[28] Nelson, "For Such a Time as This," 58.

Mexicans not only were involved in the first supernatural manifestation of the Holy Spirit at the Azusa Street Mission, but they were also the first to receive divine healing.[29] Shortly after the Apostolic Faith Mission opened, a Mexican man with a clubfoot was reportedly healed during a worship service. A.G. Osterberg stated that this was the first great miracle of the revival. The alleged healing left an indelible impression on Osterberg. He was so moved by the event that he closed his church and joined the Azusa Mission.[30]

Mexicans also participated in a number of other healing episodes at the revival. A.C. Valdez claimed to have witnessed many healings at the mission, including the healing of his father. Abundio and Rosa López also stated that divine healing was part of their ministry.[31]

The first Azusa Street participants believed that these miraculous healings were a manifestation of the long-awaited outpouring of the Holy Spirit that was prophesied to take place "in the last days" of the world. The headline of the first edition of *The Apostolic Faith* newspaper read, "Pentecost Has Come: Los Angeles Being Visited by a Revival of Bible Salvation and Pentecost as Recorded in the Book of Acts."[32] The article claimed, "The power of God now has this city [Los Angeles] agitated as never before. Pentecost has surely come and with it the Bible evidences are following, many being converted and sanctified and filled with the Holy Ghost, speaking in tongues as they did on the day of Pentecost. . . . some are on their way to the foreign fields, with the gift of the language." This supernatural outpouring of the Spirit led many at the mission to believe that God was unleashing a worldwide revival that would usher in the second coming of Jesus Christ.[33]

Cadence and Spirituality of the Azusa Street Revival

The daily schedule at the Azusa Street Revival was mind-boggling by today's standards. Services took place seven days a week for three years straight, from 1906 to 1909, and off and on from 1909 to 1913. In contrast to

---

[29] A.C. Valdez with James F. Scheer, *Fire on Azusa Street* (Costa Mesa, CA: Gift, 1980). Abundio López and Rosa López, "Spanish Receive the Pentecost," *AF,* Oct. 1906: 4. Osterberg, "Oral History."

[30] Osterberg, "Oral History," 12.

[31] Mrs. Knapp, *AF,* Sept. 1906: 2. No author, *AF,* Sept. 1906: 3. Valdez, *Fire on Azusa Street,* 27, 34, esp. 39. López and López, "Spanish Receive the Pentecost," 4.

[32] *AF,* Sept. 1906: 1.

[33] *AF,* Oct. 1906: 1. *AF,* Jan. 1907: 1. The lead articles from the October 1906 and the January 1907 editions of *The Apostolic Faith* read "The Pentecostal Baptism Restored" and "Beginning of World Wide Revival."

more traditional liturgical worship services, the Azusa Street Revival had no set format, at least not officially.

Despite the lack of an official liturgy, one could regularly expect to see enthusiastic prayer, song, testimony and preaching at almost every service. A visitor could also expect to hear singing in the Spirit, speaking in tongues, and prayer for divine healing. After the services, about 100 black, brown and white people would tread upstairs into the "Upper Room," named after the room where Jesus' disciples were baptized with the Holy Spirit on the Day of Pentecost. Here the revivalists sought the baptism with the Holy Spirit and the gift of speaking in tongues, and on other occasions spent time in quiet meditation.

It was in the "Upper Room" that the races would intermingle and lie prostrate across the floor or kneel in an attitude of prayer and supplication. Seymour and other mission leaders would cross the racial lines in that day by laying their hands on people of any race, color, gender or economic background to pray for those wishing to receive the Holy Spirit's baptism.[34]

Charles Parham and William Seymour's insistence that speaking in unknown tongues evidenced the baptism with the Holy Spirit was the Achilles' heel of the early Pentecostal Movement. Although not emphasized in contemporary Pentecostalism, most people at Azusa Street equated tongues with the God-given ability to speak a human language one had never studied. The first edition of *The Apostolic Faith* proclaimed, "The Lord has given languages to the unlearned, Greek, Latin, Hebrew, French, German, Italian, Chinese, Japanese, Zulu and languages of Africa, Hindu and Bengali and dialects of India, Chippewa and other languages of the Indians ... in fact the Holy Ghost speaks all of the languages of the world through His children."[35]

Hundreds of Azusa Street participants allegedly left the mission with the ability to speak one or more human languages previously unknown to them.[36] However, more than one returned from the foreign mission field after realizing that he or she did not in fact speak the language they thought God had given them.[37]

---

[34] Valdez, *Fire on Azusa Street*, 9-11.

[35] *AF*, Sept. 1906: 1. *The Apostolic Faith* (Portland, Oregon), "A Historical Account of the Apostolic Faith: A Trinitarian-Fundamental Evangelistic Organization" (Portland, OR: Apostolic Faith, 1965) 59.

[36] *The Apostolic Faith*, 1906-1908.

[37] Anderson argues that while we must acknowledge that it may be theoretically possible to speak in an unknown human language *(xenolalia)*, it is highly improbable and there is little evidence to substantiate this claim. Anderson, *Vision of the Disinherited*, 15-20. For an alternative view, see Wacker, *Heaven Below*, 40-57.

It was not tongues speaking, but the powerful heartfelt singing that stood out most to visitors. In the early days of the revival there were no hymnals or musical instruments. All singing was done a cappella and often from memory. Negro spirituals and Methodist and Holiness camp meeting songs were the most popular. Bartleman stated, "In the beginning in 'Azusa' we had no musical instruments. In fact, we felt no need for them. There was no place for them in our worship. Everything was spontaneous. We did not ever sing from hymnbooks. All the old well-known hymns were sung from memory quickened by the Spirit of God. We sang it from fresh, powerful heart experience."[38] Glenn Cook wrote that the singing created a "holy awe" and "indescribable wonder," and a place where "evil speaking and evil thinking was all departed."[39]

Contrary to the stereotype of the revival as a wild orgy of handwaving fanatics grasping for experiences with the sacred, there was a quieter side. Early eyewitnesses tell of long periods of soft singing, hushed prayers, and great periods of quietness at the revival, especially in the Upper Room on the second floor of the mission. Bartleman claims that the Upper Room, as he called it, was sacred, a kind of holy ground.[40] It was here that "men sought to become quiet from the activities of their own too active minds and spirits, to escape from the world for the time, and get alone with God. There was no noisy, wild, exciting spirit there. . . . It was a sort of 'city of refuge' . . . a 'haven of rest,' where God could be heard, and talk to their souls."[41]

Message and Theology of the Azusa Street Revival

Contrary to the popular perception of early Pentecostals as "ignoramuses," many were keen students of doctrine, church history, and larger social and religious trends.[42] They compared their movement to the outpouring of the Holy Spirit on the Day of Pentecost (from which they derive their name). They also saw themselves in continuity with Martin Luther's doctrine of justification, John Wesley's teaching on sanctification, and the more recent proto-Pentecostal revivals among the Quakers, Irvingites, Swedes, Irish and Welsh.[43]

---

[38] Bartleman, *How Pentecost Came to Los Angeles,* 57.

[39] A.W. Orwig, "My First Visit to the Azuzu [sic] Street Pentecostal Mission, Los Angeles, California," *The Weekly Evangel,* Mar. 18, 1916: 4. Glenn A. Cook, "The Azusa Street Meetings: Some Highlights of this Outpouring" (Belvedere, CA: Belvedere Christian Mission, ca. 1920) 2.

[40] Bartleman, *How Pentecost Came to Los Angeles,* 55.

[41] Bartleman, 82.

[42] As noted in Dayton, *Theological Roots,* 11.

[43] "The Promise Still Good," *AF,* Sept. 1906: 3.

In fact, many who joined the Azusa Street Revival had been following the quasi-Pentecostal revival in Wales directed by Evan Roberts.[44] Frequent references to theologians, Bible scholars, figures in church history, "priest-class," and "Sinatic manuscripts" also indicates a level of theological literacy and sophistication not often ascribed to early Pentecostals.[45]

Despite his surprisingly high level of theological literacy, Seymour's main message was simple transformation—spiritual, physical, intellectual and social. He taught that a person must be born again to enter the kingdom of heaven. "Now don't go from this meeting and talk about tongues, but try to get people saved," Seymour often stated.[46] His message of transformation and conversion of the body, mind and spirit is evident in his emphasis on divine healing and his radically egalitarian message that God recognized no social barriers such as race, class, gender and education.

The theology of Seymour's Azusa Street Revival represents the coming together of four major theological streams in late-19th-century U.S. Christianity:

1. The Holiness and Wesleyan idea of entire sanctification
2. The Reformed idea of power for Christian service
3. Dispensational premillennialism
4. A robust belief in faith healing.[47]

While the message had a loud sectarian ring to it, the Azusa participants did not originally see themselves as ushering in a new movement. On the contrary, they initially saw themselves as reformers seeking to restore existing denominational churches back to their New Testament roots. *The Apostolic Faith* stated, "We are not fighting men or churches, but seeking to displace dead forms and creeds and wild fanaticism's [sic] with living, practical Christianity."[48]

Indeed, Seymour and his followers believed that the spiritual gifts gave them the ability to restore the New Testament church to its original purity.

---

[44] Bartleman, *How Pentecost Came to Los Angeles,* 13, 15, 19-20, 26. See the eight additions of *The Apostolic Faith* for evidence of this theological literacy.

[45] "The Pentecostal Baptism Restored: The Promised Latter Rain Now Being Poured Out on God's Humble People," *AF,* Oct. 1906: 1. "Shall We Reject Jesus' Last Words?" *AF,* Oct. 1906: 3. Bartleman, *How Pentecost Came to Los Angeles,* 43, 45-46, 62, 65-66, 77, 89.

[46] As cited in A.W. Orwig, "Additional From Los Angeles Covering the Early Pentecostal Work," *The Weekly Evangel,* April 8, 1916: 4. "Tongues as a Sign," *AF,* Sept. 1906: 2. "The Salvation of Jesus," *AF,* Jan. 1906: 4.

[47] Shumway, "The Gift of Tongues," 172. Grant Wacker, "Pentecostalism," in *Encyclopedia of the American Religious Experience,* ed. Charles H. Lippy and Peter W. Williams (New York: Scribner, 1988) 935. Dayton, *Theological Roots.*

[48] "The Apostolic Faith," *AF,* Sept. 1906: 2.

Far from ceasing with the death of the apostles, they taught the spiritual gifts were still available to all Christians. They emphasized the spiritual gifts (charismata) listed in 1 Corinthians 12 and 14: wisdom, knowledge, faith, healing, miraculous powers, discernment of spirits, tongues, interpretation of tongues, and prophecy.

It was precisely the belief in tongues as evidence of Holy Spirit baptism that separated Pentecostalism from most other forms of Christianity. This initial-evidence theory became the hallmark of early Pentecostalism and *the* watershed that separated them from their Holiness and Methodist cousins—at least for a short while. The purpose of tongues was not self-gratification or ecstasy, as often thought, but an enduement of power to preach a transformative message of faith, repentance and conversion to Jesus Christ both on the mission field and right at home.

Seymour and his colleagues held that the outpouring of the Holy Spirit was also evidenced by "signs and wonders" and divine healing. Healing testimonies are found on virtually every page of *The Apostolic Faith* newspaper. If love, transformation and speaking in tongues were the central attractions at the Azusa Street Revival, divine healing was not far behind.[49]

People regularly prayed for divine healing at the Azusa Mission. Scores of letters and testimonials in *The Apostolic Faith* claim that God had miraculously healed them of cancer, epilepsy, tuberculosis, asthma, blindness, fever, deafness, head injuries, hemorrhages, hernias, lung infections, mental illnesses, paralysis, pneumonia, rheumatism, smoking addiction, alcoholism, drug addiction, and many other illnesses and diseases. The Azusa leaders confidently claimed that "canes, crutches, medicine bottles, and glasses are being thrown aside as God heals."[50]

One early Mexican American Pentecostal leader and participant in the Azusa Street Revival, named A.C. Valdez, said these objects hung from the walls of the mission as evidence of the miraculous healings that had taken place.[51] Confidence in faith healing was partly shaped by the conviction that Christians should not use medicine. Like Parham, Seymour stated, "Medicine is for unbelievers, but the remedy for the saints of God we will find in James

---

[49] Bartleman, *How Pentecost Came to Los Angeles,* xviii.

[50] *AF,* Sept. 1906: 2.

[51] Bartleman, *How Pentecost Came to Los Angeles,* xviii. Valdez, *Fire on Azusa Street,* 9. Nelson stated that Rev. Lawrence Catley and Mrs. Amanda Smith confirmed this in his interviews with them. Nelson, "For Such a Time as This," 206. See also *AF* 1:1, Sept. 1906: 2.

5:14."⁵² He claimed that all sickness was from the devil and that the body itself was sanctified in healing.⁵³

Pentecostal emphasis on replacing dead forms and creeds with "living, practical Christianity," tongues, the spiritual gifts, enthusiastic worship, and divine healing went beyond the pale of orthodoxy and intellectual respectability for most Protestant Christians in that day. The result was ridicule and expulsion. With no place to go, the homeless Pentecostals began to form their own missions and denominations. It was precisely their commitment to doctrine that prompted them to condemn vigorously as works of the devil similar spirit-oriented and millennial religions such as Spiritualism, Theosophy, Seventh-day Adventism, Christian Science and the Jehovah's Witnesses.⁵⁴

Conflict With the Religious Establishment and the Beginning of the Citywide Revival

While the Azusa Revival converted many non-Christians, most of those who joined the mission came from Protestant churches in Los Angeles. As pastors saw their churches dwindle in attendance and the Azusa Mission grow, many became agitated. This decline in church attendance, along with Seymour's radically egalitarian message, threatened the religious establishment and social order.

In June 1906, the Los Angeles Ministerial Association filed a formal complaint with the city against the Azusa Mission on the grounds that it was disturbing the peace and should thus be closed down. The police investigated the charge and decided not to shut the mission down because it was located in an industrial, not residential, section of the city.⁵⁵

Criticism did not end with the Ministerial Association. Pentecostals were attacked by Methodists, Holiness people, Nazarenes, Baptists, and many other Protestant denominations as the latest version of a long-prophesied Biblical plague of end-time false prophets decimating the land and ravaging the spiritually undiscerning and malnourished. These critics unleashed a barrage of verbal and occasional physical abuse on the fledgling Pentecostal Movement, some calling it "foolishness," others "fanatical," and still others "a work of the devil."⁵⁶

---

⁵² William J. Seymour, "Questions Answered," *AF*, Oct. to Jan. 1908: 2.

⁵³ *AF*, Jan. 1907: 3.

⁵⁴ "God Is His Own Interpreter," *AF*, Jan. 1907: 2. *AF*, Feb.-Mar. 1907: 1.

⁵⁵ Nelson, "For Such a Time as This," 60.

⁵⁶ "One Church," *AF*, Oct. 1906: 3-4. "Spreads the Fire," *AF*, Oct. 1906: 4. "Pentecost With Signs Following," *AF*, Dec. 1906: 1. Phineas Bresee, "The Gift of Tongues," *Nazarene*

People also had a field day mocking the revival as "darky camp meetings" where "wild theories" and "mad excitement" reigned.[57] The free newspress, although negative, attracted people seeking a deeper Christian faith or the latest religious fad. Rather than shrinking back at the barrage of criticism heaped upon the mission, the participants re-read the attacks as an indication that the revival was having a positive impact on the city. Satanic opposition only convinced them all the more that they were indeed preaching *the Truth* in the last days of the world.

The Azusa Street participants fanned out like a flashflood across a sun-scorched Los Angeles, preaching "waves of power." In April 1906, for example, Frank Bartleman personally printed and later distributed 75,000 "Earthquake" tracts throughout Southern California shortly after the San Francisco earthquake leveled the city. The revival not only attracted blacks and Mexicans such as Mack E. Jonas, Charles Mason, Garfield Haywood, Julia Hutchins, A.C. Valdez and Abundio López, but also prominent Angelenos like Rabbi Gold, Dr. Henry S. Keyes, Women's Christian Temperance Union (WCTU) leader Florence Crawford, and railroad family aristocracy Carlos Huntington.[58]

The press, reports of miraculous healings, and scores of street-corner preachers continued to attract throngs of people. Crowds of 800 to 1,000 people tried to pack their way into the mission. Reflecting the cosmopolitan mix of the city itself, eyewitness Glenn Cook reported that 20 nationalities attended the revival.[59]

Azusa Street Revival Spreads Across the United States and Around the World

The hordes of people who descended upon the revival in Los Angeles came from across the country. William H. Durham, Charles H. Mason, Ophelia Wiley, Lucy Farrow, F.W. Williams, J.A. Jeter, D.J. Young, Garfield T. Haywood, Gaston Barnabas Cashwell, Ernest S. Williams, and many others traveled from the Midwest, East Coast and South to attend the revival. Durham, who came from Chicago, described Seymour as "the meekest man I ever met. He walks and talks with God. His power is in his weakness. He seems to maintain a helpless dependence on God and is as simple-hearted as a little child, and at

---

Messenger, Dec. 13, 1906. C.W. Bridwell, "Fanatical Sect in Los Angeles Claims Gift of Tongues," *Rocky Mountain Pillar of Fire,* June 13, 1906.

[57] "Ascension Robes," *AF,* Sept. 1906: 4. Shumway, "The Gift of Tongues," 176.

[58] "Queen 'Gift' Given Many," *Los Angeles Daily Times,* July 23, 1906: 7. "Baba Bharati Says Not a Language," *Los Angeles Daily Times,* Sept. 19, 1906: 1.

[59] Cook, "Azusa Street Meetings," 1-4.

the same time is so filled with God that you feel the love and power every time you get near him."

Like the ocean winds, however, Durham's opinion would later change. For the time being, the revival became a sacred center from which Pentecostalism spread to New York (Robert and Marie Burgess); Chicago (Durham); Portland, Oregon (Crawford); Seattle (Thomas Junk); Indianapolis (Haywood); Memphis/ South (Mason, Young, Jeter); Alabama (F.W. Williams); Virginia (Lucy Farrow); North/South Carolina (Cashwell); San Diego (Abundio and Rosa López), and other locations across the United States. By 1914, Pentecostalism had spread to almost every U.S. city with a population over 3,000.[60]

The sensational newspaper coverage, traveling evangelists, street-corner preachers, foreign missionaries, and attacks by denominational leaders quickly spread the Pentecostal message around the world. Andrew Johnson, who left for Scandinavia in April 1906, was the first foreign missionary sent overseas by the mission.[61]

A.G. Garr and four others carried the Azusa Street message to China and India in July. The missionary impulse was so strong that it took Seymour only 15 minutes to raise the $1,200 Garr and his associates needed to travel overseas. A few months later, Lucy Farrow, Julia Hutchins, J.S. Mead and G.W. Batman spread Seymour's message to Liberia, while Tom Hezmalbalch carried it to South Africa. A.S. Copley took the message to Toronto, Canada, and A.C. Valdez carried the Azusa Street message to Australia and New Zealand. A.H. Post took the message to Egypt, South Africa, England, India and Sri Lanka; Lucy Leatherman carried the message to Jerusalem and the Middle East, while George and Carry Montgomery carried it to Mexico.[62]

From overseas, Thomas Barrett, a Methodist pastor from Norway, was converted to Pentecostalism in New York City by some Azusa Street participants on their way to Africa. The Anglican vicar Alexander A. Boddy, who first heard about the Azusa Revival from Barrett, traveled from England to Los Angeles to attend the revival.

By 1908, the mission claimed missionaries in over 50 nations around the world.[63] Writing in 1912, Boddy claimed that the Azusa Street Mission had

---

[60] Nelson, "For Suchw a Time as This," 62, 1.

[61] Nelson, 59.

[62] For a list of all of the countries to which the Azusa Street Mission sent missionaries see Wayne Warner, *The Azusa Street Papers* (Foley, AL.: Harvest, 1997) 69-79. Nelson, "For Such a Time as This," 59-64, 213; Valdez, *Fire on Azusa Street*, 101-10; Shumway, "The Gift of Tongues," 180-82.

[63] Nelson, "For Such a Time as This," 61-62.

become a sacred center for the growing Pentecostal Movement and was "a sort of 'Mecca' to Pentecostal travelers . . . [who] like to kneel where the fire fell." [64]

The Transformative Egalitarian Social Power of the Azusa Street Revival

One of the reasons why men and women, rich and poor, blacks, whites, Mexicans, and 17 other nationalities were attracted to the revival was because of Seymour's radically egalitarian spirit and transformative message. In a period dominated by Jim Crow segregation, the Ku Klux Klan, Nativism, Social Darwinism and racial purity, Seymour's message of racial equality and transnational multicultural global Christianity ran against the grain of U.S. society. The first edition of *The Apostolic Faith* newspaper declared, "God makes no difference in nationality. Ethiopians [blacks], Chinese, Indians, Mexicans, and other nationalities worship together." [65]

Underscoring this belief in racial egalitarianism and a global Christian consciousness, the Azusa Street leaders claimed, "It is noticeable how free all nationalities feel. If a Mexican or German cannot speak English, he gets up and speaks in his own tongue and feels quite at home, for the Spirit interprets through the face and people say 'amen.' No instrument that God can use is rejected on account of color or dress or lack of education. That is why God has so built up the work." [66]

Blacks at the Azusa Street revival also shared this sentiment. Mattie Cummings, a black participant, stated, "Everybody was just the same. It didn't matter if you were black, white, green, or grizzly. . . . Germans and Jews, blacks and whites, ate together in the little cottage at the rear. Nobody ever thought of race." [67]

Bartleman summed up the attitude of many Azusa participants when he declared, "The color line was washed away in the blood." It was precisely this kind of message of racial reconciliation that caused a number of former white supremacists such as Cashwell to "crucify" their racist beliefs at the Azusa Street Mission, where he asked blacks to pray for him.[68]

---

[64] Shumway, "The Gift of Tongues," 177. A.A. Boddy, "A Meeting at the Azusa Street Mission, Los Angeles," *Confidence,* Nov. 1912: 244.

[65] "The Same Old Way," *AF,* Sept. 1906: 3.

[66] *AF,* Nov. 1906: 1.

[67] Nelson, "For Such a Time as This," 234.

[68] Bartleman, *How Pentecost Came to Los Angeles,* xix; Ithiel C. Clemmons, *Bishop C.H. Mason and the Roots of the Church of God in Christ* (Bakersfield, CA: Pneuma Life, 1996) 45.

The Anglican vicar A.A. Boddy remarked after his visit in 1912 that the interracial activities at Azusa Street were extraordinary. He was particularly struck by how Southern whites would come to the revival, lay aside their white supremacist attitudes, and then take their racially reconciliatory message back to the South.[69]

The Azusa Street Revival was a transformative egalitarian social space, not only for racial and ethnic minorities, but also for women. Seymour claimed that on the Day of Pentecost, God "called them all into the Upper Room, both men and women, and anointed them with the oil of the Holy Ghost, thus qualifying them all to minister in this gospel. . . . In Christ Jesus there is neither male nor female, all are one."[70] He supported women in the ministry and sponsored Florence Crawford's pioneer evangelistic and pastoral work in Portland, Oregon. Women also served on the ordination committee and as evangelists, missionaries and church planters; they ran the *Apostolic Faith* newspaper and ministered at the revival. They also worked with Seymour in conducting evangelistic-social work. Susie Villa Valdez and Cena Osterberg, for example, teamed up to minister to prostitutes, alcoholics, single mothers in Los Angeles, and migrant farm workers in Riverside and San Bernardino, California.[71]

Reflecting his radically egalitarian vision and own life story, Seymour attempted to erase the deeply embedded class distinctions at the Azusa Street Revival. He stated, "These meetings are different from any you ever saw in all your born days . . . no flesh can glory in the presence of our God." He declared that God "recognizes no man-made . . . classes of people, but 'the willing and obedient.'"[72]

The importance of formal theological education, perhaps one of the most obvious class indicators at that time, was downplayed at the Azusa Street Revival. Frank Bartleman claimed, "We had no 'respect for persons.' The rich and educated were the same as the poor and ignorant, and found a much harder death to die. We only recognized God. All were equal."[73] A.W. Orwig seemed to summarize the attitude of many Azusa Street participants when he wrote, "Education and culture are at a discount in this great battle for souls. The [divine] call is not based on what we know, but what we have experienced."[74]

---

[69] Boddy, *Confidence,* Sept. 1912: 209-12. Nelson, "For Such a Time as This," 198.

[70] W.J. Seymour, "Who May Prophesy?" *AF,* Jan. 1908: 2.

[71] Valdez, *Fire on Azusa Street,* 25.

[72] "Pentecostal Faith Line," *AF,* Sept. 1906: 3.

[73] Bartleman, *How Pentecost Came to Los Angeles,* 58.

[74] Orwig, 7.

"God Is Sick at His Stomach": Parham's Reaction to the Azusa Street Revival

It was the physical contact and fears of miscegenation between the races that damned the revival the most in the eyes of Jim Crow America. Seymour's claim that the revival had been a "melting time" where "God is melting all races and nations together" conjured up images of interracial touching and miscegenation.[75]

Stories of men and women kneeling together, falling across one another, giving one another a "holy kiss," and laying hands on one another to pray for healing or to receive the Holy Spirit served as proof positive in the minds of many that Seymour's revival services were a "hot bed" of promiscuous sexual activity.[76] Pillar of Fire leader Alma White claimed Seymour was a "devil-possessed" "religious fakir" whose revival in the "worst slums" of Los Angeles was the scene of kissing and shocking familiarity between the sexes.[77]

The most scandalous accusations of all came from Charles Parham. The Azusa Street Revival had been running about six months when Parham blasted, "God is sick at His stomach!" "To my utter surprise and astonishment I found conditions [at the Azusa Street Mission] even worse than I had anticipated," Parham declared.[78] Disappointed, but not entirely surprised by Parham's reaction, Seymour tried to assuage Parham's worst fears. He considered Parham the father of the Pentecostal Movement and was hoping to receive his blessing. Threatened by Seymour's success, Parham did what any white supremacist would do; he condemned the meetings in the most vicious racial and sexual overtones possible. He stated that "a white woman, perhaps of wealth and culture, could be seen thrown back in the arms of a big 'buck nigger,' and held tightly thus as she shivered and shook in freak imitation of Pentecost."[79] Parham went on to condemn Seymour's mission by claiming that it was a "hot bed of wildfire" where "religious orgies outrivaled scenes in devil or fetish worship."[80]

---

[75] *AF*, Feb.-Mar. 1907: 7.

[76] Charles F. Parham, "Free-Love," *AF* [Baxter Springs], Dec. 1912: 4-5. "Darky camp meetings" was the expression Parham used to describe Seymour's Azusa Street Revival.

[77] Alma White, *Demons and Tongues* (Zarephath, NJ: Alma White, 1949, originally 1910) 67-70, 82, 108. Nelson, "For Such a Time as This," 83.

[78] Shumway, "The Gift of Tongues," 178. Nelson, "For Such a Time as This," 96.

[79] Parham, "Free-Love," 4-5.

[80] Charles F. Parham, "Leadership," *AF* [Baxter Springs], June 1912: 7.

Although Seymour said little in response to Parham's vicious accusations, his white elders threw Parham out of the mission. Angry and disgraced that a black man and his white friends publicly checkmated him, Parham immediately set up a rival mission in Los Angeles. Siphoning off 200 to 300 white followers from Azusa Street at first, Parham split the fledgling Pentecostal Movement in Los Angeles along racial lines. Like the tide, however, Parham's followers receded. Frustrated at his thwarted attempt to take over the mission, Parham went back to Texas to face a tidal wave of accusations.[81]

Seymour's main biographer, Douglas J. Nelson, argues that Seymour's sense of propriety and character was beyond reproach.[82] Clearly, in the minds of people such as Parham, the revival was an egalitarian social space where women and men engaged in activities that went beyond the pale of the acceptable borders and boundaries of the Victorian Era morality in U.S. society.

Parham had gone to the Azusa Street Mission at the height of his popularity, claiming 13,000 followers throughout the United States. His debacle at Azusa Street would cost him dearly. Losing hundreds of followers, he could no longer count on support for his evangelistic services among the growing number of Azusa Street daughter missions popping up throughout the United States. This fact, along with his failed attempt to take over Alexander Dowie's Zion City after Dowie's death, left Parham's public image seriously tarnished. The most devastating blow to Parham's ministry was yet to come. In December, the scandalous news broke in a newspaper that he had been accused of sodomy in San Antonio, Texas.[83]

In the morally strict world in which he lived, that accusation alone was the "kiss of death" to his ministry. Parham shouted that his enemies like Wilbur Viola of Zion City framed him and the charges were dropped. As Parham's star dimmed, Seymour's was rising. Parham spent the rest of his life living in the shadow of Seymour's "darky camp meetings" and the "sewage of Azusa Street."[84] By the time Parham died in 1929, he was largely unknown among second-generation Pentecostals.

Seymour's transformative egalitarian message had limits, however. The issue of race raised its head when Charles Parham and William Durham tried unsuccessfully to take over the Azusa Street Mission in 1906 and 1911 respectively.[85]

---

[81] Nelson, "For Such a Time as This," 95-97.

[82] Nelson, 84.

[83] Goff, *Fields White Unto Harvest,* 136-42, 223-24.

[84] Nelson, "For Such a Time as This," 61.

[85] Nelson, 208-12, 246-52.

As we shall see shortly, in 1909 Seymour ran into conflict with the Mexican contingent at the mission, whom he "ruthlessly crushed."[86]

While Seymour taught that women could exercise a prophetic voice in the ordained ministry, he also stated that they should submit to their husbands at home.[87] While contact between white women and black and brown men was frequent, Seymour placed a tremendous emphasis on sexual purity and chastity. And while Seymour downplayed status and rationality, his critics prompted him to begin running his services "decently and in order."[88]

Later, Seymour was even known to have worn a tie and a top hat, all upper-class status symbols. By 1915, and after several attempted takeovers by white leaders, Seymour reluctantly revised the Apostolic Faith Mission *Constitution* and *Articles of Incorporation* to exclude whites from the governing board and serving as bishop. This reluctance is evident in his decision to allow whites to remain on the Apostolic Faith Mission Board of Trustees.[89]

Marriage, Betrayal, and the Slow Road to Decline

By May 1908, Seymour was printing 50,000 copies per month of *The Apostolic Faith*. The newspaper was distributed around the world. Feeling on top of the world, Seymour gleefully stated, "We are on the verge of the greatest miracle the world has ever seen." Seymour spoke too soon, however. Had he known what lay ahead, he might have said otherwise.[90]

Conflict erupted in the mission immediately after Seymour unexpectedly announced that he and Jeannie Moore Evans had married on May 13, 1908. Jeannie Evans was an African American woman, revival pianist and worship leader, and lay leader in the Azusa Street Revival. Their marriage, which took place unannounced in a private ceremony conducted by Reverend Ed Lee, shocked many in the mission. Stunned by the self-gratifying act, Clara Lum (a key leader of the mission and editor of the newspaper) and other Azusa Street participants interpreted the marriage as a betrayal of their end-times message.[91]

---

[86] Bartleman, *How Pentecost Came to Los Angeles*, 145.

[87] "Who May Prophesy?" *AF*, Jan. 1908: 2. W.J. Seymour, "To the Married," *AF*, Jan. 1908: 3.

[88] W.J. Seymour, "Gifts of the Spirit," *AF*, Jan. 1907: 2. Boddy, *Confidence*, Nov. 1912: 244-45.

[89] William J. Seymour, *The Doctrines and Discipline of the Azusa Street Apostolic Faith Mission of Los Angeles, Cal.* (Los Angeles: Apostolic Faith Mission, 1915) 47, 50.

[90] Nelson, "For Such a Time as This," 62-64, 213.

[91] Nelson, 64, 216-18.

Clara Lum questioned Seymour's virtue, wisdom and spirituality. Like a jilted lover, Lum, who apparently had fallen in love with and wanted to marry Seymour, raised a hornet's nest of opposition.[92] She accused Seymour of having compromised on "sanctification," a serious accusation among the holiness-minded Pentecostals. Lum left the mission in protest to join Florence Crawford's work in Portland, Oregon, but not before she grabbed the only copies of the national and international mailing lists. Her public protest shook the mission to its very core.

As in slavery days, Seymour's tongue had been cut out. He had been symbolically castrated. Without the newspaper to spread his message, he was voiceless and invisible. Not willing to give up so easily on their dream, the newlyweds traveled north to Portland in hot pursuit of Lum and the mailing lists. After rejecting his overtures for reconciliation and Christian charity, Lum refused to see the Seymours or give them the international mailing lists. They went back to Los Angeles disappointed, but not without hope. Still, his moral and pastoral authority had taken a serious hit, one that would prove almost impossible to recover from fully.[93]

Conflict Between Seymour and the Mexican Contingent

Seymour's growing conflicts with Parham, Lum, Carpenter (who questioned Seymour's fiscal management of the mission), and other whites may have inadvertently led Seymour to misdirect his frustration at the Mexican contingent. The same year that Abundio López was ordained by Seymour in 1909, Azusa Street Revival historian and eyewitness Frank Bartleman reported that the leader of the Mission ruthlessly crushed a group of poor and illiterate Mexicans at the revival. He argued that this signaled the decline of the Holy Spirit's work at the mission.

The Spirit tried to work through some poor, illiterate Mexicans, who had been saved and "baptized" in the Spirit. But the leader *deliberately refused to let them testify, and crushed them ruthlessly.* It was like murdering the Spirit of God. Only God knows what this meant to those poor Mexicans. Personally

---

[92] Clemmons, *Bishop C.H. Mason and the Roots of the Church of God in Christ* (Bakersfield, CA: Pneuma Life, 1996) 50. C.H. Mason stated to Bishop Ithiel C. Clemmons in an interview in 1948: "Seymour told him that Clara Lum had privately made it clear that she fell in love with Seymour and wanted him to propose marriage to her. Seymour had tentatively considered the possibility and discussed the matter in its early stages with Mason, who advised him not to even think about the idea." Lum never married.

[93] Nelson, "For Such a Time as This," 217. Twenty lists were made up of subscribers in Southern California, while the other two were the national and international lists. While Seymour had the local mailing lists, he did not have the national and international lists.

I would rather die than to have assumed such a spirit of dictatorship. Every meeting was now programmed from start to finish. Disaster was bound to follow, and it did so.[94]

Regardless of why the conflict began, Seymour's ministry to Mexican Americans helped birth the Latino Pentecostal movement. As Abundio López and Juan Martínez Navarro conducted evangelistic work among Mexicans, by 1912 Genaro Valenzuela was pastoring the Spanish Apostolic Faith Mission in Los Angeles and later spread the Pentecostal message to Mexico. Azusa Street Revival participants like George and Carrie Judd Montgomery influenced a number of future pioneer Pentecostal evangelists like the Genaro Valenzuela, Juan Lugo, and Francisco Olazábal to join the movement and spread the Pentecostal message throughout the United States, Mexico and Puerto Rico.[95]

Conflict Between William Durham and William Seymour in 1911

Despite the conflict with Lum in 1908 and with the Mexican contingent in 1909, the Azusa Street Revival continued to run peacefully off and on for the next four years, although meetings were considerably smaller than during their "glory days." In 1909, the Reverend W.B. Godbey, an influential Bible scholar and leader in the Holiness Movement, attended the revival and claimed that the meetings were still running nonstop. Los Angeles was "electrified with the movement," Godbey claimed.[96]

While the conflicts with Parham, Lum, and the Mexican revivalists had taken the zest and wind out of the revival's sail, the Azusa Street Mission still attracted solid attendance until 1911, when William H. Durham led a devastating schism.

In February of that year, Durham returned to Los Angeles to serve as Seymour's interim pastor while he went on a speaking tour across the country. Durham's dynamic preaching abilities and unbounded conviction attracted hundreds of people throughout the city for approximately 10 weeks, including many who had left the mission years earlier. Unbeknown to Seymour, however, Durham was preaching "another Gospel."

Durham's "Finished Work of Calvary" denied the Wesleyan view of sanctification held by Seymour and most Pentecostals at that time. He argued that the

---

[94] Emphasis mine. Bartleman, *How Pentecost Came to Los Angeles,* 145. Nelson, "For Such a Time as This," 92.

[95] Gastón Espinosa, "'The Holy Ghost Is Here on Earth': The Mexican Contributions to the Azusa Street Revival," *Enrichment Magazine,* Spring 2006.

[96] Nelson, "For Such a Time as This," 218.

believer received complete sanctification at conversion, and sanctification was not a second-unique experience. Durham used Seymour's pulpit to propagate his own unique Pentecostal message and ridicule all other Pentecostal missions in Los Angeles. The Azusa Street Mission and the Pentecostal community in Los Angeles were divided. Unable to bite their tongues any longer, Seymour's elders wired him and requested that he return home as soon as possible. The conciliatory Seymour tried as hard as he could to find common ground with Durham and persuade him to reject the "Finished Work" theology, but Durham would not budge. In an ironic twist of events reminiscent of his own conflict with Julia Hutchins in 1906, Seymour locked Durham out of the mission. Like Parham, Durham immediately set up a rival mission in Los Angeles. It was May of 1911.[97]

Durham's spectacular preaching and controversial doctrine brought in people by the boatloads. Within just a few days, his congregation swelled to over 600 people. Durham's dogmatic zeal, impressive personality, "firm determination to rule or ruin," and nonstop campaigning to win Pentecostalism to his "Finished Work" doctrine all seemed unstoppable. For this reason his followers were shocked to hear of his sudden death on July 7, 1912. Only 39 years old, Durham had waged a tireless campaign against pulmonary tuberculosis.[98] His success had come at a devastating price, however. The schism he caused in the Apostolic Faith Mission decimated the revival and greatly reduced the number of people who attended the mission.

About two-thirds of the participants followed Durham out of the Azusa mission. Rather than return to Seymour's mission after Durham's death, many joined existing white missions or formed their own independent Pentecostal churches. By 1912, there were at least 12 Pentecostal missions preaching "the Truth." This division led A.A. Boddy to lament that the Pentecostal community in Los Angeles was hopelessly divided. Yet, it is precisely this built-in tendency to fragment that has kept the Pentecostal Movement one of the fastest-growing religious movements in the world.

Seymour and the Origins of the Oneness Controversy in 1913

If Durham's controversy had knocked what little wind was left out of the revival, the final nail in the coffin was the "Oneness" controversy. The Pentecostal Movement was permanently torn asunder between April 15 and

---

[97] Shumway, "The Gift of Tongues," 179. Nelson, "For Such a Time as This," 246-52.

[98] Nelson, "For Such a Time as This," 249. Shumway, "The Gift of Tongues," 179.

June 1, 1913, at the Worldwide Pentecostal Camp Meeting held in the Arroyo Seco campground just outside of Los Angeles. In sharp contrast to the first camp meeting six years earlier, Seymour was not invited to speak, or even sit on the stage with the rest of the ministers during the 1913 meetings. Despite the slap in the face by his Pentecostal brethren, Seymour attended the camp meeting anyway. Just as the 1,000 whites, blacks, Mexicans and other participants were about to proclaim Maria B. Woodworth-Etter's healing services a great success, controversy erupted. The controversy was not over race, but again over doctrine.

A number of Durham's followers, led by the Canadian evangelists Robert A. McAllister and John G. Scheppe, began preaching throughout the camp that the apostles baptized only in the name of Jesus Christ (Acts 2:38), not in the triune formula found in Matthew 28:19. They rejected as unbiblical the Trinitarian formula of God as one essence in three persons. The "Oneness," or "Jesus Only," Pentecostals required Trinitarians to be rebaptized in the name of Jesus only. The new controversy permanently split the Pentecostal Movement into two theological camps. Seymour was completely powerless to stop it. Most of Durham's followers embraced the "Jesus Only" position, including a number of the blacks and Mexicans.[99]

While Seymour rejected the Oneness position, his friends Glenn Cook, Frank Bartleman and G.T. Haywood all embraced the position. The movement quickly spread like a flashflood throughout emerging Pentecostal denominations such as the Assemblies of God, which it almost destroyed as nearly one-third of its ministers defected to the Oneness movement, including E.N. Bell and Howard Goss.[100]

The Azusa Street Mission in Ignominy, 1913-1936

The Oneness controversy in 1913 marked a major turning point in the history of the Pentecostal Movement. The movement, which had spent so much time preaching unity, was now permanently divided—this time over doctrine. Turning "brother against brother," the controversy further weakened the Azusa Street Mission by siphoning off valuable black and white leaders and parishioners. The controversy just about snuffed out what little flame was left in the revival. Nevertheless, Seymour and his wife continued their work as pastors of the Apostolic Faith Mission.

---

[99] Shumway, "The Gift of Tongues," 191. Nelson, "For Such a Time as This," 253-54.

[100] Nelson, "For Such a Time as This," 254. Wacker, *Heaven Below,* 147.

The conflicts with Parham, Lum and Durham prompted Seymour to make a historic decision. In 1915, he published his revised *Articles of Incorporation* and *Constitution* to state that only "people of color" could serve on the board of trustees and as bishops, although exceptions were made later. He stated, "Now because we don't take them [whites] for directors . . . is not for discrimination, but for peace. To keep down the race war in the Churches and friction. . . . We are sorry for this, but it is best [for] now."

He went on to state, "If some of our white brethren have prejudices and discrimination . . . we can't do it." The reason was that many of his white brothers and sisters had always been faithful and had never left his side during the attempted takeovers. For this reason, he said, "We love our white brethren and sisters and welcome them." Not willing to give up on his message of reconciliation and a color-blind church and society, he stated, "Our colored brethren must love our white brethren . . . and our white brethren must love their colored brethren . . . so that the Holy Spirit won't be greaved" [sic]. He concluded by noting that God transcended racial categories, "Christ is . . . neither black nor white man, nor Chinaman, nor Hindoo [sic], nor Japanese, but God. God is Spirit . . . [and] without His Spirit, we cannot be saved."[101]

Seymour wrote that some whites, like Parham, not only divided the Azusa Street Mission, but also brought in a divisive and fanatical spirit by being too dogmatic in their insistence that speaking in tongues was the only physical evidence of the baptism with the Holy Spirit. This led him to make the historic decision to reject Parham's theory that only speaking in unknown tongues evidenced the baptism with the Holy Spirit.

Seymour wrote, "Wherever the doctrine of the Baptism with the Holy Spirit will only be known as the evidence of speaking in tongues, that will be an open door for witches and spiritualists, and free lovism . . . because all kinds of spirits can come in [and] they can counterfeit the outward manifestations and practices." Despite this fact, Seymour still strongly believed in the baptism with the Holy Spirit. He wrote, "It is all right to have the signs following, but not to pin our faith to outward manifestations. We are to go by the Word of God." He simply said that speaking in tongues should not be the only defining mark of Holy Spirit baptism and Christian fellowship.[102]

Seymour's once powerful revival had, like the waves of a hurricane, receded. By 1914 the mission was reduced to about 20 to 40 black-and-white participants, many of whom were part of the original prayer group at Bonnie

---

[101] Seymour, *Doctrines and Discipline,* Preface, 8, 10, 12-13.

[102] Seymour, *Doctrines and Discipline*, Preface, 8, 10, 12-13, 47-51.

Brae Street eight years earlier.[103] Nightly meetings had been reduced to just one meeting a week—all day Sunday. Seymour continued to pastor his small flock for almost another decade. Although a bit quieter now, Seymour continued to push for Christian unity, love and cooperation in Los Angeles. As the Roaring '20s brought great prosperity to millions of Americans and growth among the scores of emerging Pentecostal denominations, the Azusa Street Mission struggled to survive. In contrast to its glory days, when Seymour could raise $1,200 in 15 minutes, now his Sunday offering amounted to barely $.75. This regression prompted Seymour, someone who had never taken an offering during the revival, to go to his congregation, hat clenched in hand, and say, "Expenses, please, at least . . ."[104]

Despite the struggle of the Azusa Street Mission to survive, Seymour was still a highly sought-after speaker across the country. Although little is known about the churches that invited him to preach, the evidence indicates that he had regular offers to preach from 1906 through the early 1920s. Whether as a means to survive or as a way to keep his message alive and avoid the hard realities of the Azusa Street Mission's decline, Seymour and his wife went on lengthy speaking engagements across the country, preaching his prophetic egalitarian vision of Pentecostalism. He regularly visited black and white churches in Indianapolis, Chicago, Cincinnati, New York, Washington, Baltimore, Houston and other places. Between 1916 and 1917 Seymour made one last attempt to bring the various Pentecostal churches and missions together in Christian unity. Only two pastors bothered to attend.[105]

In 1918, Seymour attended Aimee Semple McPherson's first Los Angeles campaign, not as a speaker but as a silent spectator. A new star was rising. Not ready to give up, the creative Seymour organized an Azusa Street anniversary celebration in 1920, although with little fanfare. A year later he went on another preaching tour across the country. On September 28, 1922, while dictating a letter to a friend, the 52-year-old Seymour died of a massive heart attack.

Despite the fact that the revival touched thousands around the world, only 200 people showed up to pay their last respects. People testified at the funeral of the impact he had had on their lives. Others shed silent tears. His body was laid to rest in Evergreen Cemetery, East Los Angeles, in a plot not far from

---

[103] Shumway, "The Gift of Tongues," 179.

[104] Shumway, "The Gift of Tongues," Nelson, "For Such a Time as This," 260-69.

[105] Nelson, "For Such a Time as This," 267-69.

where another giant would one day rest—the Mexican American Pentecostal evangelist Francisco Olazábal.[106]

After her husband's death, Jeannie Seymour took over the Azusa Street Mission, which despite one last attempt by a white man named R.C. Griffith, who claimed to be Coptic priest, remained firmly in her control until it was torn down in 1931 at the height of the Great Depression on the shoddy pretext of being a fire hazard. Afterward, she took her homeless flock back to the old Bonnie Brae Street house, where she continued to hold meetings until 1936. On July 10, 1938, Jeannie Seymour died at the age of 62. Her body was laid to rest in a simple redwood coffin next to her husband.[107]

Despite the decline of the revival, by 1914 there were an estimated 70,000 Pentecostals throughout the United States, missionaries in at least 50 countries, and literature published in at least 30 languages. Seymour's revival helped give birth directly and indirectly to the Charles Mason's Church of God in Christ, the General Council of the Assemblies of God, the Apostolic Faith (Portland, Oregon), the United Pentecostal Church, the Pentecostal Assemblies of the World, the Apostolic Assembly of the Faith in Christ Jesus, the Latin American Council of Christian Churches, the Church of God (Cleveland, Tennessee), the Church of God of Prophecy, the Fire Baptized Holiness Church, the Pentecostal Freewill Baptist Church, and many other denominations, periodicals, and independent churches and ministries across the United States and around the world.[108]

Charles Mason (the Church of God in Christ) and many other black, white, and Latino Pentecostals continued to preach and practice Seymour's prophetic theology of racial reconciliation and multicultural Christianity. Seymour's death, in relative obscurity, should not obscure the very real contributions this one ordinary prophet made to global Christianity.

Conclusions: The Significance of William J. Seymour and the Azusa Street Revival

Seymour was an ordinary prophet whose prophetic social consciousness and theology of racial reconciliation and multicultural, transformative, egalitarian Christianity created an alternative vision and message that challenged

---

[106] Gastón Espinosa, "Francisco Olazábal: Charisma, Power, and Faith Healing in the Borderlands," in *Portraits of a Generation: Early Pentecostal Leaders,* ed. James R. Goff Jr. and Grant Wacker (Fayetteville: U of Arkansas P, 2002) 177-97, 400-404. Nelson, "For Such a Time as This," 267-70.

[107] Nelson, "For Such a Time as This," 272-74.

[108] Shumway, "The Gift of Tongues," 191. Clemmons, *Bishop C.H. Mason,* 58.

the church and society to live up to its professed ideals of unity in Christ and liberty and justice for all. His vision of Pentecostalism differed greatly from that of Charles Parham. While Parham's version of Jim Crow Pentecostalism interpreted tongues (*glossolalia*) as evidence of the baptism in the Spirit with no social implications, Seymour used tongues as a means of creating what was *in his day* a prophetic egalitarian transformative message and transnational multicultural global fellowship of believers. It was precisely because he preached and practiced a message of racial reconciliation where everyone was treated equal regardless of race, class, gender or education that attracted people to Pentecostalism. No longer could a pious Christian make blacks and Mexicans sit in the last pews in the back of the church or at camp meetings. No longer could truly spiritual Christians keep the pulpit from bright, but uneducated, men and women. No longer could devout Christian men require women with a passion to preach to sit silently in their churches or at home. No longer could the kiss of peace be offered only to people of the same race. The fact that Seymour was a poor, unschooled black man has everything to do with his racially egalitarian transformative message and multiracial church that he willed to create. He was not, as early Pentecostal historians Frank Bartleman and B.F. Lawrence depicted, a cog in an inevitable divine process.[109]

While the Azusa Street Revival was not a blatant protest against the social order of the sort we are used to seeing in the post-Civil Rights Era, the Azusa Street Revival was nonetheless, in its own day, a profound populist movement and indirect critique of the religious and social order. In an era that did little to stop the lynching of over 3,400 blacks and Mexicans across the United States between the 1880s and 1920s, it is not surprising that people who were not part of W.E.B. Du Bois's "Talented Tenth" found other indirect creative ways to use their heartfelt beliefs to transform church and society. Changing hearts and minds is just as powerful and subversive a form of prophetic social transformation as is standing on the steps of the Lincoln Memorial in Washington, D.C., demanding structural change. More importantly, in Jim Crow America in the early 20th century it was the only real option for economically poor but spiritually rich unschooled working-class Southern blacks like Seymour. Although by the 1930s Parham's vision had largely won the day as denominations began to split largely along racial lines, there have always been preachers, churches and denominations both in the United States and around the world that have faithfully preached the spirit of Seymour's transformative egalitarian

---

[109] B.F. Lawrence, *The Apostolic Faith Restored* (St. Louis, MO: Gospel Publishing House, 1916) 73-80. Bartleman, *How Pentecost Came to Los Angeles,* 57.

Pentecostal message—a message that Harvard University Professor Harvey Cox now argues is in the process of reshaping global Christianity in the 21st century.[110]

---

[110] Harvey Cox, *Fire From Heaven: The Rise of Pentecostal Spirituality and the Reshaping of Religion in the Twenty-First Century* (New York: Addison-Wesley, 1995).

2

The Role of Women in the Azusa Street Revival

Estrelda Alexander

Introduction

Chances are, if you were asked to reflect on the 1906 Azusa Street Revival's place in the modern Pentecostal Movement, the names and exploits of several prominent *men* would come immediately to mind. Charles Fox Parham, William Joseph Seymour, William Durham, Frank Bartleman and Gaston B. (G.B.) Cashwell are all well-known for their roles in the revival and in the movement. These men—along with several others such as Charles Harrison Mason, Howard Goss, Alfred Garrison Garr and Frank Ewart—are renowned for their individual exploits and their collective leadership. They helped to move what began as a localized, relatively insignificant revival among "disinherited" washerwomen and maids to a worldwide movement that by some estimates now touches the lives of more than 811 million people, nearly more than one-third of the Christian world.[1]

To tell only their story, however, would be to miss out on the other half of

---

[1] "Global Statistics," in *The New International Dictionary of Pentecostal and Charismatic Movements,* ed. Stanley M. Burgess, with Eduard M. van der Maas (Grand Rapids: Zondervan, 2002) 287.

the story. There were more women than men who attended the revival, but the women who played an equally vital role in every aspect of the unfolding of the fledgling movement have not been given the same recognition as these men. The women, whose names remain largely unknown, were instrumental in initiating the revival, bringing it to fruition and ensuring that its message found its way around the country and the world.

In this chapter, I begin to address this oversight and sketch out the story of some of these women, their ties to the Azusa Street Mission and Revival, and their contribution in taking the Pentecostal message from Azusa Street to the various arenas in which it found a home. To some degree, the reasons for the oversight are understandable. Outside of the information about them contained in correspondence filed with the *Apostolic Faith* and other periodicals, little tangible data regarding their role and contribution has previously been published. As is the case for much of religious history, many primary sources did not focus on the role of women, so their stories have been largely untold.

One problem inherent in the process of researching Evangelical and Pentecostal religious movements is the lack of attention that has generally been given to identifying women. Even when these women have been mentioned, their names have frequently been misspelled in various primary and secondary resources,[2] making it difficult to sort out the data that is available. In these same sources, married women often do not stand as individual persons, but are identified only by initials or as Mrs. So-and-so in conjunction with their husband's names.

Getting to Azusa Street

The roles that these women played in bringing the revival to pass began to unfold several months before the meetings got under way. At least four of them—Lucy Farrow, Lucy Leatherman, Mabel Smith Hall and Anna Hall—had been protégés of Seymour's mentor, Charles Fox Parham, either in Kansas or Houston, where they had already had the experience of speaking in tongues.[3] Several of these women, including Lucy Farrow, Julia Hutchins, Rachel Sizelove, Anna Hall, Mabel Smith Hall and Ivey Campbell, did not come to Azusa Street as novices, but had experience in ministry as pastors and evangelists throughout the country.

---

[2] For example, Julia Hutchins' name is variably spelled *Hutchinson* and *Hutchings*. Rachel Sizelove is sometimes referred to as *Sizemore*, and Ardella Meade is *Ardel* or *Della* in some references.

[3] A.C. Valdez Sr. with James F. Scheer, *Fire on Azusa Street* (Costa Mesa, CA: Gift, 1980) 18.

Farrow had been the pastor of the church William Seymour attended in Houston before he attended Parham's Bible School in 1905. It was Farrow who introduced Seymour to the doctrine and phenomenon of the baptism of the Holy Spirit with tongues as the Bible evidence. She had heard Parham when he visited Houston, and she left her pastorate for a time, in order to work as a governess for his family in Kansas when he traveled throughout the state, holding revivals in Melrose, Baxter Springs, and Columbus. While she was serving the Parham family, she received the baptism of the Holy Spirit. During Lucy Farrow's absence from Houston, Seymour filled in as pastor at her church. When she returned to Houston, and resumed her pastorate, she shared her experience with him and explained what she had learned from Parham about the doctrine of the baptism in the Spirit with the Bible evidence of speaking in other tongues. Subsequently, she introduced Seymour to Parham,[4] thus setting up the chain of events that ultimately led to the beginning of the Azusa Street meeting.

Neely Terry was responsible for the invitation Seymour received from Mrs. Julia Hutchins, to come to Los Angeles in 1906. Terry was a Los Angeles resident who belonged to a small Holiness church founded and pastored by Julia Hutchins. While visiting with her family in Houston, she attended Farrow's church where she met Seymour when he was serving as interim pastor. On returning to Los Angeles, Terry convinced her pastor and congregation to invite Seymour to serve as pastor. It was this invitation that brought Seymour to that city.[5] Since she was a relative of Ruth Asberry, in whose home Seymour conducted his initial Bible studies, Terry may have been instrumental in his finding a place to carry out his ministry after he was rejected by the congregation.[6] It is not known, however, what role, if any, Terry actually played in the revival.

Though Hutchins and her congregation initially rejected Seymour's message of baptism in the Spirit accompanied by the Bible evidence, she later came to be a regular participant in the Azusa Street Revival and a solid supporter of Seymour's ministry. Later, she was instrumental in taking the Pentecostal message from Azusa Street to Liberia. Hutchins had previously been a member

---

[4] Farrow's and Seymour's early relationship is detailed in Susan Hyatt's, "Spirit-Filled Women," in *The Century of the Holy Spirit: 100 Years of Pentecostal and Charismatic Renewal*, ed. Vinson Synan (Nashville, TN: Thomas Nelson, 2001) 245-46.

[5] Cf. James Tinney, "William J. Seymour: Father of Modern-Day Pentecostalism," in *Black Apostles: Afro-American Clergy Confront the Twentieth Century,* ed. Randall K. Burkett and Richard Newman (Boston: G.K. Hall, 1978) 218.

[6] Robert Owens, "The Azusa Street Revival," in *The Century of the Holy Spirit: 100 Years of Pentecostal and Charismatic Renewal, 1901-2001,* ed. Vinson Synan (Nashville, TN: Thomas Nelson, 2001) 47.

and teacher at Second Baptist Church, a prominent congregation that was the first African American Baptist church and the second African American congregation in the city of Los Angeles. When she began espousing the Holiness doctrine of sanctification at this Baptist church, however, she and the families of eight fellow believers who were attracted to this doctrine were expelled from the congregation. It was from this small group that Hutchins established her Holiness congregation.

Shortly after the revival started, Hutchins was converted to the Pentecostal understanding of Holy Spirit baptism. Details of how this came about or her specific role in the Azusa Street Revival have yet to be fully explored. What was reported in *The Apostolic Faith* (Los Angeles, Calif.) is that she "received the gift of the Uganda [*sic*] language."[7]

Women in the Revival

A number of women held significant roles in the administration of the Azusa Street Mission and played vital roles in the revival. Farrow had reassociated with Seymour at Azusa Street when she and J.A. Warren Jr. came to help with his, at first, floundering meeting. By the time Farrow and Warren arrived, however, the Bonnie Brae Street house meeting was fully under way. Still, for her role in ministering in the meetings, she was described as an "anointed handmaiden" whose ministry in the revival included laying on of hands for seekers to receive the Pentecostal experience. One woman, Ethel Goss, who later encountered Farrow in one of Parham's Texas camp meetings reported, "Although colored [*sic*], she was received as a messenger of the Lord to us, even in the deep south of Texas."[8]

Though she was not initially an elder at the Azusa Street Mission, Jennie Evans Moore was one of the women present at the Bonnie Brae prayer meetings. She went with Seymour to Azusa Street and was an active participant in the revival and the leadership of the church.

Moore played an increasingly vital role in the revival. She was the first woman to receive the Pentecostal experience in Los Angeles, while the revival was still at the Bonnie Brae Street house meeting, and was one of Seymour's earliest adherents to experience tongues.[9] She immediately began to speak and prophesy

---

[7] "Testimonies of Outgoing Missionaries," *AF* [Los Angeles] 1:2, Oct. 1906: 1.4.

[8] Ethel A. Goss, *The Winds of God* (New York: Comet, 1958) 56.

[9] Some report her to be the first person to speak in tongues in the Bonnie Brae Street prayer meeting, before the group moved to Azusa Street. See Cecil M. Robeck Jr., "Jennie Evans Moore," in *The New International Dictionary of Pentecostal and Charismatic*

in Hebrew and was divinely empowered to play the piano "in the Spirit" without prior training.[10] She and Seymour married on May 13, 1908, and their marriage, in part, was the catalyst for the first major schism in the movement.

After their marriage, Moore worked alongside her husband in leading the mission. During the worship services, she could be found playing and leading in hymn singing. She was also a member of the credentialing board. Upon his death, she served as pastor of the then-dwindling mission.[11]

Two women who shared the same last name, but were not related, were active in both the ministries of Charles Parham and the Azusa Revival—Mabel Smith Hall and Anna Hall. Mabel Hall worked as a member of Parham's revival team in Houston, Texas, and was particularly noted for the gift of *xenolalia*, that is, the ability to speak in a foreign language she had not learned. The languages that were recognized when she spoke in tongues included Hebrew, German, French and Spanish. She not only spoke in tongues fluently and interpreted, but she understood naturally spoken foreign languages and responded to them in tongues. On more than one occasion, Mabel reportedly spoke in tongues while talking on the street. After one street meeting, a man came to her and offered to hire her to interpret French and Spanish for his business. He found it incredulous that she told him she did not speak those languages, but the Holy Ghost spoke through her, using her tongue.[12]

We do not know when Mabel Hall arrived at Azusa Street or how long she stayed. But by the time she came to Azusa Street, she had considerable ministry experience and was already baptized in the Holy Spirit with the Pentecostal evidence of tongues. She left Azusa Street in the fall of 1906 to help a former Dowie adherent who had relocated to Chelsea, Massachusetts. On their way east, she and her first husband, Jesse, preached nightly to "overflowing crowds" in Chicago. Her ministry there convinced William Durham, prominent pastor of North Avenue Mission, to visit the Los Angeles revival. This invitation set up a chain of events that led to a second major schism in the fledgling movement—the "finished work" controversy.

Anna Hall experienced both the baptism in the Spirit and the gift of tongues following a vision without hearing about the reality of the experience "except

---

Movements, ed. Stanley M. Burgess, with Eduard M. van der Maas (Grand Rapids: Zondervan, 2002) 906-7.

[10] Ted Olsen, "American Pentecost: The Story Behind the Azusa Street Revival, the Most Phenomenal Event of Twentieth-Century Christianity," *Christian History,* issue 58, vol. 17.2 (1998): 14.

[11] Larry Martin, *The Life and Ministry of William J. Seymour,* The Complete Azusa Street Library 1 (Joplin, MO: Christian Life, 1999) 231.

[12] H.G. Tuthill, "History of the Latter Rain," *The Faithful Standard,* July 1922: 8.

from the Word."[13] During the early 1900s Hall was closely affiliated with Charles Fox Parham and active in many of his revivals. She regularly traveled with him to hold meetings, and her gifts and abilities stood out enough above some others that she often shared his pulpit and on several occasions filled in for him at preaching engagements.[14]

Like her colleague Mabel Smith Hall, Anna Hall came to Azusa Street from Parham's ministry in Houston. After coming to Los Angeles, Hall wrote to Parham from time to time about what was going on in the meetings. Not long after Hall arrived in Los Angeles, Seymour penned a letter to Parham, saying that "Sister Hall has arrived, and is planning out a great revival in this city that will take place when you come."[15] The big meeting never took place, however. Once Parham got to Azusa Street, he was appalled by what he considered to be improper mixing of the races and unseemly behavior of the participants. With Hall's assistance, he set up separate meetings in the city. Although Hall had been an integral part of the Azusa Revival, she shared in the meeting with Parham from that point until they left the city.

While in Los Angeles, Hall used her gift of languages to preach to Armenians and Russians who were among the newer Los Angeles immigrants. At one point, Hall attended a Russian church in Los Angeles and allegedly preached to the congregation in their own language. An article in the first issue of the *Apostolic Faith*, titled "Russians Hear in Their Own Tongue," describes Hall's acumen in the gift of *xenolalia*, for Hall was one of several Azusa Street participants who claimed the ability to speak in a known tongue, but among the few who actually report being able to use that gift to minister. After leaving Los Angeles, Hall worked among the Catholic fishermen on the coast of Texas, and scores of them were saved through hearing her speak in their language.[16]

Within the revival, white women from various walks of life ministered alongside black washerwomen and household servants who had no formal training. Both were given free reign to speak in tongues, interpret glossolalic messages, prophesy, intercede and lead worship. They could also be found at the altar praying with new converts and seekers for the baptism of the Holy Spirit and for healing. One element of the revival that drew public attention, and a degree of derision from the secular press, was the regular sight of white

---

[13] "Jesus Is Coming," *AF* [Los Angeles] 1:1, Sept. 1906: 4.

[14] Alex V. Bills, "The Houston Connection: After Topeka and Before Azusa Street," paper delivered to the 30th Annual Meeting of the Society for Pentecostal Studies, Kirkland, WA, March 16-18, 2000, p. 30.

[15] James Goff, *Fields White Unto Harvest: Charles F. Parham and the Missionary Origins of Pentecostalism* (Fayetteville: U of Arkansas P, 1988) 119.

[16] "Sermon by Charles F. Parham," *AF* [Baxter Springs, KS] no. 3, April 1925: 14.

men, many of whom were somewhat prominent members of the clergy or community, kneeling alongside black women to receive Holy Spirit baptism.[17]

Further evidence of the inclusion of women in the leadership of the mission comes from an interesting sidelight. Disenchanted by the racial attitudes of some trusted whites,[18] Seymour later incorporated into the formal structure of the Azusa Street Mission, through its governing documents, directions that his successor should be a person of color.[19] He did not specify a *man* of color, leaving room that possibly the person could be a woman. Perhaps the greatest evidence of Seymour's prophetic understanding of women's role is reflected in a statement in *The Apostolic Faith:*

> Before Jesus ascended to heaven, holy anointing oil had never been poured on a woman's head; but before He organized His church, He called them all into the upper room, both men and women, and anointed them with the oil of the Holy Ghost, thus qualifying them all to minister in this Gospel. On the day of Pentecost they all preached through the power of the Holy Ghost. In Christ Jesus there is neither male nor female, all are one.[20]

But this portrait of complete disregard for the traditional boundaries of gender in the Azusa Street Revival and Mission is not the total picture. The freedom available to women in the earliest days of the revival quickly gave way to limitations on their leadership that were encoded into the very fabric of the movement and increased as the work took on more structure. Surely, Seymour was indebted to several women for making him aware of the Pentecostal experience, getting him to Los Angeles, involving themselves in and supporting his ministry. Yet within 10 years of the beginning of the mission, his apparent wariness about granting them complete equality and access to leadership was evident in at least two important moves he made in developing the mission's structure. First, the doctrinal statement Seymour

---

[17] Owens, "Azusa Street Revival," 54.

[18] Charles Parham, William Durham, Florence Crawford and Clara Lum had all disappointed Seymour in some way. Parham had spoken disparagingly about what he considered hyper-emotionalism and an inappropriate racial climate at the revival. Durham had challenged Seymour's Wesleyan understanding of sanctification and had attempted to usurp his authority within the congregation. And, Crawford and Lum had allegedly absconded with the mailing list for the Apostolic Faith newsletter.

[19] Apostolic Faith, *Amended Articles of Incorporation* (Los Angeles: The Apostolic Faith Mission, May 19, 1914) 94.

[20] Untitled item, *AF* 1:10, Sept. 1907: 3.4.

developed in 1915[21] made a clear distinction in the roles that men and women were to play in vital areas of worship and ministry leadership. According to *The Doctrines and Discipline of the Azusa Street Apostolic Faith Mission of Los Angeles*, Seymour insisted that "all ordination must be done by men, not women. Women may be ministers but not to baptize and ordain in this work."[22] The liturgy that Seymour developed for the ordination service clearly indicated that all laying-on of hands and prayer within such services were to be done by "elders."[23] This might suggest that already the levels of ministry to which women might aspire were somewhat restricted. Might it have been later, the rank of elder, and then bishop, were restricted to men, with women relegated to lower ranks with less ministerial privilege?

Secondly, though there were women on the loosely organized administrative board that operated in the earliest days of the mission, in the later years, he excluded women from positions of authority. Four of the five people who served on the board of trustees that finally had legal responsibility for governance of the mission were men. The only woman granted a position on that board was Seymour's wife, Jennie Evans Seymour. So while it could be said by an eyewitness that in the earliest days of the movement, "the color line was washed away in the blood,"[24] it is evident that the gender line was strongly bent, but not broken.

From Azusa to the World

Several outstanding women were among the many evangelists and missionaries who went out from the Azusa Street Revival to take the message of Pentecostalism across the country and around the world. Large numbers of women preachers went out from Azusa or, after visiting Azusa, went back to various parts of the world to preach what they claimed to be the "Full Gospel." Some went as single missionaries or evangelists. These included Ivey Campbell, who preached in Ohio and Pennsylvania; Mabel Smith Hall, who preached in Chicago; Rachel Sizelove, in Missouri; and Lucy Leatherman, who made a missions trip around the world, stopping in such exotic places as Egypt, Lebanon and South America.

---

[21] This was sometime after the revival had begun to wane and the mission had begun to decline in attendance.

[22] W.J. Seymour, *The Doctrines and Discipline of the Azusa Street Apostolic Faith Mission of Los Angeles* (Los Angeles: W.J. Seymour, 1915) 91.

[23] Seymour, 135-57.

[24] Frank Bartleman, *How Pentecost Came to Los Angeles* (Los Angeles: F. Bartleman, 1925) 54.

Some, including Daisy Batman, May Evans, Ardella Meade and Rosa de López, went as part of husband-and-wife teams. Still others went as part of larger missionary endeavors. Lucy Farrow and Julia W. Hutchins preached in Liberia, West Africa. Clara Lum and Florence Crawford went to Portland, Oregon. After leaving the Azusa Street meeting in August 1906, Farrow conducted preaching campaigns in Virginia, New York, North Carolina, Texas, Louisiana and England on her way to Liberia. While in Virginia, she stopped in Norfolk and nearby Portsmouth, holding successful revival services in which hundreds were saved and baptized with the Holy Spirit. By the time she left that state, two new congregations had been planted in those cities.[25]

On arriving in Africa, Farrow stayed seven months in Johnsonville, Liberia, 25 miles away from its capital, Monrovia. Reportedly, during her tenure there, she experienced the xenolalic gift of the Kru language and was able to preach at least two messages to the Kru people in their own dialect. Also, reportedly some of the Kru people to whom she ministered received the English language with their Holy Spirit baptism. After leaving Liberia, Farrow returned to Los Angeles by way of Virginia and other areas of the South.[26]

In August 1907, after returning to Los Angeles, Farrow established a ministry that was closely linked to the Azusa Street Mission. She continued to minister from a "small faith cottage" in back of the mission where people came to her for prayer for healing and to receive the baptism of the Holy Spirit. As detailed in the final issue of *The Apostolic Faith* to be produced in Los Angeles:

> The Lord had baptized a number in the little faith cottage back of the Mission. He has used our dear Sister Farrow whom He sent from Texas at the beginning of the outpouring of the Spirit in Los Angeles. In her room in the cottage, quite a number have received a greater filling of the Spirit and some have been healed and baptized with the Spirit since she returned from Africa.[27]

Julia Hutchins, her husband and her niece, Leila McKinney, were among the people who traveled with Farrow to Liberia. During her stay in Africa, Hutchins filed reports back to Azusa Street detailing the group's activities and recounting God's miraculous workings in their midst. A number of these reports were carried in various issues of *The Apostolic Faith*. Little is known

---

[25] D. William Faupel, *The Everlasting Gospel: The Significance of Eschatology in the Development of Pentecostal Thought*, JPT Supp. Series 10 (Sheffield, England: Sheffield Academic Press, 1996) 220.

[26] Untitled Item, *AF* [Los Angeles] 1:11, Oct. 1907–Jan. 1908: 1.

[27] Untitled Item, *AF* [Los Angeles] 1:13, May 1908: 2.1.

about Hutchins' ministry after her return from Africa.

One of the six female "elders" at the Azusa Street Mission, Florence Crawford,[28] received the baptism of the Holy Spirit at the revival. At the same time, she was reportedly healed instantly from a variety of ailments, including eye defects, lung problems and the residual effects of a childhood illness. Almost immediately she embarked on an evangelistic campaign. Crawford was among the earliest of the Azusa Street converts to take the Pentecostal message on the revival circuit. Beginning in Los Angeles, by September 1906, she moved on to principal cities of the Northwest—including Portland, Oregon, and Seattle, Washington. She then went east to Minnesota and to Canada.

Crawford was second only to Seymour, in the number of signed articles contributed to the *Apostolic Faith.* She was instrumental in distributing the monthly newspaper, which chronicled the events of the revival to Seymour's supporters. The extent of her influence among the revival's constituents can be attested to by the fact that in later editions of *The Apostolic Faith,* like Seymour, she resorted to using only her initials to sign articles. The assumption is that everyone knew who F.L.C. was.

Eventually, she and Seymour disagreed regarding his decision to marry. This disagreement stemmed from two possible sources. First, Crawford held the same radical understanding of Christ's imminent return to which many early Pentecostals adhered. Though she, herself, was married, she left her husband, having come to the extreme position some held that such normal activities as marriage and raising a family were counterproductive to the urgent need to reach as many as possible with the Pentecostal message before Christ's return. Secondly, since Crawford had held a somewhat prominent place in the ministry, she may have felt threatened by what the new alliance between Seymour and Moore could mean for her own leadership position. At any rate, Crawford left the Azusa Street Mission and Los Angeles and moved to Portland, where she set up her own ministry, which she named the Apostolic Faith Church. According to Crawford, however, the reason for her departure was that she felt the marriage and other stances taken by Seymour signaled compromise on the issue of sanctification.

Crawford's Portland ministry began when she established a mission that included two auditoriums with a combined seating of more than 3,000. She was, reportedly, very heavy-handed in her leadership style and her organization was extremely sectarian, to the point that members were forbidden to participate in

---

[28] Lewis F. Wilson, "Florence Crawford," in *The New International Dictionary of Pentecostal and Charismatic Movements,* ed. Stanley M. Burgess, with Eduard M. van der Maas (Grand Rapids: Zondervan, 2002) 564-65.

worship with other Pentecostal bodies. In 1935, her heavy-handed leadership style resulted in several congregations pulling away to organize the Bible Standard Churches.[29] Since Crawford placed her emphasis on evangelism rather than building a large organization, her denomination never became very large. Currently, there are fewer than 50 congregations in the United States, although there are also eight congregations in Canada and seven congregations in Europe. A large part of the constituency of the Apostolic Faith Church is in more than 30 congregations in Africa, 16 congregations in Asia, and 17 congregations in the Caribbean.[30]

Another female who played at least a minor role in the Azusa Street meeting was Mildred Crawford, Florence's then 10-year-old daughter. Mildred was an active participant in revival services and had had her own Pentecostal experience. She also traveled extensively with her mother to Florence's many evangelistic campaigns (while her older brother was left at home with his father). At one point, juvenile officials in Portland, Oregon, attempted to take Mildred away from her mother, accusing the elder Crawford of permitting her daughter to "roll around on the floor among Negroes and white men for a couple of hours every night."[31]

Before coming to Azusa Street, Clara Lum had been a servant in Parham's home and an associate of Phineas Bresee, founder of the Christian and Missionary Alliance.[32] She came to the revival in 1906, specifically seeking the baptism of the Holy Spirit. After receiving it, she became an integral part of the ministry. Besides serving on the governing board of the mission, Lum regularly participated in various aspects of the worship service. She exercised the gifts of tongues and interpretation and read the testimonies of those who wrote to the mission. Her clerical and administrative skills allowed her, among other things, to record the messages in tongues given at the revival. She served as secretary and coeditor (along with Seymour) of *The Apostolic Faith* from 1906-1908.

Reportedly Seymour and Lum had a deep friendship that both had thought might result in marriage. However, when Seymour consulted his friend,

---

[29] Robert Bryant Mitchell, *Heritage and Horizons: The History of Open Bible Standard Churches* (Des Moines, IA: Open Bible Publishers, 1982) 41.

[30] The Apostolic Faith Church—Branch Locations <*http://www.apostolicfaith.org/aboutus/branch.asp*>.

[31] Cf. "Color Line Obliterated," *The Morning Oregonian* [Portland], Dec. 31, 1906: 4. Cecil M. Robeck Jr., "Florence Crawford: Apostolic Faith Pioneer," in *Portraits of a Generation: Early Pentecostal Leaders,* ed. James R. Goff Jr. and Grant Wacker (Fayetteville: U of Arkansas P, 2002) 219-35.

[32] Edith Blumhofer and Grant Wacker, "Who Edited the Azusa Mission's Apostolic Faith?" *Assemblies of God Heritage,* 21:2, Summer 2001: 16.

Charles Harrison Mason, Mason cautioned him that a marriage between a black man and a white woman could lead to disaster for the ministry.[33] It is not surprising then that she, like Crawford, objected to Seymour's marriage to Jennie Evans Moore, left the mission, and moved to Oregon. She cooperated with Crawford in taking the national and international mailing lists to Oregon, leaving Seymour with only the Los Angeles list. After moving to Oregon, Lum joined Crawford and the two began publishing the paper under the title *The Apostolic Faith* (Portland, Ore.), at first without acknowledging that Seymour was no longer affiliated with it.[34] When Crawford established her own group, she served as editor of the adult and children's newsletters and teacher in the Apostolic Faith School.

Ophelia Wiley, a black preacher, singer and songwriter,[35] preached from time to time in the Azusa Street meetings and wrote articles for *The Apostolic Faith* (Los Angeles, Calif.) newspaper. She also served as part of evangelistic teams to spread the news of the revival in various cities throughout the northwestern United States,[36] accompanying Crawford and others on early trips to Oakland, California; Seattle, Washington; and Salem and Portland, Oregon.

Ivey Campbell preached revivals throughout Ohio and Pennsylvania and won many to the Pentecostal experience.[37] An article in *The Los Angeles Record* referred to her as "the gifts of tongues missionary."[38] Regularly, pastors and other ministers received their Pentecostal experience in her meetings. Her ministry caused such a stir in Akron that the ministers in that city passed a resolution denouncing her.[39]

Lucy Leatherman, who spoke Arabic and was the widow of a physician, traveled with Adolf de Rosa to hold meetings in Greenwich, Connecticut, where they met with considerable opposition, including charges of witchcraft

---

[33] Ithiel Clemmons, *Bishop C.H. Mason and the Roots of the Church of God in Christ* (Bakersfield, CA: Pneuma Life, 1996) 50.

[34] Cecil M. Robeck Jr., "Clara Lum," in *The New International Dictionary of Pentecostal and Charismatic Movements,* ed. Stanley M. Burgess, with Eduard M. van der Maas (Grand Rapids: Zondervan, 2002) 846.

[35] Martin, *Life and Ministry of William J. Seymour,* 229.

[36] Cf. Ophelia Wiley, "Sermon From a Dress," *AF* [Los Angeles] 1:2, Oct. 1906: 2.4; "Spreading the Full Gospel," *AF* [Los Angeles] 1:3, Nov. 1906: 1.4.

[37] "Report From Ohio and Pennsylvania," *AF* [Los Angeles] 1:6, Feb.–Mar. 1907: 5.1. "Pentecostal Meetings," *AF* [Los Angeles] 1:8, May 1907: 1.3.

[38] "Gift of Tongues' Is Satan's Work," *Los Angeles Record* [Los Angeles], Jan. 10, 1908: 2.

[39] "Gift of Tongues' Is Satan's Work."

and hypnotism.[40] She also went to the Middle East to minister to the Arabic population, and much later to South America where she was one of the earliest foreign missionaries from the Church of God (Cleveland, Tennessee). Leatherman was also one of the most prolific correspondents, reporting back regularly to such periodicals as A.A. Boddy's *Confidence* as well as to *The Apostolic Faith* (Los Angeles, California).

Besides undertaking her own ministry activities, Leatherman's actions were instrumental in furthering the ministry efforts of others who were to become prominent in the Pentecostal Movement. During a visit to New York City, Leatherman was involved in a revival meeting in which Thomas Ball Barratt encountered the Pentecostal message. After the meeting he asked Leatherman and some others to pray with him so that he might receive his Pentecostal experience. Barratt would go on to found and lead the thriving Pentecostal Movement in Norway. He also had an impact throughout Scandinavia and ministered as far away as India.

During that same meeting in New York, Leatherman, who had a fairly close relationship with Charles Parham, became aware of the need to plant a Pentecostal church in the city. She petitioned Parham to send someone to undertake such an effort. Parham dispatched Marie Burgess, who founded Glad Tidings Tabernacle. Through the following years she, and later her husband, Robert Brown, built the congregation into the largest Pentecostal body on the East Coast.

Rachel Sizelove and her husband had been long-time members of the Free Methodist Church, and she had been a Free Methodist evangelist from Springfield, Missouri, before coming to Hermon, California, to secure a better education for her children. In late spring of 1906, she and her husband visited the Azusa Street Revival. After leaving the revival in 1907, she and her family returned to minister for a short while in Springfield, Missouri, where they held cottage meetings and then returned to Los Angeles. Several years later she returned to Springfield for a visit. During this period, she reportedly had a vision of "a beautiful bubbling, sparkling fountain" in the heart of the city. According to her, it "sprang up gradually, but irresistibly, and began to flow toward the East and toward the West, toward the North and toward the South until the whole land was deluged with living water."[41] Her vision was later viewed as a prophetic witness of the future home for the headquarters of the Assemblies of God.

---

[40] Martin, *Life and Ministry of William J. Seymour,* 229.

[41] Rachel Sizelove, "A Sparkling Fountain for the Whole Earth," *Word and Work* 56, no. 6 (June 1934): 1.

Prominent among the couples who went out from Azusa Street were Samuel and Ardella Mead. These two were well-known pioneer Methodist missionaries to Africa before attending the Azusa Street Revival. They both received the Holy Spirit baptism there and stayed at the revival for some time, identifying what they heard from several tongues speakers as African dialects. Ardella claimed to speak in an African dialect.[42] They returned to Africa with G.W. and Daisy Batman and another couple, Myrtle and Robert Shideler.[43]

A.G. Garr and his wife, Lillian, went to Danville, Virginia, and then on to India, five weeks after receiving their Holy Spirit baptism. From India, they went on to China, where their meetings drew great crowds. They also paid a great personal price. While they were in China, they lost two children to the plague. That both felt a call and commitment to the ministry can be attested in a testimony that Lillian sent to *The Apostolic Faith*:

> God has put quite a burden on my heart for India's hungry souls. The Spirit has groaned through my soul for hungry ones until the pain was like travail. Oh how grateful we are for His working with us in this needy field.[44]

After returning to the United States in 1911, Lillian traveled with her husband in itinerant evangelistic work until her death in 1913.

G.W. and Daisy Batman traveled with their three children to Liberia, along with Julia Hutchins and Lucy Farrow. The Batmans' story as reported in an issue of *The Apostolic Faith* is an example of how this couple was viewed as a ministry team, not simply as a minister and his wife.

> They started with faith in God though they were taking their three little children and their destination is called the "white man's graveyard." They did not have more than their fare to New York. They have the gift of healing and we believe God will wonderfully use them among those darkened souls.[45]

The sense of purpose these women found in the ministry and the joy it produced are evident in the testimony that Daisy Batman filed back to Azusa Street while she was in New York with her husband, on the way to Liberia:

> Three years ago . . . the Lord gave us the call to Africa. At first I thought I would . . . let my husband go, but He said, "No, you must go too.". . . When

---

[42] Ardell[a] K. Mead, "Sister Mead's Baptism," *AF* [Los Angeles] 1:3, Nov. 1906: 3.2.

[43] Myrtle Shideler, "Received Her Pentecost," *AF* [Los Angeles] 1:5, Jan. 1907: 3.1.

[44] Sister A.G. Garr, "In Calcutta, India," *AF* [Los Angeles] 1:7, Apr. 1907: 1.1.

[45] "En Route to Africa," *AF* [Los Angeles] 1:4, Dec. 1906: 4.1.

He saw I was willing to spend my life in Africa for precious souls, He revealed to us that He would tell us when to go. And three months after we received our baptism, He said, "Now go to Africa." O glory to God, I am so glad I got to the place where the blessed Lord's will is my will.[46]

The Batmans exemplify the dear cost early Pentecostals were willing to pay to spread their newly found fervor. While in Africa, the entire family—Daisy, George and their children contracted a fever and died.

G.W. and May Evans both served as part of the credentialing committee.[47] May Evans had been healed of a debilitating condition 12 years before the revival. She was the first white person to receive the baptism of the Holy Spirit under Seymour's ministry. The couple accompanied Florence Crawford as part of a team to Oakland, where they stayed and preached for six weeks, and then traveled to Portland. They then accompanied her to Salem and Seattle.

Abundio de López and his wife, Rosa, both received the Pentecostal experience in the early months of the revival. Soon after, they began "preaching the gospel in open-air meetings on the Plaza"—that is, they held street meetings on *La Placita*, which lay at the heart of the Mexican area of Los Angeles, in order to reach the Latino population that had begun to come to the city.[48] They were also involved in "helping Mexicans at the altar" in the Azusa Street Mission.[49] The López family traveled to other areas, such as San Diego, with sizeable Latino populations.[50]

The Afterglow

In the waning years of the Azusa Street Mission—between 1910 and 1922—Jennie Seymour served at the helm of leadership with her husband, William, over a small but faithful remnant. During that period, the couple traveled together to the various camp meetings in which William was invited to speak. It was also during this time that William made Jennie the only female member of the official board of trustees for the mission. Before William J. Seymour died, September 28, 1922, he placed the ministry in his wife's hands. Upon his death, Jennie Evans Seymour assumed the pastorate over the even smaller remnant.

During her tenure as pastor, Jennie Seymour withstood several blows to the ministry that ultimately proved fatal to its very existence. First, in 1930,

---

[46] "En Route to Africa."

[47] Fred Corum, *Like As of Fire* (n.c.: privately published, n.d.), preface.

[48] "Spanish Receive the Pentecost," *AF* [Los Angeles] 1:2, Oct. 1906: 4.3.

[49] "Preaching to the Spanish," *AF* [Los Angeles] 1:3, Nov. 1906: 4.3.

[50] "From Los Angeles to Home and Foreign Fields," *AF* [Los Angeles] 1:4, Dec. 1906: 4.1.

she and the congregation were successful in withstanding an attempt by R.C. Griffith to take over the ministry and replace her as pastor. Griffith claimed to be a Coptic priest. The resulting battle was resolved in the courts, with Mrs. Seymour retaining leadership of the group. However the legal proceedings were costly for the small congregation and many of the remaining members sided with Griffith and left.[51]

Unfortunately, they could not withstand the resulting financial problems that beset the ministry. After vacating the building, Jennie Seymour moved her small congregation of the last faithful few into her home on Bonnie Brae Street (almost directly across the street from where the revival started). She continued to hold worship services there until her health failed in February 1936. At one point, Pastor Seymour mortgaged her home, attempting to save the mission. She later sold the mortgages on the mission and her home to a Los Angeles bank. When she could no longer make payments, the bank foreclosed.

Jennie Evans Seymour died July 2, 1936, five months after she relinquished leadership of the church. She had served as pastor for 11 years. With her death, one segment of the legacy of women's leadership in the life and ministry of the Azusa Street Mission came to an end.

One woman who attempted to preserve the memory of the Azusa Street Revival and keep its message alive for a later generation was Emma Cotton. Cotton attended the revival as a young woman, along with her husband, Henry. Apparently, they played no major role in the revival itself, but were eyewitnesses to the spiritual unfolding that made a lasting impression on their personal lives and public ministries.

Thirty years after the revival ended, Cotton published the first of what were to be several installments of her own remembrance of the services. Her remembrance is one of the few that presents the female perspective of the events of the Azusa Street Revival. Her recollection gave significance to the place of women in the leadership of the revival. In it, she reserved a special place for the prominence of Lucy Farrow.

At the time of its publication, Cotton was affiliated with the Church of God in Christ (COGIC) and was the pastor, along with her husband, of a large congregation in Los Angeles. Eventually, this congregation became one of the most important local COGIC bodies for much of the late 20th century.

---

[51] Douglas Nelson, "For Such a Time as This: The Story of Bishop William J. Seymour and the Azusa Street Revival, a Search for Pentecostal/Charismatic Roots" (Ph.D. diss., U of Birmingham, England, 1981) 273.

Conclusion

The legacy of the Azusa Street Revival has yet to be fully explored—especially as it relates to the ministry of women in the Pentecostal Movement. It is important that the task of such exploration be vigorously pursued, since Pentecostal women are beginning to reclaim their place in the leadership of a movement they were so vital in shaping. The women of Azusa Street were not bystanders or merely supporters. Their lives, works and words portray a level of commitment and involvement in every facet of ministry, despite restrictions that had found their way into the Pentecostal Movement in its earliest stages.

3

Pentecostal Healing at the Mission

Kimberly Ervin Alexander

One of the salient features of Pentecostalism is its emphasis on healing of the sick.¹ Indeed, most portrayals of Pentecostals—especially those in the worlds of literature, drama and film—will most often paint the picture of the Pentecostal healing minister.² Through the medium of television, Pentecostal healing ministries have been brought into the homes of millions of Americans. Occasionally, on the American terrain, one still sees a tent pitched on the outskirts of town where the revivalistic atmosphere builds to a crescendo, often resulting in a prayer line for the healing of the sick.³ And in many American

---

¹ See Donald Dayton, *Theological Roots of Pentecostalism* (Peabody, MA: Hendrickson, 1987) 115. Dayton argues, "Perhaps even more characteristic of Pentecostalism than the doctrine of the baptism in the Spirit is its celebration of miracles of divine healing as part of God's salvation and as evidence of divine power in the church."

² For instance, *Elmer Gantry*, Sinclair Lewis's thinly cloaked picture of Pentecostal Aimee Semple MacPherson, shows "Sister" involved in the healing ministry. This was also portrayed in the film version of the movie. This was, of course, the idea behind the comedy *Leap of Faith*. The film which most accurately depicts American Southern Pentecostalism, *The Apostle*, interestingly, does not emphasize the healing role of the evangelist, though the belief and practice is certainly understood as a part of the Pentecostal community in the film.

³ See David E. Harrell, *All Things Are Possible: The Healing and Charismatic Revivals in Modern America* (Bloomington: Indiana UP 1975) for a study of the itinerant healing

*Scripture references in this chapter are taken from the King James Version.

communities, a Pentecostal church is the destination of one wanting to receive prayer for healing.[4] While it may be available at a growing number of mainline or liturgical churches, a person would know that type of prayer could be received at a Pentecostal church.

From its inception, the Pentecostal Movement has preached a gospel that includes healing for the whole person. Healing miracles were expected, and the demonstrations of God's power to heal became the "drawing cards" for many missionary and evangelistic efforts.[5] The testimonies which arose in the Pentecostal community and circulated in the wider geographic community were in most cases word-of-mouth advertising, utilized by the growing movement. In fact, these healing miracle stories were a major reason for the explosion of the movement.

While belief in healing is actually one of the doctrines connecting Pentecostalism to historical Christianity, in modernity, healing became one of the doctrines that *divided* the movement from the mainstream, where skepticism demanded scientific proofs and verifiability. Pentecostals, for the most part, did not think in those terms and saw no reason to offer such proof.[6] In postmodernity, however, it is possible that healing practices may once again be the theme that brings Pentecostals to the table, or to the festival, as it has been described.[7] With this in mind, an exploration of healing theology and practice at the pivotal Azusa Street Revival proves to be informative.

---

evangelists. See also Stephen J. Pullum, *"Foul Demons, Come Out!"—The Rhetoric of Twentieth-Century American Faith Healing* (Westport, CT: Praeger, 1999) for a more recent treatment of these evangelists and their healing rhetoric.

[4] One student of Pentecostalism observes that he has come to expect "a period of intense prayers for healing" as part of the pattern of Pentecostal worship services. Cf. Harvey Cox, *Fire From Heaven: The Rise of Pentecostal Spirituality and the Reshaping of Religion in the 21st Century* (Reading, MA: Addison-Wesley, 1995) 6.

[5] See Gary B. McGee, "Pentecostal Strategies for Global Mission: A Historical Assessment," in *Called and Empowered: Global Mission in Pentecostal Perspective,* ed. Murray A. Dempster, Byron D. Klaus, and Douglas Petersen (Peabody, MA: Hendrickson, 1991) 203-24; and L. Grant McClung Jr., ed. *Azusa Street and Beyond: Pentecostal Missions and Church Growth in the Twentieth Century* (South Plainfield, NJ: Bridge, 1986).

[6] See Ronald A.N. Kydd, *Healing Through the Centuries: Models for Understanding* (Peabody, MA: Hendrickson, 1998). Kydd delineates various models of healing theology and practice dating from antiquity to the present. See also my review of this work in *Journal of Pentecostal Theology* 16 (Apr. 2000): 117-27. Here I argue that verifiability, which Kydd calls for, would have been impossible and unthinkable in the early years of the movement because of the way Pentecostals generally distrusted doctors and medicine.

[7] See Cheryl Bridges Johns, "'Partners in Scandal': Wesleyan and Pentecostal Scholarship," *Pneuma: The Journal of the Society for Pentecostal Studies* 21, no. 2 (Fall 1999): 183-97. See also Harvey Cox, *Fire From Heaven.*

Though the revival has often been described in terms of phenomena associated with it, recent scholarship has shown there was a carefully delineated theological framework out of which early Pentecostalism was birthed.[8] Steven J. Land has shown that the earliest American Pentecostals, like those at Azusa Street, came to the Pentecostal revival with a clearly understood doctrinal rubric, the fivefold gospel: Jesus is Savior, Sanctifier, Spirit-Baptizer, Divine Healer, and Soon-Coming King. Land identifies five theological motifs at the heart of the movement's theology:

1. Justification by faith in Christ
2. Sanctification by faith as a second definite work of grace
3. Healing of the body as provided for all in the Atonement
4. The premillennial return of Christ
5. The baptism in the Holy Spirit evidenced by speaking in tongues.[9]

Students of the 19th-century Holiness Movement may readily observe that these early Pentecostals were heirs of that movement's theological heritage. As Dayton has demonstrated, from the Wesleys and their children in Holiness circles the Pentecostals had inherited a belief in a definitive work of sanctification; a belief in healing in the Atonement may be traced to Wesley's daughters and sons in the healing movement; and from the premillenialists, they had adopted a statement regarding the return of Jesus.[10]

To understand the depth of thought with regard to healing theology in early Pentecostalism, there is no better source than the revival's periodical publication, *The Apostolic Faith*.[11] A thorough reading of the testimonies, sermons and revival reports therein reveals that healing was regarded as much

---

[8] See Dayton's *Theological Roots*. Also see D. William Faupel, *The Everlasting Gospel: The Significance of Eschatology in the Development of Pentecostal Thought*, JPT Supp. Series 10 (Sheffield: Sheffield Academic Press, 1996) for an exploration of the eschatology which became a kind of catalyst for the movement. The most recent contribution to the search for Pentecostal roots has been that of Laurence W. Wood, *The Meaning of Pentecost in Early Methodism* (Lanham, MD: Scarecrow, 2002).

[9] Steven J. Land, *Pentecostal Spirituality: A Passion for the Kingdom*, JPTS Series 1 (Sheffield: Sheffield Academic Press, 1993) 18.

[10] See Dayton, *Theological Roots*.

[11] See Kimberly Ervin Alexander, *Pentecostal Healing: Models of Theology and Practice* (Leiden, The Netherlands: Deo Publishing, 2005). This paper relies heavily upon the research findings reported in this work, which provides an analysis of healing theology and practice found in the two major branches of the movement, the original Wesleyan groups and the later Finished Work groups.

more than a phenomenon; healing in the Atonement was an integral part of Pentecostal soteriology.

The Origins of Illness

Like their mothers and fathers in the 19th-century healing movement, Seymour and his followers saw Satan to be the author of illness and disease, though God sometimes allowed or permitted it. *The Apostolic Faith* boldly declared, "Sickness is all the work of Satan [sic]."[12] Sickness and disease were unknown, foreign to humanity, until "that unholy visitor came into the garden" and, as a result, sickness now is passed on through the human condition. Apparently, sickness is inherited, just as sin is inherited: "Every drop of blood we received from our mother is impure. Sickness is born in a child just as original sin is born in the child." But just as the remedy for sin is found in the work of Christ, so is the remedy for illness. Indeed, Jesus "was manifested to destroy the works of the devil."[13]

In this view, Christians become sick because of "sins of omission or commission," "overexertion," or "getting on his [Satan's] territory."[14] Breaking covenant with God may result in sickness, or a state "worse than the first."[15] Like the man at the pool, observers were instructed to "sin no more, lest a worse thing come upon thee."[16] In the Old Testament, the people of God knew healing for their diseases until they trusted in "the arm of the flesh," beginning with the reign of Solomon, who was understood to have brought in occultic practices, "whoring after familiar spirits."[17]

Though these statements seem to be fairly straightforward, with sickness in the believer being the result of sin, these early Pentecostals were able to hold in tension the fact that some were sick as a result of natural circumstances. When writing of David's belief in healing (based on a reading of Psalm 103), *The Apostolic Faith* concludes that David was healed of rheumatism, "perhaps contracted in the caves where he hid himself from his pursuers."[18]

Sickness and disease then, are the result of the Fall and a part of the fallen human condition; sickness is the work of Satan, but may be permitted by God

---

[12] *AF* 1.5, Jan. 1907: 1.
[13] *AF* 1.10, Sept. 1907: 2.
[14] *AF* 1.5, Jan. 1907: 1.
[15] *AF* 2.13, May 1908: 2.
[16] *AF*
[17] *AF* 1.10, Sept. 1907: 2.
[18] *AF*

as a correction for disobedience; and finally, some illness may be the result of natural, but cursed, circumstances in the world.

God's Remedy for Sickness: The Atonement

As has already been stated, the Azusa leadership saw a remedy for sin and sickness in the blood of Jesus. From the inaugural issue of *The Apostolic Faith*, in the statement of faith, Matthew 8:16 is referred to as support for God's ability to heal.[19] This statement was reprinted in every issue. The article which follows that initial statement is titled "The Precious Atonement." It is addressed to "Children of God, partakers of the precious Atonement."[20] The benefits of the Atonement are listed: forgiveness, sanctification, healing of our bodies, and "baptism with the Holy Ghost and fire upon a sanctified life."[21] Seymour proclaims in this article:

> ... how we ought to honor that precious body which the Father sanctified and sent into the world, not simply set apart, but really sanctified, soul, body and spirit, free from sickness, disease and everything of the devil. A body that knew no sin and disease was given for these imperfect bodies of ours. Not only is the Atonement for the sanctification of our souls, but for the sanctification of our bodies from inherited disease.[22]

Reading Isaiah 53, Seymour writes that the fulfillment came with Jesus. He instructs that the best translation of "He hath borne our griefs" is "He hath borne our sickness."[23] Why then should we bear them, he concludes. This he proclaims is "full salvation."[24] Christ's sacrifice was "twofold": "He gave His blood for the

---

[19] *AF* 1.1, Sept. 1906: 2.

[20] *AF*

[21] *AF*

[22] *AF*

[23] This preference for the "sicknesses" translation may indicate that Seymour was here using the Revised Version. In an 1891 edition of the *RV*, a margin reference for both verses 12 and 14 of Isaiah 53 indicates that the Hebrew is "sickness." Whether or not Seymour got this information on the "better translation" from a margin reference or from a commentary, it is indicative of his ability to choose a translation which serves his purpose. See John Christopher Thomas, "Women, Pentecostals and the Bible: An Experiment in Pentecostal Hermeneutics," *Journal of Pentecostal Theology* 5 (1994): 41-56, where Thomas points out James' preference, in Acts 15, for the LXX translation of Amos 9:11, 12 over a more exclusive translation as found in the Hebrew text (pp. 46, 47). This example from the *Apostolic Faith* is in keeping with this type of Pentecostal hermeneutic.

[24] *AF* 1.1, Sept. 1906: 2.

salvation of our souls, and He gave a perfect body for these imperfect bodies of ours."[25] This twofold salvation is referred to in testimonies recorded in the periodical. John Waterson testified, "I can testify to this world that there is power in the blood of Jesus Christ to cleanse from all sin and all dread diseases. Two days before I received your letter I was made well and my shoulder went up into its place. All I can say is, praise the Lord for ever and ever."[26]

Christ's sacrifice is likened to the Passover lamb, which, when eaten by the Israelites, gave them "strength and health" as they went out of Egypt. As the Jews look back to the Passover, we look back to Calvary. The Lord's Supper observance remembers "twofold salvation," and the body of the Lord is taken for health. When the body is not properly discerned, that is, not believing in full salvation, illness or death results.[27]

Eating the flesh and drinking the blood do not only occur as we partake of the Lord's Supper, however. By "faith in His Word for salvation, health and healing," one is allowed to partake of the flesh and blood on a daily basis. Because His perfect body never saw corruption, one may have healing. His body was prepared by God "from heaven by the Holy Ghost and sent down into this world to be the Bread of Life."[28] Here, the work of Christ is a Trinitarian event.

For Seymour, honoring the blood and the body of Jesus is accepting and preaching this full salvation, the river of living water which Jesus offers the woman in John 4. In this river is "healing, health, salvation, joy, life—everything in Jesus."[29]

Health and healing are intricately linked to salvation and are actually the results of sanctification of the body. Commenting on Paul's prayer in 1 Thessalonians 8:23, *The Apostolic Faith* concludes: "That prayer is being prayed by the Holy Ghost for us today. Jesus prayed that the Father would keep us from evil, which means sickness and all the works of the devil. All sickness is the work of Satan, and we have just as much right to look to Jesus for the health of these bodies as for the saving

---

[25] *AF* 1.4, Dec. 1906: 2.

[26] *AF* 1.9, June-Sept. 1907: 3. Seymour still holds to this interpretation of Christ's sacrifice in 1915. He writes, "They were to kill the lamb and take its blood and sprinkle it over the door overhead and the sides to save them from the destroyer. But in the very house they were instructed to eat the body. The blood saved them from the destroyer, but the body of the lamb saved them from disease and sickness. Glory to His name! May we obey God's Word and voice and we shall be saved through Jesus from sins, and feasting on His perfect body" (W.J. Seymour, *The Doctrines and Discipline of the Azusa Street Apostolic Faith Mission of Los Angeles, CA,* 1915), 95.

[27] *AF* 1.4, Dec. 1906: 2.

[28] *AF* 1.6, Feb.-Mar. 1907: 2.

[29] *AF* 1.3, Nov. 1906: 2.

and sanctifying of our souls."[30] The writers can assert, "We ought to claim perfect health through the Atonement of Jesus."[31]

Like their predecessors in the 19th century, salvation is for service. Therefore, the life in Christ of which one is witness is to be one which exhibits the fruit of that life, "a perfect monument of His truth and witness to the healing and sanctification of our body, soul, and spirit."[32]

The Holy Spirit and Healing

Being baptized in the Spirit so encompassed the lives of the individuals who were a part of the Azusa Street Revival that the whole direction of their lives was changed as a result. A Chinese missionary, Antoinette Moomau, wrote, "To sum it up, the baptism of the Spirit means to me what I never dreamed it could this side of Heaven: victory, glory in my soul, perfect peace, rest, liberty, nearness to Christ, deadness to this old world, and power in witnessing."[33] Florence Crawford, a leader at Azusa, wrote, "I never was so determined as now to stand in all the fullness of this great Gospel." And so, empowered by the Spirit, they served.

From their foremothers and forefathers in the healing movement, they had inherited a doctrine of divine healing in the Atonement. But how did a new understanding of and experience in the Holy Spirit effect that doctrine?

Baptism in the Spirit is referred to often in relation to healing. Revival reports and testimonies refer to those who are healed at the time of their Spirit baptism.[34] One writes of feeling the "streaming" through his body and comments "I suppose the healing power."[35]

For Clara Lum of the Apostolic Faith Office, the Holy Spirit provided better health and a source of strength during illness: "Oh, it was so sweet to have Him talk and sing through me when I was sick, during the night seasons. Sometimes I sang for hours and in a new voice and it did not tire me."[36]

---

[30] *AF* 1.4, Dec. 1906: 2.

[31] *AF* 1.11, Jan. 1908: 3. This positional understanding is atypical of most Azusa Street theology of healing, but may be the influence of such 19th-century adherents as Carrie Judd Montgomery. The "fault line," which begins to have influence in the 19th-century healing movement is here evident.

[32] *AF* 1.6, Feb.-Mar. 1907: 6.

[33] *AF* 1.11, Jan. 1908: 3.

[34] See *AF* 1.1, Sept. 1906: 2, 3; 1.4, Dec. 1906: 4; 1.5, Jan. 1907: 4; 1.6 Feb.-Mar. 1907: 3, for examples.

[35] *AF* 1.4, Dec. 1906: 4.

[36] *AF* 1.6, Feb.-Mar. 1907: 8.

One account describes a person who was praying for the healing of a sick sister and asked the Holy Spirit to pray through him, "instead of praying in the old way." When the message, "The Lord for the body and the body for the Lord" came, the sister was instantly healed and convicted of the need for a deeper walk with the Lord. The Holy Spirit's empowerment allowed for more effective work for God, including praying for the sick. The man in this account reportedly said he could "accomplish a hundred times as much in a day and much more easily than formerly. It is simply letting the Holy Ghost do the work."[37]

The gift of healing, a gift of the Spirit, was discussed by some participants. A report from the revival in India reported that healing, along with other gifts listed by Paul, were being given "by the Holy Ghost to simple, unlearned members of the body of Christ."[38] Seymour and the other leaders taught that the gifts listed in 1 Corinthians 12 are in the Holy Spirit, and when the Spirit dwells in the human heart "in all His fullness," the gifts are resident there as well.[39]

Baptism in the Holy Spirit allowed the Christian worker an added dimension of effectiveness as well as strength. With the fullness of the Spirit came gifts, including healing. As a further benefit of the Atonement, the Spirit-filled person had more of the fullness of salvation. As for those who were healed simultaneously with the experience of Spirit baptism, the receptivity on their part allowed for them to receive all the fullness of God.

Signs Following Believers

A prominent healing text, which was more often than not omitted by the 19th-century movement, is Mark 16:16-18. This text comes to the forefront with the advent of the Pentecostal revival. Under Parham's influence, Seymour and others had become convinced that speaking in tongues was the "Bible evidence" of being filled with the Holy Ghost. Those gathered at Bonnie Brae Street had waited for this evidence, as had Agnes Ozman in Topeka. With that sign came others. The Mark 16 text promised exorcism of demons, deliverance from snakes and poison, speaking with new tongues, raising the dead, and healing. It stood to reason that because tongues were following the believers at Azusa, the rest would also follow. Issue number 3 reported that all the signs had followed at Azusa except raising the dead. The issue reported that they were waiting on that sign, because it would prove God to be true and would "result in the salvation of many souls."[40]

---

[37] *AF* 1.8, May 1907: 3.

[38] *AF* 1.3, Nov. 1906: 1.

[39] *AF* 3.

[40] *AF* 4.

The Mark 16 text became a support text for *The Apostolic Faith* statement on healing. In the inaugural issue, the text is quoted as support for the phenomena appearing at Azusa. The signs confirmed the Word and confirmed what was happening in Los Angeles.[41]

The Apostolic Faith was not unfamiliar with text critical problems associated with these verses. They offered the following apology:

> Why do they reject these verses? Because Dr. Godbey, in his commentary and translation has left them out. Why did he leave them out? Because they were not in the Sinaitic [sic] manuscript from which he translated. It was a manuscript found in later years in a mission on Mount Sinai. The man who found the manuscript, a German by the name of Tischendorf, said that some sheets of it had already been thrown into a receptacle for kindling wood. In this or some other way, a part may have been lost from that manuscript.[42]

The writer who had once followed Godbey's word on the reliability of the text had come to believe that these were Jesus' last words because of what had been experienced and heard through the Spirit at Azusa. For those at Azusa, Word and Spirit were the guide! African-American Christians, according to James Cone, already had a hermeneutic that placed Scriptural interpretation in the context of "a gift of the Spirit," rather than "intellectual encounter with the text."[43]

In a later issue, one finds a statement which reveals the Spirit's role in Pentecostal hermeneutics: "This Bible becomes a new book to those baptized with the Holy Ghost. You absolutely lose your own judgment in regard to the Word of God. You eat it down without trimming or cutting, right from the mouth of God. You live by every word that proceedeth out of the mouth of God."[44] Land, in answering the question "Do Pentecostals place Spirit above the Scripture?" writes:

---

[41] *AF* 1.1, Sept. 1906: 2.

[42] *AF* 1.2, Oct. 1906: 3. For a more extensive study of the use of the longer ending of Mark in early Pentecostalism, see John Christopher Thomas and Kimberly Ervin Alexander, "'And the Signs Are Following': Mark 16:9-20—A Journey into Pentecostal Hermeneutics," *Journal of Pentecostal Theology* 11, no. 2 (2003): 147-70.

[43] James Cone, "Black Worship," in *The Study of Spirituality,* ed. Cheslyn Jones, Geoffrey Wainwright, and Edward Yarnold (Oxford: Oxford UP, 1986) 489. Cone gives as an example the rejection by blacks of white interpretations of Scripture which endorsed slavery. They understood themselves as not being "merely taught by the Book" but by the Spirit.

[44] *AF* 1.5, Jan. 1907: 3.

> The answer is "Yes" and "No." Yes, the Spirit is prior to the written Word of God, but the Spirit inspires, preserves and illumines the Word within the communion of those who are formed, corrected, nurtured and equipped by the Word. Yes, the Spirit does not exist only to illumine Scripture and apply the benefits of salvation to the believer. The gifting and guiding of persons in community and the community as a whole is the ongoing, daily task of the Spirit. The signs and power of the Spirit are not an optional addition for a church that would engage principalities and powers and suffer unto death.[45]

Not to accept the final words of Jesus would be trimming or cutting, thereby rejecting what came out of the mouth of God.

"Signs following" became the litmus test for a movement of God. *The Apostolic Faith* boldly proclaimed in headlines that these signs were following at Azusa.[46] These signs were the subject of songs given by the Holy Spirit[47] and of messages in tongues interpreted by the Holy Spirit.[48]

Charles H. Mason testified that before his experience at Azusa, he had seen the sign of healing many times but had not understood the sign of tongues. As he began to "hunger and thirst" for more, he accepted that tongues was a sign of baptism in the Spirit. The sign came as he totally surrendered his whole being to God. Tongues, then, became a sign of responsiveness and surrender to God just as healing had been a sign of his acceptance of God's power to heal.[49]

In its 11th issue, *The Apostolic Faith* published a series of questions and answers. One of those questions asked what was the real evidence of the baptism of the Holy Ghost. The answer follows:

> Divine love, which is charity. Charity is the Spirit of Jesus. They will have the fruits of the Spirit. Galatians 5:22: "The fruit of the Spirit is love, joy, peace, longsuffering, gentleness, goodness, meekness, faith, temperance; against such there is no law. And they that are Christ's have crucified the flesh with the affections and lusts." This [is] the real Bible evidence in their daily walk and conversation; and the outward manifestations; speaking in tongues and the signs following: casting out devils, laying hands on the sick and the sick being healed, and the love of God for souls increasing in their hearts.[50]

---

[45] Land, *Pentecostal Spirituality*, 39.
[46] *AF* 1.4, Dec. 1906: 1.
[47] *AF* 1.8, May 1907: 2.
[48] *AF* 1.4, Dec. 1906: 3.
[49] *AF* 1.6, Feb.-Mar. 1907: 7.
[50] *AF* 1.11, Jan. 1908: 2.

For the Azusa leadership, these signs followed the person whose life was filled with the fruit of the Spirit. The signs were outward manifestations of inward experiences. So they were not just phenomena poured out by God, but were the natural outflow of the Spirit-filled life, the life that participates in God. This is why those who experienced an inward flow, or streaming of the Spirit, could assume it to be healing power.

Means of Healing

The scripture most often referred to in regard to the method of healing or the practice of healing is James 5:14. The text is used to support the statement of faith with regard to seeking healing. Reports in the first issue support this doctrinal statement. The last page of the first issue carries the story of one who was anointed and prayed for and whose deafness was healed.[51] G.B. Cashwell, a North Carolina Holiness minister who was baptized in the Holy Spirit at Azusa, reported cases where the sick were anointed with oil throughout the southeastern United States, just as he had been anointed at the meeting in Los Angeles.[52] No explanation of what oil symbolizes, or what occurs as the oil is applied, is offered. The practice seems to be in obedience to Scripture and seems to be accompanied by the faith that God's healing power will be present.

For others, Mark 16 was understood as a mandate: "They shall lay hands on the sick and they shall recover." Many testimonies are offered in which the sick have hands laid on them, or are touched in some way by the one doing the praying, and the sickness disappears. A.G. Garr and his wife, early recipients at Azusa, went back to their home in Danville, Virginia, and reported on the healings that had taken place there. Garr writes, "Soon after we arrived, a lady sick with dropsy came to the meeting. She got out of bed to come; had been sick a long time. As she told us how glad she was to see us back in Danville and of her long sick spell, I said: 'God will heal you,' and took her hand. She immediately shouted that she was healed. I felt the healing power flow into her body."[53]

For others, it was possible simply to pray the prayer of faith, according to James 5, and see the results. The person need not be present to be healed. If two agreed in prayer together, healing could take place.[54]

---

[51] *AF* 1.1, Sept. 1906: 4.

[52] *AF* 1.7, Apr. 1907: 4; and 1.4, Dec. 1906: 3.

[53] *AF* 1.2, Oct. 1906: 3.

[54] *AF* 1.9, June-Sept. 1907: 3.

The altar became a place of healing. Here, just as one could be saved, sanctified or Spirit-baptized, one could receive healing.[55] At the altar, one could be anointed with oil or have hands laid on them.

Healing also came as a result of spiritual or charismatic experiences. Several issues report visions of light, clouds, heaven or of Jesus, which culminate in the healing of an individual.[56] In an issue from September 1907, a report is given of a girl who had been "laid out for burial" and who was hours later "raised from the dead." While in this unconscious state, she had a vision of Jesus and heaven. It was reported that the child was completely healed as a result.[57]

One of the most common means of healing for Azusa followers was the anointed handkerchief. Taking Acts 19:12 as their cue, handkerchiefs were brought to Pentecostal meetings to be prayed for and anointed with oil. Others would send the handkerchief to *The Apostolic Faith* office in order that it be anointed and mailed back to the sick ones. Readers reported that they were healed as a result, often as they removed the cloth from the envelope. A Canadian reader wrote:

> I feel led by the Holy Spirit to testify to the glory of God what He has done for me and my wife. The Lord has wonderfully healed me from catarrh of nine years standing. Glory! Glory! Glory! Glory be to my dear Redeemer's name! Soon as I received the handkerchief, or as soon as I opened the letter, such power went through my whole being as I have never felt before, and I praise Him, I feel the healing balm just now go through soul and body. Glory to King Jesus, the Great Physician of soul and body.[58]

The power to heal did not reside in the handkerchief, nor the oil used to anoint, but "through the simple faith of the dear ones who brought them." *The Apostolic Faith* staff wrote that they prayed for the handkerchiefs and "the power of God comes upon us in praying for them."[59] As with anointing with oil, there is a sacramental quality to this type of observance. The presence of God is manifested through a common element according to the faith of those praying and receiving.

---

[55] *AF* 1.1, Sept. 1906: 4.
[56] *AF* 1.3, Nov. 1906: 4; 1.5, Jan. 1907: 3.
[57] *AF* 1.9, June-Sept. 1907: 4.
[58] *AF* 3.
[59] *AF* 1.6, Feb.-Mar. 1907: 1.

A final and important word must be said about the means of healing. For the Azusa participants, Jesus is the Great Physician and to take medicine is, like Solomon and those after him, to trust in the arm of the flesh. The Azusa leaders contended that medicine and doctors could come between a person and the Atonement.[60] They warned, "The doctor gives you poison and you die because you dishonor the Atonement. You are sickly, you fall asleep. You come to the Lord's table and yet you do not believe in full salvation for soul and body. You take the cup and eat the bread, and yet deny the body of the Lord for health and salvation. So you are sick because you do not discern the body of the Lord Jesus."[61]

Numerous testimonies attributed healing to trusting in Jesus as healer and not in medicine. *The Apostolic Faith* advised the healed not to keep "crutches, medicine bottles, and glasses" as "souvenirs" lest one be tempted to use them again.[62] This advice may be a critique of those like Alexander Dowie who displayed such articles as healing trophies.

With 15 references in 13 issues to this matter, it seems evident that there was no room for any other means of healing than that coming through Jesus directly. If medicine is "poison," then clearly Jesus would not use this method to heal. If one was "in the way," then he or she took Jesus as healer and Great Physician. This strict stance, of course, is not peculiar to the Pentecostal Movement. It was inherited from those in the healing movement before them.

Conclusion

In Seymour's 1915 *Doctrines and Discipline,* one witnesses the evolution of the Azusa Street congregation. Seymour alludes to divisions within the Pentecostal Movement, especially those along racial lines, which had rocked the congregation at 312 Azusa Street. This document also provides a glimpse into the movement's transformation in the area of governance. Further, Seymour comments on "fleshly doctrines" and practices which had sought to invade the movement.[63] One of the effects of these challenges is Seymour's apparent contextual reflection on the doctrine of Spirit baptism and the accompanying signs in which he broadens his view.[64]

---

[60] *AF* 1.4, Dec. 1906: 2.

[61] *AF.*

[62] *AF.*

[63] Specifically, he refers to non-Trinitarian baptism, "artificial dancing," soul sleep, Sabbatarianism, triple immersion in baptism, "holy kisses" between male and female believers, divorce and remarriage questions, and annihilation of the wicked.

[64] See Kimberly Ervin Alexander, "'Gracious Pentecostal Showers': Experiences of Spirit Baptism on Azusa Street" (forthcoming).

An overlooked later reflection is in Seymour's expansion of his statement of faith regarding healing. Earlier editions of the statement quoted Exodus 15:26 and included references to classic healing texts (James 5:14; Psalm 103:3; 2 Kings 20:5; Matthew 8:16, 17; Mark 16:16-18). The earlier statement had also included a quotation of Jeremiah 32:37, "Behold I am the Lord, the God of all flesh; is there anything too hard for me?"[65] But in 1915, Seymour follows the Jeremiah citation with a reference to Luke 24:52, 53 and the phrase "with great joy."[66]

In spite of the constraints of organization, controversies, personal hurt and division, it seems that the elder Seymour felt a need to comment on the results of his understanding and experience of Pentecostal healing; this truth had brought him "great joy."

May the heirs of Azusa ever experience the same.

---

[65] AF 1:1, 1:2, 1:3, and 2:2.
[66] Seymour, *Doctrines and Discipline*, 93.

4

Spiritual Hunger "on the Apostolic Faith Line"

Daniel Woods

Part One: Gaston Barnabas Cashwell Travels to Los Angeles Hungry

About two months ago, I began to read in the Way of Faith *the reports of the meetings in Azusa Mission, Los Angeles. I had been preaching holiness for nine years, but my soul began to hunger and thirst for the fullness of God* (G.B. Cashwell, late December 1907).[1]

Because there are no extant issues of *The Way of Faith* from the early Azusa Revival, we can not be certain exactly what Reverend G.B. Cashwell read that stirred a "hunger and thirst" strong enough to draw him from eastern North Carolina to Southern California. As veteran holiness preacher, first in the Methodist Episcopal Church (South) and after 1903 as minister in the breakaway Holiness Church of North Carolina, Cashwell had long believed that the "baptism with the Holy Ghost" was another name for the "second blessing" of sanctification. Yet something in the reports issuing from Los Angeles convinced him that Spirit baptism was a separate "third blessing"

---

[1] G.B. Cashwell, "Came 3,000 Miles for His Pentecost," *Apostolic Faith* [Los Angeles], Dec. 1906: 3. [Hereafter cited as *AF*.] Emphasis added.

he had not experienced, and he began to long for "the fullness of God." The hunger was so strong that Cashwell set out for Azusa Street with only enough money for a one-way ticket, fasting his way across the continent to seek the true "baptism with the Holy Ghost."

Cashwell headed directly to the altar upon arriving at the Apostolic Faith Mission, but he "struggled from Sunday till Thursday" before his hunger was satisfied. As with many pilgrims, especially those who had been active in the Holiness ministry, Cashwell had to experience a deeper level of purification before speaking in tongues, the "Bible sign" that one had indeed been baptized in the Holy Spirit. Though he had to "die to many things" during this "new crucifixion," Cashwell's primary hindrance was apparently racial prejudice. Though he must have read about the biracial composition of the revival's leadership and multiethnic nature of the crowds, the bevy of black altar workers attempting to impart Spirit baptism by laying their hands on white seekers offended his Southern sensibilities. After days of seeking God in "an upstairs room in the Mission," Cashwell saw "the windows of heaven" open and the "light of God" instantly clarified his thinking. After returning to the meeting hall, Cashwell began to speak in tongues that he described variously as German, Greek and "unknown."

Cashwell steamed out of Los Angeles a blessed man. He had been delivered from chronic rheumatism and catarrh at a special healing service. Furthermore, the Azusa saints had collected enough money to purchase his return fare, and he had enough left over to buy the new suit of clothes he had been praying for. Most of all, Cashwell headed home with what he had come for: "I am filled with His Spirit and love, and I am now feasting and drinking at the fountain continually and speak as the Spirit gives utterance." Experiencing what Azusa pastor William J. Seymour called "the full gospel," Cashwell left his hunger in California and returned home a full man.[2]

According to a brief news item in *The Apostolic Faith*, Cashwell departed for North Carolina "rejoicing to carry the good news of the Pentecost to the hungry souls there." Clara Lum, Seymour's "silent partner" in producing the Azusa Revival's official paper, probably wrote these words.[3] She understood the spiritual hunger that drew seekers like Cashwell to Azusa Street. In the late

---

[2] This account draws on Cashwell, "Came 3,000 Miles," 3; an untitled news item in *AF,* Dec. 1906, 3: and Vinson Synan, *The Holiness-Pentecostal Tradition: Charismatic Movements in the Twentieth Century* (Grand Rapids: Eerdmans, 1997) 112-14.

[3] Edith L. Blumhofer and Grant Wacker make a persuasive case for Lum's editorial role with the paper in "Who Edited the Azusa Mission's *Apostolic Faith?*" *Assemblies of God Heritage*, Summer 2001: 15-21.

1890s, she had left her teaching position in California to move to Shenandoah, Iowa, the headquarters of the World's Faith Missionary Association, a radical Holiness enterprise headed by Charles Hanley. In July 1898, a powerful experience of "Christ in me" led her to declare, "I can never be hungry any more." Yet by May 1906, when she visited the emerging Azusa Revival, Lum felt she had lost her experience, and she longed for the spiritual intimacy and power she witnessed in that humble place. Soon Lum was speaking in tongues, the one sure sign that a seeker was filled with the Holy Ghost, and claiming the additional spiritual gifts of healing, exorcism and anointed writing.[4]

Beginning in 1899, Lum had served as the associate editor of Hanley's paper, *The Firebrand*, choosing testimonies and writing news items that magnified God's willingness to satisfy the longings of those whose faith could break through the restraints of traditional religious forms and doctrines. She assumed the same position and purpose with *The Apostolic Faith* when Seymour launched the paper in September 1906. She used her writing and editorial responsibilities to celebrate God's ability and willingness to satisfy the desires of hungry saints, always with the goal of stirring even more spiritual hunger wherever her news traveled. Like J.M. Pike of *The Way of Faith* and many other radical Holiness editors of the time, Lum served as a mediator of spiritual hunger, both reflecting and shaping expectations with every issue.

In this light, it is important to return to the moment when G.B. Cashwell finally experienced his Pentecostal baptism. When his struggle ended successfully in the mission's "upper room," Cashwell descended into the main meeting hall to find Clara Lum reading to the assembled seekers "of how the Holy Ghost was falling in other places." After listening briefly as Lum previewed material from the upcoming edition of *The Apostolic Faith*, Cashwell suddenly began "speaking in tongues and praising God." Since this kind of thrilling news originally stirred him to travel "by faith" to Los Angeles, it seems appropriate that the consummation of Cashwell's pilgrimage occurred to the sound of widespread Pentecostal testimonies so fresh that they had yet to make it into print.[5]

These reports, more than the sermons, statements of faith, and exegetical articles that quickly began to proliferate in the burgeoning Pentecostal press, provide a window on the spiritual longings of the people who gravitated to the

---

[4] Blumhofer, "Clara E. Lum," *Assemblies of God Heritage*, Summer 2001: 17-18.
[5] Cashwell, "Came 3,000 Miles," 3.

Azusa Revival.[6] While editors like Lum exercised considerable control over the material by their selection, editing, and summarizing of testimonies and revival reports, they drew their exemplars from behavior they observed and accounts they heard and read. From this perspective, the relationship between the producers of the revival (like Seymour and Lum) and its consumers (like Cashwell and countless others who either traveled to Los Angeles or corresponded with the revival's leaders) appear to be more symbiotic than linear, with publishers and readers building each other's desires and expectations.

Part Two: Feasting on Azusa Fare

People from all over the country are sending in letters of inquiry, having heard that Pentecost has come to Los Angeles. . . . *Souls are hungry all over the land* (Clara Lum, September 1907).[7]

Seymour and Lum produced 13 issues of *The Apostolic Faith* between September 1906 and May 1908. One constant in the paper, evident in both the direct testimonies of the newly baptized Pentecostals and the mediating words of the editorial staff, was the prevalence of "hungry/filled" imagery. In the inaugural issue of the paper, for example, anonymous editorials and news briefs rooted the stunning success of the revival in its ability to stimulate and satisfy spiritual hunger. One anonymous front-page article traced the revival's origins to "five years ago last January" when a female student in a short-lived Kansas Holiness school operated by Charles Parham spoke in tongues after she and her colleagues had "tarried" for "true Pentecostal power." "This made all the Bible school *hungry,* and three nights afterward, 12 students received the Holy Ghost, and prophesied, and cloven tongues could be seen upon their heads."[8] Then early in 1906, "the Lord sent" Seymour and two others associated with Parham in Houston to Los Angeles "as messengers of the *full* gospel."[9]

---

[6] What amounted to a statement of faith for the Apostolic Faith Movement appeared in the initial *AF* issue under the title "The Apostolic Faith Movement" (*AF,* Sept. 1906: 2). The three core experiences were salvation, sanctification and Spirit baptism—the latter identified as "a gift of power upon the sanctified life" that is always accompanied by tongues, "the same evidence as the Disciples received on the Day of Pentecost." In addition, Azusa leaders emphasized that all true believers should forsake their "sinful ways" (even making "restitution" when appropriate) and that they "must believe that God is able to heal" the sick. The same list of beliefs appeared in several of the 13 *AF* issues published under Seymour's oversight between September 1906 and May 1908 with only slight changes in wording.

[7] "Good News Spreads," *AF,* Sept. 1906: 4. Emphasis added.

[8] "The Old-Time Pentecost," *AF,* Sept. 1906: 1.

[9] Untitled news item, *AF,* Sept. 1906: 1.

After the revival broke loose in California, according to a brief note titled "Message from God," one "sister had a vision of God's people as vessels that were *full*, and the Lord said, 'The vessels must be emptied and I will *fill* them.'"[10] Within a few months, missionaries had headed across the city and the globe to carry the news that "the last Pentecostal revival to bring our Jesus" had commenced in a humble "barn-like building on Azusa Street."[11]

One woman "spoke to the Russians in their church in Los Angeles in their own language as the Spirit gave the utterance." "They are a simple, pure, and *hungry* people for the *full* gospel," the unnamed reporter added.[12] Another report told of "Brother and Sister A.G. Garr . . . preaching to *hungry* souls" in Danville, Virginia, while on their way to carry the Azusa message to India.[13]

The purpose of the paper was also couched in the figurative language of *hunger*. According to a short notice titled "Good News Spreads," publication of *The Apostolic Faith* had become necessary because "souls are *hungry* all over the land." "People from all over the country are sending in letters of inquiry, having heard that Pentecost has come to Los Angeles. Some have come long distances and report that the half had not been told them. Through this paper we answer inquiries, as it would be impossible to write to each."[14] Readers of the first issue learned that subscription to the paper was free and that they were encouraged to send in the addresses of "any *hungry* souls to whom you wish the paper sent."[15]

The voices, if not the names, of *The Apostolic Faith* staff come through clearly from the first issue. Equally burdened to satisfy spiritual hunger where it already existed and to heighten it everywhere else, they labored to represent the sound of "unknown tongues" and to capture other miraculous events "beyond description" in ordinary but compelling words.[16]

Since this unarticulated editorial policy guided the selection, shrinking and summarizing of so many firsthand testimonies, scholars interested in the spirituality of early Pentecostals must be aware that they are often listening to two voices speak at once. At times, especially when multiple versions of testimonies have survived, one might disentangle the voices in insightful ways. For the most part, though,

---

[10] *AF,* Sept. 1906: 4.

[11] Untitled news item, *AF,* Sept. 1906: 4. "The Same Old Way," *AF,* Sept. 1906: 3.

[12] "Russians Hear in Their Own Language," *AF,* September 1906, 4.

[13] "Good News from Danville, Va.," *AF,* Sept. 1906: 4.

[14] *AF,* Sept.1906: 2.

[15] "Sample Copies," *AF,* Sept. 1906: 4.

[16] "Pentecost Has Come," *AF,* Sept. 1906: 1.

students of the movement can safely accept these two voices as one testimony resonating from a place of deep agreement about the needs of God's people as Christ's return approached. They found expression in print, in other words, when the producers and consumers of the revival spoke convincingly to each other about the particulars of their spiritual hunger. And these testimonies deliver a wider range of acceptable desires and gratifications than the more narrowly focused and internally consistent doctrinal statements and sermons that have attracted so much of historians' attention to this point.[17]

A sampling of six such testimonial duets, also drawn from the September 1906 issue of *The Apostolic Faith*, illustrates the value of these painfully brief and disembodied reports, each one mapping a point where the spiritual dynamic of the Azusa Revival intersected with the needs and longings of the everyday (and often unnamed) folk who gravitated to the emerging Pentecostal Movement.

These testimonies also allow scholars to consider the experiences of people outside Southern California, like G.B. Cashwell, who read these or similar reports and "began to hunger and thirst for the fullness of God." While most could not emulate Cashwell's pilgrimage to Los Angeles, their hunger in many cases proved strong enough to draw the Azusa spirit from the printed text and release it to where they lived.

The first testimony, occupying a bare seven lines on the front page, announces: "A brother who had been a spiritualist medium and who was so possessed with demons that he had no rest, and was on the point of committing suicide, was instantly delivered of demon power. He then sought God for the pardon of his sins and sanctification, and is now filled with a different Spirit." Whether he was a "brother" who had become possessed or a possessed man who was now a brother, this man's apparently lightning-quick reversal of fortunes spoke to several levels of spiritual longing: the mainstream evangelical desire to see sinners saved (or backsliders reclaimed); the holiness desire to see the redeemed experience the "second blessing" of sanctifying grace; the radical evangelical desire to see the reality of demonic power both confirmed and cast out; and, the Pentecostal desire to steal one from the Spiritualists, rivals they believed were offering a seductive but counterfeit path to supernatural power.

---

[17] For an exceptional recent use of testimonies, see Grant Wacker's *Heaven Below: Early Pentecostals and American Culture* (Cambridge and London: Harvard UP, 2001). Also see Daniel Woods, "The Royal Telephone: Early Pentecostalism in the South and the Enthusiastic Practice of Prayer," in *Religion in the American South: Protestants and Others in History and Culture,* ed. Beth Barton Schweiger and Donald G. Mathews, eds. (Chapel Hill and London: U of North Carolina P, 2004) 125-52.

Only as a last note does the reader learn that the delivered man had also been "filled with a different Spirit."[18]

Readers and writers of *The Apostolic Faith* shared a similar passion for quick and impressive changes in individuals' lives. A second testimony tells of a "young man who a year ago was in the chain gang," but "is now baptized with the Holy Ghost and preaching everywhere. He was "a Catholic but God took all the Romanism out of him."

The few selected details in this short item effectively met readers at several points of spiritual hunger. The young man had been changed by an encounter with a living God, they were assured, not by the power of education or social reform. Also, some readers may have perceived him as one of the "new immigrants," mostly Roman Catholics, Orthodox Christians and Jews who had arrived from Eastern and Southern Europe during the last two decades. It must have reassured many anxious Evangelicals to read about God using Pentecostal power to punch "all the Romanism out" of one of these strangers. Furthermore, the ex-convict's deliverance promised to multiply itself because the experience of Spirit baptism had empowered him with the boldness to preach the full-gospel message everywhere, including places where he was "struck and spit upon in the face."

One other detail in this brief testimony was calculated to speak to the passions of many readers: "He is telling the Catholics to get their own Bibles and the Protestants to get to God and not lean on preachers." Early converts to the Azusa message often lived several hours of each day in their Bibles. People of the Spirit, they also longed for a revival of faithful devotion to the Word, especially one that stressed the responsibility of each believer to discover Biblical truths firsthand. True saints of God would not rely on the revelations of a denominational hierarchy, or even of some red-hot preacher; they could only stand on what they heard directly from the Lord. Theirs was a Biblicism with a decidedly populist and individualist streak.[19]

A third testimony presents an even more rapid-fire sequence of supernatural events in the life of an anonymous youth: "In about an hour and a half, a young man was converted, sanctified, and baptized with the Holy Ghost, and spoke with tongues. He was also healed from consumption, so that when he visited the doctor he pronounced his lungs sound." In a span no doubt shorter than the duration of many fruitless sermons the readers had endured, this young man had his past sins wiped from his record and the root of inbred sin pulled

---
[18] Untitled news item, *AF*, Sept. 1906: 1.
[19] Untitled news item, *AF*, Sept. 1906: 2.

from his heart. Additionally, he had spoken in tongues, the "Bible sign" that he had indeed been filled with the Holy Ghost, and was instantly freed from the plague of consumption. Readers hoping for proof of the Azusa Revival's authenticity would have latched on to the physician's confirmation (though few early Pentecostals placed much stock in doctors otherwise).

This miniscule narrative does not stop with the young man's dizzying first few minutes as a Christian. The last sentence adds what must have been the most intriguing part of the story: "He has received many tongues, also the gift of prophecy, and writing in a number of foreign languages, and has a call to a foreign field." An alert reader in 1906 would have unpacked the following claims from this loaded sentence: (1) Glossolalia is not just a "heavenly language" that signals Spirit baptism; it is also the "gift of tongues"; (2) this gift can open the door to other charisms mentioned in 1 Corinthians 12, such as prophecy; (3) the restoration of tongues as the ability to speak (and apparently write) actual foreign languages one had never learned could speed up the eternal timetable of world evangelization—and, consequently, of the Second Coming; (4) these gifts may be accompanied by a ministerial "calling" that could free Pentecostal saints from the drag mundane of responsibilities and give their lives an exalted purpose. Once unpacked, these implications demanded responses from expectant readers—responses that could range from vitriolic rejection to immediate acceptance.[20]

The fourth reported testimony shares several features with the first three. Writer and subject remain anonymous in this 12-line paragraph, which again features a flurry of miraculous experiences:

> A young lady who came into the meeting unsaved, went to the altar during the sermon, under deep conviction, and was saved in about five minutes. Before that evening was over, she was sanctified and baptized with the Holy Ghost and had the gift of the Chinese tongue and was singing in Chinese in the Spirit.

In a variation on a theme, this young woman rushed through the emerging Pentecostal *ordo salutis* and evidenced her Spirit baptism by speaking and then

---

[20] Untitled news item, *AF*, Sept. 1906: 1. For an example of the latter response, see the letter from Oregon Holiness editor M.L. Ryan: "When I finished reading in your letter of what God was doing in Los Angeles, I fell on my knees and agonized Godward a bursting soul of appreciation; a great and blessed conviction seized me." The private reaction soon turned public as he "rushed out of the office shouting and praising God. The fire had struck my soul. I then read the wonderful works of God in Los Angeles to others and a little crowd gathered around me; they too caught the fire of the Spirit in the letter and some shouted and some wept" (untitled news item, *AF*, Sept. 1906: 2).

singing in Chinese. This particular detail apparently struck a deep chord with many readers. Surviving Pentecostal periodicals from the movement's first few years feature multiple accounts of "singing in the Spirit." Reported variously as familiar tunes sung in unlearned foreign tongues, as "wordless songs" intoned in "heavenly languages," as the corporate rendition of a "new song" in tongues (often accompanied by others "playing instruments in the Spirit"), and even as the sound of an unseen angelic choir, supernatural music captured the imagination of early converts to Pentecostalism as little else did.[21]

Furthermore, this young woman witnessed the beginning of something else that readers of *The Apostolic Faith* desired—a revival at home. Her mother, who rushed to the altar close on her daughter's heels, "has also been saved, sanctified, baptized with the Holy Ghost, and healed of asthma and heart trouble, which the doctors said was incurable." The significance lay more in the implication than the particulars of this sentence: Those unmoved by the testimonies of strangers, may well respond when Pentecostal consequences strike close to home. The sight of a beloved family member weeping repentantly at an altar or singing confidently in Chinese held the potential to stimulate spiritual hunger in those who otherwise appeared unaffected by the swirl of manifestations taking place around them.[22]

Other reports tell of individuals who actually received their Azusa experiences at home so that family members who would not venture down to the Apostolic Faith Mission were forced to witness the results of Spirit baptism.[23] One clear goal of Azusa spirituality was to "set homes on fire."[24]

The next testimony differs from the previous four in that the subject is named and, after an editorial introduction, allowed to speak for herself. "Sister Anna Hall," had recently come to assist in the Los Angeles revival from Houston, where "the Lord led her into the Pentecostal baptism and gift of tongues without her hearing the truth except from the Word." Hers was one of the first of many testimonies in *The Apostolic Faith* and other early Pentecostal periodicals from people claiming to have previously spoken in tongues solely in response to a Scriptural insight. Hall and others served as reassuring precursors of the current revival. It also spoke to

---

[21] For a pioneering effort to place "singing in the Spirit" at the core of Pentecostal-Charismatic spirituality, see Richard M. Riss, "The Heavenly Choir," *International Pentecostal Holiness Church Legacy,* Summer 1996: 1-3, 6.

[22] Untitled news item, *AF,* Sept. 1906: 3.

[23] E.g., the front page of the first *AF* told of an octogenarian Nazarene who broke out in tongues at home. His son, a physician, "came to see if he was sick, but found him only happy in the Lord." Another "Nazarene brother" received Holy Ghost baptism "in his own home in family worship." He began to tell of feeling "an abounding love" so great "that it almost seemed to kill me."

[24] Untitled news item, *AF,* Sept. 1906: 1.

the Pentecostals' conviction that their movement was not altogether new, but a restoration of the New Testament pattern. All Christians who sincerely sought for "clear light on God's Word," they believed, would soon see that the Bible sanctioned the Azusa message.

Hall may have discovered the truth of Pentecostalism by *sola scriptura*, but her testimony relates a "wonderful vision and revelation" God had given her firsthand. Only a few weeks before leaving Texas, she awakened to a sense of God's imminent presence. Then in a blurring of natural and supernatural realities that clearly resonated with many new Pentecostals, Hall described hearing "the beautiful warbling of a bird" that "seemed way down in my soul." Then she "saw a little infant face," as the bird's song "began to ripple . . . like water running over pebbles." Then it "increased till it sounded like many waters, and the face enlarged till it was a full-grown face." Amid these transformations, Hall exclaimed, "Surely this is a messenger from the holy country." The sound and the face merged to answer her, "Yes and I have come to tell you that Jesus is coming. Go forward in My name, preach the gospel of the Kingdom, for the King's business demands haste."[25]

Hall's testimony demonstrates two other tenets of Azusa spirituality. First, Biblical authority for the revival was insufficient by itself. Visionary experiences, prophetic statements, and interpreted tongues messages fill the pages of most early Pentecostal papers, confirming and directing the inchoate movement. Second, extra-Biblical revelations served primarily to locate contemporary events on the eternal timetable. Easily more than half of all divine messages during the heady days of Pentecostalism's birth exclaimed in one way or another that "Jesus is coming" and the "fields are white unto harvest." The hastening of world evangelization through the restoration of the gift of tongues, therefore, was not merely an opportunity, it was the only hope for a lost humanity hurtling blindly toward the end of time. Because the "King's business demands haste," many readers of revelations like Hall's felt unprepared to meet the task at hand and began to hunger for increased spiritual energy. And while most efforts at self-definition in *The Apostolic Faith* and other early Pentecostal papers appear at first glance to point to some past ideal—whether to the manifestations of the apostolic age or merely to the "old-time religion" of the early 19th-century camp meetings—a more contextualized reading makes plain that this movement faced forward, looking back in time only long enough to recapture the levels of power and purity demanded by the challenges of living in the final stage of history.[26]

---

[25] "Jesus Is Coming," *AF*, Sept. 1906: 4.

[26] Cf. these two anonymous editorial statements in the September 1906 issue of *AF*: "The Apostolic Faith Movement" (p. 2) identifies the revival as restoration-oriented and

The last example covers the spread of the movement to Hermon, "a small Free Methodist settlement in the hills near Los Angeles." The anonymous report uses the experiences of several unnamed believers to highlight several more emerging Pentecostal commitments.

First, although *The Apostolic Faith* leaders stated clearly that the Azusa spirit aimed not "to tear down churches but to make new churches out of old ones," their insistence on displacing "dead forms and creeds" meant that the very spiritual dynamism their revival generated would by necessity create a considerable amount of division.[27] The witness from Hermon illustrates this process: "At cottage prayer meetings being held there, the Holy Ghost has manifested His presence in a marvelous way. The church people stand aloof to a great extent, but God is overthrowing all opposition. . . . Two nights afterward, at another cottage prayer meeting, the house was filled to overflowing with people." Pentecost came to Hermon in a home, not in a church, because the local Holiness leaders fought the Azusa message. Pentecostals prayed for these stubborn resistors to God's move—and celebrated whenever one succumbed to the "full gospel"—but they functioned in testimonies and reports primarily as foils, as proof that end-time truth was reserved for those hungry enough for "strong meat."

The Hermon report also makes clear that eating such "strong meat" could overwhelm the physical body of believers, subjecting them to hours, even days, of being shaken or "slain in the Spirit" before they broke forth speaking in tongues. Occurring more often than not in public, these manifestations demonstrated the level of humility a seeker of Spirit baptism must achieve, provided a deeply satisfying corporate experience Pentecostals described as "the power falling," and caused a sensation in the broader community that forced nearly everyone to take a position for or against God's move.

At a "meeting recently held in a cottage near the church" in Hermon, for example, "one sister was baptized with the Holy Ghost on the front porch. She lay under the power of God for something like two hours, praising God and speaking in an unknown language. Two nights afterward, at another cottage prayer meeting, the house was overflowing with people" and "two sisters lay under the power of God until after one o'clock, speaking and singing in unknown tongues. The singing could be heard over the hills. This is stirring the people."

---

does not mention premillenial eschatology as one of the revival's doctrinal commitments; while "Ascension Robes" (p. 4) makes clear the Azusa leaders' awareness that Jesus could return at any moment.

[27] Untitled news item, *AF*, Sept. 1906: 4. "The Apostolic Faith Movement," *AF*, Sept. 1906: 2.

The conclusion of the Hermon report explains that the Holy Spirit "recognizes no man-made creeds, doctrines, nor classes of people, but 'the willing and obedient shall eat the good of the land.'"[28] This remarkable sentence implies that the shapers of the Azusa Revival—both its producers and its consumers—were willing to endure alienation from family, church and community in exchange for the promise of a supernaturally effective ministry in the "last days." This was the center of their common spiritual hunger. But they would not have to eat alone. Whether enjoyed in person or in print, there existed a growing society of like-minded seekers. Traditional barriers of age, gender, region, nationality, race, ethnicity, denominational, education or income promised to be obliterated by the Spirit. All the hungry could anticipate sitting down together at a different type of Last Supper, one that prepared the true church "for her last march to meet her beloved."[29]

Part Three: Brother Cashwell Returns Home Full

At Dunn, N.C., about 50 have received the baptism with the Holy Ghost, about 15 preachers among them. Since we closed here, the work has spread into other states, Georgia, South Carolina, Virginia, and many parts of North Carolina. The power is falling and hundreds both white and colored, are receiving the real Pentecost. Some are receiving one gift, and some another. . . . Many of our people are speaking in divers kinds of tongues, and some are making arrangements for their fields of labor. Several missions are being opened up in the South on the *Apostolic Faith* line. Brethren, pray much, and push the work of making up the Bride, for the Bridegroom is coming (G.B. Cashwell, February 7, 1907).[30]

Barely a month after leaving Azusa Street, G.B. Cashwell rejoiced that all kinds of hungry Southerners were "receiving the real Pentecost." As in Los Angeles, the "power was falling" on seekers without regard to traditional distinctions of class, color or church affiliation. Pentecostalism was spreading throughout the South "on the Apostolic Faith line." Cashwell's choice of words here is suggestive. By "Apostolic Faith line," he no doubt referred to the bundle

---

[28] "Fire Falling at Hermon," *AF,* Sept. 1906: 3.

[29] Untitled news item, *AF,* Sept. 1906: 4. A brief item on page 1 cogently illustrates this obliteration of barriers by lumping the testimonies of "Bro. Campbell, a Nazarene brother, 83 years of age" and "Viola Price, a little orphan colored girl eight years" together in one brief paragraph (untitled news item, *AF,* Sept. 1906: 1).

[30] G.B. Cashwell, "The Fire Spreading in the South," *The New Acts* (Alliance, Ohio), Feb. 1907: 4. [Hereafter cited as *NA.*] Emphasis added.

of beliefs and manifestations transplanted from Azusa Street by the witness of religious periodicals and of returning pilgrims like himself. His phrase also carried a second meaning: The Holy Spirit was quickly establishing a network of Pentecostal "missions" throughout the South. In much the same way modern transportation and communication systems were rapidly shrinking the world by accelerating the movement of people and information, this emerging series of spiritual stations would carry the last great revival to every corner of the region, nation and globe with supernatural efficiency.

One of the most effective conduits of the Azusa message, Cashwell carried the essence of the revival to his native region in person and in print.[31] In his letter dated February 7, 1907, for example, Cashwell cogently combined several key elements of the emerging Pentecostal ethos. Only the holy, humble and hungry would give witness to Holy Ghost baptism by speaking in tongues, and as the "Bride of Christ," only they would be invited to the upcoming Wedding Supper of the Lamb. As time was short, all who received the Acts 2 *gift* of the Holy Spirit should expect to manifest one or more of the 1 Corinthians 12 *gifts* of the Spirit. "God has blest me," Cashwell explained, "in casting out devils, healing the sick and in discerning of spirits."[32]

Most often, though, the gift was "divers kinds of tongues," an instantaneous ability to speak in one or more foreign languages. Furthermore, because such divine powers uniquely equipped the Spirit-baptized to reap the end-time harvest, they should listen carefully for the location of their particular "fields of labor," which could just as easily be across town or on the other side of the world.[33]

Cashwell also brought home the full range of experiences that satisfied the hungry seekers in Los Angeles. The testimony of Florence Goff, who was Spirit baptized during the first week of Cashwell's Dunn meetings, illustrates the contact between Azusa spirituality and preexisting spiritual hungers that fueled the spread of the Pentecostal revival. Goff recalled that soon after her sanctification in 1896, "God blessed me in working for Him, gave me dreams and visions, and so powerfully anointed me with the Holy Ghost until I was sure I had the baptism."

---

[31] While other Southerners traveled to Los Angeles and helped bring Pentecostalism back home, only C.H. Mason had such a widespread impact on the region.

[32] Cashwell made this claim in a letter to *The Apostolic Faith* dated January 24. See "Hundreds Baptized in the South," *AF*, Feb.-Mar. 1907: 3.

[33] E.g., later in 1907, a young South Carolina farmer-preacher who attended the Dunn meetings visited Los Angeles on his way to becoming the first Pentecostal missionary in China. See Daniel Woods, "Failure and Success in the Ministry of T.J. McIntosh: The First Pentecostal Missionary to China," *Cyberjournal for Pentecostal-Charismatic Research* 12 (Jan. 2003), *www.pctii.org/cyberg/*.

Several years later, she embraced B.H. Irwin's mercurial Fire-Baptized movement and "received such an anointing that my flesh tingled as it were with heavenly fire," an experience she understood at the time as the authentic "third blessing." Following Irwin's moral failure in 1900, Goff found her ministry limited by a combination of serious physical illnesses and a nagging confusion about the reality of Spirit baptism.

Cashwell's return from Azusa Street facilitated a powerful encounter with the Holy Spirit that simultaneously—and unmistakably—resolved Florence Goff's theological and physical afflictions. Having read accounts in religious papers of the events in Los Angeles, and facing the prospect of another risky surgical procedure, Goff announced upon arriving at Cashwell's meetings that she had come "for the real baptism of the Holy Ghost and my body healed."

On January 5, 1907, and in the days to follow, her multivalent hunger found deep satisfaction when she came face-to-face with a messenger from Azusa Street:

> Brother Cashwell said, "Come to the altar." I went, several hands laid on me, the power fell, the Holy Ghost came and healing with him. They told me to say, "Praise the Lord!" I wanted to but my jaws were stiff, my hands drawn, but after a moment my jaws were loosed, I said "Praise the Lord!" two or three times, I felt like my tongue was coming out, it was going so fast. I knew he had come. I lay down on my left side and slept that night for the first time in months. Glory! Since then I have gained strength and weight. God has given me 12 languages, enabling me to write several, and play beautiful anthems with the words on the piano.... Often he interprets through me....
> In the battle till Jesus comes, robed and ready.[34]

Appearing in the initial issue of Cashwell's *The Bridegroom's Messenger*, Florence Goff's staccato testimony exemplifies how closely the doctrinal and experiential dynamics of Azusa spirituality were reproduced in countless—though probably never identical—baptisms in settings as diverse as Boston, Calcutta and Dunn.

Cashwell was only one such builder of "the Apostolic Faith line," many of whom never visited Los Angeles in person but acquired their mastery of Azusa spirituality from some combination of contacts with emissaries from Los Angeles and reading reports in sympathetic periodicals.[35]

---

[34] "Mrs. H.H. Goff's Letter," *The Bridegroom's Messenger* [Atlanta] Oct. 1, 1907: 4.

[35] For an excellent discussion of the first Pentecostal periodicals, including reprints of two early title lists, see Gary B. McGee, "Periodicals," in *The New International Dictionary of Pentecostal and Charismatic Movements,* ed. Stanley M. Burgess, with

Most of these papers, following the example of *The Apostolic Faith,* featured multiple reports and testimonies from around their regions and beyond, the sheer volume of which functioned to validate the spirituality of the Azusa Revival's central tenets and expressions. Editors and subscribers alike used these publications to track the establishment of a literal "Apostolic Faith line" as well. Freely reprinted from one paper to another, these witnesses provided readers with a mental map of the expanding Pentecostal network, as if the places they read about were stations linking a global connection of trains, telegraph operators or electrical generators in the spiritual realm.

The Massachusetts-based Holiness paper *Word and Work* typifies this genre, featuring detailed accounts of Pentecostal outpouring throughout New England but also delivering tantalizing snippets concerning developments around America and the world. Readers of the September 1907 issue, for example, learned of "a wonderful outpouring in Korea" and "marvelous things in the island of Java, here and there in China [and] Sweden." They also read that "unearthly music . . . of angels" was heard during a Holiness gathering in New York, that one Georgia man received the Holy Ghost after the Lord instructed him to write "27 letters to different ones, confessing wrongs or telling them of his desire to pay them money due them," and that a Seattle woman "fell under the power of the Spirit and conversed with some who interpreted, warning the people to prepare for the coming of the King of kings." They were invited to celebrate with many in Denver, Spokane and Winnipeg who had recently spoken in tongues and to intercede for "hungry little" clusters of small-town seekers in Missouri, Michigan and New Hampshire who had yet to break through. And, despite this ever-widening outpouring, they noted that "people still go to Azusa Street Mission in Los Angeles from long distances to get their Pentecost."[36] Readers of *Word and Work* (and most other Pentecostal papers) learned to plot what one contributor called "bright spots" as a way of building their confidence and focusing their prayers.[37]

Others headed for these "bright spots" in person once the Pentecostal revival moved closer to their homes. When Massachusetts evangelist A.J. Rawson, for example, read that Ivy Campbell had brought Pentecostal manifestations from

---

Eduard M. van der Maas (Grand Rapids: Zondervan, 2002) 975-78. Complete (or nearly complete) runs of some of these papers are currently available to scholars. For many other titles, though, only scattered issues or reprinted selections in other papers survive.

[36] "Extracts From Exchanges," *Word and Work,* Sept. 1907: 247-48. [Hereafter cited as *WW.*]

[37] E.g., in "Spread the Fire," G.L. Packard wrote, "New England is now dotted over with bright spots, over which the Holy Spirit is brooding, and where groups of saints are . . . receiving 'the promise of the Father' (*WW,* June 1907: 181)."

Los Angeles to Ohio, he boarded the first train for Akron. After receiving his baptism, Rawson announced, "This very year will witness the coming of Jesus and we shall see mighty miracles in the next few months."[38]

Such expectancy could push Pentecostal mapmaking into the prophetic. Soon after returning to New England, Rawson delivered a "message in tongues" on the nearness of the end which caused his wife to see "what seemed to be a map of the United States." In the midst of this vision, she exclaimed, "I can see bright places here and there, where the Pentecostal blessings are going to be."[39]

One month later, the Rawsons used their newfound prophetic gifts to clarify the existing map as well, removing sites of "fanaticism" and validating those where "the true work" had taken hold. In a written interpretation of her husband's message in tongues, Sister Rawson indicated the primary direction of the revival and highlighted its capital cities. It "started with those humble children in California," she explained, "and extended East." The revivals in the Akron and Alliance area of northeastern Ohio would now take center stage, and the movement "from there will extend to all parts of the world." "God wants us all," she concluded, "to keep in full touch with . . . headquarters in Ohio."[40]

Even if such overt efforts to project or edit the emerging map of the "Apostolic Faith line" failed to gain broad acceptance, the Azusa Revival's amazing spread convinced most Spirit-filled saints that their world was shrinking. Both the *end* of time and the *ends* of the earth were getting closer to them. In this emerging Pentecostal worldview, the increasingly faster transference of people, messages and power in the natural realm foreshadowed a corresponding development in the spiritual.

A.J. Rawson once more provides an exaggerated example of this logic. When one man "preached in Chinese," he "seemed to see" in a vision "four converted . . . and baptized." Rawson informed the audience that by means of "what is called Pentecostal wireless telegraphy," the brother was actually witnessing a real event as it occurred in China. One mission worker in attendance was greatly relieved. "She had been praying in the African language, but thought it of no use, since she could not go to Africa." Now she understood that the Holy Spirit had been broadcasting her prayers instantly across the Atlantic "by a Pentecostal wireless method, corresponding to the Marconi system." Rawson apparently got this idea

---

[38] Quoted in Addie M. Otis, "The Apostolic Faith Movement," *WW*, Feb. 1907: 51.

[39] "Good News From New England," *NA*, Feb. 1907: 2.

[40] Following divine direction, A.J. Rawson sent the translated tongues message to *The New Acts*, "for it is for all the people to know" ("Momentous Message," *NA*, Apr. 1907: 3). S.G. Otis, publisher of *Word and Work*, immediately reprinted the text in full ("The Apostolic Faith Work in New England," *WW*, Apr. 1907: 113).

from a speculative piece in *The Apostolic Evangel,* a Georgia paper edited by one of Cashwell's biggest conquests, Fire-Baptized leader J.H. King. The next issue of *Word and Work* reprinted the entire article to enlighten its largely New England readership, illustrating once more the importance of emissaries and editors in promoting hunger for the Azusa experience as they simultaneously extended and reshaped the "Apostolic Faith line."[41]

The movement's early fascination with "missionary tongues," whether delivered in person or over the Holy Ghost radio, gradually faded from the front pages of most Pentecostal periodicals. So too did hopes for an easy perfection and unity of all Spirit-filled Christians—and even the expectation that the end could not be more than a year or two away.

Reports of corporate singing in tongues also became less frequent, as did witnesses to racial equality. By late 1908, after Clara Lum had moved to Oregon and taken *The Apostolic Faith* with her, events on Azusa Street began to recede from the larger view.[42] In 1909, frustrated by the lack of unity, giftedness and ethical purity among Pentecostals, G.B. Cashwell returned to Methodism.[43]

Yet the short-lived satisfaction readers drew in early 1908 from the prospect of "Pentecostal Wireless Telegraphy" illustrates more than the enthusiastic naiveté of the revival. It also expresses the core value evident from the beginning of the Azusa outpouring: believers' hunger to feel God's Word coursing through their bodies to touch a lost and hurting world with supernatural effectiveness before Christ's return. And a century later, this longing continues to attract seekers from all classes, cultures and churches and to locate them on the increasingly visible Pentecostal map of the world.

---

[41] "Apostolic Faith Mission, 260 Maple Street, Lynn, Mass.," *WW,* Jan. 1908: 18. The last quote comes from "Pentecostal Wireless Telegraphy," attributed to *Apostolic Evangel* and reprinted in *WW,* Feb. 1908: 36-38. *The Apostolic Evangel* had ceased publication by September 1907, but Rawsons had ministered with King prior to this time and presumably had access to his publications ("The Outlook Bright," *NA,* June 1907: 7).

[42] Historians disagree on the impact of Lum's actions on the Los Angeles revival. See Blumhofer and Wacker, "Who Edited the Azusa Mission's *Apostolic Faith*?"

[43] This assessment is based on my reading of Cashwell's articles in *The Bridegroom's Messenger* in 1908 and early 1909.

5

From Azusa to Cleveland

The Amazing Journey of G.B. Cashwell and the Spread of Pentecostalism

David G. Roebuck

On March 18, 1916, A.J. Tomlinson, general overseer of the Church of God, published an announcement of the death of G.B. Cashwell. Tomlinson wrote:

> As we go to press we have just learned of the death of brother G.B. Cashwell, of Dunn, North Carolina, having departed this life the 4th [of this month]. Well I do remember that on the 12th day of January, 1908, while this dear brother was standing behind the sacred desk delivering the message the Holy Ghost fell upon this servant of the Lord, and after about three hours of wonderful manifestations, I knew I had received the Holy Ghost because I spoke in tongues as the Spirit gave utterance.

Tomlinson continued:

> To brother Cashwell is due the honor of carrying the Pentecostal message, first to many of us in the southeastern states eight years ago, having preached in his own state North Carolina, Georgia, Florida, Alabama and Tennessee, besides some of the western states. Though his career as a Pentecostal preacher was of short duration, he set the match to the prepared material, and the fire he started is still blazing higher and spreading.[1]

---

[1] A.J. Tomlinson, "G.B. Cashwell Passes Over," *Church of God Evangel,* Mar. 18, 1916: 2.

This brief death announcement revealed the influence of G.B. Cashwell on the spread of Pentecostalism throughout the southeastern United States. Although it specifically recounted Cashwell's influence on A.J. Tomlinson in Cleveland, Tennessee, it is illustrative of both the rapid spread of the movement and Cashwell's role in its expansion. There are, of course, many other stories of men and women leaving the Azusa Street Mission in Los Angeles and taking the Pentecostal message to their constituencies, or to those in other parts of the world. But few had the explosive success that Cashwell experienced.

Along his journey, Cashwell significantly influenced people and movements that came to make up some of the largest Pentecostal denominations in the United States. Added to Cashwell's extraordinary geographical journey, the story of Tomlinson is an illustration of how Holiness leaders altered their theological understanding of Spirit Baptism from that taught by the Holiness Movement, to that taught by the emerging Pentecostal Movement.

Religious Activity in Bradley County, Tennessee

The story of Cashwell's journey from Azusa Street to Cleveland, Tennessee, begins with the account of how Tomlinson came to live in Cleveland. Ambrose Jessup Tomlinson can be characterized as a missionary and a seeker. Born into a Quaker farm family in Westfield, Indiana, he was converted shortly after his marriage in 1889, and soon became convinced of the doctrine of entire sanctification. Seeing great needs among the "mission field" in the mountains of western North Carolina, eastern Tennessee, and northern Georgia, perhaps as early as 1894, Tomlinson traveled to that region as a colporteur and missionary evangelist.[2]

By 1899, the Tomlinson family had settled in Culberson, North Carolina, to establish a ministry base there. Culberson was a small village located in western North Carolina, just north of the Georgia state line and along a railroad. Soon Tomlinson founded a school for children, a Sunday school, a clothing distribution center and an orphanage. As a means of appealing for financial support, Tomlinson published a periodical titled *Samson's Foxes*. He envisioned the children to whom he ministered as potential firebrands of the gospel among the

---

[2] The best biography of Tomlinson is R.G. Robins, *A.J. Tomlinson: Plainfolk Modernist* (New York: Oxford UP, 2004). Much of Tomlinson's journal is in the Manuscript Division of the Library of Congress in Washington, D.C. Tomlinson's son, Homer, edited and published the journal in three volumes. See Homer A. Tomlinson, *The Diary of A.J. Tomlinson*, 3 vols. (Queens, NY: The Church of God, 1949-1955). A typescript of part of the journal is located in the Dixon Pentecostal Research Center in Cleveland, Tenn., and will be referred to as A.J. Tomlinson, "Journal of Happenings," which is the heading of the first extant volume of the original manuscript.

Appalachian people. This periodical, along with a later one titled *The Way*, featured news from the Divine Healing and Holiness movements, as well as appeals for help for the "mountain missionary work." These periodicals reveal Tomlinson's early theological position as clearly within the Holiness Movement.[3]

By 1903, after years of searching and seeking God, this man of vision, passion and ability discovered a home among a small congregation known as the Holiness Church in the nearby community of Camp Creek, North Carolina. There Tomlinson covenanted with fellow travelers who deeply wanted to please God and restore God's church.

Perhaps Tomlinson was reflecting in part on the Camp Creek community when he noted in his 1916 announcement of Cashwell's death that Cashwell had "set the match to the prepared material." The Holiness Church at Camp Creek was the result of a revival that had occurred in 1896. Holiness evangelists had preached the message of sanctification in the community's Shearer Schoolhouse, and there were many converts to the belief that one can experience a second work of grace that allows the believer to live a victorious life free from bondage to sin.

Revival fires burned beyond the protracted meeting, and in the weeks and months that followed, the group held Sunday school and prayer meetings under the leadership of W.F. Bryant. According to Tomlinson's 1913 account, during these meetings, the Holy Spirit fell upon the seekers, more than 100 were filled with the Spirit and spoke in tongues, and many experienced healings. Tomlinson's report laments that the absence of a church structure led to both a falling away and fanaticism. Finally, a remnant of the group harkened to the pastoral wisdom of R.G. Spurling, who, along with R. Frank Porter, organized the Holiness Church in Bryant's home on May 15, 1902.[4]

Of course, speaking in tongues was not unique to the Camp Creek community

---

[3] Extant copies of both publications are available at the Dixon Pentecostal Research Center in Cleveland, Tennessee.

[4] Tomlinson's account is the earliest history of these events. Although he does not seem to have been an eyewitness, he was a close personal friend of R.G. Spurling and W.F. Bryant at the time he published his history. R.G. Spurling and his father, Richard Spurling, had organized the Christian Union just across the Tennessee state line in 1886. Tomlinson's 1913 account identified the Holiness Church as a continuation of the Christian Union, but under a new name. See A.J. Tomlinson, *The Last Great Conflict* (Cleveland, TN: Press of Walter E. Rodgers, 1913; repr. New York: Garland, 1985) 188-91. Tomlinson does not describe the nature of the error and fanaticism, but there are tantalizing clues that the group may have been involved in Benjamin Hardin Irwin's Fire-Baptized Movement described below. Certainly the many baptisms and ascetic practices noted by Charles W. Conn in his history of the Church of God resemble the Fire-Baptized Movement, and Harold D. Hunter notes some likely connections as well. See Charles W. Conn, *Like a Mighty Army: A History of the Church of God, Definitive Edition, 1886-1995* (Cleveland, TN: Pathway Press, 1996) 47-52; and Harold D. Hunter, "Beniah at the Apostolic Crossroads: Little Noticed Crosscurrents of

in 1896. Emphases on holiness and divine healing were prevalent throughout the United States and the Southeastern states, particularly during the closing years of the 19th century. The results were an explosion of Holiness congregations, associations and denominations, including the nearby East Tennessee Holiness Association.[5] There were numerous reports of speaking in tongues as the 19th century drew to a close. One of the best known of these was Daniel Awrey, who spoke in tongues in Delaware, Ohio, in 1890, and was living in Beniah, Tennessee, just nine miles north of Cleveland, Tennessee, by 1896.[6]

Subsequent events in and around Beniah, along with the rise and fall of the Fire Baptized Movement in east Tennessee in particular, must have been a factor leading to Tomlinson's relocation to Cleveland. The history of the brief-lived Beniah is intrinsically tied to the ministry of Benjamin Hardin Irwin. Searching for more of God and His blessings than he had previously experienced, Irwin was a lawyer-turned-preacher who founded the Fire Baptized Holiness Association. His sanctification experience had prompted him to join the Iowa Holiness Association, and his study of John Wesley's protégé, John Fletcher, and his "baptism of burning love" led to Irwin's seeking an experience of fire subsequent to sanctification.

Enhancing his personal search was his uncanny ability to incorporate developments of culture and science at the time, which provoked him to use newly coined scientific and pseudoscientific terms to describe spiritual experiences—such as "baptisms of fire," "dynamite," "lyddite," "oxidite" and "selenite." Once Irwin established the Fire Baptized Holiness Association in Anderson, South Carolina, in 1898, it quickly influenced and often divided other Holiness associations, including the one in east Tennessee.[7]

With the growth of the Fire-Baptized Movement, Bradley County in

---

B.H. Irwin, Charles Fox Parham, Frank Sandford, A.J. Tomlinson," *Cyberjournal for Pentecostal Charismatic Research,* 1, *http://www.pctii.org/cyberj/table.html* (Jan. 1997).

[5] One of the best-known accounts of the rise of the Holiness Movement is Vinson Synan, *The Holiness-Pentecostal Tradition: Charismatic Movements in the Twentieth Century* (Grand Rapids: Eerdmans, 1997).

[6] D. Woods, "Awrey, Daniel," in *The New International Dictionary of Pentecostal and Charismatic Movements,* ed. Stanley M. Burgess, with Eduard M. van der Maas (Grand Rapids: Zondervan, 2002) 344. Harold D. Hunter provides the most complete discussion of Beniah to date in his article "Beniah at the Apostolic Crossroads" and a review of speaking in tongues through the centuries in "Tongues-Speech: A Patristic Analysis," *JETS* 23, no. 2 (June 1980): 125-37.

[7] I am indebted to conversations with Wade H. Phillips for this connection between Irwin's spiritual search and cultural, scientific and pseudoscientific developments of his day. For more information on Irwin, see Vinson Synan, *Old-Time Power: A Centennial History of the International Pentecostal Holiness Church* (Franklin Springs, GA: LifeSprings Resources, 1998) 44-56.

east Tennessee became central to future events related to the spread of Pentecostalism. Cleveland was the county seat and located in the center of the county, while the river town of Charleston was just 12 miles to the north. Situated along the Southern Railroad that connected Cleveland and Charleston was a growing community called Beniah.

In Beniah, Irwin found supporters who joined with him in plans to build a school of the prophets and a headquarters for the Fire-Baptized Association. These included the previously mentioned Daniel Awrey, who had attended the 1898 organizational meeting in Anderson, South Carolina, and served as a Fire-Baptized "Ruling Elder" in east Tennessee. It is possible that had Irwin's plans been successful, Beniah might have become the center of Fire-Baptized activities. But those plans were tragically interrupted with news that Irwin had fallen into sin. As a result, several Fire-Baptized congregations in Bradley County and the surrounding area were swept upon the shores of despair.

When Tomlinson covenanted with the Holiness Church at Camp Creek in 1903, the small congregation already knew and loved him. They immediately selected him as their pastor. But Tomlinson's vision and mission could not be contained within the valleys of the Unicoi Mountains, however, and he sought to establish other congregations. By the end of 1904, Tomlinson appeared to be serving as an itinerating pastor of three additional congregations.[8]

In December of 1904, Tomlinson relocated to Cleveland, Tennessee, which was 50 miles to the west of Culberson. In November, he had recorded in his journal, "I am arranging to move to Cleveland, Tennessee, and take charge of churches at Drygo and Union Grove and mission work in Cleveland."[9] His son Homer later wrote that the move was out of a desire for good schools for his children,[10] and the fact that Cleveland was along a major north-south rail line was also a factor. But it should not be overlooked that most of the congregations that called Tomlinson to pastor—Union Grove, Luskville and Drygo in particular—were located in communities near Beniah that had likely been home to Fire-Baptized congregations.[11]

---

[8] Tomlinson, *The Last Great Conflict*, 192.

[9] Tomlinson, "Journal of Happenings," Nov. 8, 1904.

[10] Homer A. Tomlinson, *The Great Vision of the Church of God* (Queens, NY: Homer A. Tomlinson, 1939) 7.

[11] See A.J. Tomlinson, "Journal of Happenings," Dec. 8, 1903, and Nov. 8, 1904. Might Tomlinson have been part of the Fire-Baptized Movement himself? Hunter raised this possibility in "Beniah at the Apostolic Crossroads." Evidence to suggest at least an influence includes the fact that Tomlinson opposed the use of pork at Culberson, and the men are not wearing neckties in the best-known photo of the Culberson ministry. R. Frank Porter, who served as a Ruling Elder with the Fire-Baptized Movement, was one of the elders involved in setting the Holiness Church at Camp Creek in order, and

Thus, it is probable that Tomlinson's success among a remnant of Fire-Baptized people was a major factor in his move to Cleveland, which was the closest town of any size to those congregations.

The Journey of G.B. Cashwell

The importance of Gaston Barnabas Cashwell to the spread of the Pentecostal Movement throughout the South has been well-documented in Vinson Synan's *The Holiness-Pentecostal Tradition* and *The Old-Time Power*. Originally a Methodist minister, Cashwell joined the Holiness Church of North Carolina in 1903. When he read about the events occurring at the Apostolic Faith Mission on Azusa Street in 1906, he traveled to Los Angeles to see the revival for himself. The revival at the Azusa Street Mission not only provided a life-changing experience for Cashwell, but its newspaper, *The Apostolic Faith*, served as a key outlet for reports of his activities and, as such, a critical source of our knowledge concerning his subsequent travels and ministry.

Cashwell's letters to *The Apostolic Faith* document both his spiritual and geographical journey. He wrote:

> I began to read in the *Way of Faith* the reports of the meetings in Azusa Mission, Los Angeles. I had been preaching Holiness for nine years, but my soul began to hunger and thirst for the fullness of God. The Spirit led me more and more to seek my Pentecost. After praying and weeping before God for many days, He put it into my heart to go to Los Angeles to seek the Baptism with the Holy Ghost.[12]

Upon arriving at the Azusa Mission, Cashwell found that before he could have his own Pentecost, he had to "die to many things"[13] including his personal racism toward the Azusa leadership of African-Americans, such as William J. Seymour. But Cashwell persevered and received his Spirit baptism after five days of seeking for the blessing.

Tomlinson used the Fire-Baptized term "Ruling Elder" to refer to his own serving as moderator of the first Church of God General Assembly in 1906. See *Samson's Foxes* 1, no. 1 (Jan. 1901): 4; Lillie Duggar, *A.J. Tomlinson: Former General Overseer of the Church of God* (Cleveland, TN: White Wing Publishing House, 1964) photographs; M.S. Lemons, "History of the Church of God" (unpublished manuscript, ca. 1937) 4, 5, 10; and Tomlinson, "Journal of Happenings," Jan. 30, 1906.

[12] G.B. Cashwell, "Came 3,000 Miles for His Pentecost," *The Apostolic Faith*, Dec. 1906: 3.

[13] Cashwell, 3. Although several periodicals, including one edited by Charles Fox Parham, used the title *The Apostolic Faith*, all references here are to the Los Angeles publication.

When Cashwell returned home to Dunn, North Carolina, he was determined to preach the truth of his new experience and quickly became what Vinson Synan called the "Apostle of Pentecost" to the South.[14] The December 1906 issue of *The Apostolic Faith* carried an account of his victorious trip to and from the Azusa Street Mission:

> Brother G.B. Cashwell, who came from North Carolina for his Pentecost, has returned on his way rejoicing to carry the good news of the Pentecost to the hungry souls there. He had faith in God that the money would be provided for his fare to return, and the Lord provided it, and he trusted the Lord for a suit of clothes and the Lord gave him a suit. So the trip was one of faith, and the Lord made it a great blessing.[15]

Cashwell's revival in Dunn, which began on December 31, 1906, and lasted three weeks, is one of the great stories of both the early Pentecostal Movement and the International Pentecostal Holiness Church in particular. According to Synan, "Every Holiness preacher on the East Coast, it seemed, wanted to investigate the new doctrine and to actually see and hear for himself an Azusa recipient as he spoke in the strange new tongues."[16] During the Dunn revival, preachers such as G.F. Taylor and A.H. Butler received their Pentecostal experience as well.

Cashwell's own account of the revival appeared in the January 1907 issue of the Azusa newspaper. He wrote:

> This is only the third day, here, and already about 10 have received their Pentecost. Five preachers received the baptism and some of them have two or three languages already and can preach sermons and pray in the tongues. The church is filled to overflow and people come from all over the country. Sinners are being converted and others repenting. This town of about 2,500 has never seen Pentecost before, but praise God, it has come and the town is stirred from center to circumference. People have laid aside eating and business to a great extent and are going down before God in earnest. How I praise God for this wonderful salvation. All the signs follow me since I received Pentecost.[17]

Cashwell's letter continued with a report of the rapid expansion of the revival:

---

[14] Synan, *The Holiness-Pentecostal Tradition,* 113.

[15] *The Apostolic Faith,* Dec. 1906: 3.

[16] Synan, *Old-Time Power,* 98.

[17] Cashwell, "Pentecost in North Carolina," *The Apostolic Faith,* Jan. 1907: 1.

> Many have come from South Carolina and Georgia and have received their Pentecost and gone back, and there some have received the baptism. The fire is spreading. The meeting continues here in greater interest. Nearly every service, someone receives their Pentecost and speaks in tongues. Some of our preachers have preached, sung and prayed in unknown tongues, and without speaking a word of English, have awakened sinners.[18]

News of Cashwell's trip to the Azusa Mission in Los Angeles and the Dunn revival made Cashwell a celebrity of sorts, and invitations came from numerous places across the southern United States throughout 1907. In February, Cashwell preached in Bonneau, South Carolina, where F.M. Britton was brought into the Pentecostal Movement. Later that month, he preached at Toccoa, Georgia, where General Overseer J.H. King of Fire-Baptized Holiness Church received his Spirit baptism. He then traveled to Royston, Georgia, and on to Anderson, West Union, Iva and Greenville, South Carolina. Along the way, N.J. Holmes and his Altamont Bible and Missionary Institute were brought into the Pentecostal Movement. Later preaching engagements included Atlanta, Birmingham, Memphis and Cleveland (Tennessee). In the February/March 1907 issue of *The Apostolic Faith*, Cashwell enthusiastically declared, "Hundreds of precious souls in the South have received the Baptism with the Holy Ghost and speak in other tongues."[19] A May 1907 page-one report from Memphis added, "The Lord our God is with us at this place, and the saints are receiving their Pentecost."[20]

In April 1907, Cashwell described the variety of manifestations of the Spirit that were being exhibited. The names and places mentioned would eventually become heroes of the faith in the International Pentecostal Holiness Church and accentuate the extraordinary role that his journey played in the development of that denomination. He reported:

> Pentecost has come to the South. The power is falling from the Atlantic to the Mississippi river. The cities and country are filled with the glory of God, healing, working of miracles, divers kinds of tongues, interpretation of tongues. Oh, how I praise God. The Falcon school near Dunn, N.C., has received Pentecost in full. Some of the students speak in tongues. Some interpret and write several languages and interpret it. The principal, Reverend J.F. Taylor, speaks in tongues, interprets, sings and plays in the power of the Spirit.
>
> Our meeting at Toccoa, Georgia, was a complete victory, at Royston,

---

[18] Cashwell, "Pentecost in North Carolina," 1.

[19] Cashwell, "Hundreds Baptized in the South," *The Apostolic Faith*, Feb./Mar. 1907: 3.

[20] Cashwell, "In Memphis, Tenn.," *The Apostolic Faith*, May 1907: 1.

Georgia, was the same, and there were miracles of healing I never saw before. Brother King and myself anointed and prayed for a 72-year-old sister that had not walked a step in 18 months. She rose up and shouted in every room of the house, and went to the service on Sunday and exhorted and preached, and warned the people to make ready for Jesus was coming. She was of the Primitive faith, but now filled with the Holy Ghost. The power is falling at this place and people are receiving their Pentecost and speaking in tongues, for they all speak in tongues that receive the baptism as they did on the Day of Pentecost.[21]

The January 1908 issue of *The Apostolic Faith* was the last to include news of Cashwell's travels. This issue was the next-to-last one published in Los Angeles. Meanwhile, he had begun his own publication titled *The Bridegroom's Messenger* the previous October. According to *The Apostolic Faith,* he was living in Atlanta and preaching with F.M. Britton in Arcadia, Florida. Cashwell wrote, "This truth in the South is spreading as never before and will keep spreading as [we] praise our God! Pray much and be true to Jesus. Many of us are now suffering much persecution, but our God is fighting our battles. Praise His dear name!"[22]

M.M. Pinson and the Birmingham Connection

The journey of G.B. Cashwell from the Azusa Street Mission in Los Angeles to Cleveland, Tennessee, in 1908, cannot be told without including events that occurred in Alabama during the spring of 1907.[23] While passing through Birmingham, Cashwell made the acquaintance of a traveling evangelist by the name of Mack M. Pinson, who would prove to be significant in the development of the Assemblies of God. Pinson had been a student of Presbyterian-turned-Holiness preacher J.O. McClurkan in Nashville, Tennessee, and had

---

[21] Cashwell, "Pentecost in the South," *The Apostolic Faith,* Apr. 1907: 4.

[22] Cashwell in "Arcadia, Fla., and Through the South," *The Apostolic Faith*, Jan. 1908: 1.

[23] According to one source, Miss Irene Stuckey was one of the first persons to receive the baptism in the Holy Spirit in Alabama when she spoke with tongues in the summer of 1902, during a revival where the doctrine of sanctification was being preached. This fits the pattern of numerous reports of people speaking in tongues without yet understanding the later doctrine of tongues as the evidence of the baptism in the Holy Spirit. Stuckey and others in the late 19th and early 20th centuries likely saw tongues speech as one of a variety of manifestations of the sanctification experience. Stuckey is an interesting part of our story because she became the organist for Pinson. From her testimony, we know that Cashwell was preaching that speaking in tongues was an actual human language given for the purpose of evangelizing the world. According to Stuckey, Cashwell's sermon the first night she heard him denigrated the study of a foreign language and suggested that a missionary candidate who chose the study of a language over the gift of tongues "would be better off at home plowing with an ox." Information about Stuckey and Alabama events is taken from Robert H. Spence, *The First Fifty Years: A Brief Review of the Assemblies of God in Alabama (1915-1965)* (n.p.: n.d.) 5ff.

traveled throughout Alabama preaching that the experience of sanctification was the equivalent of Spirit Baptism. That is until he met G.B. Cashwell.[24]

Earlier that spring, Pinson had traveled to Bowling Green, Kentucky, where he was holding a revival in a Methodist church. According to Pinson's "Life Sketch," he was on the way to the post office one day when he heard a voice as certainly as if it had been audible, saying, "Go to Birmingham, Alabama." While he was discerning what course of action he should follow, he arrived at the post office where he received a letter from Sister Daniels, telling him that G.B. Cashwell would be coming to Birmingham on his way to Memphis. Sister Daniels asked Pinson to come to Alabama, meet Cashwell, and then continue the revival services following Cashwell's departure.

In response to the invitation, Pinson and his family packed their belongings and traveled to Birmingham, where he found Cashwell preaching to the Holiness people there. Intrigued, but still convinced that the sanctification experience was the Biblical equivalent of the baptism in the Holy Ghost, Pinson decided to travel to Memphis with Cashwell in order to hear more about the Pentecostal message.

According to Pinson, Cashwell preached one night in Memphis that Christians are sanctified outside the gate but filled with the Holy Spirit in the Upper Room. Thus, the experiences of sanctification and Spirit baptism are distinct from one another. Upon hearing this sermon, Pinson was persuaded of the new Pentecostal theology and began to seek the baptism with the Holy Spirit, which he received in his room on May 8, 1907, while in prayer with his friend H.G. Rodgers.[25]

Retuning to Birmingham, Cashwell arranged with the pastor of a Holiness mission in the southern part of the city to use their facilities for revival services. The ministerial party, including Pinson, stayed in a rooming house above the hall where the services were being held. They also rented "a few hundred chairs as it was a large hall."[26]

Although the crowds were large at first, a variety of circumstances kept the revival fro, growing as they had hoped. First, the local street-car company locked out its workers who had taken that summer to organize into a union. This made it difficult for Birmingham's citizens to get to the meeting and made travel at night somewhat dangerous as well. Added to this, the local Holiness

---

[24] Pinson's story is related in B.F. Lawrence, *The Apostolic Faith Restored* (St. Louis, MO: Gospel Publishing House, 1916) 90-95; and Mack M. Pinson, "Sketch of the Life and Ministry of Mack M. Pinson" (unpublished, 1949), Dixon Pentecostal Research Center, Cleveland, Tenn.

[25] Pinson, "Life Sketch," 8,9.

[26] Pinson, 10.

pastor seemed to resist the Pentecostal message. According to Pinson's account, upon hearing Cashwell complain, Pinson decided that perhaps the two of them should part company.[27] Pinson recollected that Cashwell agreed to a plan for Pinson and some of the others to pitch a tent in the city of North Birmingham, while Cashwell continued the services in the Holiness hall.

Pinson later wrote that the Lord blessed the services at the tent in North Birmingham. "We had numbers of others saved and filled with the Holy Spirit. A number of them were students from the Bible School in Nashville, Tenn. . . . The meeting ran several weeks; a blessed revival."

Among those who visited Pinson's tent revival in North Birmingham were Church of God leaders, A.J. Tomlinson and M.S. Lemons. Pinson recalled, "I remember that Tomlinson from Cleveland, Tennessee, and I believe a brother named Lemons came to my meeting there. . . . They didn't stay long."[28] There is no indication that Tomlinson met Cashwell while he was in Alabama, but his experience in North Birmingham both solidified changes in his theology and prompted him to invite Cashwell to come to Cleveland.[29]

Meanwhile, experiencing less success in the Holiness hall and still receiving many invitations to preach, Cashwell departed Birmingham for Atlanta. Sometime about the middle of June, Pinson left North Birmingham to pitch his tent in Coffee Springs, Alabama.[30] His encounter with Cashwell had moved him from the ranks of the Holiness Movement into the Pentecostal Movement and, through Pinson, had influenced Tomlinson. Pinson went on to spread the Pentecostal message throughout Alabama, Tennessee and other states, as well

---

[27] Pinson did not report what Cashwell was complaining about, but his description of Cashwell is in keeping with Joseph Campbell's report that Cashwell was somewhat temperamental in nature. See Joseph E. Campbell, *The Pentecostal Holiness Church, 1898-1948* (Franklin Springs, GA: Pentecostal Holiness Church, 1951) 240.

[28] Pinson, "Life Sketch," 10.

[29] Both Pinson and Rodgers were active participants in the fourth General Assembly of the Church of God in 1910. Pinson mentions Tomlinson two times in his "Life Sketch" and clearly disparages Tomlinson's ecclesiology. M.S. Lemons suggested in an interview with H.L. Chesser that Pinson wanted to join the Church of God in 1910, but because he was "a little radical," Tomlinson wanted to wait. Pinson was unwilling to wait, and thus they went separate ways. It is probable that these "radical" differences related to ecclesiology and perhaps the doctrine of sanctification as well, both of which proved to be differences between the Church of God and the Assemblies of God. Tension over either of these issues along with personality conflicts might explain both Pinson's comments about Tomlinson and Tomlinson's failure to mention Pinson in his *The Last Great Conflict*. See Church of God, *General Assembly Minutes 1906-1914* (Cleveland, TN: White Wing, 1992) 74-83; Pinson, "Life Sketch," 5, 10; W.F. Bryant and M.S. Lemons, interview by H.L. Chesser, ca. 1948, transcript, Dixon Pentecostal Research Center, Cleveland, TN, 17.

[30] His organist, Irene Stuckey, traveled with him, along with Miss Ellen Treppard, Miss Daniels, and Bro. Todd, who led the singing. See Pinson, "Life Sketch," 10-11.

as being a key leader in the formation of the General Council of the Assemblies of God at Hot Springs, Arkansas, in 1914.

A.J. Tomlinson and the Baptism in the Holy Spirit

We do not know when Tomlinson first heard of the Pentecostal doctrine of Spirit baptism as an experience subsequent to sanctification and with the evidence of speaking in tongues. It is difficult to imagine that he had not heard either reports or actual instances of speaking in tongues while visiting Frank Sandford's Shiloh in Maine, from his close personal relationships with participants in the 1896 revival in Camp Creek, North Carolina, or during his ministry to the remnant of Fire-Baptized believers in and around Bradley County. Whatever he had heard about speaking in tongues, he did not yet understand tongues to be the "Bible evidence" of Spirit baptism as the new Pentecostal Movement taught. Like many others, he may have equated sanctification and Spirit baptism, all the while viewing speaking in tongues as an occasional manifestation of the sanctification experience. This was certainly true of Cashwell and Pinson before they came into the Pentecostal Movement. It can be said of so many of that day, what Charles W. Conn has said of the 1896 Camp Creek believers who testified of a Spirit-Baptism experience. "It would be somewhat later that even those baptized would understand the doctrine, person and nature of the Holy Spirit."[31]

Elsewhere Harold D. Hunter has suggested that Tomlinson may have first read about events at Azusa Street in J.M. Pike's *The Way of Faith* or perhaps *The Apostolic Faith*.[32] We might add to the list Martin Wells Knapp's *The Revivalist*. It is likely that Tomlinson was reading a number of accounts. *The Apostolic Faith* was widely read among Holiness people, and Pike's *The Way of Faith* was publishing reports of Cashwell and others regarding the new Pentecostal doctrine. Knapp's *The Revivalist* was reporting on the new Pentecostal Movement, albeit unlike Pike was taking a negative stand on the revival.

M.S. Lemons, a constant friend and companion of Tomlinson, was asked in later years when he had first "heard of someone preaching the baptism of the Holy Ghost." Although Lemons' memory failed him regarding the exact date, his recollection pointed to the events in North Birmingham.

---

[31] Conn, *Like a Mighty Army,* 31. Harold Hunter has suggested that the presence of tongues speech at Sandford's Shiloh, Beniah, and other places might possibly displace Charles Fox Parham's role in the historical development of contemporary Pentecostal doctrine. Although Hunter's evidence is suggestive, it is not yet conclusive. See Hunter, "Beniah at the Apostolic Crossroads."

[32] Harold D. Hunter, "A Portrait of How the Azusa Doctrine of Spirit Baptism Shaped American Pentecostalism," *Enrichment* (forthcoming at the time of this writing).

> When I first got sanctified I thought I had the Holy Ghost, and taught it for a little while, but I found I didn't. Around the year 1900, we heard about a meeting in Birmingham, held by Pinson and Rogers, where people were receiving the Holy Ghost. When we heard about it we began to check it. We got on the long train (me and Tomlinson) and went down to the meeting. I did not get through, but we were satisfied in our minds about the doctrine.[33]

In this same interview, Lemons also reported that Tomlinson had sought the baptism in the Holy Spirit in Birmingham.[34] Tomlinson's diary for June 14, 1907, clarifies the date and confirms the significance of the trip. He wrote, "Returned home today from Birmingham, Alabama. I have been for a week in a meeting with Brother M.M. Pinson. Glorious results. Speaking in other tongues by the Holy Ghost."

This entry is the first discussion of speaking in tongues in Tomlinson's extant journal, and from that day forward, the journal clearly shows that Tomlinson had been convinced of Spirit baptism as an experience distinct from and subsequent to sanctification, along with the belief that tongues is the evidence of that experience. Tomlinson had completed a shift from a Holiness to a Pentecostal understanding of the baptism in the Holy Spirit.[35]

In his 1913 book, *The Last Great Conflict,* Tomlinson credited Seymour with uncovering the Pentecostal doctrine, which Tomlinson believed had been covered over by the apostasy of Christianity that followed the Council of Nicea.[36] Also in *The Last Great Conflict,* he described the process by which he had adopted the new doctrine:

> In January, 1907, I became more fully awakened on the subject of receiving the Holy Ghost as He was poured out on the Day of Pentecost. That whole year I ceased not to preach that it was our privilege to receive the Holy Ghost and speak in tongues as they did on the Day of Pentecost. I did not have the experience, so I was almost always among the seekers at the altar. . . . By the close of the year I was so hungry for the Holy Ghost that I scarcely cared for food, friendship or anything else. I wanted the one

---

[33] W.F. Bryant and M.S. Lemons, interview by H.L. Chesser, 12-13, 15.

[34] Chesser, 15.

[35] A.J. Tomlinson, "Journal of Happenings," June 14, 1907–Jan. 13, 1908. One example is July 17, when Tomlinson wrote, "Sunday I preached three searching sermons and there were fifteen professions besides the other good that must have been done. Some spoke with other tongues Sunday afternoon."

[36] Tomlinson, *The Last Great Conflict,* 156.

thing—the baptism with the Holy Ghost. I wrote to G.B. Cashwell . . . and asked him to come to our place for a few days.[37]

When the program for the third (1908) General Assembly of the Churches of God was printed, plans for Saturday and Sunday showed an expectancy regarding the new Pentecostal message: "Saturday, January 11th. 7:00 p.m. Service on Pentecostal lines. We expect Brother G.B. Cashwell, of Dunn, N.C. . . . Sunday, January 12th. 10:40 a.m. Preaching or Pentecostal Service . . . 7:00 p.m. Service on Pentecostal lines."[38]

In a later letter to *The Bridegroom's Messenger*, Tomlinson reported on the events leading up to the Assembly: "We [had] been holding 'tarrying meetings' occasionally for several weeks. As the old year was closing and the new year coming in, we held meetings on 'Pentecostal' lines as near as we could without having the experience. We were so hungry. One had received the baptism and spoke in tongues under my ministry, but that did not satisfy my hungry soul."[39]

Cashwell arrived in Cleveland on Friday and preached at least the Saturday evening and Sunday morning services. His report of the services was brief: "I gave only a few minutes talk, and asked all those who wanted the baptism of the Holy Ghost to come to the altar. The altar was full in a minute and many knelt in the aisle. We are expecting great things here if everybody will stay out of the way of the Holy Ghost."[40] Four received the baptism of the Holy Spirit, including Tomlinson.

Tomlinson's testimony included many of the spiritual manifestations that were common occurrences in the early Pentecostal Movement. According to Tomlinson, while Cashwell was concluding his message, "The Spirit came on me and down I went on the floor, right by the side of the stand on the rostrum."[41] Tomlinson continued, "My mind was clear, but a peculiar power so enveloped and thrilled my whole being that I concluded to yield myself up to God and await results."[42] Those results for Tomlinson were dramatic. They included shaking, rolling, tossing and a sense of levitation. He recorded, "As I lay there great joy

---

[37] Tomlinson, 232-33.

[38] Church of God, *Annual Assembly of the Churches of East Tennessee, North Georgia, Western North Carolina* (Information Files, Dixon Pentecostal Research Center, Cleveland, TN) 4.

[39] Tomlinson, "The Work at Cleveland, Tenn.," *The Bridegroom's Messenger*, Feb. 1, 1908: 4.

[40] Cashwell, "Report of Work," *The Bridegroom's Messenger*, Jan. 15, 1908: 2.

[41] Tomlinson, *The Bridegroom's Messenger*, Feb. 1, 1908: 4.

[42] Tomlinson, *The Last Great Conflict*, 211.

flooded my soul. The happiest moments I had ever known up to that time. . . . Oh, such floods and billows of glory ran through my whole being."[43]

These waves of joy were then followed by a vision in which Tomlinson traveled to many areas of the world including all the inhabited continents. In his vision, Tomlinson believed that his tongues speech was in fact the languages of the native peoples of the countries he was visiting. This was a common belief among many early Pentecostals who were convinced that the purpose of the latter-day rain was to provide the church with supernatural tools to win the lost in the last days.

Also in Tomlinson's vision, devils were cast out, people were saved, and he was reminded of Mark 16 and signs following believers. In his journal Tomlinson concluded, "This was really the baptism of the Holy Ghost as they received Him on the Day of Pentecost, for they all spake with tongues. With all I have written it is not yet told, but judging from the countries I visited, I spoke in 10 different languages."[44]

Conclusion

Within a few short months following the opening of the Azusa Street Mission in Los Angeles, Cashwell, Pinson, Tomlinson, and countless others like them made the theological journey from the Holiness Movement into the newly emerging Pentecostal Movement. They added to their deep conviction of sanctification as a second work of grace a subsequent blessing of Spirit baptism accompanied by the "Bible evidence" of speaking in tongues.

As a result of Cashwell's preaching tour, leaders (or future leaders) of denominations such as the International Pentecostal Holiness Church, the Fire-Baptized Holiness Church of the Americas, General Council of the Assemblies of God, and Church of God were brought into the Pentecostal Movement. Although Cashwell's famous tour lasted only a little more than a year, and although Tomlinson never visited most of the countries he saw in that vision on January 12, 1908, since that time the fruit of their ministries has spread around the world.

---

[43] Tomlinson, 212.

[44] Tomlinson, "Journal of Happenings," Jan. 13, 1908.

6

"Networks and Niches"

The Worldwide Transmission of the Azusa Street Revival[1]

David Maxwell

Brother and Sister G.W. Batman to Go to Monrovia, Liberia

After that I received baptism in the Holy Ghost and fire and now I feel the presence of the Holy Ghost, not only in my heart but in my lungs, my hands, my arms and all through my body and at times I am shaken like a locomotive steamed up and prepared for a long journey (*The Apostolic Faith* [Los Angeles], December 1906).

> The burning message of another Pentecost is now flying to the ends of the earth. "The Apostolic Faith" edited in Los Angeles has only published three numbers, the last of which was a 30,000 edition! (*The Apostolic Light* [Salem, Oregon], November 1906).

Rising at the dawn of the 20th century, the Pentecostal Movement crossed the globe within the first decade of its existence. At that stage, it was known

---

[1] This chapter is taken from my forthcoming book, *African Gifts of the Spirit: Pentecostalism and the Rise of Zimbabweam and Transnational Religious Movement* (Oxford: Jones Cursey; Ohio UP).

variously as the Fourfold or Foursquare Gospel, the Apostolic Faith, the Latter Rain of the Holy Spirit or the Holy Ghost Revival, and its adherents spent little time reflecting on its origins. Instead, they were preoccupied with the task of proclaiming their new message, which bore a resemblance to the Acts of the Apostles.

Struck by the seeming spontaneity of the Revival and its rapid dissemination, most were content to assume that its origins were supernatural, an act of God beyond the bounds of ordinary human history.[2] This sense of spontaneity and divine intervention infused the first written histories of the Movement a decade or two after its foundation.[3] A "providential" interpretation of Pentecostal origins later found its way into more scholarly accounts of the Movement written by Pentecostal ministers, church officials and more detached scholars. Thus, one historian from the Assemblies of God, U.S.A., asserted that Pentecostals had "no earthly father," the Movement being a "child of the Holy Ghost."[4] Nevertheless, a formal academic historiography of Pentecostalism has emerged. Its most influential strand, termed *the genetic approach*, stems from the recognition that early Pentecostalism shared many of "its doctrinal beliefs, leadership and organizational polities, behavioural practices and social thought" with prior 19th-century Protestant movements.[5] Hence, scholars have written intellectual histories debating the strength and significance of the various theological strands and traditions in Pentecostalism's genealogy. Vinson Synan and Donald Dayton stressed the Wesleyan Holiness roots of the Movement, while Edith Blumhofer emphasized its Reformed and Keswick influences.[6]

The second category of Pentecostal historiography, known as the "multicultural approach," has focused on the African-American and Latino histories of Pentecostalism. It explored the black origins of the Azusa Revival, and sought

---

[2] A. Cerillo Jr. and G. Wacker, "Bibliography and Historiography," in *The New International Dictionary of Pentecostal and Charismatic Movements*, ed. Stanley M. Burgess, with Eduard M. van der Maas (Grand Rapids: Zondervan, 2002) 390-405.

[3] A key example is F. Bartleman, *Azusa Street* (South Plainfield, NJ: Bridge, 1980 [1925]).

[4] C. Brumback, *Suddenly... From Heaven: A History of the Assemblies of God* [1961], cited in Cerillo and Wacker, "Bibliography and Historiography," 397. Donald Gee, a prominent figure in the British Assemblies of God, contended that Pentecostalism was "a spontaneous revival appearing almost simultaneously in various parts of the world." See Gee, *Wind and Flame* (London: AoG, 1967) 3.

[5] Cerillo and Wacker, "Bibliography and Historiography," 400.

[6] H.V. Synan, *The Holiness-Pentecostal Movement in the United States* (Grand Rapids: Eerdmans, 1971). D. Dayton, *Theological Roots of Pentecostalism* (Grand Rapids: Francis Asbury, 1987). E. Blumhofer, *Restoring the Faith: The Assemblies of God, Pentecostalism and American Culture* (Urbana: U of Illinois P, 1993).

to redefine Pentecostalism as a multicultural, rather than white religion. Lastly, historians have taken a functional approach to Pentecostalism, connecting it "to its cultural setting and Pentecostal adherents to their place in . . . social and economic structure." The functional approach is exemplified by the important work of Robert Anderson who demonstrated the appeal of Pentecostal thought and practice to marginalized poor farmers, working and lower class city dwellers, new immigrants and black Americans in rapidly industrializing and urbanizing America.[7]

The genetic, multicultural and functional interpretations offer important insights into the origins of Pentecostalism. But it is worth returning to notions of spontaneity and rapidity that animated the accounts of participants in the first histories of the Movement. The propensity of witnesses to resort to naturalistic imagery of the wind, rain and fire to describe the appearance of the early Movement highlights an important gap in Pentecostal historiography concerning modes of transmission. This chapter charts the hitherto much-neglected material history of the Movement. Focusing on the movement of people and religious literature, it will analyze how existing networks of radical Evangelical Protestantism, often sustained by the British Empire, facilitated Pentecostalism's rapid uptake.

Pentecost Across the World

The Pentecostal Movement spread rapidly across the globe. As early as March 1907, *The Apostolic Faith,* the periodical of the Azusa Street Revival, reported that Pentecost had spread to Hawaii in the West and England, Norway, Sweden and India in the East.[8] As remarkable as the initial numerical growth of the Pentecostal revival was, its impact on the lives of ordinary people was greater. Within a decade, hundreds of previously "humble folk" were scattered across the globe as missionaries. Some left Los Angeles almost immediately. At the turn of 1907, Alfred and Lillian Garr were in Calcutta on their way to China. In August 1907, Brother A. Post left for Ceylon, and by May 1908, only "one and a half years after his Pentecost," G.S. Brelesford left Colorado Springs for Egypt. Many of the first missionaries were single women, for example, Sister Nelson and Sister Johnson, who left for Calcutta in 1910.[9]

---

[7] Cerillo and Wacker, "Bibliography and Historiography," 401-5. R. Anderson, *Vision of the Disinherited: The Making of American Pentecostalism* (New York: Oxford UP, 1979).

[8] *AF* [Los Angeles], Mar. 1907.

[9] G. McGee, "From East to West: The Early Pentecostal Movement in India and Its Influence in the West," ms. (n.d.), 1. *AF* [Los Angeles], May 1908. *The Upper Room,* Nov. 1910.

The very first Pentecostal missionaries were of the independent or "faith" variety and traveled overseas without pledged support and the backing of traditional mission societies, believing that God would supply their needs. They stood in a tradition of faith missions that had emerged from the 1880s onward in response to the teachings of radical Evangelical A.T. Pierson, who had popularized the watchword "the evangelization of the world in this generation." Their renouncing of salaries and pastoral appointments represented a rejection of Western materialism, an affirmation of supernaturalism in theology and history, a dependence on God's daily providence, and a belief that they were fulfilling Biblical prophecies.[10] Some of these were rugged individualists or mavericks and positively shunned ties with mission organizations.[11] However, formal Pentecostal missionary societies were founded to coordinate the activities of faith-based missionaries.

In the United States, the Pentecostal Missionary Union (PMU) emerged from the Pentecostal Camp Meetings in Alliance, Ohio, in 1909. This initiative floundered within a year. Nevertheless, it helped spur over 185 Pentecostals overseas in that short space of time. Its sister organization, the PMU of Great Britain, took things a little more slowly, founding missionary homes and Bible schools. Two women, K. Miller and L. James, immediately sailed for India under its aegis, having previously worked there with other societies. The first missionaries trained completely by the PMU were dispatched to China in September 1910. By 1925, the PMU had sent out 60 missionaries, 36 women and 24 men. By this time, at least half a dozen other Pentecostal mission societies had formed in Europe and the United States.[12]

All these missionaries and those who supported them financially and in prayer had been captured by the key ideas of the Foursquare Gospel, the most significant being adventism. Many literally believed that they lived in the "last days" and had a duty or "burden" to spread the Christian message

---

[10] Dana Robert, *Occupy Until I Come: A.T. Pierson and the Evangelization of the World* (Grand Rapids: Eerdmans, 2003) 181.

[11] D. Bays, "Indigenous Protestant Churches in China, 1900-1937: A Pentecostal Case Study," in *Indigenous Responses to Western Christianity,* ed. S. Kaplan (New York: New York UP, 1995) 137. G. McGee, "The Azusa Street Revival and Twentieth-Century Missions," *International Bulletin of Missionary Research* 12 (Apr. 1988): 58-61, 59. G. Wacker, "Searching for Eden With a Satellite Dish: Primitivism, Pragmatism and the Pentecostal Character," in *The Primitive Church in the Modern World,* ed. R.T. Hughes (Urbana and Chicago: U of Illinois, 1995) 151.

[12] *Confidence,* Nov. 1909. P. Kay, "Cecil Polhill, The Pentecostal Missionary Union, and the Fourfold Gospel With Healing and Speaking in Tongues: Signs of a New Movement in Missions," North Atlantic Missiology Project, Position Paper no. 20, (1996) 4. McGee, "Azusa Street Revival," 59.

before Christ's return. Importantly though, Christ's return did not depend on the wholesale conversion of the world.

Many Pentecostals followed Pierson in believing that the Great Commission commanded believers simply to proclaim the gospel to the world, not to convert everyone. "[T]he purpose of missions was to gather out Christians from all nations, not to Christianize the nations themselves."[13] Nevertheless, the millennial urgency to spread the gospel in end times drove many Pentecostal missionaries forward.

In 1907, a writer in the Washington-based periodical *The Apostolic Light*, noted that missionaries from Minnesota were leaving for Japan, China, the Philippines and Korea. He went on to observe, "The pleading cry to hasten the gospel message to the ends of the earth is being answered, and the Holy Ghost has in wrought the Pentecostal '60' [Revival] into humble followers."[14] After recounting the events at a Pentecostal conference in Fyzabad, North India, the indefatigable missionary Alfred Garr wrote: "The Rapture will be wonderful. It will take all the oil we can hold to be able to partake in its wonders. Pray for us, and let us keep humble, for His coming draweth nigh."[15] Others were spurred on by the signs of the time, of which they were continually reminded in Pentecostal broadsheets:

We know that He is near.

> Signs of the Last Days: Signs on the Heavens—The Jews Return—Earthquakes and Judgements—Preparation for a World War—Increase of Riches and of Crime—The Great Falling Away—The Anti-Christ Spirit—The Latter Rain.[16]

Other aspects of the Pentecostal faith also fired the missionary impetus. A number of the early missionaries believed in the existence of missionary tongues, or *xenolalia*, "the ability to speak an actual, though unstudied foreign language, at will." Early accounts of the revival list instances of missionaries writing in Syriac and Armenian, singing in Chinese and speaking in Basotho.[17]

Such accounts were short on detail, and Wacker's analysis of them cast doubt on their veracity. Missionaries ultimately had to submit themselves to the discipline of foreign language study if they were to succeed. Nevertheless,

---

[13] Robert, *Occupy Until I Come*, 136.

[14] *The Apostolic Light*, Aug. 1907.

[15] *The Upper Room*, July 1910.

[16] *AF* [Portland], no. 20 ca. 1912.

[17] *AF*, Mar. 1907. *The Upper Room*, Nov. 1910.

between 1906 and 1909, "more than a dozen zealots journeyed" to the mission fields "armed with the conviction that they would be empowered to speak the native language when they arrived."[18] Moreover, accounts of miraculous missionary tongues doubtless stimulated interest in "regions beyond," as described in *The Upper Room,* and countered the prevailing impression created by social Darwinism that non-Western cultures were unintelligible.

More generally, missionaries such as Brother G.W. Batman (cited at the beginning of this chapter) were "steamed up" by the Holy Spirit, empowered for Christian witness. In addition, those who attended the revival services believed the "apostolic signs and wonders" that had characterized the advance of early Christians in the Book of Acts had been restored in the "last days."[19]

The gifts of the spirit—prophecy, divine healing, exorcism, as well as tongues—had been given for the advance of the gospel. And such gifts were more than an adequate substitute for the formulaic mission strategies adopted by the established missionary societies. The power of the mantra "the evangelization of the world in this generation" was the simplicity of notion of evangelism. Rather than mission being a complex operation requiring theological formation, the construction of schools and hospitals, the creation of indigenous leadership, and the eradication of regressive social customs, evangelism simply meant the preaching of the gospel to all.

Success was not to be measured in terms of the number of converts. Communicating the gospel was sufficient. "At stake was not the conversion of the world, but the faithfulness of the church to Christ's mandate."[20] In his *Practical Points Concerning Missionary Work* (1916), Cecil Polhill, founder of PMU, warned missionaries "to consider yourself an evangelist throughout your term of service. Let others educate, doctor, do philanthropy ... avoid also the incubus to the evangelist of day schools, orphanages, and the 101 things which may be accumulated in station life."[21] This outlook did not sit well with the British colonial project.[22]

Networks and Niches

Although missionary enthusiasm contributed to the global spread of the

---

[18] Grant Wacker, *Heaven Below: Early Pentecostals and American Culture* (Cambridge: Harvard UP, 2001) 44-51.

[19] McGee, "Azusa Street Revival," 58.

[20] Robert, *Occupy Until I Come,* 154.

[21] C. Polhill, *Practical Points Concerning Missionary Work* (1916), cited in Kay, "Cecil Polhill," 9.

[22] See Maxwell, *African Gifts,* ch. 2.

Pentecostal message, the speed of its movement across frontiers and its rapid assimilation cannot be attributed to their agency alone. Given that the American revival flowed from converging streams of "Wesleyan and Keswickian teachings with faith healing and dispensational premillennialism;" it was hardly surprising that radical evangelical Christians all over the world were swept along by similar currents.[23]

Protestant Europe, its mission fields and their indigenous progeny experienced a similar convergence of pietistic ideas and shared a climate of expectancy. All were seeking a more profound and immediate religious experience not present in their particular denominations. Many of the doctrinal and experiential streams that flowed into the Azusa Revival originated from Europe: Wesleyan Holiness, Keswick, the Plymouth Brethren and the Welsh Revival of 1904. Indeed, the Azusa Pentecost may well have not happened in 1906 without the events in Wales two years earlier.

Joseph Smale, Minister of the First Baptist Church, Los Angeles, returned hot-footed from the Welsh Revival, adding to the sense of expectation in the city. But that story was repeated across the world. Missionaries working as far away as Madagascar read of the Welsh Revival and prayed for it with the same sense of expectancy.[24] There was a clear link between Wales and Azusa Street in the minds of many Pentecostal pioneers.[25]

By 1906, the world was a deeply interconnected place. People, ideas and texts moved rapidly across frontiers, aided by the structures of empire, crucially the British Empire in what has been called the first globalization. Such movement was made possible by the 19th-century communications revolution of the steamship and the telegraph that accompanied the industrialization of steel and electricity, oil and chemicals.[26] The 1858-1859 revivals in America and Britain touched the rest of the globe within a year.[27] Many radical Evangelicals had attended the globe-trotting Torrey/Alexander revival campaigns at the turn of the 20th century. The Protestant world was well-primed for revival in 1906.

Moreover, given the truth of David Martin's observation that Pentecostalism

---

[23] McGee, "From East to West," 7.

[24] *Revival News,* Mar. 1907.

[25] See Bartleman, *Azusa Street*; C. Polhill, *A China Missionary's Witness* (c. 1908); A. Boddy, *Pentecost at Sunderland* (c. 1907).

[26] See P. Atterbury, "Steam and Speed: Industry, Transport and Communications," in *The Victorian Vision: Inventing New Britain,* ed. J. Mackenzie (London: V&A, 2001) 147-73; G. Barraclough, *An Introduction to Contemporary History* (Harmondsworth, England: Penguin, 1967) 43-64.

[27] D. Austin-Broos, *Jamaica Genesis: Religion and the Politics of Moral Order* (Chicago: Chicago UP, 1997) 55.

emerges in certain socioeconomic contexts or "niches," there were many locations across the world ready for Pentecostal take-off. As capitalism disrupted agrarian economies, relocating people in industrial agglomerations and their homes in large conurbations, so citizens were ready for a new religion that created new communities patterned on new sets of social relations.[28]

Although Pentecostalism often escaped missionary control appropriated by local Christians, missionaries were usually the first points of connection in its global spread. They had greater freedom of movement, returning home on furlough or attending missionary conferences funded by mission boards and faith offerings. Missionaries also had greater access to new ideas and developments. They often received the first letters from Pentecostal friends and the first literature from Pentecostal organizations. And mission stations were often the first port of call for new Pentecostal missionaries with their radical fourfold message. Indeed, converts to Pentecostalism often began by encouraging the revival among their home mission societies. Former China Inland Missionary (CIM) Cecil Polhill sought to do so indirectly through the formation of a council of missionary societies working in China, while the Anglican minister, Alexander Boddy, often described as the Father of British Pentecostalism, actively proselytized the Church Missionary Society (CMS). At one meeting in Sunderland in 1910, he chided a gathering of CMS clergy for their lack of faith in the miraculous, reminding them that . . .

> The Lord's healings were not through medicines. Paul used no medicine in healing dysentery. Peter and John did not use a galvanic battery to make the lame man leap at the Beautiful Gate of the Temple. They simply used the mighty name of the Lord Jesus himself.[29]

Because of the prior circulation of revival literature, Pentecostal missionaries sometimes encountered open church doors when they arrived in the mission field. Thus, H.M. Turney and his wife traveled to Honolulu within a year of the Azusa Street outpouring and were given free range of an unnamed mission. Pentecost soon followed.[30]

At other times, missionaries began to preach the Pentecostal message within the historic missionary societies, sometimes with painful consequences. One local missionary, D.E. Dias Wanigasekera, working in Colombo, Ceylon, wrote to *The Upper Room* to tell of his dismissal from the CMS after he had taught the fourfold gospel. Undeterred, he stayed on as a missionary, surviving

---

[28] David Martin, *Pentecostalism: The World Their Parish* (Oxford: Blackwell, 2002).
[29] *Confidence*, Mar. 1910.
[30] *AF* [Los Angeles], Mar. 1907.

on faith. He had prayed for three-and-a-half years to receive the baptism in the Holy Spirit. His prayers were finally answered after traveling 2,500 miles to a missionary conference in Fyzabad, North India.[31]

India was a prime example of how a rich combination of existing networks, traditions and Pentecostal missionaries could come together for revival. As Gary McGee notes, there were earlier Pentecostal-like revivals in Tinnevelly (1860-1865) and Travacore (1873-1881), but the first stirrings of the 1905 revival occurred in March of that year among people of the Khassia Hills. At stations staffed by Welsh Calvinist missionaries, Christians began to confess their sins in noisy "prayer-storms" that continued for hours.

Revival also occurred in the Mukti Mission at Kegon, a Christian community founded by the remarkable Pandita Ramabai, a former high-caste Hindu who had converted to Christianity. At one of its high points, revival erupted in the girls' dormitories. Witnesses reported powerful manifestations of the Holy Spirit as flames of fire. A keen participant in the Mukti Revival was Minnie Abrams, a former Methodist missionary and staunch supporter of Ramabai. Moved by what she witnessed, she wrote *The Baptism of the Holy Ghost and Fire* (1905), which was serialized by two major Christian newspapers, *The Bombay Guardian* and *Christian Patriot* (Madras), as well as the Methodist journal *The Indian Witness*.[32]

News of the revival thus spread rapidly so that when Pentecostal missionaries Kate Knight and a Miss Gardener arrived in Gujarat in February 1907, they found the missionaries in situ "a prepared people and earnestly expecting the Holy Spirit." By November 1908, *The Apostolic Messenger* could report that more than 20 mission stations had been "flooded with Pentecostal power and light," and that 50 missionaries had received "Pentecost." Many of these missionaries accepted the message of a restored Apostolic Faith and received the baptism in the Holy Ghost in a series of conferences held in Calcutta and Fyzabad 1909-1910. Examples of converts to Pentecostalism were: Mrs. Agnes Hill, general secretary of the Young Women's Christian Association (YWCA) India; a Miss Luce of the CMS, a Miss Mudge of the Women's Union Missionary Society of New York, and many "local lady school teachers."[33]

Soon, mission publications carried accounts of Pentecostal revival throughout India, particularly in the South. The revival spread dramatically across denominations embracing Anglicans (usually associated with the CMS); the Christian

---

[31] *The Upper Room*, Feb. 1910; *The Latter Rain Evangel*, Oct. 1911.

[32] McGee, "From East to West," 5-6.

[33] *AF* [Los Angeles], May 1908; *The Apostolic Messenger*, Nov. and Dec. 1908; *The Upper Room*, Mar. and May 1910.

Missionary Alliance (CMA), the London Missionary Society (LMS), the Church of Scotland, the Open Brethren, Danish Lutherans, the Young Men's Christian Association (YMCA), American Methodists, Presbyterians, Reformed and Wesleyan Methodists among others. "Along with confessions of sin and prayer storms (the most striking features)," other salient characteristics of the Indian outpouring were "dancing, visions, dreams, reception of the 'burning' (purifying work of the Spirit), repayment of debts, and even miraculous provisions of food."[34]

The Calcutta Revival of January 1907, which began at a conference of missionaries addressed by Alfred and Lillian Garr from Los Angeles, was often credited in Pentecostal histories as the first general outpouring of the Spirit in India.[35] But it is now perfectly clear that regions of India had been "awakened by the Spirit" well before the Garrs arrived on the scene.[36] Even the phenomenon of tongues had occurred prior to their arrival, first recorded at a CMS-sponsored conference in Aurangabad in April 1906. This occurrence of *glossolalia* had involved the ministry of Minnie Abrams and a "prayer band" from Mukti Mission, where revival occurred the following December. Nevertheless, the arrival of the Garrs, fresh from Azusa Street, had the effect of differentiating the prior Indian Pentecostal revival from the classical Western model, a model that came to set the benchmarks for the global movement.

Although Abrams and Ramabai endorsed the experience of speaking in tongues, neither saw it "as indispensable evidence of Spirit baptism." There were other differences too. While ecstatic phenomena such as visions and prophecies were central to the Indian movement, "divine healing and premillennialism never found the levels of acceptance that they did in the West." McGee explains the low incidence of divine healing in terms of the "intimidation of praying for the sick" in India, where the suffering was of enormous proportions. He puts the weakness of a premillennial outlook down to the local strength of postmillennial thinking, particularly in Methodist missionary traditions.[37]

After an intensive period in India, preaching the Pentecostal message of the Los Angeles vintage, the Garrs moved to China, the other major target of Pentecostal missionary endeavor. They arrived in Hong Kong in October 1907, where they joined a group of single Pentecostal women who had arrived from Seattle, U.S.A., a few months earlier. Alfred Garr was to have "a considerable impact" in Hong Kong, preaching from a base in a Congregational Church of

---

[34] McGee, "From East to West," 5.

[35] *The Apostolic Herald,* Feb. 1909.

[36] See *Apostolic Light,* Nov. 1906, with a story titled, "Pentecost in India."

[37] McGee, "From East to West," 5-8.

the American Board. Hong Kong was one of the three places Pentecostal missionaries put down roots in China. The second was Hebei Province in the north of the mainland. Here, a Mr. Berntsen had been working as a missionary since around 1904. In late 1906, he came across one of the first issues of the Azusa Street publication, *The Apostolic Faith,* and was so gripped by its description of the Revival that he immediately sailed for the United States and headed for Los Angeles. Having received baptism in the Holy Spirit, he gathered around him a dozen Pentecostal missionaries and returned to found a new independent mission in Zhengding, Hebei.

In addition to Hong Kong and Hebei, a third early Pentecostal group was established in Shanghai. Again, there were oblique connections with Azusa Street. In the summer of 1906, Pastor M.L. Ryan heard of the events in Los Angeles and was profoundly moved by them. He relocated to Spokane, Washington, where he founded a Pentecostal congregation. Within a year, a band of Pentecostal missionaries led by Ryan left the Spokane gathering for Asia. By 1910, a number of them, along with missionaries who had left other congregations, had founded a Pentecostal work in Shanghai.

Daniel Bays has shown how a dynamic indigenous Pentecostal church soon emerged from this missionary initiative. Once again, Protestant networks were crucial. Like their missionary leaders who rapidly changed allegiance, "the earliest Chinese participants in the Pentecostal Movement . . . were nearly all already Christians, but searching for a deeper and more immediate religious experience that they did not find in particular denominations." Thus, early adherents came from a variety of backgrounds: Methodist, China Inland Mission, Congregational, Seventh Day Adventist.

From this predominantly radical Evangelical context, indigenous leaders emerged to found Chinese Pentecostal movements, often blending key aspects of their prior denominational formation with classic Pentecostalism. Thus, the strongly Sabbatarian character of the True Jesus Church owed much to the Seventh Day Adventist background of some of its founders. But there were also continuities with non-Christian religion. Bays argues that the dynamism of the Chinese Pentecostalism also owed a good deal to its congruence with "traditional Chinese popular sectarian 'heterodox' religion," which centered upon millenarianism, self-interpreting direct divine revelation and divine healing. These continuities help explain the intense millennial character of the True Jesus Church and the startling visions and prayers of one of its founders, Paul Wei. They also help explain the preponderance of remarkable healing miracles described by Berntsen in the periodical *The Upper Room*.[38]

---

[38] Bays, "Indigenous Protestant Churches," 127-38; *The Upper Room,* Mar. 1910.

Given the foundational role of Protestant, especially radical Evangelical networks in the global Pentecostal Movement, it is not surprising that India and China received the greatest attention from Pentecostal missionaries and their churches back home. India and China had been the classic mission sites for the historic mission churches and remained so for Pentecostals well into the 1930s, as illustrated by their profiles at the World Missionary Conferences held in Edinburgh in 1910, and Tambaram, Madras, in 1938. Nevertheless, Pentecostalism did spread elsewhere.

Close behind the two big Asian mission fields came South Africa. Within Africa, Pentecostal missionaries also quickly gained footholds in Sierra Leone and Liberia, and were well-established in Belgian Congo by the 1910s.[39] Beyond Asia and Africa, Jamaica was primed as well for Pentecostal revival as mainland America. In March 1907, a local periodical described how Browns Town Baptist Chapel "caught fire," along with "half a dozen other chapels" and one or two Episcopalian churches.[40] Latin America was also rapidly initiated. The story surrounding the Chilean Pentecost is particularly noteworthy. In late 1906, Minnie Abrams, a leading figure in the Indian Revival, revised her book, *The Baptism of the Holy Ghost and Fire*, to include the restoration of tongues and sent it to a former classmate from Bible school in Chicago, May Hoover. Mrs. Hoover and her husband, Dr. Willis, were Methodist missionaries in Valparaiso, Chile. Indeed, Dr. Hoover was the leading missionary in the church, Superintendent of the Central district and pastor of the largest parish. Moved by Abrams's account, he encouraged Chilean Christians to seek a similar experience. When forced out by missionary opposition, he helped found the National Methodist Church in 1910, a Pentecostal brand of Methodism.[41]

Conclusion

The Azusa Street Revival was crucial in shaping the worldwide Pentecostal Movement, although there were other epicenters of revival, such as Oslo, Sunderland, Calcutta, and Hong Kong. Los Angeles may not have been the place where Pentecostalism was first born, but the Azusa Street Revival was certainly the dynamo, and most subsequent revival emerged directly or indirectly from its tutelage. Questions concerning exactly where, when and who

---

[39] See for example, *AF* [Los Angeles], June 1906; *The Apostolic Messenger*, Nov./Dec. 1908; *Confidence*, June 1911, Oct. and Dec. 1916.

[40] *Revival News: Being the Organ of the Revival League of Jamaica*, Mar. 1907.

[41] *The Upper Room*, May 1910. McGee, "From East to West," 11. E.L. Cleary and J. Sepúlveda, "Chilean Pentecostalism: Coming of Age," in *Power, Politics and Pentecostals in Latin America*, ed. E.L. Cleary and H.W. Stewart-Gambino (Boulder, CO: Westview, 1997) 99-100.

were involved in the first manifestation of the apostolic faith are of secondary importance. Such a quest is driven by the Pentecostal fascination with issues of birth and rebirth, rather than by a desire to understand the Movement's causation. The key to the Movement's rapid spread across the globe lay in the religious networks already in place.

Energized by holiness and revivalist ideas, radical Evangelicals were actively seeking what was to be the Pentecostal experience. Once the revival took place, it was spread by the movement of missionaries and pious adventurers, but more importantly, by a well-established tradition of religious print, underpinned by the communications revolution in the latter half of the 19th century.

The center of this worldwide revival was the United States. There were, of course, European missionaries and Pentecostal print operations scattered even further afield, aided in Africa and Asia by the structures of empire, particularly the predominantly Protestant British Empire. But the bulk of the resources came from North America. In this third wave of Pentecostal and Evangelical missionary activity (following the earlier Established and Nonconformist movements), we begin to see a shift from Europe to America as the major source of missionary enterprise. The shift became far more apparent in the last three decades of the 20th century. But from the outset, it is important to consider North America, the metropole and the colony in the same analytic field, exploring how developments in one shaped the other.

7

What Good Can Come From Los Angeles?

Changing Perceptions of the North American Pentecostal Origins in Early Western European Pentecostal Periodicals

Cornelis van der Laan

Introduction

At the beginning of the 20th century, the "baptism with the Holy Spirit" or similar expressions were in the air among Evangelicals in Great Britain, Holland, Germany and Switzerland. The Keswick Conventions, the Welsh Revival and the visit of Reuben Arch Torrey paved the way for the expectation of a postconversion experience of Spirit baptism as an enduement of power for service. News of the Azusa Street Revival in 1906 and the subsequent revival meetings led by the Methodist minister T.B. Barratt in Oslo were initially received with great enthusiasm.

Barratt's contact with the Azusa Street Revival during his fund-raising journey in America in 1906 is well-known. Back in Norway, he started the first Pentecostal meetings in Europe in December 1906. From Oslo, the movement spread to other Scandinavian countries and to Germany, Switzerland and Great Britain.

This article focuses on the importance of the Azusa Street Revival for Western Europe. It presents a survey of how early Pentecostals in Great Britain, the Netherlands and Germany perceived the North American Pentecostal origins. In the English and Dutch papers, the Azusa Street Revival is clearly seen as the North American Pentecostal origin, from where it spread to Europe. The German Pentecostals, however, are more cautious to point to Azusa Street for their origin. The German Evangelicals had stigmatized Los Angeles as a rendezvous of spiritism! What good can come from such a place?

Great Britain

There are several ways the Pentecostal message crossed the Atlantic. First, it was by the circulation of *The Apostolic Faith* since September 1906, but also by correspondence, direct contact with the revival and by eyewitnesses. The preceding Welsh Revival had already resulted in connections with believers in Los Angeles. Joseph Smale, a Baptist pastor from Los Angeles, had visited Wales and led his church into prayer for a revival in Los Angeles. Frank Bartleman corresponded with Evan Roberts.

Once the Azusa Street Revival started, it did not take long to get the message across the ocean. Most important has been Barratt's acquaintance with the Azusa Street Revival during his stay in America in 1906. Alexander Boddy, Anglican vicar in Sunderland, persuaded Barratt to come over to England in 1907. Sunderland became a center for seekers of the Spirit baptism and Boddy, the most prominent leader of early Pentecostalism in Great Britain. In April 1908, Boddy started the publication of *Confidence,* which frequently referred to Los Angeles. Boddy visited Los Angeles twice and wrote extensive reports in *Confidence.*

A word search in the digitalized *Confidence* 1908-1926 showed no references to Topeka or Parham, but plenty to Los Angeles (or Los Angelos) and Azusa (also spelled as *Azuza* or *Asuza*). All eight references to Seymour (not including the one referring to Seymour Road) were found in Boddy's account of his visit to Azusa Street in 1912 and in the historical overview by Bartleman in 1916. The story of the outpouring at Topeka and the role of Parham does not present itself at all in *Confidence.*

We will follow the references in *Confidence* to Los Angeles to determine the importance of the Los Angeles Azusa Street Revival and how Sunderland in turn influenced the saints in Los Angeles.

Confidence 1908-1926

Mrs. Catherine Price, wife of a London banker, became the first person known to receive the Pentecostal baptism with tongues in January 1907. Her home at 14 Akerman Road in Brixton, hosting the first Pentecostal meetings, was according to Boddy "the first centre in Great Britain."¹ Boddy speaks of her as the "first thus visited by our God in England," and "her heart had been stirred by the Welsh Revival and the manifestation of the Spirit in speaking in tongues in Los Angeles, U.S.A., April 1906."²

Every issue of *Confidence* records the subscription gifts received, listing only the initial of the surname and the place of residence. Regularly, this list includes people from Los Angeles. For instance, in September 1912, we find a certain S., an A. and another S. from Los Angeles—adding up a total of 10 shillings and 1 penny. One S. probably refers to the Englishman George B. Studd, who lived at Los Angeles and was in regular correspondence with the editor of *Confidence*.

The first reference to Los Angeles is found in a letter from the same G.B. Studd, published in May 1908. Boddy noticed that now "Sunderland and Los Angeles are linked together, by receiving and by handing back testimonies of God's love and wonder-working power."

Another letter from Studd published in June 1908 mentioned 10 names belonging to the "little band" of Studd at Peniel Hall, 227 South Main Street, praying for Sunderland. Two months later Studd reports:

> The work here in Los Angeles is growing in size and in power. We have a splendid assembly in a Hall (327 So. Spring Street) under the leadership in God of Rev. E. Fisher. . . . This hall is in a central location on one of the best streets, and is in addition to Azusa Street, which is entirely controlled (humanly speaking) by the coloured people, though white people attend there. They had splendid meetings at Azusa Street on Sunday last. Praise God for all He is doing here.³

In August 1909, Studd reports to have mailed copies of the new Pentecostal paper *The Upper Room*, edited by E.K. Fisher and G.B. Studd, to Boddy.

It was in the house of Studd, that another prominent British leader of Pentecostalism, Cecil H. Polhill, received his Spirit baptism. Polhill visited the revival in Los Angeles in February 1908, returning from a trip to China. In August 1908, Boddy introduces "our dear brother" Cecil Polhill to the readers: "He received his 'Pentecost' in a quiet meeting in a house in Los Angeles, and he believes 'Pentecost' is a call to and an inducement for evangelistic work."⁴

---

[1] "London, S.W.," *Confidence*, Apr. 1908: 7.

[2] "Echoes From Heathfield," *Confidence*, Oct. 1916: 167, as told by Rev. T. Hackett.

[3] George B. Studd, "Los Angeles," *Confidence*, Aug. 1908: 10.

[4] "Brief Items," *Confidence*, Aug. 1908: 13.

Polhill and Boddy founded the Pentecostal Missionary Union in 1909. From 1911, Polhill edited the periodical *Flames of Fire*.

Harry E. Cantel, overseer of Dowie's Zion Church in Great Britain, heard of the Pentecostal outpouring in Zion City in 1907. He traveled to Zion City and soon received his Pentecostal Spirit baptism. Before returning to London, he married Margaret Fielden. William Hamner Piper of Chicago conducted the marriage ceremony. His former Dowie following in London now turned Pentecostal (early 1908).[5] After Harry Cantel's death in 1910, Mrs. Cantel continued the work, opening the missionary guesthouse *Maranatha* in Highbury New Park, London, in 1912, where Donald Gee would receive his Spirit baptism.

The brothers, Stanley and Arthur Frodsham of Bournemouth, joined the Pentecostal Movement in England, but later both moved to North America. In Bournemouth, Stanley had started the periodical *Victory* in April 1909. Stanley married a lady worker from Dr. Yoakum's Pisgah Home in Los Angeles and subsequently moved to Los Angeles in 1913. From there, he kept in contact with the Pentecostals in England.

In 1911, Arthur Frodsham reported his journey in Canada, British Columbia and the Western States. In Los Angeles, he first met George Studd and Elmer Fisher and then, he continues:

> Of course we had to visit Azusa Street Mission, the place where the fire first fell. Situated in a poor locality, off the main street, and in an old building, yet God had set His seal on the place by first pouring out His Holy Spirit, the latter rain, which has now enveloped the world. The mission has not been flourishing of late, but now there are signs of abundance of rain, and many are blessed. Coloured and white folks worship freely together in this meeting place. (Shortly after this was written there was a revival at Azuza Street, like old times. Pastor Durham, of Chicago, was greatly used.)[6]

In the Special Supplement to *Confidence*, May 1908, we find a letter from H.G. Garr, writing from Hong Kong. Garr relates his baptism with the Spirit in "Los Angelos" two years before. Someone present at the time told him he spoke in several languages of India. Once in India, he learned speaking in tongues was not meant for this goal, but it did not shake his faith. Garr writes: "So far I have not seen anyone who is able to preach to the natives in their own tongue given with the Holy Ghost."[7]

---

[5] Gordon P. Gardiner, "Out of Zion . . . Into All the World," *Bread of Life* 31, no. 7 (July 1982): 7, 10, 11, 15.

[6] W. Frodsham, "A Pentecostal Journey in Canada, British Columbia, and the Western States," *Confidence,* June 1911: 139.

[7] "A Letter From Bro. Garr," *Confidence Supplement,* May 1908: 1-3.

In the same supplement of *Confidence,* we find a letter from Robert J. Kerr from Belfast, Ireland, who writes: "We have been waiting for a Pentecostal outpouring of the Holy Spirit ever since we heard how the Lord was pouring out His Spirit, in Los Angelos."[8] After a visit from Boddy to Belfast, so Kerr reports, seven or eight had now "received their Pentecost and are speaking in tongues . . . hallelujah."

In August 1908, W.H.S. from Bracknell, Berkshire, writes after two years of "soul-hunger":

> When accounts first reached England of the outpouring of the Holy Spirit at Los Angeles, I had the inward witness in my spirit that the work was of God. . . . When news came in September last that many were entering into the blessing at Sunderland . . . my wife and I went with the full determination to obtain the blessing if possible.[9]

In November, meetings were commenced at their house, and now 10 had received the "Baptism of the Holy Ghost with signs following."

In *Confidence*, January 1909, we find a report of the Hamburg Conference in December 1908. Brother Andrew Johnson (or Jansen) of Sweden had been "present at the beginning of the glorious revival at Azusa Street Mission, but he believes that he had received the Baptism of the Holy Ghost with signs before that revival commenced." At Los Angeles "he saw all kinds of people come for the blessing. Many preachers came. A message came that he was to witness at Jerusalem. He soon saw that this meant Sweden, his homeland."[10]

At the Hamburg Conference, Beyerhaus, from Charlottenburg, addressed the motive to seek the sign but, at the same time, reflected existing feelings of superiority toward blacks:

> We must not aim at being some great one, but be very childlike. God cannot give to a man who seeks a great renown. He begins with very humble people. He began at Los Angeles with Negroes, a despised race.[11]

Other contacts in Los Angeles, writing to *Confidence*, include E.L. Yoder,

---

[8] "Good News From Ireland: A Message from Bro. Kerr, of Belfast," *Confidence Supplement,* May 1908: 3.

[9] W.H.S. "Berkshire: A Report From Bracknell," *Confidence,* Aug. 1908: 8, 9.

[10] "German Conference," *Confidence,* Jan. 1909: 8. From Los Angeles, Johnson went to New York, from there to Gibraltar, then to Naples, then to England. He left England on November 10, 1906, in a steamer to Gothenburg and went to his home at Sherboro. He attended meetings in a Baptist chapel and was now at the Bible School at Oreboro [sic].

[11] "German Conference—Continued," *Confidence,* Feb. 1909: 36.

who received his Spirit baptism on February 28, 1907;[12] Dr. Yoakum of Pisgah Home;[13] and M.B. Hinsdale of the Soldiers Home, who distributed Pentecostal literature among soldiers.[14]

Visitors With Eyewitness Accounts From Los Angeles

At the International Congress at Sunderland, June 1909, some visitors with eyewitness accounts from Azusa Street were present, like A.H. Post from Los Angeles, Daniel Awrey of Oklahoma, Mr. and Mrs. Lockhardt of Winnipeg, and Mr. and Mrs. Carrie Judd Montgomery.[15]

Mr. Montgomery gave an account of his visit to Azusa Street and testified of his receiving the latter rain. Awrey also testified of his visit to Los Angeles. In 1910, Frank Bartleman visited Sunderland. Boddy wrote down some of his "trenchant aphorisms," like "There is only one way up, and that is down."[16] In April 1916, *Confidence* published an extensive report of the Azusa Revival from Bartleman. On the 1911 Conference, Pastor and Mrs. Kellaway from Los Angeles witnessed of Azusa Street, but also saw a need for sound teaching. Boddy reports:

> The story of Azuza Street was never more real than when Sister Kellaway, brimming over with life and joy, told us of the sawdust where they knelt to get the blessing, and the light shining out of black faces in the early day of Pentecost at Los Angeles. "But now," she said, "what we want at Los Angeles is just such teaching as you get right here."[17]

On a visit in Bunde, North Germany, in the house of Pastor Voget, Boddy met Pastor Hettiarachy of Colombo, Ceylon. Hettiarachy, in a sermon, gave testimony of a visit to Azusa Street. At Los Angeles, he had heard Brother Seymour say that before the revival commenced, someone had had a dream in which he had seen a grave two miles deep, and at the bottom sprang up a spring of clear water. Those who were buried deep in Christ were the nearest to great blessing.[18]

---

[12] E.L. Yoder, "Los Angeles," *Confidence*, May 1909: 121.

[13] "Pentecostal Items," *Confidence*, June 1911: 141.

[14] "Pentecostal Items," *Confidence*, Jan. 1912: 18.

[15] Anton B. Reuss, "Impressions of the World's Congress at Sunderland," *Confidence*, June 1909: 136-37.

[16] "Sunderland," *Confidence*, July 1910: 165.

[17] "Convention Jottings," *Confidence*, June 1911: 129.

[18] A.A. Boddy, "Days in Germany—Continued," *Confidence*, Feb. 1912: 41.

J.H. King, of North Carolina, was at the Sunderland Conference in June 1912. He testified to reading in *The Apostolic Faith,* in September 1906, of the Holy Spirit falling upon the people at Los Angeles with the sign of tongues. When he did not receive the same, he decided it was a delusion that needed to be exposed. Eventually, in February 1907, King received the Spirit baptism with tongues and became an advocate of the movement.[19]

Daniel Awrey from Los Angeles was present at the Sunderland conferences in 1909, 1910 and 1911. "Since the Pentecostal outpouring in 1906, Brother Awrey has traveled around the world three times."[20] *Confidence* reported Awrey's death in December 1913, in West Africa.

On the Sunderland Conference in June 1913, Dr. Florence Murcutt from Los Angeles gave her testimony as to the healing of the sick.[21]

Boddy's Visit to Los Angeles

In August 1912, Boddy visited Azusa Street in Los Angeles. He found Seymour not at home, but conversed with Mrs. Seymour:

> I set out to find Azusa Street Mission as soon as possible. Readers of *Confidence* will remember that it was here that the tongues as a sign of the Pentecostal baptism came so much before the public . . . the Azusa Street Mission became the scene of great blessing, though sometimes, in the absence of leaders, there was some confusion and counterfeit as elsewhere.[22]

Pointing to global importance of the Azusa Street Mission, Boddy writes:

> Thence it spread and was carried all over the world, including Europe and Great Britain, where at Sunderland, in the North, the outpouring began afresh under different conditions, and some hundred received the baptism of the Holy Ghost, the sign of the heavenly tongue.[23]

Other contacts Boddy met in Los Angeles included: Reverend Samuel P. and Mrs. Mead; G.B. Studd (with whom he had corresponded for years); the Garrs; and Dr. Finis Ewing Yoakum of Pisgah Home. Boddy's following visit to the United States was in June through August 1914. Due to the war, he had

---

[19] J.H. King, "The Testimony of an Opposer," *Confidence,* July 1912: 153-55, 158.
[20] "Daniel Awrey: His Home Call in West Africa," *Confidence,* Feb. 1914: 35.
[21] "Sunderland Convention," *Confidence,* June 1913: 115.
[22] A.A. Boddy, "At Los Angeles, California," *Confidence,* Oct. 1912: 232.
[23] Boddy, 233.

to cancel his week of meetings in Los Angeles and, therefore, did not visit Azusa Street.

Flames of Fire 1911-1917

The *Flames of Fire,* with which is incorporated *Tidings From Tibet and Other Lands,* is the periodical of the Pentecostal Missionary Union. During 1911-1917, no mention is made of Topeka or Parham, nor of Seymour or Azusa, but Los Angeles is mentioned.

Gerard A. Bailly, CMA missionary in Caracas, Venezuela, testifies of his Spirit baptism on June 28, 1907 in the Apostolic Faith Mission on Bunker's Hill, Los Angeles, while on furlough.[24] Andrew Ursham, addressing the London Conference on June 15, 1916, testified of how Pentecost fell in an Evangelical church in Chicago after a certain Brother St. Clare had come back from his visit to Los Angeles.[25]

Elim Evangel 1919-1931

In *Elim Evangel,* Parham or Topeka is not mentioned during 1919-1931, nor is Seymour. The city of Los Angeles is mentioned frequently, but mostly in connection with Aimee Semple McPherson. However, several times the Azusa Street Revival is alluded to as the commencement of the Pentecostal Movement.

E.C. Boulton, in his report of the visit he and Jeffreys and other Elim ministers made to the United States in 1924, wrote: "We could not leave Los Angeles, which might be termed the *Mecca of the Pentecostal Movement*, without paying a visit to the beautiful Angeles Tempe, of which Mrs. McPherson is the gifted pastor."[26] This peculiar description of Los Angeles might be an allusion to the Azusa Street Revival as the place where it all began, but perhaps his Mecca was Mrs. McPherson!

More clearly is T.E. Hackett in June 1921: "When in April 1906, this movement commenced in Los Angeles...."[27] A.F. Johnson gives an overview of the Pentecostal work in Sweden in 1925. In 1905 and 1906, believers in Sweden were praying for a revival:

---

[24] Gerard A. Bailly, "God's Sovereignty in Diversity," *Flames of Fire,* Oct. 1913: 2-4, and Dec. 1913: 2, 3.

[25] Andrew Ursham, "Pentecostal Revival," *Flames of Fire,* Aug. 1916: 3-5.

[26] E.C. Boulton, "Back to the Homeland," *Elim Supplement,* Oct. 1924: 46.

[27] T.E. Hackett, "The Nearing Advent of Our Lord," *Elim Evangel,* June 1921: 43.

They had been reading about the great Welsh Revival and thought God could do the same in Sweden. Then the reports came from Los Angeles that God was pouring out His Spirit and they prayed that He would visit the Scandinavian countries too, and the Lord began to answer prayer.[28]

Elizabeth Sisson portrays the Azusa Street event as the start of a worldwide revival.[29] In an article on the Spirit baptism, Charles Robinson uses Azusa Street as a paradigm for how to receive the Spirit baptism ("When the Spirit Fell in Los Angeles").[30]

Beulah Argue compares the ringing of the high-priestly bells in the Temple with the speaking in tongues of the Day of Pentecost and of the same in the present Pentecostal outpouring. Azusa Street is seen as the beginning from where it spread over the world. The bells had ceased ringing for 2000 years, but now . . .

> Out in Los Angeles, in an old barn on Azusa Street, which they had cleaned up and white-washed, God sent another Pentecost to His people. The bells rang loudly until the sound of them resounded throughout the world, and drew great numbers of people.[31]

Redemption Tiding 1924-1939

Redemption Tidings started its publication in July 1924. Contrary to the other periodicals studied above, this periodical does give attention to the Topeka event, but only once mentions Parham.

The opening issue contains an anonymous article, "Speaking With Tongues and Other Gifts: Pentecost to 1924."[32] It is a remarkable article, which was also translated into Dutch and published in *Spade Regen*. The year 1906 is of special significance to the author by linking the Azusa Street Revival to the findings of old manuscripts in Egypt containing the longer ending of Mark 16. The article opens like this:

---

[28] A.F. Johnson, "The Pentecostal Work in Sweden," *Elim Evangel*, Mar. 2, 1925: 49.

[29] Elizabeth Sisson, "Reminiscences," *Elim Evangel*, Aug. 16, 1929: 245.

[30] Charles Robinson, "The Spirit's Baptism," *Elim Evangel*, Apr. 25, 1930: 266.

[31] Beulah Argue, "The Ringing of the Golden Bells," *Elim Evangel*, Aug. 28, 1931: 553.

[32] In the editorial "The Last Twelve Verses of Mark xvi" of *Redemption Tidings*, Feb. 15, 1934, John Carter quotes from an article from Frodsham in *Victory*, which is exactly the same as part of the anonymous article in 1924. The quote corresponds with the first part of the 1924 article. I have not been able to trace the article in *Victory* to check whether the second part in which Topeka is mentioned can also be found in *Victory*. Perhaps the author of the 1924 article only used Frodsham for his first part and added to this his second part from another source.

> God is always on time to vindicate His truth. In the Spring of 1906, away in Los Angeles, California, in an obscure building, and amongst the despised negroes, was being witnessed a wonderful phenomenon.... Since then, tens of thousands have received the same filling of the Holy Spirit and are "edifying themselves" by speaking in tongues, not to men, but unto God (1 Corinthians 14:2).[33]

The author claims that opponents of this latter rain have tried to explain away the thing, and some preachers, students and leaders have been only too glad to point out that some of the earliest manuscripts of Mark's Gospel leave out verses 9-20 of the 16th chapter.[34]

At this time, when God's Word is being questioned, the author somewhat passionately continues:

> Buried for centuries, hidden away from man during the terrible times that Egypt went through, yet at last they are brought forth at the very time, 1906, when most needed. God proves His Word to the unbelieving "believer," that those who "believe" in Christ would speak in new tongues, lay hands on the sick and they should recover and cast out demons in His name.[35]

The second part of the article has a sketch of Charismatic occurrences in church history, which ends with Topeka and names Parham. Although the author writes of Topeka from which it has circled the earth, the article closes with the observation that the past 18 years "God is doing a wonderful thing in the earth" and, therefore, comes back to 1906 as the beginning of the Pentecostal Movement.

All other references in this periodical to Topeka relate to Stanley Frodsham's *With Signs Following*, published in 1926. In his review, Donald Gee assumes that Topeka will be new to most of his readers:

> It will come as a surprise to many to read the account of the first shower of latter rain outpouring at Topeka, Kansas, in 1900. Most of us look to Asuza Street Mission, Los Angeles, in 1906, as the beginning of the present outpouring. But one specially valuable feature of the book is the number of instances it gives of those who received the baptism in the Holy Spirit and spoke with tongues not only before 1906, but before 1900.[36]

---

[33] "Speaking With Tongues and Other Gifts: Pentecost to 1924," *Redemption Tidings*, July 1924: 11-14.

[34] "Speaking With Tongues."

[35] "Speaking With Tongues."

[36] Donald Gee, "An Eagerly Awaited Book: A Review," *Redemption Tidings*, May 1927: 5.

From this, Gee draws the conclusion that the Pentecostal experience has never entirely ceased in the church. He maintains that Azusa was the start of the new revival, where Pentecost became the experience of the *many,* in contrast to the *few,* from before 1906:

> All that has happened during the last 20 years has simply been, that what before was the experience of the few, has now become the experience of the many.[37]

Neither Gee nor Frodsham mention Parham, probably because of Parham's falling into disgrace. Although the Topeka story is told, it is not presented as the origin of the Pentecostal Movement. Gee, who visited the Azusa Street Mission in 1930, in his *The Pentecostal Movement: A Short History of Its Rise and Development* (September 1932), does not mention Topeka, but extensively relates what really happened at Azusa. On the cover is a photo of the Azusa Street Mission with the following text:

> "Where the Fire Fell": A picture of the rough wooden hall, as it is today, in Asuza Street, Los Angeles became famous through the Revival that broke out there in 1906, when hungry souls flocked there from all over the world. Colored people now run it under the name of "Apostolic Faith Gospel Mission."[38]

Stanley Frodsham in 1934, then editor of *Pentecostal Evangel,* comes close to presenting Topeka as origin, but even then, Azusa is the place from where it spread throughout the world:

> It was when, at a later date, this Pentecostal revival spread to Los Angeles, California, that it received a good deal of publicity. Many Christian workers visited that city and waited on God in an old barn-like building on Azusa Street. As they returned to their various churches, filled with the Spirit of God, revivals came to a great many cities throughout the States and Canada, and many thousands received a baptism in the Spirit similar to that which the 120 received on the Day of Pentecost. These were called *Pentecostal Revivals.*[39]

Stanley's brother, Arthur, in an address on a convention in Sunderland, 1935, gives us an interesting anecdote:

---

[37] Gee, 5.

[38] *Redemption Tidings,* Sept. 1932: cover.

[39] Stanley H. Frodsham, "The Pentecostal People, and What They Believe: The Distinctive Testimony of the Movement," *Redemption Tidings,* Jan. 1, 1934: 3.

We do thank God for the visitation God gave to Sunderland years ago. I go back in thought to Los Angeles. If you lived there, you would hear about when the fire fell in Azuza Street. I went down to Azuza Street and found the place closed, unfit for habitation. I thought, *Wouldn't it be wonderful if we could re-erect this place.* So I wrote to my brother, and this was his reply: "Pentecostal people don't believe in relics."[40]

In 1935, the Finish pastor Ensio Lehtonen tells of the strong desire in Finland for a fresh outpouring of the Spirit in the beginning of the century:

Then wonderful news was heard from Wales and Los Angeles. The newspapers told about them, while we continually prayed and expected the outpouring of the Spirit. Then some persons belonging to the "Laestadio" awakening traveled to Oslo, Norway, where brother T.B. Barratt had joined the Pentecostal revival.[41]

For years, E.W. Moser prayed for a special Spirit baptism:

One day somebody pointed out to us a short paragraph in the *Christian Herald*, reporting that some black people in Los Angeles had received an outpouring of the Holy Ghost with the Scriptural sign of speaking in other tongues. . . . Soon after papers arrived from America reporting news of a wonderful revival. . . . It was all so Scriptural, and to us inspiring. The doctrines set forth in those papers were precisely what we believed and taught ourselves: "Justification by faith," "Sanctification by consecration and faith," and "Baptism (immersion) in water, and the Baptism of the Holy Ghost with the sign, or initial evidence, of speaking in other tongues, as recorded in the Acts."[42]

William Burton in 1930 gives us another example how Los Angeles had captured the attention of believers in England:

One day I overheard a conversation between two Sunday School teachers: "What do yer think of the 'ere tongues as some niggers from Los Angeles is speakin' with, sayin' as 'ow they've got the Holy Spirit same as 'em at Pentecost." How my heart leaped at the news! . . . Pentecost, Tongues! Power from on High! Later I heard that others even in England

---

[40] Arthur Frodsham, "Wait for the Moving of God," *Redemption Tidings,* Oct. 15, 1935: 4.

[41] Ensio Lehtonen, "My Spirit in the North Country: Pentecostal Revivals in the History of Finland," *Redemption Tidings,* May 1, 1935: 5.

[42] E.W. Moser, "My Personal Testimony to Pentecost," *Redemption Tidings,* Mar. 1930: 5.

were filled with the Spirit just as those in the Bible, and were praising God with other tongues.[43]

J. Roswell Flower's description of 1927 fits well with the general picture of how Topeka and Los Angeles are interpreted:

> Pentecost was in existence in 1900, but it did not receive its impetus until in 1906 when the outpouring came down in Azusa Street in Los Angeles. From there it spread all over the world.[44]

The Netherlands

Gerrit and Wilhelmine Polman were the founders of the Pentecostal Movement in the Netherlands.[45] They had been Salvation Army officers before they joined Dowie's Christian Apostolic Church in Zion. In 1903, they moved to Zion City, where they stayed until January 1906. The prayer group they started in Amsterdam after their return would develop into a Pentecostal assembly. Initially, Polman remained in contact with Zion City, but after Dowie's removal from power in April 1906, Polman decided to move on more independently.[46]

In the afterglow of the Welsh Revival, they longed for a new awakening in the Netherlands. They realized that it would have to start in their own hearts, so they were praying for a baptism with the Holy Spirit. Then they received news of the Pentecostal revival at Los Angeles:

> In 1906 we heard of wonderful tidings from America. Some papers were sent to us where we read that God had again visited His people as in the times of old. We learned that God was pouring out His Holy Spirit and people were speaking in other tongues as the Spirit gave utterance.[47]

A letter from Polman cited in *The Apostolic Faith* makes clear that the Pentecostal message came to him through this paper: "The blessings of the latter

---

[43] Wm. F.P. Burton, "My Testimony to 'The Baptism in the Holy Spirit,'" *Redemption Tidings*, Apr. 1930: 4.

[44] J. Roswell Flower, "The Present Position of Pentecost," *Redemption Tidings*, Oct. 1927: 4.

[45] See my *Sectarian Against His Will: Gerrit Roelof Polman and the Birth of Pentecostalism in the Netherlands*, Studies in Evangelicalism (Metuchen, NJ: Scarecrow, 1991).

[46] Polman's last change of address reported to Zion is dated in the records of Zion as April 10, 1906. His next change of address on June 6, 1907, was never reported.

[47] G.R. Polman, "The Pentecostal Work in Holland," *The Pentecostal Evangel*, May 29, 1926: 2. Idem, "De Heere heeft groote dingen bij ons gedaan: dies zijn wij verblijd!" *Spade Regen*, no. 29 (Mar.-May 1912): 1.

rain came to us through your paper first."[48] Comparing the new information with Biblical data led them to anticipate the Holy Spirit in like manner. This expectation was further strengthened by correspondence with those blessed in this way and by the swift multiplication of the Pentecostal experience around the world. During the summer of 1907, the Pentecostal Movement had come from Norway to Germany, England and Switzerland.

In October 1907, Mrs. Polman was the first to receive the Spirit baptism in this way. Polman identifies this event, on October 29, 1907, as the definite break with the Zion church and the start of the Pentecostal work in the Netherlands.[49]

In April 1908, Polman started publication of *Spade Regen* (*Latter Rain*), which would be printed until 1931. Throughout the period of *Spade Regen*, Azusa Street or Los Angeles is seen as the beginning of the worldwide Pentecostal Movement. Polman saw the significance of the interracial aspect and of the equality in Christ.

In the first issue of *Spade Regen* (April 1908) the new work of the Spirit was seen as the latter rain, God adorning the Bride with costly ornaments (that is, spiritual gifts) in preparation for the eschatological wedding feast. The universal significance, and the equality and unity in Christ were stressed. The revival touched "blacks and whites; old experienced preachers as well as children, pastors and members of all kinds of churches and organizations."[50] And, "where God's Spirit is poured out, all separations fall away and one unites at the feet of the Cross and one just looks at the Savior of all men."[51]

The Spirit baptism itself was called a baptism of praise, love and power. *Praise*, because it "elicits from us beauteous choruses of praise, existence of which we had never dreamed and which can only find expression in the languages descending from the areas of heavenly glory."[52] Next, it enabled them to love God and Jesus more than ever before, and "we learn to appreciate our

---

[48] *AF* no. 18, Jan. 1909: 1; then published in Portland.

[49] *AF* The formulation by G.A. Wumkes gives room for the possibility that it was the content of the prophecy that made it clear to definitely break with Zion. In May 1912, just before the opening of the new hall, Polman, in his brief account of the history, dated the beginning with "a good 4 1/2 years ago." This confirms that, in the eyes of Polman, the movement started with the event of October 29, 1907.

[50] "Wat zal dit toch zijn?" *Spade Regen*, no. 1 (Apr. 1908): 1. Also in R. van Oosbree, *Valiants for Truth We Have Known: Eighty Years of Holy Ghost Revival* (Pasadena, CA: Ravano, 1986): 1-6.

[51] *Spade Regen*, no. 1: 4.

[52] *Spade Regen*, no. 1: 1.

neighbor, view him amiable in Christ, like He once taught us."[53] Lastly, it gave them power to be a witness wherever Jesus called. Evidently, the personal experience of the Spirit baptism was not confined to the individual, but also had a collective significance of equality and unity in Christ. The renewed vertical relation with God had horizontal effects in producing a fresh appreciation of one's neighbor.

A good number of *Spade Regen* were sent to South Africa, to the Dutch Indies and some to Los Angeles. In a letter from Pasadena, Mrs. Dr. Harry Ronde testified of her Spirit baptism in August 1907. She had left Holland 24 years ago and now requested 100 issues of *Spade Regen*. Much pleased, Polman comments:

> The first stream of English papers, containing the good news, came from California. From there now comes a call for Dutch literature for our countrymen there and elsewhere—praise Him! [54]

Another letter from Los Angeles came from Henry Smith, who had moved from Belgium to America in 1893. After his conversion in 1909, he had received his Spirit baptism.[55] Ties with Los Angeles were also strengthened by two visits from Frank Bartleman (1910 and 1913). Other American visitors in those early days included Daniel Awrey (1910), J.H. King (1912) and a certain John Matthews from Los Angeles (1912).

Throughout the period under Polman, the Azusa Street Revival is viewed as the origin. Although, as we shall see, Polman was aware of the Topeka story, it is never alluded to in his publications.

Germany

Contrary to the early British and Dutch Pentecostals, the German Pentecostals show a mixed picture of the impact of the Azusa Street Revival. Next to a positive reflection of Azusa, there is a critical account of spiritistic influences. German Pentecostals even point to Parham as the originator of Pentecostalism as early as 1909. Why this difference?

Evangelicals in Germany, as in England and Holland, at first warmly welcomed the news of the outpouring of the Holy Spirit in Los Angeles and Oslo. The tide in Germany soon changed after the tumultuous meetings led by Heinrich Dallmeyer in Kassel in July and August 1907. After the meetings had

---

[53] *Spade Regen*, no. 1.
[54] *Spade Regen*, no. 6, Jan.-Feb. 1909: 2.
[55] *Spade Regen*, no. 35, Nov. 1913: 4.

been stopped by the police, Dallmeyer denounced the Pentecostal Movement as from the devil. In his revocation in October 1907, Dallmeyer stated that the "driving Spirit in the Los Angeles Movement is not the Spirit of God, but a Lying Spirit."[56] German Evangelicals were strongly divided over the issue. B. Kuhn, editor of the *Evangelischen Allianzblatt,* started to warn against the Pentecostals. In September 1907, the *Allianzblatt* published a letter of warning from Johan Seitz to the Azusa Street Mission.[57]

The same month, Kuhn describes the Pentecostal Movement as a disease that with "epidemic might and dynamite power" had spread from Los Angeles, and by way of Oslo, to Germany, causing splits and divisions.[58] Missionary G.F. Nagel wrote critical reports from India about the Garrs from Los Angeles who had traveled from Calcutta to Kumur. These Azusa Street missionaries were accused of false teachings. They claimed that resistance against the Spirit baptism with tongues led to losing one's justification and that Jesus himself had spoken in tongues at the cross.[59]

Two years after Kassel, the majority of the Evangelicals agreed with the Berlin Declaration that rejected the Pentecostal Movement as diabolic. The Berlin Declaration of September 15, 1909, summarized the arguments used before, in which Los Angeles is portrayed as a city of demonic activity. The exceptional negative focus on Los Angeles among Evangelicals since Kassel explains for the different view the German Pentecostals developed on Azusa.

The German Pentecostals had by then become a movement distinct from the German

Evangelicals. In February 1909, the Pentecostal periodical *Pfingstgrüsse* was launched, edited by Jonathan Paul. The first issue included a remarkable article on the history of the Pentecostal Movement from Thomas G. Atteberry of *The Pentecostal Witness.*

---

[56] Dieter Lang, *Eine Bewegung bricht sich Bahn* (Brunnen: Brunnen Verlag, 1979) 185. Paul Fleisch, *Die Pfingstbewegung in Deutschland* (Hannover: Heinr. Feesche Verlag, 1956) 65.

[57] Johannes Seitz, "Brief nach Los Angeles (Kalifornien)," *Allianzblatt,* no. 33 (Sept. 1, 1907), cited in B. Kuhn, *Die Pfingstbewegung im Lichte der heiligen Schrift und ihrer eigenen Geschichte* (Gotha: Missionsbuchhandlung P. Ott [1909]). The letter is dated July 7, 1907, the day the Kassel meetings started.

[58] Kuhn, *Die Pfingstbewegung,* 27, taken from *Allianzblatt* 1907.

[59] Kuhn, 51-56, taken from *Allianzblatt;* Fleisch, *Pfingstbewegung,* 16, 17. After India Garr went to China, from where he wrote a letter to *Confidence,* Boddy shows awareness of the accusations against Garr: "So much was written against him" (*Confidence Supplement,* May 1908: 3), but nevertheless seems to accept his ministry. Boddy would later meet Garr in Los Angeles. In May 1916, Stanley Frodsham in *Confidence* reports the death of Mrs. Lilian Garr.

In the article, Topeka, Kansas, is presented as the origin of the Pentecostal Movement with Parham as its leader. Before the Pentecostal Movement came to Los Angeles, it had already spread to every state of the Union and had been kept from "fanaticism and wild fire." Los Angeles is described as a city of false religions and of many spiritistic mediums that had become a meeting place for evil spirits. The leadership in Los Angeles is presented as incapable:

> As the leadership of the movement lacked wisdom and discernment, soon psychics and persons with hypnotic and mesmeric powers connected with the work. The results of their operations were multiple forms of fanaticism in spiritistic manifestations. As a result of these strange bodily demonstrations, of which a number were caused by hypnotic influence and magnetic streams that were taken into the meetings, others also by demonic powers, splits occurred.[60]

During the first months missionaries went out, they took with them, according to Atteberry, the "Los Angeles-Spirit." Before the end of the first year, the leadership in Los Angeles acknowledged their error, but the evil had already been done.

The Pentecostal Witness was edited by Thomas Atteberry and Daniel Bryant from Zion City, Illinois.[61] Bryant had been overseer of the Zion Church in South Africa. In the article, Atteberry mentions that at the time of the Azusa Revival, he was pastoring a church in Los Angeles "in the line of the full gospel." The only issue of *The Pentecostal Witness* that could be traced (November 1908) unfortunately did not contain the article used by *Pfingstgrüsse*.[62] While in Los Angeles, Atteberry edited *The Pentecostal Truth,* of which some copies are present at the Flower Heritage Center. Atteberry had apparently come to a skeptical position toward Azusa. His argument corresponds very well with Parham's assessment of the Azusa Street Mission during his visit in October 1906.

Pfingstgrüsse also contains positive references to Los Angeles, for instance, when visitors give account of their experience in or with Azusa Street, like Cecil Polhill and Andrew Johnson. Alexander Boddy's report of his visit to Azusa Street in 1912 is published, but when Jonathan Paul visited the United States

---

[60] Thomas G. Atteberry, "Zur Geschichte der Pfingstbewegung," *Pfingstgrüsse,* Feb. 1909: 12.

[61] See "Apostolic Faith Directory," in *The Pentecost,* Dec. 1908: 16.

[62] *The Pentecostal Witness* 15 (Nov. 1908), was found in the Donald Gee Centre with thanks to Desmond Cartwright. From this issue, we learn that the church Atteberry was pastoring while in Los Angeles was the People's Church.

in 1912, he did not include Los Angeles.⁶³ After the deception of World War I, contacts with Pentecostals from abroad were slowly restored. In December 1919, *Pfingstgrüsse* gladly announced a letter received from the brethren in Los Angeles confirming the unity among believers.⁶⁴ The silence is broken.

The Los Angeles Connection Reconsidered

The stigmatizing of Los Angeles in the Berlin Declaration was already present in the letter of invitation to the Berlin conference, where the declaration would be made:

> The Tongue movement of 1907 has come to us by way of Christiana-Hamburg from Los Angeles. Los Angeles has, however, in an article brought by the movement's own organ, . . . been drawn as a rendezvous of spiritistic spirits and as an area that has become fatal for the movement. This origin also explains the mournful character the movement with us carried.⁶⁵

The "movement's own organ" might refer to Atteberry's article in *Pfingstgrüsse*, but it can also point to Charles Parham's paper, also called *Apostolic Faith*, since Parham presented himself as the founder of the movement. The description of the revival as becoming overpowered by "spiritistic spirits" is typical for whites like Parham and Alma White, who condemned the Azusa Revival because of its interracial character. This same prejudice, even if it was unaware, might explain the German Evangelical disproportionate negative emphasis on the Los Angeles connection.

In 1910, Eugen Edel writes an apology of the Pentecostal Movement. In a clear attempt to refute the repudiation based on the Los Angeles origin, he wrote:

> Often one finds the view represented as if the origin of the Pentecostal Movement lies in Los Angeles in America. From this has the rumor about the "Los Angeles spirit" been constructed. But the earthly origin of the Pentecostal Movement was actually in Topeka, Kansas.⁶⁶

---

⁶³ "Ein Reisebericht über Amerika," *Pfingstgrüsse* 5, no. 3 (20 Oct. 1912): 20-22. Paul reports visits to Union Hill near New York (Mrs. Mok), Montwait near Boston, New York (Simpson), Rochester (Mrs. Baker's Elim Faith House), Detroit, Chicago (Mrs. Piper's Stone Church), New York (Glad Tidings Hall). On his way back to New York, he visited Mennonites in Illinois and Indiana.

⁶⁴ "Von unsern Brüdern aus America," *Pfingstgrüsse* 11, no. 25 (14 Dec. 1919): 107.

⁶⁵ Ernst Giese, *Jonathan Paul, Ein Knecht Jesu Christi*, 2nd ed. (Altdorf: Missionsbuchhandlung und Verlag, 1965) 155.

⁶⁶ Eugen Edel, *Die Pfingstbewegung im Lichte der Kirchengeschichte* (Brieg: by the author, 1910) 66-67.

In 1915, the Dutch Reformed pastor G.A. Wumkes was writing a monograph on the Pentecostal Movement. Polman had provided him with literature. When Wumkes in his first draft on the basis of Edel's description introduced Parham as the founder of the movement, Polman corrected him by letter:

> Parham has indeed said that he was the founder of the movement, but that was a political move of his and later it has become apparent that his motives were not sound.... The Pentecostal Movement has her origin in Los Angeles (1906), in a circle of converted coloreds, who came together and prayed for the baptism with the Holy Spirit, like the first disciples received it in the beginning. Their prayer was answered and from there it has spread itself.[67]

Polman is not afraid to side with the black origin of Azusa Street in spite of refutation. Himself an illegitimate child, he knew what it meant to be despised for your descent.

We may conclude that in the early British and Dutch periodicals, the Topeka event and Parham are completely absent, while Azusa Street plays a very important role as the place where the fire first fell and from where it spread over the world. The strong repudiation by the German Evangelicals of the Los Angeles origin prompted the German Pentecostals to prefer Topeka as the origin, an alternative that was offered to them by white American Pentecostals.

---

[67] G.R. Polman to G.A. Wumkes, Amsterdam, 27 Feb. 1915. As a true historian, Wumkes, in his final draft, presented both versions side by side: G.A. Wumkes, *De Pinksterbeweging voornamelijk in Nederland* (Utrecht: G.J.A. Ruys, 1916) 4.

8

Azusa Missionaries in the Context of the Caste System in India

Paulson Pulikottil

What happened in Los Angeles in 1906 is undoubtedly a watershed in the history of Christian missions. Hundreds of missionaries going out to the various parts of the world from one location is unprecedented in the history of the Christian church. Iain MacRobert pointed out that within the first two months of the movement, 38 missionaries went out from the Azusa Street Mission and in the first two years, the missionaries from Azusa Street were serving over 50 nations worldwide.[1]

India, more than 8,000 miles away from Azusa Street in Los Angeles, was among the many nations that was a favorite destination of the missionaries who went out as a result of this revival. Some of them were guided to India by the supernatural intervention of God. Alfred G. Garr spoke in Bengali when he was baptized in the Holy Spirit, and that made him sail to Calcutta.

While at prayer in the Azusa Street Mission, someone spoke to George E. Berg in Hindustani, which made Berg consider India as his mission field. Though detailed biographical information or reports of the work of all Azusa

---

[1] Iain MacRobert, "The Black Roots of Pentecostalism," in *Pentecost, Mission and Ecumenism: Essays on Intercultural Theology: Festschrift in Honor of Professor Walter J. Hollenweger*, ed. Jan A.B. Jongeneel (Frankfurt am Main: Peter Lang, 1992) 79.

Street missionaries is not available to us even 100 years after the event, here is an attempt to explore some aspects of the work of these missionaries. The special focus is on how the Azusa Street Revival impacted the work of missionary work among the Dalits in India.

Azusa Missionaries

The term *Azusa missionaries* is used in this section to describe three different groups of Pentecostal missionaries to India. The first group is those who were physically present at the Azusa Street Revival meetings, and having received the baptism in the Holy Spirit in these meetings, went from Azusa Street Mission directly. Alfred Goodrich Garr Sr. and George E. Berg belong to this group.

Alfred G. Garr was the pastor of the Burning Bush Mission in Los Angeles when he received the baptism in the Holy Spirit on June 14, 1906, at the Azusa Street meetings. Guided by the fact that he spoke in Bengali when he was baptized in the Holy Spirit, he decided to go to Bengal in India as a missionary. He set out for India with the funds raised at the Azusa Street meetings and arrived in Calcutta in 1907.

A.G. Garr was more an itinerant revival preacher than a missionary. Garr mainly worked among the missionaries in conferences and other meetings. In these meetings, he expounded the Pentecostal doctrines, especially that of the baptism in the Holy Spirit.[2] His focus was not mainly on evangelism but renewal. He also ministered in Pandita Ramabai's Mukti Mission. He preached in Bombay, India, and in Colombo, Sri Lanka. However, his stay in India was brief (for a few months) as he left India for Hong Kong in October 1907.[3]

George E. Berg is another significant missionary who belongs to this group. G.E. Berg arrived in India on February 28, 1908. He visited Mukti Mission where the revival was going on, later worked in Bombay and then moved to the southern part of India.

The second group involved those who had their Pentecostal experience or exposure to the Pentecostal experience in Azusa Street, but waited some more time (in some cases years) before they went to India. So, they were not sent directly from the Azusa Street, but went out either as independent missionaries

---

[2] Gary B. McGee, "The Calcutta Revival of 1907 and the Reformulation of Charles F. Parham's Bible Evidence," *Asia Journal of Pentecostal Studies* 6, no. 1 (2003).

[3] McGee, "Garr, Alfred Goodrich, Sr. (1874-1944)," *Dictionary of Pentecostal and Charismatic Movements,* ed. Stanley M. Burgess and Gary B. McGee, with Patrick H. Alexander, assoc. ed. (Grand Rapids: Zondervan, 1988) 660.

or missionaries of some sending bodies. Robert F. Cook is representative of this second category of Azusa missionaries. Robert F. Cook, a Russian immigrant to the U.S., and his wife were introduced to Pentecostalism at the Azusa Street Revival in 1908. However, Cook received the Holy Spirit baptism at home.[4] In 1913 he and his first wife, Anna Cook, traveled to India as independent missionaries. He was briefly associated with the Assemblies of God but later became a missionary in the Church of God (Cleveland, Tenn.). After the death of Anna, he married Bertha in 1918. Though we cannot say that Cook went out from Azusa Street, we can say he was part of the missionary force influenced by the Azusa Street Revival.

The third group is those who received their baptism in the Holy Spirit during the days of Azusa Street Revival and went out to serve in India during this period. In the case of some of these missionaries, we may not have evidence to say if they were physically present in the Azusa Street meetings. It is highly probable in the case of many who lived near Los Angeles, to be physically present there, but we do not have information about their connection to Azusa Street. Probably they were influenced by the Azusa Street Revival directly, or indirectly through the various Pentecostal writings, or preachers who went out from the Apostolic Faith Mission.

An example is Thomas Ball Barratt, who received the Baptism away from Azusa Street but with the advice and prayer support of the Azusa Street Mission. Having heard about the revival that was going on in Azusa Street while he was in New York raising funds for his mission in Norway, Barratt wrote a letter to the mission in Azusa Street, asking how to receive the blessing they were receiving. His letter was duly replied when he was told to tarry for the Holy Spirit, and the participants of the Azusa Street meetings promised to pray for him. He received the baptism in the Holy Spirit on October 7, 1906, while he was still in the city of New York.[5] Barratt took the Pentecostal message to his own denomination in his own country and traveled worldwide, including India, carrying the Pentecostal message. Though Barratt did not put in long years of missionary service in India, he was one of those early Pentecostal preachers from the West who visited India.[6]

---

[4] L.F. Morgan, "Cook, Robert F.," in *The New International Dictionary of Pentecostal and Charismatic Movements,* ed. Stanley M. Burgess, with Eduard M. van der Maas (Grand Rapids: Zondervan, 2002) 560. Also see Robert F. Cook, *Half a Century of Divine Leadings and Thirty-Seven Years of Apostolic Ministry in South India* (Cleveland, TN: Church of God Foreign Missions Department, 1955).

[5] Lester Sumrall, *Pioneers of Faith,* First Indian ed. (Secunderabad, India: Ben Publishing, 1995) 26.

[6] Sumrall, 31.

Another representative of this group is Dorothy L. McCarty, of whom scanty biographical details are available. She received the baptism in the Holy Spirit while the Azusa Street Revival was still on, but may not have been present in the Azusa Street Mission. She wrote to *The Pentecost* in September 1908, "I was baptized with the Holy Ghost and spake in tongues as they did on the day of Pentecost."[7] She traveled to India as an independent missionary sometime in 1910 and worked in various places in India including Bhogalpur, in the state of Uttar Pradesh.[8]

THE SOCIAL CHALLENGE OF INDIA
Social Reality of India

India posed a great challenge to Western Pentecostal missionaries. It was not merely the diversity of cultures and languages that puzzled them. India presented to them social realities they were not accustomed to. Though the Western world was divided along color lines, a bipartite social reality in the United States and most of Europe, India's unique caste system was strange to Western missionaries. India has a social system called *castes* that has economic and political implications. As Ghurye has presented it, the Hindu society is "ruled by a social philosophy of caste, unaffected by the modern ideas of rights and duties."[9] This philosophy of caste not only stratified people but used this stratification for exploitation and oppression.

One of the major issues in caste system is the fate of the low castes and Dalits. Dalits were generally understood as those who were so low in the social stratography that they were considered outside the caste system. The word *Dalit* literally means "oppressed, broken people." It denotes those who are "outcastes, exterior castes, or the depressed classes."

> They were placed socially, economically, culturally and politically at the very bottom of a hierarchical society. That be their permanent place; every effort was made to keep them there through enforced poverty and social degradation; and they knew it. Why were they Dalits? Not out of choice. They were Dalits because it suited the convenience of the "higher castes" to keep them at the bottom.[10]

---

[7] D.L. McCarty, "Testimonies: Mrs. D.L. McCarty," *The Pentecost* 1, no. 2 (1908) 3.

[8] (Miss) D.S. McCarty, "Another Call From India," *The Latter Rain Evangel*, Jan. 1913: 24.

[9] G.S. Ghurye, "Features of the Caste System," in *Social Stratification,* ed. Dipankar Gupta, Oxford in India Readings in Sociology and Social and Cultural Anthropology (Delhi: Oxford UP, 1991) 36.

[10] John C.B. Webster, *A History of the Dalit Christians in India* (Delhi: ISPCK, 1992), 31.

Approaching a society with a strange system of social organization with the gospel of Christ was an immense challenge. Just as their predecessors in India, Azusa missionaries had to face this challenge of a considerable segment of the population deprived of their rights, due their placement in the society.

Dalits in Indian Christianity

A great number of Dalits had already become Christians before the first Azusa missionary arrived in India. Protestant missionary work in India had a history of 200 years when the Azusa Revival broke out. As the Catholic missionaries arrived, followed by the Protestant European missionaries who presented the gospel to them, the Dalits responded to it enthusiastically. The main reason for this enthusiasm according to Webster is that for them, religious conversion "represented a rejection of a hierarchy which kept Dalits down. During the final quarter of the 19th century, increasing numbers of Dalits saw this as the way of liberation and chose to follow it."[11] He further points out:

> By the outset of World War I approximately one million Dalits had converted to Christianity and many more were to follow in the 1920s and 1930s. So great was the impact of those mass movements that they changed the course of the history of Christianity in India and pushed the Dalits movements on to the next stage.[12]

In India, when they became Christians, Dalit had their names changed. They were protected by the white missionaries and lived under the ecclesiastical hegemony of the Western missions because they were unable to develop their own distinctness.

The Azusa missionaries thus had to meet two social realities. One is that of a layered social system where those at the lower layer of social organization were oppressed and exploited. The other is another social group, that is, Christians, mainly from the low castes who embraced Christianity and enjoyed the protection of the European missionary or the church.

Models of Engagements With the Caste System

As in the case of other countries, the foreign missionary efforts in India can be considered as taking place in three waves.[13] The first wave is of the Catholic mission efforts in India. The second being the Protestant missions,

---

[11] Webster, 31.

[12] Webster, 33.

[13] See Paul A. Pomerville, *The Third Force in Mission* (Peabody, MA.: Hendrickson, 1985).

which began in the beginning of the 18th century. The third is the various Pentecostal missions, which entered the land of India as the result of the Azusa Street Revival. The Western missions who came to India, whether they were part of the Catholic mission or Protestant missions, had to respond to India's age-old caste system. The Pentecostal missions emerging from the Azusa Street were directly or indirectly influenced by it. They had the advantage of being latecomers. They could learn from the models that earlier missions, both Protestant and Catholic, had experimented with. They had the choice of following one of those models or developing one of their own.

The Catholic Mission

The early Catholic missionaries did not see caste as a religious system but a social one and chose to work within the caste system. L. Stanislaus explains that the Catholic missionaries "viewed it [the caste system] by and large in terms of the European Estates system and considered it one more case of legitimate stratification."[14] The Catholics allowed caste distinctions to continue and the ministers were assigned according to the castes. This is exemplified in the Madurai mission of Robert de Nobili:

> The Madurai Mission of Robert de Nobili not only allowed distinctions between high and low castes to continue in the Church but even divided the Mission itself between Brahman *sanyassis* who ministered to the high castes and *pandaraswamis* who ministered to the low.[15]

Protestant Missions

Protestant missionary activity in India begins with the Tranquebar mission by the arrival of Bartholomeus Ziegenbalg in 1706. However, it was the arrival of William Carey in 1793 that marked the great influx of missionaries to India. In Protestant missionary activity that ensued, missionaries representing diverse denominations and countries baptized people from various castes.

Protestant missionaries were not targeting any specific caste, with the exception of the work of Alexander Duff, the Scottish missionary educator. He was successful in converting high-caste Bengali elite through his education mission. However, the rest of the missionary force were not competent to do such specialized work and evangelized anyone who came on their way. Webster observes that the congregations formed as the result of such missionary

---

[14] L. Stanislaus, *Liberative Mission of the Church Among Dalit Christians* (Delhi: ISPCK, 1999) 146-47.

[15] Webster, 35.

endeavors were "comprised of individuals often from widely diverse social backgrounds."[16]

One important aspect of Protestant missions and the major difference with the Catholic mission is that the majority of Protestant missionaries considered caste as a religious institution and condemned it among many other aspects of Hinduism that they considered as evil.[17] So, the converts of Protestant mission efforts left their respective castes and joined a new mixed group.

Seeing the caste system as a religious system that had to be done away with along with many other "pagan ways," the early Protestant missionaries actively opposed it. Protestant missionaries tried to overcome the barriers of caste by mixing people of various castes and including Dalits in their schools with students of high caste. They also involved actively in protesting against caste-related practices; they opposed restrictions in the use of public roads, public wells, and in the south against prohibition of wearing "breast cloth."

The Protestant missions also spent lots of energy in evolving strategies for approaching the reality of caste. The mass movements among the Dalits made the Third Decennial Missionary Conference, held in Bombay in 1892, to devote considerable discussion to this issue. They considered questions like, should mission efforts be focused on improving the social condition of the Dalits, should they limit their work to Dalits who have become Christians or all the Dalits, and so on.[18]

THE FORMATION OF THE AZUSA MISSIONARIES

Ministering in a society that is structured along caste lines, with a considerable number of them already baptized into Christianity, was the social reality the Azusa missionaries faced. However, their encounter with this reality was very much conditioned by their missionary formation, which in fact was part of their spiritual formation. There are at least three aspects of this spiritual formation of the Azusa missionaries significant in this context.

Emphasis on Evangelism

Azusa Street Mission had a great impact on evangelism. Though Pentecostalism is a renewal movement challenging the church to return to the apostolic faith, evangelism of the lost was the foremost goal. The often-quoted words of

---

[16] Webster, 35.

[17] Stanislaus, *Liberative Mission,* 148.

[18] Webster, *History of the Dalit Christians in India,* 38. See also *Report of the Third Decennial Missionary Conference Held at Bombay* (Bombay: 1893).

William J. Seymour, "Now, do not go from this place and talk about tongues; but try to get people saved,"[19] illustrates the emphasis on evangelism that Azusa Mission maintained throughout its existence. The emphasis on evangelism was the hallmark of Azusa missionaries.

For obvious reasons in the early days of their ministry, some of the Azusa missionaries in India had to focus on the distinctive Pentecostal doctrines that evolved between Topeka Revival (1901) and Azusa Street. It may even appear as if the early Azusa missionaries ignored Seymour's admonition and continued to "talk about tongues" in India. A.G. Garr's work in Calcutta, and then in Bombay, was to convince the non-Pentecostal missionaries and believers about the Pentecostal experience of baptism in the Holy Spirit and speaking in tongues. However, Garr's stay in India was only for a short period—less than a year.

At least in the beginning of his ministry in India, George Berg was focusing on the existing Christian workers and did a work of renewal. His ministry in Bombay was characterized by "the sick are being healed, demons are cast out, sinners are saved, believers sanctified and baptized with the Holy Ghost and fire."[20] Probably, Berg had to focus on those who were already Christians because he felt the need for renewal, as he observed: "I have travelled much since coming to India to find many a hungry soul among the dear missionaries as well as among other classes."[21] In Bombay particularly, he focused not only on the Western missionaries, but also used the door that was opened for him among "the native Christian preachers and workers in that city."[22]

However, Berg's work among those who were already Christians was only for a few months after his arrival in India. He soon moved away from the work of revival among the believers to evangelism among the unreached, which remained his focus for the rest of his life. He would look back two years after his arrival in Bombay in 1908 and remark that his mission was to "carry the blessed Pentecostal truths to the missionary and the benighted heathens."[23] Robert F. Cook from day one was fully involved in evangelism among the economically poor and social outcasts.[24]

---

[19] Quoted in Thomas F. Zimmerman, "The Reason for the Rise of the Pentecostal Movement," in *Azusa Street and Beyond: Pentecostal Missions and Church Growth in the Twentieth Century,* ed. L. Grant McClung Jr. (South Plainfield, NJ: Bridge, 1986) 60.

[20] George E. Berg, "Salvation for India," *The Pentecost,* Dec. 1908: 2.

[21] Berg, 2.

[22] Berg, 2

[23] Berg, "Echoes from the Jungles of India," *The Latter Rain Evangel,* Apr. 1910: 15.

[24] See Cook, *Half a Century.*

Azusa Mission and Racial Equality

Another significant emphasis of the Azusa Street Revival was that racial equality also had formative influence on the Azusa Street missionaries. Seymour's insistence that the evidence of baptism in the Holy Spirit is racial equality was unprecedented in history and so radical. The white and the colored being filled with the Holy Spirit and worshiping together in the Jim Crow days was unimaginable. This made one of the eyewitnesses of these meetings, Frank Bartleman, say, "The 'color line' was washed away in the blood" of Jesus.[25]

The missionaries who went out from the United States carried this message of racial equality, though at least some of them found it difficult to translate it into ground reality in their mission field. Though J.G. Lake in South Africa found it practically difficult, his correspondence to *The Pentecost* indicates that American missionaries in South Africa were still holding on to this emphasis of Azusa Street. In 1909, he wrote from Johannesburg, "One of the curses of American missionaries is that they teach race equality. Now the African native is a very different man from the American Negro."[26]

The emphasis that the blood of Jesus has washed the color line away was part of the missionary formation of the Azusa Street missionaries, which equipped them for dealing with another social reality called *caste*, the system in India. The Pentecostal churches that emerged in India as a result of the work of Azusa Street missionaries were churches where believers of all castes were integrated.

However, a blemish on the history of the Pentecostals in India is the division of the Church of God (Cleveland) along caste lines. But, it was only in 1972 that the Church of God (Cleveland) was divided along caste lines in the state of Kerala. This has to be considered as an exception, and the Church of God in other states of India and no other Pentecostal missionary church followed suit.

The Mukti Complement: "Baptism of Love"

Another important aspect of the formation of the Azusa missionaries, which has implication for their work among the Dalits in India, is the influence of Mukti Mission in Pune (also spelled as "Poona" in earlier documents). Holy Spirit revivals were happening all over the world prior to the Azusa Street

---

[25] Frank Bartleman, *Azusa Street* (South Plainfield, N.J.: Bridge, 1980 [1925]) 54.

[26] John G. Lake, "Important Instructions for Missionaries to South Africa," *The Pentecost,* June 1909.

Revival, and India also witnessed many such revivals. The revival that took place at Mukti Mission, run by Pandita Ramabai in Pune a few months before the Azusa Street Revival, made a great impact on Pentecostal missionaries. The revival in Mukti was widely publicized in the Western Christian media.

The publicity given to Mukti Revival resulted in many in the West and expatriate missionaries working in India to visit Mukti. In another sense, Mukti acted as a Pentecostal magnet. The visitors from Azusa Street to Mukti Mission includes A.G. Garr, George E. Berg, Thomas Ball Barratt, and others. Many Pentecostal preachers and missionaries to India also visited Mukti and even ministered there. A number of Western missionaries working in India, who belonged to various denominations, also received their Pentecostal experience in Mukti, and some even changed their affiliation (some were forced) to Pentecostal missionary organizations.

The Pentecostal revival and the visits and consequent reports from visitors to the Western media resulted in the Mukti Mission being considered as a Pentecostal mission. Various Pentecostal publications began to raise funds for Mukti. At certain points, their support to Mukti had overtaken their support to individual Pentecostal missionaries to India. The work of the Mukti Mission was reported regularly in the Pentecostal papers, considering Pandita Ramabai, her daughter, Manorama, and others in Mukti Mission as Pentecostals.

Ramabai's emphasis on the "Baptism of Love" that should follow baptism in the Holy Spirit was a significant contribution to the formation of Azusa missionaries. This had a significant impact on the praxis of mission in early Pentecostalism where compassion became an integral part of Pentecostal mission. The British Pentecostal newspaper, *Confidence*, reported that Barrat's visit found it significant to quote Ramabai's position on the baptism in the Holy Spirit. After the baptism in the Holy Spirit, she insisted that all need a baptism of love.

> Pandita Ramabai and Dr. Yoakum, alike emphasise *LOVE* as being the great result of "Pentecost." It would be surely better to have a real Baptism of Love than anything else, but we have not found in our personal experience that the Seal of "Tongues," when from God, lessened the LOVE. No more loving people have we met than the great proportion of those who have received this Seal.[27]

This love, in the context of Mukti Mission, manifested in service of compassion to the poor and the underprivileged. Mukti Mission was the place where

---

[27] Editor, "After 'Pentecost': Love," *Confidence,* Apr. 1908: 16.

Christ's love for the lost and the downtrodden was displayed and a place where mission as compassion was manifest. At the time of revival there were more than 1,500 inmates at Mukti Mission, most of them young widows.

The visitors to Mukti Mission and those who read about the work of Mukti Mission realized the need for this double baptism, one that empowers for witness, the other that empowers for service to the poor. This concept of double baptism shaped the mission methodology and the praxis of the Azusa missionaries. George Berg wrote in a letter published in *The Pentecost* in 1908 (probably after his visit to Mukti), "I wanted to be flooded more with pure, unselfish love. This will never fail to win souls and draw them to Jesus Christ."[28] In the very beginning of his missionary work in India, Berg was convinced that "unselfish love" is sure to win souls, and he kept to this path very closely as we will see below.

The work of D.L. McCarty is another example of how the love for the downtrodden became the hallmark of Pentecostal missions to India. Her attitude to the people whom she served was very different from that of some non-Pentecostal missionaries. In one of her dispatches, she narrates an event that illustrates her attitude to the people whom she served:

> One dear missionary who has been in India nearly quarter of a century came to visit me and when my poor, dirty, ragged neighbors came in to see my friend (the second white face most of them had ever seen) she said. "You must not let these people come into your home. Don't let them come farther than the veranda." I felt bad to think she did not approve, but I had gone too far and could not change. How many poor souls have sat on the floor with their heads in my lap, and wept and telling me their trouble. They did not beg. They wanted love and sympathy, and many a mother has put her oiled, naked baby in my arms, even in the street when I was passing, not thinking of my clean, white dress, and I have knelt and prayed for them in the street.[29]

This is not intended to suggest that compassion was the monopoly of the Azusa missionary; pre-Azusa missionaries were busily involved in compassion ministries. However, the purpose of quoting this anecdote is to show the "baptism of love" had influenced their outlook and explain the ministries of compassion that they founded.

---

[28] Berg, "Salvation for India," 3.

[29] D.L. McCarty, "India," *The Christian Evangel,* Aug. 29, 1914: 4.

MISSION METHODOLOGIES OF THE AZUSA MISSIONARIES

In this section I would like to focus on the unique methodological contributions the Azusa missionaries made in the context of caste system. There are at least two distinct approaches that we can discern in their work in relation to the reality of caste and ensuing socioeconomic deprivation.

Top-Down Approach

The first is what could be termed as the "Top-Down" approach. *Caste* is a social system of stratification and hierarchy. This vertical organization is evident in terms used such as "high caste" and "low caste." Not only were those different castes unequal in their social status, but those at the lower rung of the caste system were also controlled by those on the higher rung. This vertical arrangement was used to justify the social and economic inequalities and injustice. We have already seen that with the exception of few missionaries, like Alexander Duff, Protestant missionary energy before the arrival of Azusa missionaries was poured into evangelism and education of Dalits.

In evangelizing a caste-ridden society, it was important to ask where to start. The options were limited too: either at the bottom of the caste hierarchy or at the top. Some Azusa missionaries, like D.L. McCarty, had conscientiously used the "Top-Down" approach when she focused on reaching out to the high-caste Hindus.

One main methodological problem in identifying the converts of McCarty is her practice of changing their original Hindu names to Christian (mostly Biblical names). However, there are indications that the people she focused on were high-caste Hindus. In McCarty's postings to *The Christian Evangel*, many of the inmates of her home had Christian names, but there are indications that they came from the top of the caste structure. They were still wearing the tuft when they came to her. Keeping a tuft is a custom of the male members of the Brahmin caste and a mark of spirituality for other caste Hindus.

> I was so amused at the boys when Joseph came. Paulus said to him the second day, "If you are going to live with mamma, cut off your pig tail (they let a bunch of hair grow on the crown to give the gods a hold to pull the spirit out of the body), so he got the scissors and Paulus cut it off.[30]

While it was rather easy to evangelize the lower castes, who saw conversion

---

[30] D.L. McCarty, "Promising Work Among the Lowly of India," *The Christian Evangel*, Mar. 28, 1914: 3.

as a way out of the caste system and for social and economic betterment, evangelism among high castes was difficult. In the first place, there were no social or economic motivations for conversion. Secondly, conversion meant losing the high social standing that was theirs by birth. This made McCarty observe: "On account of the caste system it is very hard for them to step out and confess Christ."[31]

Her approach was not an accident but a conscious strategic one. She was convinced that reaching out to the high-caste Hindus was the best way to evangelize people of all castes: work from the top to the bottom. Conversion of people of lower castes had invited unspeakable persecution and opposition to the mission work.

Having learned from her predecessors (the Protestant missionaries of the pre-Azusa period), she adopted a strategy of converting the potential persecutor so that the persecution and opposition could be avoided. She said:

> Scripture is being fulfilled in our midst. Some want to be baptized on our big day (they mean Easter), and I am willing after they are taught that long. All are of high caste that are being instructed. It is easy to get the little fish after you have caught the larger ones as it is the high caste that do the persecuting of the low caste.[32]

How many of the Azusa missionaries adopted her method is a matter of further investigation. However, McCarty was indisputably an innovator in this area!

Evangelism, Then Education

Protestant missionaries of the pre-Azusa period used education as a means for evangelism. Education was certainly part of the church's mission, as was health care, and so on. However, education as a means to evangelism, and thus to conversion, was a very common approach. This explains the numerous schools and colleges that sprang up in the colonial era of missions in India. "Schools are the means for the expansion of the Kingdom," as one Christian journal put it.[33]

Another Azusa missionary, George E. Berg, reversed this popular model. He emphasized both evangelism and education. However, he did not use education as a means of evangelism; at the same time, he did not ignore the need to educate the people. His approach was evangelism, followed by education.

---

[31] McCarty, "Another Call From India," 24.

[32] McCarty, "Promising Work," 3.

[33] Arun Shourie, *Missionaries in India: Continuities, Changes, Dilemmas* (New Delhi: ASA, 1995) 82, quoting *Gharbandhu,* Jan. 1952.

Within a year of writing to *The Pentecost* about what he was doing among those who were already Christians, Berg surprised us with another letter where he expressed his desire to reach out to jungle tribes in the most formidable part of India, which he described as the "Fever District." These are the areas in the present state of Tamil Nadu where typhoid fever claimed hundreds of lives every year. He also noted this was an area that was ignored by other missionaries, being a place where "wild elephants and many other wild beasts, also plenty of serpents [were present] among them."[34]

In a letter dated February 17, 1910, Berg was able to tell his Pentecostal readers that he had started his work among the tribes of Nilgiri Hills and had won about 20 souls by then. His work was not limited to evangelism, but also primary education for the tribal children and adult literacy program. He was planning for school buildings and then "gospel" halls in the tribal settlements. These gospel halls would be used for gospel meetings at night and as reading rooms during the day for education, primarily literacy programs. The priority given to evangelism was evident where he wrote about his proposed school. The school would be a place where the "old people will first get converted and then filled with the Spirit and then learn to read and write."[35]

One important dimension of the work of Berg here is that he did not stop with people being converted and filled with the Holy Spirit, but educated them further. While the pre-Azusa Street missionaries took education as a preparation for evangelism, George Berg considered education as a contribution for a better life that the missionary makes to the lives surrendered to Jesus. The underprivileged tribals of the Nilgiri Hills and the outcasts in areas where he worked, received not just salvation or just education, but they were saved, empowered and equipped for a better life.

Conclusion

We have to compile the biographies of each of the missionaries to India from Azusa Street to complete a study of their contribution to India and the models that were evolved through their service in India. However, from what we know now, it is clear that the work of the Azusa Street missionaries in India is a typical example of how lives surrendered to God's will and empowered by the Holy Spirit can break barriers of color, class and caste. We also realize that the Spirit of God not only empowers people to witness in faraway countries, but also makes them innovators as well.

---

[34] George E. Berg, "In the Fever District," *The Pentecost* 1, no. 9 (1909): 5.

9

Revivals and the Global Expansion of Pentecostalism After Azusa Street

Allan Anderson

Revivals in the Early 20th Century

The Azusa Street Revival was not an isolated or unique occurrence, neither was it the only revival significant in the early expansion of Pentecostalism. The first decade of the 20th century produced revivals in various parts of the world—including the Wonsan Revival in Korea in 1903, the Welsh Revival from 1904, the various Indian revivals from 1905, the Madagascar Revival of 1905, the "Korean Pentecost" from 1907, the Chilean Revival from 1909, and the Manchurian Revival in 1910.

These revivals were characterized by various common features, including ecstatic emotionalism and the manifestation of spiritual gifts. All were regarded as being evidence of the coming of the Holy Spirit in power in the "last days." To a greater or lesser degree, all these revivals contributed to the rapid dissemination of Pentecostal ideas and practices throughout the Evangelical Protestant world, fires fueled as they were by the premillennialist expectations of the time. Reports from the Azusa Street newspaper, *Apostolic Faith*, reveal the essence of the radical Evangelical missionary vision at the beginning of the 20th century. The time was short, but the power of the Spirit in a latter-day worldwide revival was now given to enable the gospel to be preached to all nations before the Lord's return.[1] Pentecostals thus continued the end-time revivalist emphases of the forms of Evangelicalism from which they had emerged, convinced that a worldwide revival was preceding the imminent coming of Christ. Some of the revivals in different parts of the world had a decidedly "Pentecostal" character, with gifts of the Spirit like healings, tongues, prophecy and other "miraculous" signs.[2] Frank Bartleman, a participant in Azusa Street, wrote, "The present worldwide revival was rocked in the cradle of little Wales. It was brought up in India, following; becoming full-grown in Los Angeles later."[3] While Bartleman's impressions of the "progression" of these revivals may be open to question, it was these three that had particular significance for Pentecostalism.

The Welsh Revival (1904-05) emphasized the Pentecostal presence and power of the Spirit, where meetings were long, spontaneous, seemingly chaotic and emotional, with "singing in the Spirit" (using ancient Welsh chants), simultaneous and loud prayer, revelatory visions and prophecy—all these phenomena emphasizing the immediacy of God in the services and in personal experience.

Indirectly, the revival in the Welsh chapels also facilitated a resurgence of the Welsh language and the indigenization of Christianity in that country. Revival leader Evan Roberts (1878-1951) taught a personal experience of Spirit baptism to precede any revival. Although Pentecostalism's emphases were found in the radical and less common manifestations of this revival, early Pentecostal leaders (especially in Britain) drew inspiration from it and saw their movement as growing out of and continuing it.[4] Importantly, Joseph Smale, a Los Angeles Baptist pastor visited the revival and instituted a similar one in his church in 1905, resulting in a wider acceptance of Pentecostal ideas there before the Azusa Street Revival broke out. Some of Smale's members were later involved in Azusa Street. In the Keswick Convention of 1905, the emotionalism of 300 Welsh delegates influenced an unofficial all-night prayer meeting that went, according to an observer, "out of control." A.T. Pierson described the meeting

---

[1] *AF* 1 [Los Angeles], Sept. 1906, 1.

[2] Gary B. McGee, "'Latter Rain' Falling in the East: Early Twentieth-Century Pentecostalism in India and the Debate Over Speaking in Tongues," *Church History* 68, no. 3 (1999): 650.

[3] Frank Bartleman, *Azusa Street* (S. Plainfield, N.J.: Bridge, 1980 [1925]) 19.

[4] Eifon Evans, *The Welsh Revival of 1904* (Bridgend, U.K.: Evangelical Press of Wales, 1969) 190-96. D.D. Bundy, "Welsh Revival," in *The New International Dictionary of Pentecostal and Charismatic Movements*, ed. Stanley M. Burgess, with Eduard M. van der Maas (Grand Rapids: Zondervan, 2002) 1187-88. Dana Robert, *Occupy Until I Come: A.T. Pierson and the Evangelization of the World* (Grand Rapids, MI/Cambridge, U.K.: Eerdmans, 2003) 260.

and the manifestations of speaking in tongues there as "disturbing anarchy" and "a Satanic disturbance."[5]

Indian Christians had heard of the Welsh Revival, but Pentecostal-like movements had been in South India since the revival under the CMS preacher John Christian Aroolappen in 1860. The Welsh Revival spread to other parts of the world through Welsh missionaries, and in 1905 revivals broke out in the Khasi Hills in northeast India where Welsh Presbyterian missionaries were working.[6]

The separate revival at Pandita Ramabai's Mukti Mission for young widows and orphans in Kedgaon, near Pune, commenced in 1905 and lasted two years. This was characterized by tears of repentance and confession; emotional and prolonged prayer meetings; powerful demonstrations of the Spirit including healings, speaking in tongues, prophecy and interpretation; and above all, the evangelistic teams of hundreds of young women empowered by the Spirit to witness in the surrounding villages. Once again, when A.T. Pierson wrote against the manifestations of this revival (especially the tongues) as being the ravings of "a few hysterical women," Ramabai was quick to the defense. She wrote that she was "convinced more and more" that those given the gift of tongues had been "greatly helped to lead better lives" and were more effective in prayer and evangelism as a result of their experience.[7] The revival certainly made the Mukti Mission a very important Pentecostal center of international significance,[8] it preceded the Azusa Street Revival in chronology, and was a precedent for a widespread alternative form of Pentecostalism.[9]

The Mukti revival had at least four far-reaching consequences. First, it is clear that Bartleman, Azusa Street leader William Seymour, and the writers of *The Apostolic Faith* saw the Indian revival as a precedent to theirs. The "Pentecost" had come to India. The Pentecostal press soon began reporting on the revival and clearly situated it within the emerging Pentecostal Movement. The *Apostolic Faith* had major articles in it, including one by Albert Norton, a Methodist missionary working near the Mukti Mission, two from Max Wood Moorhead's *Cloud of Witnesses,* published in Colombo, Sir Lanka, and extracts

---

[5] Robert, *Occupy Until I Come,* 261-62.

[6] T. Nongsiej, "Revival Movement in Khasi-Jaintia Hills," in *Churches of Indigenous Origins in Northeast India,* ed. O.L. Snaitang (Delhi: ISPCK, 2000) 32-34.

[7] *Mukti Prayer-Bell,* Sept. 1907: 3-8.

[8] Allan Anderson, "'The Present Worldwide Revival . . . Brought Up in India': Pandita Ramabai and the Origins of Pentecostalism," paper given at the SPS Annual Meeting, Regent University, Virginia Beach, U.S.A., Mar. 2005: 10-12.

[9] McGee, "Latter Rain," 651, 656-57, 664.

from Ramabai's own periodical, the *Mukti Prayer-Bell*. All these attest to the importance placed on this revival by the Azusa Street Mission. The revival and the work of the Mukti Mission was reported on in *Confidence*, the British Pentecostal periodical, and American Pentecostal periodicals *The Pentecost* and the *Latter Rain Evangel*, in the latter case from 1909 to 1913.

The first report of the revival in India titled "Pentecost in India" was carried in the third issue of *The Apostolic Faith* in Los Angeles. This was a reprint from *India Alliance*, a paper of the Christian and Missionary Alliance in India:

> News comes from India that the baptism with the Holy Ghost and gift of tongues is being received there by natives who are simply taught of God. The India Alliance says, 'Some of the gifts which have been scarcely heard of in the church for many centuries, are now being given by the Holy Ghost to simple, unlearned members of the body of Christ, and communities are being stirred and transformed by the wonderful grace of God. Healing, the gift of tongues, visions, and dreams, discernment of spirits, the power to prophecy and to pray the prayer of faith, all have a place in the present revival.' Hallelujah! God is sending the Pentecost to India. He is no respecter of persons.[10]

The importance of this report is that it referred to speaking in tongues occurring in the Bombay (Mumbai) area before news of Azusa Street had reached India.[11] The first missionaries to India (Calcutta) from Azusa Street, Albert and Lillian Garr, reached there late in December 1906.[12]

Second, women played a more prominent role in the Indian revival than in the American one. Ramabai was an already famous social reformer and Evangelical Christian, an Indian woman who resisted both patriarchal oppression in India and Western domination in Christianity. The Mukti revival was preeminently a revival among young women led by women, motivating and empowering those who had been marginalized and cast out by society.[13] This was an example of Pentecostalism's early social activism, empowering the oppressed for service and bestowing dignity on women leaders. In this the Mukti revival and Ramabai herself were pioneers within global Christianity and without precedent.

---

[10] *AF* [Los Angeles] 1.3, Nov. 1906: 1.

[11] McGee, "Latter Rain," 654-56.

[12] Gary B. McGee, "The Calcutta Revival of 1907 and the Reformulation of Charles F. Parham's 'Bible Evidence' Doctrine," *Asia Journal of Pentecostal Studies* 6, no. 1 (2003): 123, 126.

[13] *Pentecostal Evangel* 543, Apr. 19, 1924: 9.

Third, both Ramabai in her ministry and the revival she led demonstrate an openness to other Christians, an ecumenicity and an inclusiveness that stands in stark contrast to the rigid exclusivism of many subsequent Pentecostal movements.

The fourth important consequence was its impact on Latin American Pentecostalism. Ramabai's right-hand worker, Minnie Abrams, contacted her friend and former Bible school classmate in Valparaiso, Chile, Mrs. Willis Hoover, with a report of the revival in Mukti. This was contained in a booklet she wrote in 1906 titled *The Baptism of the Holy Ghost and Fire,* which in its second edition included a discussion of the restoration of speaking in tongues, the first written Pentecostal theology of Spirit baptism. As a result of Abrams' booklet, the Methodist churches in Valparaiso and Santiago were stirred to expect and pray for a similar revival, which began in 1909 and led to Willis Hoover becoming leader of the new Chilean Methodist Pentecostal Church.

Today, the vast majority of Pentecostal churches in Chile, statistically one of the most Pentecostal countries in the world, are descendants of this revival. The point is that Chilean Pentecostalism has its roots in the Mukti revival rather than in Azusa Street. This was specifically a Methodist revival that did not promote a doctrine of "initial evidence." An alternative to the "initial evidence" form of Pentecostalism centered in the United States was developing globally, and Mukti was its earliest expression.

There were other revivals like the "Korean Pentecost" of 1907-08,[14] with features that still characterize Protestant (and Pentecostal) churches in Korea today: daily and all-night prayer meetings, simultaneous prayer, Bible study, and an emphasis on evangelism and missions. But beyond this are more characteristically Pentecostal practices like healing the sick, miracles and casting out demons.[15]

These revivals continued for several decades and were sometimes quite unconnected with Western Pentecostalism. Healing revivals that began in the Ivory Coast and Ghana in 1914-1915 under the ministry of the Liberian William Wade Harris and in Nigeria under Garrick Braide and Joseph Shadare (among others) between 1915-1922 resulted in hundreds of thousands of conversions to Christianity and independent Pentecostal churches all over West Africa. Azusa Street missionaries were already active in Liberia in 1907, and we can assume that Harris must at least have heard about them and their characteristic practices.

---

[14] William N. Blair and Bruce Hunt, *The Korean Pentecost and the Sufferings Which Followed* (Edinburgh: Banner of Truth Trust, 1977) 71, 75.

[15] Young Hoon Lee, "The Holy Spirit Movement in Korea: Its Historical and Doctrinal Development" (Ph.D. thesis, Temple University, 1996) 80-90.

The revival in Yorubaland under Joseph Babalola in 1930 resulted in the formation of the Christ Apostolic Church, one of the largest Pentecostal churches in the region. In China, Pentecostal missionaries began propagating their ideas from 1907 onward. The Shandong revival in China from 1930 to 1932 was a specifically Pentecostal outpouring among Baptists and Presbyterians, resulting in the eventual emergence of independent Pentecostal churches.[16] The revival in post-Sukarno, Indonesia, in the 1960s resulted in hundreds of thousands of new additions to Pentecostal churches. These examples could be multiplied in several other countries.

Pentecostal Missionaries and "Missionary Tongues"

From its beginning, Pentecostalism placed emphasis on evangelism and missions as a result of the experience of Spirit baptism. People came to the United States from far away and went back with the baptism, including the founder of Pentecostalism in Europe, T.B. Barratt of Oslo, Norway, and especially various Evangelical missionaries from different parts of the world. From Azusa Street and other centers (including those in other continents), "Apostolic Faith" missionaries were sent out to places as far away and diverse as China, India, Japan, Egypt, Liberia, Angola and South Africa within two years.[17]

This was no mean achievement, and was the beginning of what is arguably the most significant global expansion of a Christian movement in the history of Christianity. These missionaries were convinced that they had been given "missionary tongues" through the baptism in the Spirit, and that when they reached their destinations they would be able to speak miraculously languages of national people without having to undergo the arduous task of language learning. Apart from isolated instances when it was claimed this had happened, most admitted that they were unable to speak in the languages of the nations, and some returned to the United States disillusioned.

The early 20th-century migrants who carried the Pentecostal message all over the world were most often poor, untrained and unprepared for what awaited them; but they sometimes left comfortable homes for lives of relative deprivation to spread their newfound faith. Many did not return. Some missionaries went out "by faith" without any income. The disasters that befell the Batman family in Liberia and the team that went with M.L. Ryan to Japan

---

[16] Allan Anderson, *An Introduction to Pentecostalism: Global Charismatic Christianity* (Cambridge: Cambridge UP, 2004) 115-21, 133, 136-37.

[17] D. William Faupel, *The Everlasting Gospel: The Significance of Eschatology in the Development of Pentecostal Thought* (Sheffield Academic Press, 1996) 182-86, 208-9, 212-16.

without financial support are now legendary. John G. Lake wrote an exasperated letter home in 1909 about sending missionaries to South Africa without funds, as one of them had arrived in Cape Town without the necessary minimum of $100 and a guarantee of support. To get him through to Johannesburg had cost them "a great deal of trouble and expense," Lake complained.[18]

Vinson Synan speaks of these early Pentecostal missionaries as "missionaries on a one-way ticket."[19] They went out to live "on the faith line," to bring "light" into "darkness," and in some cases they had no fixed plans for their arrival—for they were led to their destinations by the Spirit, and the Spirit would show them what to do when they got there. As one of these missionaries, May Law, put it, speaking of her team in Hong Kong: "Three young women, and one of mature years, left their homes of wealth, and comfort . . . and their beautiful native State of Washington, for dark S. China."[20] Two of these three young women died there soon afterward from tropical diseases—and this was the fate of many of these unprepared missionaries who would refuse to take medicines.

Many of the first missionaries were independent, without organizational backing, and related only in a loose way to fledgling Pentecostal congregations in their home country. As Antoinette Moomau in Shanghai put it, "Jesus is doing much more for us than any board could do, and we are happy to know that we are free creatures in Him."[21] However, these Pentecostal migrants did remain in regular contact with their home countries and sending organizations (as much as they *were* organizations), with letters going back and forth between missionaries and home churches, the latter producing periodicals often issued free of charge to these missionaries, keeping them abreast with the developing movement both at home and around the world. Often the only link with any form of organization was through these periodicals, which served the threefold function as home bases for the missionaries, the means of disseminating information about them, and for raising funds to support them.

The periodicals were also important vehicles for internationalizing and creating norms for Pentecostal beliefs and values. They were perceived by the missionaries as being the primary sources of both their own identity and that of their converts. Later, Bible schools were established to further normalize Pentecostal identity. More recently, the printed periodical that was all-important at the beginning of the 20th century has been replaced by a host of other media,

---

[18] *Pentecost* 1, no. 7 (June 1909): 3.

[19] Vinson Synan, *The Holiness-Pentecostal Tradition: Charismatic Movements in the Twentieth Century* (Grand Rapids: Eerdmans, 1997) 129.

[20] E. May Law, *Pentecostal Mission Work in South China: An Appeal for Missions* (Falcon, NC: Falcon, 1915) 2.

[21] *Pentecost* 1, no. 7 (July 1909): 5.

like videotapes, television programs, books and music recordings that have further accelerated the promotion of a transnational Pentecostal meta-culture.

There were at least three factors creating impetus for the international movement of hundreds of early independent Pentecostal missionaries. First was their premillennialist eschatology that posited the urgency of the task of world evangelism at the end of time before the imminent return of Christ. Second, they had a firm belief in their experience of Spirit baptism by which they had been given "foreign languages" to preach their gospel to the nations of the world. Pentecostalism, common with other Christian revivalist movements at the time, held that their ecstatic manifestations were evidence of the end-time outpouring of the Spirit given to evangelize the world within the shortest possible time. The Pentecostals would seek to identify which particular language they had been given (usually through some member of the assembly who would be familiar with a foreign language) and then they would make arrangements to go to that country as soon as possible. And third, these missionaries often met up with other, more experienced missionaries once on the field, especially when they discovered that God had *not* given them the ability to speak the languages of the peoples to whom they had gone. The missionary networks were very significant in the spread of Pentecostal ideas throughout the world and in particular (but certainly not exclusively), that of the Christian and Missionary Alliance, especially in Asia.

Following the earlier ideas of Charles Parham, almost all the first Pentecostals universally believed that when they spoke in tongues, they had spoken in known languages *(xenolalia)* by which they would preach the gospel to the ends of the earth in the last days. There would be no time for the indeterminable delays of language learning. Early Pentecostal publications were filled with these missionary expectations, often referring to the gift of tongues as the "gift of languages." In the first issue of Azusa Street's *Apostolic Faith* (September 1906), the expectations of early American Pentecostals were clear. They fully expected through Spirit baptism to be able to speak "all the languages of the world" in order to preach the gospel "into all the world":

> The gift of languages is given with the commission, "Go ye into all the world and preach the gospel to every creature." The Lord has given languages to the unlearned Greek, Latin, Hebrew, French, German, Italian, Chinese, Japanese, Zulu and languages of Africa, Hindu and Bengali and dialects of India, Chippewa and other languages of the Indians, Esquimaux, the deaf mute language and, in fact the Holy Ghost speaks all the languages of the world through His children.[22]

---

[22] *AF* [Los Angeles] 1, Sept. 1906: 1.

Like Wesley, the whole world was indeed their parish. When "the Holy Ghost fell on a preacher" at Azusa Street, reported this paper, he was able to speak "Zulu and many tongues more fluently than English." In keeping with common practice of Pentecostals at that time, this unnamed preacher probably turned up in South Africa to work among the Zulu. On another occasion, a missionary from Central Africa recognized some of the languages spoken at Azusa Street as being African "dialects," confirming his need to return there with these new linguists.[23]

The growth of Pentecostalism was greatly facilitated by the network of Evangelical and Holiness missionaries already on the field who played a major role in the dissemination of Pentecostal ideas, as well as those who went out as a direct consequence of Pentecostal revivals. The Azusa Street Revival was probably the most well-known of the earliest centers of Pentecostalism in North America and was also the source of the first wave of Pentecostal missionaries. This revival turned what was until then a fairly localized and insignificant new Christian sect into an international movement.

Early Pentecostals were convinced they would overcome all obstacles through the power of the Spirit and thereby defeat Satan and conquer his territory, the "world." This was the transnational, universal orientation that was an essential part of Pentecostalism from its beginnings. The first paragraph of the first issue of the Azusa Street newspaper, *Apostolic Faith,* virtually bristled with the excitement of the event. A countless number had been "converted, sanctified, and filled with the Holy Ghost," it declared. But even more significant is what it perceived as the result, where these same people were "daily going out to all points of the compass to spread this wonderful gospel."[24]

Clearly, this new "Apostolic Faith" was a missionary movement and the "going out" from Azusa Street was immediate in ever-widening circles. Hundreds of visitors came to see what was happening and to be baptized in the Spirit. Many of these began Pentecostal centers in various North American cities and eventually in other continents.[25]

Some scholars have referred to the "myth" of Azusa Street that has overlooked the importance of other centers and have suggested that its role was not as central as has been generally accepted.[26] There *were* other important early North

---

[23] *AF*, 2-3.

[24] *AF*, 1.

[25] Faupel, *Everlasting Gospel,* 202-5, 208.

[26] Joe Creech, "Visions of Glory: The Place of the Azusa Street Revival in Pentecostal History," *Church History* 65 (1996): 405-24.

American centers of Pentecostalism independent of Azusa Street, but what cannot be denied is that for three years, Seymour's Apostolic Faith Mission was the most prominent center of Pentecostalism on the continent. That this was a predominantly African-American church rooted in the African slave culture of the 19th century is significant, particularly for the spread of Pentecostalism into other parts of the world where so-called primal religions were dominant.[27] Its emphasis on healing facilitated the spread of its message to people expecting power demonstrations to accompany religious leaders. Pentecostal missionaries were sent out all over the world, reaching nations as far away as China, India, Japan, Egypt, Liberia, Angola and South Africa. This was no small achievement.

Centers of Pentecostalism in Latin America and Europe

As a result of the efforts of Azusa Street missionaries and their converts, new revival centers spread Pentecostalism from places like Hong Kong, Oslo, Sunderland, Johannesburg, Lagos, Valparaiso, and Belém (Brazil),[28] where there are now more Pentecostals than in any other country. With roots in the ministry of William Durham in Chicago, his associate Luigi Francescon (1866-1964) established Italian congregations in the United States and Argentina in 1909. He formed the first Pentecostal church in Brazil in São Paulo in 1910, the Christian Congregation.

The Assembly of God in Brazil began with two Swedish immigrants, Gunnar Vingren and Daniel Berg, also associated with Durham, who went to the northern Brazilian state of Pará in 1910. They founded the Apostolic Faith Mission, registered in 1918 as the Assembly of God. By 2000 it was the largest non-Catholic church in Latin America. A second phase of 20 to 30 new Brazilian Pentecostal denominations were started after 1952, the most important being Brazil for Christ, God Is Love, and Foursquare Gospel Church. After about 1975, a third type of Pentecostal Movement began, the largest being the Universal Church of the Kingdom of God, a prosperity-oriented movement founded in 1977 in Rio de Janeiro by Edir Macedo.[29] The countries of Brazil, Chile and Argentina have the biggest Pentecostal churches on the continent,

---

[27] Douglas J. Nelson, "For Such a Time as This: The Story of William J. Seymour and the Azusa Street Revival" (Ph.D. thesis, University of Birmingham, 1981) 157-58. Walter J. Hollenweger, *Pentecostalism: Origins and Development Worldwide* (Peabody, MA: Hendrickson, 1997) 18-19.

[28] See Anderson, *Introduction to Pentecostalism,* for the details.

[29] David Martin, *Tongues of Fire: The Explosion of Protestantism in Latin America* (Oxford, U.K.: Blackwell, 1990) 66. Mike Berg and Paul Pretiz, *Spontaneous Combustion: Grass-Roots Christianity Latin American Style* (Pasadena, CA: William Carey Library, 1996) 101-9.

but nearly every other Latin American and Caribbean country has also been affected by this phenomenon, often with the aid of Western missions.[30]

Most Western European Pentecostal churches have their origins in the revival associated with T.B. Barratt (1862-1940), Methodist pastor in Oslo, Norway, who visited New York in 1906, and was baptized in the Spirit with the help of Pentecostal missionaries on their way to Africa and the Middle East. Barratt sailed back to Norway, a zealous Pentecostal destined to become the founder and prime motivator of Classical Pentecostalism in Europe. The revival in his Filadelfia Church in Oslo was a place of pilgrimage, and spread to other parts of Europe. Pentecostals in Scandinavia became the biggest churches outside the Lutheran state churches, sending missionaries all over the world. Lewi Pethrus' (1884-1974) Filadelfia Church in Stockholm, Sweden, with its own extensive mission program and social activities, was probably the largest Pentecostal congregation in the world until the 1960s.

Alexander Boddy (1854-1930), Anglican vicar in Sunderland, England, visited Barratt's church and invited him to his church in September 1907. This became the most significant early Pentecostal center in Britain, and annual Whitsun conventions from 1908 to 1914 drew Pentecostals from all over Europe. Boddy, who remained an Anglican vicar all his life, edited the influential periodical *Confidence* (1908-1926), which reported on Pentecostal revivals and expounded Pentecostal doctrines. He also supported Cecil Polhill in the creation of the Pentecostal Missionary Union in 1909, an interdenominational missionary movement that mainly worked in western China and central India. In Belfast in 1915, George Jeffreys founded the Elim Pentecostal Church, now the largest Pentecostal denomination in Britain.[31]

The Assemblies of God in Great Britain and Ireland emerged in 1924 as a congregational association of autonomous churches. Donald Gee (1891-1966) was its chairman from 1948 until his death in 1966, traveling internationally and organizing the European Pentecostal Conference held in Stockholm in 1939 and the first Pentecostal World Conference (PWC) in Zürich in 1947. He was one of the most influential Pentecostal leaders of his time.[32]

Pentecostalism spread from England to France in 1926 and began among the Roma (Gypsy) people in 1952. In France and Spain, about a quarter of the Roma population belongs to a Pentecostal church today. Portuguese Pentecostalism

---

[30] Berg and Pretiz, *Spontaneous Combustion*, 41-42, 69, 70-79. Martin, *Tongues of Fire*, 51. Anderson, *Introduction to Pentecostalism*, 79-81.

[31] Walter J. Hollenweger, *The Pentecostals* (London: SCM, 1972) 184-85. P. Johnstone and J. Mandryk, *Operation World: 21st Century Edition* (Carlisle, U.K.: Paternoster, 2001) 650.

[32] William K. Kay, *Pentecostals in Britain* (Carlisle, U.K.: Paternoster, 2000) 74.

has its roots in Brazil, from where José Placido da Costa and José de Mattos returned to Portugal in 1913 and 1921 respectively as Pentecostal missionaries. Swedish missionaries planted Pentecostalism in Spain in 1923.[33] Italy now has the second-largest population of Pentecostals in western Europe after Britain. Francescon sent Giacomo Lombardi to Italy from Chicago in 1908, and the Pentecostal Christian Congregations and the Italian Pentecostal Christian Church trace their origins to Lombardi.[34]

The Pentecostal Movement has been relatively more successful in Eastern Europe, where it has grown in the face of severe persecution. Ivan Voronaev commenced a Russian Pentecostal church in New York and in 1920 established congregations in Bulgaria, Ukraine and Russia. Voronaev's church in Odessa soon had 1,000 members, and in 1927 he was appointed president of the Union of Christians of Evangelical Faith.

Pentecostals enjoyed the favor of the Communist state that had liberated them from Orthodox persecution, but after the passing of antireligious laws in 1930, Voronaev and 800 pastors were sent to Siberian concentration camps, after which Voronaev disappeared, and by 1940 was presumed dead. The Christians of the Evangelical Faith (Pentecostal) unsuccessfully approached Soviet leaders Kruschev in 1957, and Brezhnev in 1965 for religious freedom, only realized in 1991. In Ukraine, the Evangelical Pentecostal Union is one of the largest Pentecostal denominations in Europe, with some 370,000 members in 2000. By this time, there were some 400,000 Russian Pentecostals and 780,000 Ukrainians—the highest number of Pentecostals in any European nation. There are over 300,000 Pentecostals in Romania, where the Pentecostal Apostolic Church of God is the largest denomination, founded in 1922 and since 1996 known as the Pentecostal Union. Since the disintegration of Communism, there has been more freedom for Pentecostals in Eastern Europe, but new Pentecostal groups from the West have flooded into former Communist countries with evangelistic techniques that have brought opposition from Orthodox churches and national governments.[35]

The Impact in Africa and Asia

Possibly 11 percent of Africa's population in 2000 were "Charismatic," a significant form of Christianity on the continent. Classical Pentecostals

---

[33] Johnstone and Mandryk, *Operation World*, 529, 583.

[34] Hollenweger, *The Pentecostals*, 251. Johnstone and Mandryk, *Operation World*, 365.

[35] Hollenweger, *The Pentecostals*, 267-69, 274, 281. Johnstone and Mandryk, *Operation World*, 540, 644. Anderson, *Introduction to Pentecostalism*, 98-101.

have been operating there since 1907, when missionaries from Azusa Street arrived in Liberia and Angola. In South Africa in 1908, several independent Pentecostal missionaries arrived in Johannesburg and founded South Africa's biggest Classical Pentecostal denomination, the Apostolic Faith Mission, in racially integrated services. But white leaders passed racist laws and kept all significant positions for themselves, contributing to the many schisms that took place. Most Classical Pentecostal denominations in South Africa were divided on racial grounds until 1996.[36]

Nicholas Bhengu (1909-1986) was one of the most influential South African Pentecostals and leader of the "Back to God" section of the Assemblies of God. British independent Pentecostal missionary William Burton (1886-1971) worked in the southern Congo from 1915 to 1960, and founded what became the Pentecostal Community of the Congo. In East Africa, most of the numerous independent churches place an emphasis on the Holy Spirit as a result of various revival movements.

German evangelist Reinhard Bonnke began his ministry in southern Africa in 1967 and has since preached throughout Africa to some of the biggest crowds in Christian history. His "Christ for All Nations" organization, now based in Frankfurt, has been highly effective in promoting Pentecostal practices in Africa.

Pentecostalism has become one of the most prominent Christian movements across West Africa. The first Azusa Street missionaries to Liberia in 1907 were African-Americans. Three of the largest Pentecostal denominations in Ghana have origins in the work of a remarkable Ghanaian, Peter Anim (1890-1984) and his Irish contemporary James McKeown (1900-1989).[37]

Nigeria today has some of the largest Pentecostal congregations in the world, with vigorous outreaches both nationally and internationally. Divine healing through laying on hands for the sick (and sometimes accompanied by ritual symbols) has always been a prominent part of Pentecostal practices in Africa.

Within a relatively short time, a complex network of Pentecostal missions was established all over India. The Assemblies of God in India formed a regional council for South India in 1929 and has had independent districts with Indian leadership since 1947. K.E. Abraham (1899-1974) became a Pentecostal in 1923. Because of disagreements with missionaries, he founded the Indian Pentecostal Church of God. This and the Assemblies of God are the

---

[36] Johnstone and Mandryk, *Operation World*, 21. Anderson, *Introduction to Pentecostalism*, 106-10.

[37] Anderson, *Introduction to Pentecostalism*, 115-21. Johnstone and Mandryk, *Operation World*, 241, 421, 488.

two largest Pentecostal denominations, with some 750,000 affiliates each in 2000. The best known of the Indian Charismatic healing evangelists is D.G.S. Dhinakaran of Tamilnadu (member of the Church of South India), whose Jesus Calls Ministry has extensive campaigns with huge crowds.[38]

Myanmar, Thailand, Malaysia and Singapore have vibrant Pentecostal and Charismatic churches, but the greatest Pentecostal expansion in Southeast Asia was in Indonesia. Dutch American Pentecostal missionaries arrived there in 1922. Over 2 million Javanese became Christians between 1965 and 1971, during the "Indonesian Revival," despite heavy persecution from Muslim extremists. By 2000 there were 9 million to 12 million Pentecostals and Charismatics, 4 percent to 5 percent of the total population in a country 80 percent Muslim.[39] Pentecostal churches were founded in the Philippines in 1928 by Filipinos converted in the United States, where the three largest churches today are the Jesus Is Lord Church, founded by Eddie Villanueva in 1978, the Jesus Miracle Crusade (both Filipino-founded churches), and the Assemblies of God.[40]

Pentecostal missionaries were active in China from 1907. The McIntoshes and the Garrs from Azusa Street were among the first. Although there were only some 5 million Christians in mainland China at the time of the exodus of Westerners in 1949, estimates of membership of unregistered independent Chinese movements in 2000 vary between 20 million and 75 million. China may now have the largest number of Charismatic Christians in Asia, especially in unregistered independent house churches, which have developed in isolation from the rest of Christianity for at least 50 years and despite severe opposition. The True Jesus Church, founded by Paul Wei in 1917 in Beijing, and the Jesus Family, founded by Jing Dianying at Mazhuang, Shandong, in 1927, are Pentecostal churches, the former both Oneness and Sabbatarian. These and other "old three self" churches were banned during the 1950s until the end of the '70s, after which there was rapid growth. By 2000, an estimated 10 percent of Protestants

---

[38] Roger Hedlund, "Indigenous Pentecostalism in India," in *Asian and Pentecostal: The Charismatic Face of Christianity in Asia*, ed. Allan Anderson and Edmond Tang (Oxford: Regnum Books; Baguio, Philippines: APTS Books, 2005) 215-44. Roger Hedlund, *Christianity Is Indian: The Emergence of an Indigenous Christianity* (Delhi: ISPCK, 2000) 160-61.

[39] Gani Wiyono, "Pentecostals in Indonesia," in *Asian and Pentecostal: The Charismatic Face of Christianity in Asia*, ed. Allan Anderson and Edmond Tang (Oxford: Regnum Books; Baguio, Philippines: APTS Books, 2005) 307-28. Johnstone and Mandryk, *Operation World*, 339.

[40] Johnstone and Mandryk, *Operation World*, 521. Joseph Suico, "Pentecostals in the Philippines," in *Asian and Pentecostal: The Charismatic Face of Christianity in Asia*, ed. Allan Anderson and Edmond Tang (Oxford: Regnum Books; Baguio, Philippines: APTS Books, 2005) 345-62.

in China were members of the True Jesus Church, and most Christian groups in central Shandong province were of Jesus Family background.[41]

In 1932, Mary Rumsey, baptized in the Spirit at Azusa Street and a missionary in Japan, established the first Pentecostal church in Seoul, Korea, with Heong Huh, the first Korean Assemblies of God national chairman. David (formerly Paul) Yonggi Cho (1936) and his future mother-in-law Jashil Choi (1915-1989) began a small tent church in a Seoul slum area in 1958. Thirty years later, his Yoido Full Gospel Church with 700,000 members under 700 pastors had become the largest Christian congregation in the world, and Pentecostalism had become the second-largest form of Protestantism in Korea.[42] Space does not allow an exhaustive treatment of the expansion of Pentecostalism, but these examples illustrate the global trend.

Challenges in the Present Century

By the 1930s, there were very few countries without some Pentecostal witness—a truly remarkable achievement.[43] Pentecostalism in all its multifaceted variety, including the "Pentecostal-like" independent churches and the Catholic Charismatics, is one of the most significant forms of Christianity in the 21st century. According to oft-quoted but controversial estimates, there may have been over 500 million adherents of these movements worldwide in 2000,[44] found in almost every country of the world and spanning all Christian denominations. In less than 100 years, Pentecostal, Charismatic and associated movements have become the major new force in world Christianity. The Azusa Street Revival stands at the forefront of this 20th-century development.

This is not cause for triumphalism however, as Pentecostalism has been beset with blemishes that remain after 100 years. Among the most pressing are those of fragmentation, individualism and patriarchalism. One of the greatest challenges is that of disunity and exclusivism. Doctrinal and organizational differences emerged early, sometimes based on race and class, but more often

---

[41] Gotthard Oblau, Deng Zhao Ming, and Edmond Tang, "Christianity in China," in *Asian and Pentecostal: The Charismatic Face of Christianity in Asia,* ed. Allan Anderson and Edmond Tang (Oxford: Regnum Books; Baguio, Philippines: APTS Books, 2005) 411-88.

[42] Martin, *Tongues of Fire,* 135, 146. Johnstone and Mandryk, *Operation World,* 387. Anderson, *Introduction to Pentecostalism,* 136-39.

[43] Johnstone and Mandryk, *Operation World,* 83-84, 250, 480, 509-10, 627.

[44] David B. Barrett and Todd M. Johnson, "Annual Statistical Table on Global Mission: 2003," *International Bulletin of Missionary Research* 27, no. 1 (2003): 25. This statistic, although widely quoted, is impossible to verify and depends on how "Pentecostalism" is defined. The majority of those included in this figure are independent churches worldwide and Charismatics in older churches.

because of petty differences and dogmatism. The legacy is that Pentecostals have been responsible for more divisions than it has taken the rest of Christianity 2,000 years to produce. Ironically, the more Pentecostals divided, the more they multiplied, but this does not absolve guilt in the tearing apart of the body of Christ. Some of the most acrimonious schisms in church history have taken place among Pentecostals. No serious efforts are being made to restore broken relationships, with few exceptions.

Not only do Pentecostals need to draw closer to themselves, but also to their sisters and brothers in older churches. In a time when there is much greater openness to the working of the Spirit, it is tragic that many official Pentecostal organizations eschew pursuing relationships with national and international ecumenical bodies like the World Council of Churches. It is not all gloom, however. The various dialogues taking place, especially the Catholic-Pentecostal dialogue, are the beginning of change. The Society for Pentecostal Studies provides one of the most ecumenical forums in North America for creative scholarship and conversation between Pentecostals and Charismatics of all kinds. Recently, the World Council of Churches had a series of exploratory conferences with Pentecostals,[45] culminating in an international Conference of World Mission and Evangelism on the Holy Spirit, healing and reconciliation in Athens, Greece, in May 2005.

For the first time, a significant number of Pentecostals were full delegates in a major ecumenical conference. The involvement of Pentecostal denominations in the ecumenical movement could pave the way for dynamic changes in the international face of Christianity and promote the healing of the ruptured body of Christ.

Along with the challenge of fragmentation is that of a leadership that has often been far from exemplary. Although Pentecostalism may not have the monopoly on religious charlatans, its recent history has provided numerous examples of how far from perfect Pentecostal luminaries are. The "health and wealth" gospel, in particular, has spawned a rapidly growing global Pentecostal culture that has questionable practices tantamount to exploitation in the name of "God's blessing," linked to an equally questionable theology. Many present-day Pentecostal leaders are accountable to nobody and are a law unto themselves. Unfortunately, Pentecostal ecclesiology has lent itself to such rampant individualism.

Patriarchalism exists in several areas of Pentecostalism today. Not only does

---

[45] Allan Anderson, "Pentecostals, Healing and the Ecumenical Movement," *International Review of Mission* 93:370/1 (July/Oct. 2004): 486-496.

this reveal itself in the very limited opportunities for ministry and leadership for women (who form the large majority of Pentecostals), but in far too many places expatriate missionaries manipulate national churches and theological colleges through control of financial resources raised in richer countries.

Only when this practice stops will Pentecostals have come of age. It is doubtful whether there will ever be solutions to these problems as long as sin abounds, but the greater cooperation and networking of Pentecostals globally will certainly do much to address these pressing issues.

The worldwide revivals of the early 20th century, of which Azusa Street is the best known, were instrumental in helping create a new form of Christianity in the 20th century. This global expansion of Christianity has so transformed the face of world religion that we may no longer speak of Christianity as a "Western" phenomenon, or even of Pentecostalism as originating in North America. With the vast majority of Pentecostals today living in Latin America, Africa and Asia, the new challenges to Western Pentecostalism will come from outside its borders, and surely we will be far the richer for it.

10

Constructing Different Memories
Recasting the Azusa Street Revival

Anthea Butler

In 2004, I attended a meeting in Malaysia of Asian Church Historians, sponsored, in part, by the Henry Luce foundation. At the last minute I was asked to discuss some aspects of Pentecostalism in my capacity as the President for the Society for Pentecostal Studies. In my remarks, I happened to mention the Azusa Street Revival, and was immediately challenged by historians who hailed from China and India. They challenged me on the notion that Azusa Street could be perceived as the "center" of the Pentecostal Movement. How could I and others think that the Azusa Street Mission could be construed as the center of the movement, they countered, when believers in Asia had spoken in tongues in the late 1800s and movements had been established, long before the missionaries from Azusa Street came to evangelize their countries, who believed they had the gift of *xenolalia*? The ensuing verbal assault became so intense and heated that I unexpectedly broke into tears.

What I said then, perhaps, struck even me. But I believe that it was an important insight on how we remember Azusa Street and how we understand its salience for persons of African decent. In my final comment to the group, I remarked that as an African-American who had experienced racism firsthand,

Azusa Street was important, not because I had some great American agenda to "own" Pentecostalism, but rather, that the Azusa Street Revival, headed by an African-American, speaks to the core experience of racism and oppression in the United States. The fact that the leader of the revival was William J. Seymour, an African-American man, who did not have much education, who had been the "last" in many ways, said more to me about the

nature of what Pentecostalism should be than it has become. It should not be a movement about power and hegemony, but about inclusion, openness, and racial reconciliation. To this day, I do not know if my detractors were moved by my arguments that day. I was moved, however, to reconsider the ways in which historians have used Azusa Street to put forth similar justifications.

The question is, then, to whom does Azusa Street belong? Most Pentecostals would say that it belongs to the worldwide movement of Pentecostalism, or even more judiciously, to the entire Christian world. For African-American Pentecostals, however, Azusa Street belongs to us. Before the reader becomes offended by this statement, let me clarify what I mean.

For years, academics that study Pentecostalism have had an ongoing argument about the origins of Pentecostalism. Some choose to think of Pentecostalism arising out of old stock whites of the 19th century and the Holiness Movement in the United States and abroad. Some called it a Restorationist Movement, arising out of the millennial fervor of the 19th century. Still others hold that the antecedents of the revival lay within the African-American religious experience during slavery and the reconstruction period.[1]

This chapter will not take up any of those banners, however. Azusa Street belongs to all Pentecostals, even if they are uncomfortable with Azusa Street's hegemony as the "origin" of the Pentecostal Movement. My argument goes a bit deeper. It is my contention that the Azusa Street Revival belongs to African-Americans and African-American religious history for its beginnings as an all-black prayer meeting that convened at 214 North Bonnie Brae Street in Los Angeles, its pastoral leadership provided by William J. Seymour, and its eventual end as a church that welcomed all races. It finished as it began—as a black church. For African-American Pentecostals, Azusa Street cannot be thought of outside a discussion of racism, racial hierarchies, Social Darwinism, and an inequitable justice and economic system that placed African-Americans at the lowest end of the spectrum in 1906. Azusa Street acts as a mirror for us—a mirror in which we can interrogate religious leadership in the African-American community. It allows us to ask questions about the role of slave religion in Pentecostal worship, and it provides a

---

[1] For a good summary of these particular historiographic arguments, see Augustus Cerillo Jr., "Interpretive Approaches to the History of American Pentecostal Origins," *Pneuma: The Journal of the Society for Pentecostal Studies* 19 (1997): 29-52.

resource for the pride that early Black Nationalists felt when they found themselves in the Scripture in passages such as, "Ethiopia shall soon stretch out her hands unto God" (Psalm 68:31). The Azusa Street Revival may belong to Pentecostalism, but the mission's memory and purpose belongs to African-Americans.

When Frank Bartleman wrote that "the color line was washed away in the blood," he could write with the enthusiasm as a white man who was thrilled with the experience of having whites and blacks mix together without overt racism in a worship service.[2] Yet the perspective of the African-Americans at the Azusa Street Revival might have been summed up in the line prior to Bartleman's declaration, which is not so often quoted. That line read, "There were far more white people than colored coming."[3] And so it has been with the myriad interpretations, popular and academic, of the Azusa Street Revival and race relations.

In order to interrogate the meaning of the memories of Azusa Street for African-American religion, the place to start is not with Bartleman's declaration of the color line being washed away in the blood, but with W.E.B Du Bois's declaration that the problem of the 20th century was the color line.[4] In *The Souls of Black Folks*, Du Bois recognized the religious traditions of African-Americans within the confines of the racial realities that faced African-Americans of the day. Jim Crow, lynching, and violence against African-Americans coupled with the constrained opportunities for advancement, stood as an indictment against the promised freedom that emancipation should have bought at the end of the Civil War. For African-American Pentecostals, these realities did not change with the advent of the Azusa Street Revival. In a sense, they were magnified. The very nature of the revival, its origin as a black prayer group and its blossoming into a full fledged revival led by William Seymour, not only controverted racial stereotypes and morays of the day, it also complicated the ways in which persons of different races had to interact with each other.

In lauding the interracial nature of the revival, too often writers forget that the principles of social Darwinism were held, not only by rich industrialists and nations, but also by many who looked upon African-Americans as inferior. Many of those persons who embraced social Darwinism were Christians. It is no surprise then, that when the revival began to attract the notice of the local newspapers that racial stereotypes came into full view—the stony optics of the colored exhorter, the colored mammy, and others similar derogatory descriptions.[5]

---

[2] Frank Bartleman, *Azusa Street: The Roots of Modern-Day Pentecost* (Plainfield, NJ: Bridge Publishing, 1980), 54.

[3] Bartleman.

[4] W.E.B. Du Bois, *The Souls of Black Folks* (Chicago: A.C. McClurg, 1903), vii.

[5] "Weird Babel of Tongues," *Los Angeles Daily Times,* Apr. 18, 1906: 1.

Bartleman's line perhaps has been looked upon as the utopia that Pentecostal wanted to achieve, but the reality for blacks at the Azusa Street Revival was that the color line had been delineated in blood . . . the blood of black people. Phenotypes were a way to become pejorative about the leadership of the revival, and African-American participation was reduced to caricatures about worship and black leadership. No surprise then, that the "progenitor of Pentecost," Charles Parham, who had taught Seymour for a time, spoke of racial hierarchies in his writings after being dismissed from the revival following his attempted takeover.[6]

Unfortunately for the most part, Pentecostalism has been divided racially ever since, in both scholarship and practice. Despite Seymour's best efforts, Parham rejected the revival with virulent words about its worship styles. Participants from the South, black and white, found themselves separated through Jim Crow laws. Latinos and Latinas were either coopted or ostracized—both on a racial basis and as the result of a language barrier. Research on Pentecostals labeled their religion under such categories as deprivation theory or even insanity. And the inexorable climb toward Pentecostals respectability that led toward the formation of the Pentecostal Fellowship of North America was reconstituted as the Pentecostals and Charismatic Churches of North America (PCCNA) in 1994. The formation of the PCCNA was both the apology and the reparation for years of racial division between Pentecostal groups.

For all of the apologies, however, the core of Azusa Street, the contingent of African-Americans, Jennie Evans Moore, Ruth and Richard Asberry, William J. Seymour, and others, have been overlooked in order to serve the needs of the larger narrative that has been constructed about Azusa Street and its interracial constituency that wavered over time. What might we discover if we leave this argument behind, and look at why the African-American core of the revival was already at odds with the "black church" and its leadership of African-American religious life in the early 20th century?

The initial participants of the Bonnie Brae prayer meeting and the Azusa outpouring were, in fact, only a small segment of the population of Los Angeles at the time. African-Americans however, were having a larger debate within their own constituency about whether to leave the trappings of 'slave religion' behind, and to mainstream themselves in a manner that would bring them greater respect from the white community.

Du Bois's assessment of the black church in *The Souls of Black Folks* was

---

[6] Charles F. Parham, "Free-Love," *AF* [Baxter Springs, KS] 1.10, Dec. 1912: 4-5; untitled item, *AF* [Baxter Springs, Kans.] 1.8, Oct. 1912: 2.

that "the Negro church of today is the social centre of Negro life in the United States."⁷ Given that the revival started out in a home prayer meeting, the core participants at the start of the revival were somewhat outside the mainstream of black religious life. The search for the experience of the Holy Spirit not only would put them at odds with hegemonic white power structures; it also left them out of the mainstream conversation among African-American churches of the day. Large black churches in urban areas such as Philadelphia and Detroit would soon come to ridicule Southern religiosity and practices of slave religion as uncivilized, and during the interwar period would work hard to root these practices out from church members.⁸

Seymour and his cohort from Bonnie Brae Street participated in a revival that included shouting, falling out, prophecies and the like—behaviors Du Bois saw at a rural black church and described as a feeling of "suppressed terror hung in the air" that "seemed to seize us—a pythian madness, a demoniac possession."⁹ African-Americans then, both at the beginning of the revival, as well as those who attended throughout, were engaged in an argument about respectability of worship and race relations they did not even realize. Allowing for open worship, women's leadership, and healing stood in direct contradiction to the majority of Baptist and African Methodist Episcopal churches of the day.¹⁰

Black participants, such as Charles Harrison Mason, cofounder of the Church of God in Christ, had been dismissed from a Baptist fellowship in part because of beliefs about sanctification that allowed for these types of worship practices.¹¹ The issue of what sanctification actually was had already been a hot topic

---

⁷ W.E.B. Du Bois, *The Souls of Black Folks*, 136.

⁸ Victoria Wolcott, *Remaking Respectability: African-American Women in Interwar Detroit* (Chapel Hill: U of North Carolina P, 2001) 198.

⁹ Wolcolt., 134.

¹⁰ Indeed, there was a struggle for the recognition of blacks in Los Angeles, but within the African-American community the struggle between middle-class religion and what might be termed *folk* religion, such as was present at the Azusa Street Mission. When, in 1909, the *Los Angeles Daily Times* included an entire section of the newspaper with coverage of African-Americans in Los Angeles. Some were of the articles were on the contributions that local African-Americans were making in education, the military, professional life, construction, or some other aspect of everyday life. G.R. Bryant wrote the article on "Religious Life of Los Angeles Negroes," *Los Angeles Daily Times,* February 12, 1909, 3:2. That article listed 10 African-American congregations, including a couple of small Presbyterian and Episcopalian congregations with membership of near 25 people. The Azusa Street Mission, which from 1906-1908 had been larger than every congregation mentioned, received no mention at all.

¹¹ Ithiel Clemmons, *Bishop C.H. Mason and the Roots of the Church of God in Christ* (Bakersfield, CA: Pneuma Life, 1996). Also see E.C. Morris, *Sermons, Addresses and Reminiscences and Important Correspondence, with a Picture Gallery of Eminent Ministers and Scholars* (Nashville, TN: National Baptist Publishing Board, 1901) 32-35.

within black Baptist churches and resulted in schisms that would evolve into the African-American wing of Holiness Pentecostalism. The black participants at Azusa, engaging in the discussion and teachings regarding sanctification, were once again at odds with much of the African-American church.

In many ways, black participation in the revival at Azusa Street was not about modeling the traditional black church that was rising to prominence despite the era of Jim Crow. It was an alternative pathway to spiritual renewal that connected its participants, not just to the present and the millennial fervor of the day, but also back to their African past in worship that was unrestrained, free and oriented toward the miraculous rather than the scientific.

To be a black person at Azusa Street was not only transgressive to whites, it was also transgressive to the dominant expressions of the black church of its time. It is little wonder that the heirs of the revival and their storefront churches in Chicago and Detroit would be written about and reviled by both black sociologists and Works Progress Administration personnel alike.[12]

Perhaps the most intriguing element of this departure from the ongoing project of constructing a new black religious norm is Seymour's leadership in the revival. Seymour's leadership was very unlike the average black pastor of the day. Pastors exerted both a spiritual and a practical position of authority with their black congregations, in part because it was one of the few leadership roles open to African-American men who were uneducated during the early 20th century. Rather than exerting a heavy charismatic hand over the revival, Seymour chose not to be an overbearing leader. He often yielded the pulpit in the revival to others and was often described as meek, humble and unassuming.[13] His assumed meekness would cause trouble in later years as differing personalities would try to usurp Seymour's role from the pulpit, but his leadership style stands out as being a rather intriguing departure from the almost deified role of the black pastor during this period.

Seymour also did not outwardly seem to exhibit the same types of patriarchal leadership that developed in the black church during the Reconstruction Period. Both black and white women were members of the Azusa Street Mission staff, notably Jennie Evans Moore, Clara Lum, Florence Crawford and Sister Prince. In many black churches of the day, these women would not have been allowed to operate in a capacity of leadership, nor would they have been allowed to step into

---

[12] Anthea Butler, "Observing the Lives of the 'Saints': Sanctification as Practice in the Church of God in Christ," in *Histories of American Christian Practice* (Baltimore, MD: John Hopkins, 2006).

[13] Cecil M. Robeck, Jr., *The Azusa Street Mission and Revival: The Birth of the Global Pentecostal Movement* (Nashville: Thomas Nelson, 2006), ch. 3.

the pulpit. This simple modeling of cooperative leadership disregarding gender was both progressive and Biblical at the same time. For Seymour, if the "Spirit had been poured out on all flesh" that meant that both sexes would be able to lead within the revival. The configuration of the leadership would eventually house the demise of the mission's effectiveness when Clara Lum absconded with the mailing records of the Apostolic Faith.[14] For all of that, Seymour remained committed to women's participation in the Azusa Street Mission.

The interracial component of the mission would also fly in the face of the norms for black churches of the time. Seymour's openness to have an interracial revival was not merely to provide a model for whites, it was also about modeling what blacks were calling for during this time period. African-American leadership such as W.E.B. Du Bois and Booker T. Washington faced the complex issue that both wanted their churches to remain autonomous, while at the same time asking for equal rights in the workplace, equitable wages, the justice system and education. If black churches could remain autonomous, they would be able to become centers of black life and education—free from the oversight of whites. They would also become places to teach racial self-determination, an important part of the struggle against Jim Crow laws and social and economic discrimination.

Seymour's willingness to make the mission interracial opened up criticism from blacks and whites alike, a departure from what other black leaders were striving for during the time period. That is not to say that Seymour saw the mission as totally integrated. Seymour writes in *The Doctrine and Disciplines of the Apostolic Faith Mission*, about the revival's fortune that arose from the beginnings at the prayer meeting on North Bonnie Brae Street:

> In 1906, the colored people of the City of Los Angeles felt they were led by the Holy Sprit that they decided to have Elder W.J. Seymour, of Houston, Texas, to come to Los Angeles, California, and give them some Bible teaching. . . . From his teaching one of the greatest revivals was held in the city of Los Angeles. . . .Very soon division arose through some of our brethren, and the Holy Sprit was grieved. We want all of our white brethren and white sisters to feel free in *our* churches and missions, in spite of all the trouble we have had with some of our white brethren in causing diversion, and spreading wild fire and fanaticism. Some of our colored brethren caught the disease of this spirit of division also.[15]

---

[14] Robeck Jr., ch. 7.

[15] William J. Seymour, *The Doctrines and Discipline of the Azusa Street Apostolic Faith Mission of Los Angeles, CA 1915* (Los Angeles: privately published, 1915) 12 (emphasis mine).

Seymour's account of the division of races at Azusa Street was one that obviously was painful, but it is interesting to note that he does not say that he considered the church or the initial mission to be an "interracial church." It was a work where all were welcomed, but its very beginnings arose out of a black prayer meeting. By highlighting "the colored people of Los Angeles" when he began his historical account of the mission, Seymour may have wanted his readers to remember the context in which the mission first arose, his openness for all to participate in the mission, and the eventual tensions that arose from that quest to integrate.

Many Black churches of the time would have considered it to be a disaster to invite whites into the congregation, especially in Southern churches, where churches were suspected of being hotbeds of black sedition. Despite the fact that blacks and whites did mix together for worship in the South, it was often under the auspices of white oversight and leadership. Azusa, with both its geographic placement and its leadership, attempted to model something very different to both blacks and whites. Even so, it was met by resistance from both parties.

Once again, Seymour's quest for interracial partnership put him squarely in opposition to the trajectory of black religion of the time period. While other churches were either calling for civil rights, equal facilities, or a complete departure from white American life into a black nationalist stance, Seymour attempted to hold both worlds together by modeling traditional forms of black worship and pursuing interracial leadership even though taking a moderate approach to pastoral leadership was a radical departure from the trajectory that the black church was taking during the early 20th century.

In this sense, then, by recasting Azusa Street, not simply as an interracial revival, but as a challenge to the traditional historical writing and trajectory of African-American Christianity, we find within it some promising seeds for both renewal and change. Seymour's emphasis on equality in leadership, regardless of gender, points to the deconstruction of the role of patriarchy in both African-American Pentecostalism and the black church broadly defined. By seeking interracial cooperation, Seymour's inclusion of all peoples at the revival and in its nadir, points to the eventuality of equality for African-Americans. The participation of representatives from all social classes in this revival, speaks to the salience of the revival for all persons, no matter what their economic situation. It may also come as no surprise that many African Methodist Episcopal and Baptist churches have resumed ecstatic worship that once they eschewed at the beginnings of the 20th century. By reconstructing Azusa Street to act as a counter to African-American religious history then, the true quest for civil rights, the retention of African spiritualities, and a black-centered but racially inclusive spiritual space, helps to place Azusa Street missions not at the margins of African-American religion, but close to many of the central issues it still needs to engage. Azusa Street is for all of us, but especially for the black church. It points toward a reality we still need to press, without fail.

Part II
The Legacy of the Azusa Street Revival

11

Signs of Grace in a Graceless World
The Charismatic Structure of the Church in Trinitarian Perspective

Frank D. Macchia

The Charismatic Structure of the Church in a Graceless World

We live in a graceless world. This statement is one-sided, but true nevertheless. Though natural life is graced by God to an extent, it often confronts us as quite ambiguous, especially when grace seems eclipsed by darkness. This ambiguity is especially evident in the realm of social relationships. As Christopher Lasch has noted in his book, *Haven in a Heartless World*, the structures of capitalist society have come increasingly to dominate even the life of the family, which has served traditionally and ideally as a "haven" in the midst of an impersonal world. Families are losing their role as a haven and are becoming less and less influential in imparting values, caring for their young and elderly, and upholding human dignity and worth.

Family members share little in common, since they spend most of their time serving different institutional interests. Moreover, familial relationships often seem as graceless as the institutions that have influenced them. For example,

---

*Scripture references in this chapter are taken from the New King James Version.

seemingly ungrateful children are sometimes reminded of the need to obey in return for the shelter, food, clothing and other "services" granted by parents as providers, as though parenting can be reduced to the provision of various goods and services![1]

And the media is quick to sell the illusion that a haven may yet be found through increased purchasing power. Marketing experts have done sufficient research to know what kind of consumers to make of us and how to instruct us effectively in the task of measuring one's attainment of personal worth by the level of consumption achieved. Socialist societies have not historically been any more liberating, since one in such contexts was generally judged by how well he or she could "produce" for the state or, ideally, the "common good." Indeed, the principalities and powers of human social life seek to make us into one-dimensional beings fit for a particular social function and disposable if shown to be unfit for use. A certain social worth is only granted to those who benefit most from a complex interplay of values shaped by the dominant culture.

In our personal struggles to be loyal to Christ, we tend to keep our private sins a secret. This secrecy can increase the power of these sins in our lives. We feel alone and ashamed. As our situation worsens, we feel there is no one in whom we can confide. In the midst of this growing "gracelessness," we often feel bound by "flesh" and desperately groan for the grace of God and the liberty of life in the Spirit. Where can graced existence and graced community be found?

It should be found in the church! Martin Luther once called the church the "infirmary of the sick."[2] This is true, not only because we are wounded sinners, but also because we are wounded healers, gifted to heal and to strengthen one another by helping each other in unique ways to be receptive to the grace of God. The church should pulsate with ever-increasing gifts of helps and edification. The people of God are not to fall short of any gift while waiting for the Lord's return (1 Corinthians 1:9). John Koenig stated that the church is to be a "gift-evoking" fellowship.[3] Is this what the church has become?

Answer: In part, but we still have a long way to go. Part of the process of becoming a gift-evoking fellowship is to appreciate the source of our charismatic life *in God.* It is not coincidental that the two passages that deal most prominently with spiritual gifts in the New Testament, 1 Corinthians 12 and Ephesians 4, speak of *God as triune,* even though the contexts of these texts do not require it (1 Corinthians 12:4-6; Ephesians 4:4-6).

---

[1] Christopher Lasch, *Haven in a Heartless World: The Family Besieged* (New York: W.W. Norton, 1978, 1995) 12-21.

[2] *Lectures on Romans,* trans. Wilhelm Pauck (Philadelphia: Westminster, 1961) 130.

[3] John Koenig, *Charismata: God's Gifts for God's People* (Philadelphia: Westminster, 1978) 123.

The church from early on saw the source of their corporate life fundamentally in the story of Jesus, which was Trinitarian in structure. Jesus is the One raised from the dead by the Father "according to the Spirit of holiness" (Romans 1:4)*. Jesus also bestows the Spirit, who proceeded from the Father on others (John 20:22). The church that pulsates with gifts of new life cannot help but connect this new life with the life of God as Father, Son and Spirit. It is thus fitting to explore the Trinitarian context for spiritual gifts a bit further.

The Trinitarian Context

There is no Spirit without Word, nor Word without Spirit. Both Spirit and Word are the "left and right hands" of the Father (Irenaeus). In the beginning, God spoke the Creation into being, but that spoken word was carried on the very breath of God (Genesis 1:1-3). In Ezekiel 37, hopeless Israel was promised that the word of prophecy would join with the winds of the Spirit to raise Israel up from the grave in order to make her into a living nation for God.

This outpouring of the Spirit was also attached to the future coming of the Messiah (Isaiah 61:1-3). When the Son of God was born as the Word of the Father (John 1:1-18), He was conceived in the Virgin Mary, through the "hovering" of the Spirit in a way similar to the hovering of the Spirit at the Creation (Luke 1:35). Jesus preached and healed the sick as the man of the Spirit (Luke 4:18), gave His life on the cross "[by] the eternal Spirit" (Hebrews 9:14), and was raised from the dead "according to the Spirit of holiness" (Romans 1:4).

It is from this experience of the Spirit in communion with the Father that Jesus bestowed the Spirit on the church. The Old Testament foresaw that the Messiah would be anointed by the Spirit (Isaiah 61:1-3). Unprecedented was the idea that the Messiah would *bestow* the Spirit of God. Indeed, Christ's deity was revealed in His role as *Bestower* of the Spirit. Jesus as the man of the Spirit reveals His lordship after the Resurrection by breathing the Spirit upon the disciples (John 20:22), for only God can breathe the divine breath upon creation (Genesis 2:7). Jesus, as the Word of the Father and the resurrected Lord, exercises the divine right of breathing the Spirit forth, an act that culminates in Luke's account of Pentecost. Indeed, "the first man, Adam, became a living being; the last Adam became a life-giving spirit" (1 Corinthians 15:45, *ESV*).

Jesus' anointing was thus unique in that it involved His incarnation as the divine Word of the Father. The church does not represent an extension of this Incarnation in the world (as a *Christus prolongatus*). That assumption would only serve to deify the church! But the church does represent an extension of the anointing of Jesus in the world in the sense that the church is sanctified and empowered by the Spirit to proliferate Christ's gracious presence in the world. Though Jesus' anointing is in a sense unique, it is also paradigmatic in its *charismatic specificity* for the church. Through the charismatic structure of the church, the church builds itself up in love as members help each other receive and grow in the grace of Christ that comes to us through gospel and sacrament. It also helps the church spread that grace to others.

In spreading grace to others, we walk the self-sacrificial path of the cross. Jesus poured out the Spirit not only from His risen life, but also from His crucified life as well. Thus, we cannot interpret Jesus' charismatic life, nor that of the church, in a triumphalistic way that neglects the path of the cross or the cost of discipleship. The charismatic life of Jesus was part of His proclamation of the year of the Lord's favor to the suffering of the world (Luke 4:18). Ripped from this Christological setting, spiritual gifts can seem triumphalistic and separated from the hope that the gifts inspire for those who suffer.

The church in spiritual gifts must bear one another's burdens and seek solidarity with those who suffer everywhere, offering help and hope. Hope sometimes finds courage in a strength that is hidden and not affirmed by extraordinary signs. Moreover, there are ordinary gifts blessed by the Spirit, along with extraordinary ones in the church. But extraordinary signs reveal that hidden strength can sometimes reach by God's grace for a visible foretaste of the victory to come.

The point here is that the Christological foundation of the church is not only to be found in church office, sacrament or proclamation. Christ is also present in multiple gifts and signs of the Spirit in the fellowship of the church. Neglected to an extent in ecumenical documents on the nature of the church is the way in which the gifts of the Spirit *(charismata)* proliferate and diversify Christ's presence through the church in the world. A juridical or sacramental understanding of the church that lacks an appreciation for the church's charismatic structure can seem Spiritless, overly institutional, abstract and monolithic. Even the preaching of the church without the power and gifts of the Spirit can seem overly cerebral and abstract.

The fact is that the Christological source of the church is not to be seen in church office, sacrament and preaching in isolation from the church's charismatic structure. Christ's outpouring of the Spirit upon the people of God had the effect of producing multiple and diverse giftings. In what may be termed Paul's description of Pentecost, Ephesians 4:8 states that Christ "ascended on high" in order to "give gifts to his people." The ultimate goal of this outpouring of divine gifts upon the people of God at Pentecost is that Christ would one day "fill all things" (v. 10). The creation that is presently under the reign of sin and death is to one day become the very temple of God through Christ and the Spirit (cf. 1 Corinthians 15:20-28; Revelation 21:3). Indeed, the church is presently filled with God's Spirit in order to be the harbinger in the world of this final indwelling of God in all of creation, which will be the final victory of life over death. Pentecost inaugurates the time when God will expand God's dwelling place among mortals and make all things new (Revelation 21:3-5).

What is interesting about the Ephesians 4:8 text noted above is the fact the outpouring of the Spirit at Pentecost "gives gifts unto people." The message of this text is clear: Christ poured out the Spirit at Pentecost in a way that is not generic nor monolithic but rather particularistic and diverse. Paul notes that we exercise gifts "according to the grace. . .given to us" (Romans 12:6), implying that grace is experienced in ways unique and particular to a person's gifting.

The outpouring of the Spirit at Pentecost proliferates among the people of God in the specific form of diverse gifts so that all of the people of God can become unique channels of grace to one another in the midst of a world characterized to a significant degree by graceless relationships. Spiritual gifts are the specific means by which the church becomes a graced community ever more faithful to its ministry and its mission as it becomes ever more faithful to Christ. Through the cultivation of spiritual gifts, the church grows toward the "full stature of Christ" in the world (see Ephesians 4:13).

Christ bestowed the Spirit upon the church from the ultimate context of His loving communion with the Father. Jesus' life in the Spirit was actually a drama played out from His loving relationship with the Father. The Father lovingly and lavishly bestowed the Spirit on the Son to show forth His good pleasure in the Son (Matthew 3:16,17; John 3:34). The Son responded in the Spirit by showing uncompromising devotion to the Father, even to the point of obedient death on the cross (Philippians 2:8; Hebrews 9:14). In response to the Son, the Father raised Him from the dead "according to the Spirit of holiness" (Romans 1:4; Philippians 2:9). In the story of Jesus, as well as correspondingly in God, the Spirit is the *bond of love* between the Father and the Son. When Jesus bestowed the Spirit upon the church, He showed that His loving communion with the Father was not closed, but open to others. The Spirit poured out from this love is also that bond between us and God (Romans 5:5).

Why does the Trinitarian drama of redemption played out in the story of Jesus lead to the establishment of the church? The Trinitarian drama in the story of Jesus has to do with loving communion, or a *mutual* participation in life *(koinonia)*. Thus, redemption through the mutual working of Word and Spirit brings about a loving and gracious *fellowship* as the locus of witness and new life. The church is thus not an accident of history, nor is it supplemental to the drama of redemption. The fellowship of the church is vital to the redemption of the world since God wills that we "comprehend with all the saints" the depth of the love of Christ (Ephesians 3:18). The charismatic structure of the church facilitates the *koinonia* at work in this *mutual* comprehension of Christ's love.

The church as participant in the fellowship of the Father and the Son through the Spirit implies that spiritual gifts are *relational, interactive and governed by the love of God*. As Michael Welker has shown us in his book *God the Spirit*, the gifts of the Spirit are *interactive and relational*. Discernment guides prophecy; interpretation explains tongues; wisdom guides the proper use of knowledge; evangelism points those who are healed to the good news to which the healing bears witness; faith keeps scholarship loyal to the proclamation of the church, and scholarship keeps faith open up to critical questions, and so forth. In spiritual gifts, church members interact in ways that are grace-filled and edifying. Since spiritual gifts are relational and interactive, they represent the fundamental structure of the church.[4]

As a result of Pentecost, the church was formed with a *charismatic structure*. This structure is fluid and relational, because spiritual gifts are graced ways of relating to each other that depend on the will of the Spirit at work among us and the contextual needs of the ministry of the Word of God (1 Corinthians 12:11). Spiritual gifts signify and facilitate the graced relationships necessary to expand our capacities to receive and apply the grace that comes to us through Word and sacrament. We can take this to mean that the *charismata* (spiritual gifts) represent the formation of edifying relationships in the church that inspire us in many different and unique ways to bear one another's burdens, affirm one another's dignity and worth before God, and build one another up in Christ. Spiritual gifts open the church to God's grace and show forth signs of this grace in a graceless world.

Placed within the framework of the charismatic structure of the church, the ordained ministry in relation to preaching and sacraments can be explained in ways that avoid the problems that accompany clericalism, or an understanding of the church dominated by the clergy. The *koinonia* of the Spirit experienced in the interactive charismatic life of the church implies a mutually accountable and edifying ministry in the church, involving all of the people of God. We will conclude this paper with a reflection on preaching and sacrament in relation to the charismatic structure of the church.

---

[4] Michael Welker, *God the Spirit* (Minneapolis: Augsburg/Fortress, 1994) 148.

Preaching, Sacrament, and the Charismatic Structure of the Church

There is no way to overestimate the significance of preaching and Scripture in channeling God's grace to the church. The gospel of Jesus and the Scriptural witness come to us through the very breath of God so that we may have the wisdom and the power to be saved through faith in Jesus Christ (2 Timothy 3:15,16). The Scriptures are inspired, but not in the sense of representing a static deposit of revealed truths that we can systematize into idols of ink and paper.

This fundamentalist illusion of Scripture as a static deposit can cause the church to presume that it has the final word on all of life's questions and challenges. There is no need under this modernist illusion to dialogue or to learn, to grow or to change. Following 2 Timothy 3:15, 16, the Scriptures should be embraced as a living witness to Jesus Christ through the Spirit of God, inspiring ever-increasing faith in Jesus and granting us ongoing wisdom and power to serve one another and the world in Christ's name. As breathed by the Spirit, the Scriptures are a living guide or measure of our worship and witness and not a static deposit to master and control according to our own self-serving ends.

Because of the living breath of God, the gospel of the Scriptures bursts forth with signs of life in the charismatic structure of the church. Spiritual gifts, then, help to keep the apostolic Word of the Scriptures alive and relevant within the ongoing gracious and gifted interactions of the people of God as they grow up into the full stature of Christ. Furthermore, spiritual gifts are always accountable to the living witness of the apostolic Word of the Scriptures as Paul clearly notes in his struggle with the pneumatically gifted members of the Corinthian congregation (1 Corinthians 14:37).

Within the charismatic structure of the church, the Spirit functions through the Scriptures as a living book of both freedom and order to guide our gracious interactions with one another. In fact, the Scriptures themselves are a universally relevant and binding gift of the Spirit to the church in order to guide the particular and diverse charismatic structure of the church in its ongoing life and mission.

My approach to Scripture might be regarded by some as dangerously vague. Some might see in my description of Scripture a fluid and imprecise understanding of how the Scriptures speak to us. Are there not truths clearly revealed in Scripture on which we can rely? Certainly. As Karl Barth reminds us, the revelation of God is *verbal* as well as personal.[5] Many Evangelicals have misread Barth on this point. Barth did not deny that revelation through

---

[5] Karl Barth, *Church Dogmatics* I/1 (T&T Clark Publishers, 1956) 139.

Scripture is verbal; he only denied that this verbal witness can be viewed as a static deposit to be mastered and placed at the disposal of our systems and ideologies. Notice what Barth states: "The personal character of God's Word means, not its deverbalizing, but the posing of an absolute barrier against reducing its wording to a human system." For Barth, God's placing divine revelation at our disposal in this way "would mean his allowing us to gain control over His Word, to fit it into our own designs, and thus to shut up ourselves against Him to our own ruin."[6]

The Bible is verbally inspired and does contain truths that we confess and live by. But this text and its truths are living and active, constantly channeling the power and wisdom of the Spirit to us by the grace of God in diverse ways in the midst of gifted interactions among the people of God. Those ordained as leaders among us preach and teach the Word of God in a way that constantly places Christ and His Biblical witness before us as the foundation of our gifted interactions and ministries. Yet, these leaders are also gifts among other gifted members of the congregation, despite their special functions as ministers among us. They are accountable to us as we are to them. Ultimately, the canonical witness through the Spirit inspires, empowers and guides us all in our gifted praise and service.

The charismatic structure of the church also serves to expand the field of the grace that comes to us in the gospel. Without this structure, preaching tends to become intellectualistic and abstract. In the Protestant focus on the Word of God, pneumatology has tended to be dominated by the exposition of the Biblical text and the inward illumination of the text in the mind of the believer. This dominant emphasis on the *noetic* function of the Spirit has dogged Protestant theology from Schleiermacher to Barth and has hindered the believer's participation in the full breadth of the Spirit's work by focusing on the illumination and subsequent knowledge of revelation.

More recent Protestant theologians have attempted to refer to the Spirit's work along the lines of a more holistic and transformational "new creation" motif in an effort to transcend the limitations of confining the work of the Spirit to the revelational and the noetic. A greater role for a diversity of *charismata* in our understanding of the ministry of the church to serve a multiplicity of needs will go far in enhancing this positive trend toward a more holistic pneumatology understood in the context of new creation.

In addition, the restriction of the Spirit's work to the realm of the noetic has tended to avoid or devalue the ecstatic and depth experiences of God in favor of the cognitive and the rational responses to the Word. Gordon Fee has

---
[6] Barth, 139.

expressed the view of many Pentecostals when remarking that "contrary to the opinion of many, spiritual edification can take place in ways other than through the cortex of the brain."[7]

More of an emphasis on the gifts of the Spirit among all the people of God will allow for a broad spectrum of gifted activity that will involve the divine claim on the whole person, including the depths of the subconscious mind, the life of the body, and the disciplines of rational thinking.

We need to say something about the sacramental life of the church as well. By the power of the Spirit, the gospel is further proclaimed with sacramental signs of baptism and Eucharist. We participate in the grace of this gospel through baptism and Eucharist. Because Christ was baptized in solidarity with sinners, a solidarity that led Him to the cross, we can now identify with Christ in His death and resurrection through baptism. The Eucharist extends this participation in God's grace in the ongoing life of the Christian.

Again, the charismatic structure of the church expands the field of the receptivity of grace that comes to us in the sacraments. In sacramental traditions, the temptation has been to objectify the grace of God in the giving of the sacrament, which resulted in a "ritual distancing of God" from the laity. More of an emphasis on the *charismata* will open the sacraments up as wellsprings of a communal life that involve all the people of God as active participants. As Clark Pinnock stated so well:

> As well as receiving the sacraments from the Spirit, we need to cultivate openness to the gifts of the Spirit. The Spirit is present beyond liturgy in a wider circle. There is a flowing that manifests itself as power to bear witness, heal the sick, prophesy, praise God enthusiastically, perform miracles and more. There is a liberty to celebrate, an ability to dream and see visions, a release of Easter life. There are impulses of power in the move of the Spirit to transform and commission disciples to become instruments of the mission.[8]

Also, as Karl Rahner has pointed out, the gifts of God's presence in the church can serve to "shock" the institutional life of the church and throw it back to the very core of its life in the presence of God, reminding it also that its existence and purposes are penultimate and relative to the coming kingdom of God in power.[9]

---

[7] Gordon Fee, *God's Empowering Presence: The Holy Spirit in the Letters of Paul* (Peabody, MA: Hendrickson, 1994) 129.

[8] Clark Pinnock, *Flame of Love: A Theology of the Holy Spirit* (Downers Grove, IL: InterVarsity, 1996) 129.

[9] Karl Rahner, "Religious Enthusiasm and the Experience of Grace," *Theological Investigations 16* (New York: Seabury, 1979) 35-59.

Conclusion: The Word of Grace in a Graceless World

The charismatic structure of the church participates in the *koinonia* of God as Father, Son and Spirit. Founded on Christ and filled with the Spirit, the charismatically diverse church reaches by the Spirit for this *koinonia* and seeks to open it up redemptively to the world. This *koinonia* of diverse gifts provides the context in which the ordained clergy can lead and guide the church into the mysteries of Christ through preaching and sacrament. The Spirit works through the gifts to help the church receive gospel and sacrament in diverse and relational ways that are specific, concrete and contextual.

This is finally the purpose of the charismatic structure of the church. The Spirit fills us in a way that enhances our unique reception of grace through preaching and sacrament so that we might variously help others be receptive as well. This is how we build one another up in God's love. May all things be done unto the diverse edification of the body of Christ so that the church can show forth signs of grace in a graceless world.

12

Encountering the Truine God

Spirituality Since the Azusa Street Revival

Simon Chan

Introduction

Philip Turner, the former dean of Berkeley Divinity School at Yale, reveals that what effectively weaned him from the liberal theology he was fed as a student in an Episcopal seminary was his spending 10 years in Africa as a missionary, where he encountered Nicene Christianity as a living reality.[1] Turner's experience of theological liberalism is not peculiar to ministers in the ECUSA (Episcopal Church in the United States of America); the scenario is played out in most mainline Protestant denominations in the West in varying degrees. At the same time, we also see many examples of people like Turner whose exposure to a vibrant Christianity has decisively changed their theological paradigm. A friend of mine doing his Ph.D. at a very liberal seminary in California (which I will not name) told me the story of one of his professors whose comfortable Christianity was thrown into confusion after a summer's visit to Cambodia, where he saw a kind of Christianity very different from his own. The Spirit of God continues to move in surprising ways.

These stories of conversion illustrate the power of a lived theology or spirituality. It is *as* spirituality that the true strength of Pentecostalism is to be

---

[1] Philip Turner, "An Unworkable Theology," *First Things,* June-July 2005: 10-12.

found. Pentecostal spirituality arose from a desire of many Christians for a fuller reality of God's presence, and they found it in the powerful working of the Holy Spirit. Today, Pentecostalism is a highly globalized, grassroots movement. Its theology is firmly grounded in the living faith of the church and in the mission field. Pentecostals must never lose sight of this fact. Whatever secondary theology Pentecostal scholars develop, they must help the church to sustain its primary theology. That is to say, our reflections cannot be too far removed from the living faith of the millions of Pentecostals scattered throughout the world. This approach gives rise to two implicit questions I would like to address in this paper:

1. What does reflection on the living faith of Pentecostals entail?
2. How does global Pentecostalism affect our theological reflection?

These two questions have to do with the "content" and "form," or the "text" and "context," of Pentecostal spirituality respectively. I use the terms *content* and *form* or *text* and *context* very loosely, because they are not so easily separated from one another. The content of the Pentecostal faith always assumes a certain form; it always exists within a specific context.

Pentecostal Spirituality as a Distinctive Understanding of the Holy Spirit

Ask any Pentecostal what distinguishes him or her from other Christians and the instinctive response is likely to be "the special work of the Holy Spirit in my life." He or she may not be able to explain what is so special about the work of the Holy Spirit, but will be able to describe in some detail what happened before and after being "filled with the Spirit." In some inchoate way, the filling of the Spirit is also linked to the four- or fivefold gospel. This level of conceptualization may be called *primary theology*.[2] What are we to make of the Pentecostal's primary theology? Here is where the work of the theologian comes in.

Pentecostals give special focus to the third person of the Trinity. But how is this to be understood theologically? The distinct person of the Spirit emerges in His creating the divine narrative, the story of the triune God with respect to the future; and this divine narrative includes His indwelling of believers

---

[2] The distinction between *primary* and *secondary* theology is more frequently employed in the field of liturgical theology, perhaps because of one of its central concerns, namely, the relationship between *lex orandi* and *lex credendi*. See, e.g., Geoffrey Wainwright, *Doxology: The Praise of God in Worship, Doctrine and Life* (London: Epworth, 1980), chs. 7 and 8; and Aidan Cavanagh, *On Liturgical Theology* (New York: Pueblo Publishing, 1984).

and the church.³ Putting it differently, what this focus does is that it heightens and advances the gospel trajectory. The work of the triune God takes on greater depth and intensity as the gospel story continues to unfold with the Holy Spirit's descent upon the church on the Day of Pentecost to constitute an assembly of ordinary people into the body of Christ and to direct her toward final consummation as the bride of Christ.

In understanding the distinctive work of the Spirit in the church, we also deepen our understanding of the work of the Father and the Son. The Spirit who is sent from the Father to indwell the body of Christ is the Spirit of sonship by whom we cry, "*Abba,* Father" (Romans 8:15). The Spirit's work as third person fulfills the work of the Father and the Son, or better still, the work of the Father through the Son (hence, the four/fivefold gospel). Jesus speaks of "greater works" the disciples will do because of His going to the Father. This has usually been understood as a reference to the coming of the Spirit. That is to say, the coming of the Spirit alters the believers' relationship to the Father and the Son in such a way that what the disciples of Jesus do after the Pentecost event could be said to be something different: "greater works." However, that phrase itself is understood.

What made Pentecostals different from other Christians is the way they appropriate the work of the Spirit into their Christian lives, and in so doing, they give to the person and work of the Spirit a distinct focus. This is encapsulated in the classical doctrine of baptism in the Holy Spirit. As I have noted elsewhere, the early Pentecostals may have been quite mistaken in their *explicit* theology of Spirit baptism, but their spiritual instinct was basically sound. *Through* this doctrine they were seeking to articulate something of the "empowering presence" of the Spirit in the Christian life.⁴ They might have expressed the truth rather badly, but it was not, for that reason, any less real.

The challenge for later generations of Pentecostals who have acquired the conceptual tools to articulate their faith in more precise terms is to press ahead from where their forebears had left off. The Holy Spirit, naturally, remains central to the Pentecostal theological enterprise. This focus on the Spirit opens many new vistas for Pentecostals. The recent work of Amos Yong has highlighted the importance of the pneumatological question in dealing with critical issues facing the 21st-century church, like religious pluralism, Christianity and

---

³ Cf. Robert Jenson, *Systematic Theology: The Triune God,* vol. 1 (New York/Oxford: Oxford UP, 1997): "To say that the Holy Spirit is without qualification 'one of the Trinity' is to say that the dynamism of God's life is a narrative causation in and so of God" (p. 160).

⁴ Simon Chan, *Pentecostal Theology and the Christian Spiritual Tradition* (Sheffield, England: Sheffield Academic Press, 2000) 40-72.

science, and globalization.⁵ But undergirding these concerns is a critical question: How has the distinctive identity of the Spirit in the economy of the triune God been addressed? Any theology, including a theology of religions, will not be true to Pentecostal spirituality if it does not take full cognizance of the distinctive identity of the Spirit.

Amos Yong's pneumatological approach to other religions may be cited as an example of this failure.⁶ While I think that Yong has raised the right questions, I am not as certain that he has provided the way forward for Pentecostals. For one thing, his Trinitarian theology of the religions fails to take seriously the concrete narrative of the triune God; rather, what we see is a Trinitarian *pattern* of working expressed in terms of metaphysical principles as a way of finding common ground with other religions. For example, Word and Spirit are understood as the poles of concreteness and dynamism that are necessary for discerning the divine presence and activity (the pneumatological) in other religions.⁷ While Yong does not deny the status of the Spirit as the third person of the Trinity, his pneumatological approach to the religions tends to treat the Spirit modalistically, largely as God's action in the world. This is manifestly inadequate. As Ralph del Colle has pointed out in another context, our pneumatology remains incomplete if the Spirit is seen only as presence and power and not *also* as third person.⁸ But what is distinctive of the Spirit as third person, especially in relation to human beings? Del Colle introduces the concept of the *enhypostasia* of the Spirit. This is analogous to the two enhypostases of the Son. First, the Son is generated by the Father immanently, and in the economy of God the Son as a human person comes through generation (from the Virgin's womb).

But there is a second enhypostasis of the Son: "The eternal Son now incarnate . . . in his human nature undergoes an in-personing in the Spirit,"⁹ that is, He was anointed by the Holy Spirit for the mission of God. Analogously, we are born as persons, but by the indwelling Holy Spirit we become more fully the persons we

---

⁵ Amos Yong, *The Spirit Poured Out on All Flesh: Pentecostalism and the Possibility of Global Theology* (Grand Rapids: Baker Academic, 2005). Yong is probably the one Pentecostal theologian who has done more than any other to engage global issues from a pneumatological perspective, but essentially from within the framework of late modernity. See work cited below and his earlier book *Spirit-Word Community: Theological Hermeneutics in Trinitarian Perspective* (Aldershot, England: Ashgate, 2002).

⁶ *Beyond the Impasse: Toward a Pneumatological Theology of Religions* (Grand Rapids: Baker, 2003).

⁷ *Beyond the Impasse*, ch. 2.

⁸ Ralph del Colle, "The Holy Spirit: Presence, Power, Person," *Theological Studies* 62, no. 2 (2001): 322-40.

⁹ Colle, 336.

are meant to be. In Christ, we experience full personhood. In short, to recognize the distinctive work of the Holy Spirit as third person is to see the necessity of His work of making us into Christ-conformed persons (no longer "I" but Christ living in me), being indwelled by the One who is the "giving gift," so that we become persons-in-communion and God's gift to the world.

Spirit as presence and power culminates in Spirit as person, so that "the teleology of presence and power culminates in love . . . a love enabled by the divine personhood that in the Spirit's self-effacing modality of being person constitutes the church as persons-in-communion."[10] The mission of the Spirit is essentially to draw people into communion with the Trinity, to make them *ecclesial* people. What Yong's pneumatological approach to the world religions lacks is an equal emphasis on the personhood of the Holy Spirit, along with the Spirit as God's presence and activity. Without it, our Trinitarian theology of religions is incomplete.[11]

The issue could be restated as a question of the relation between the church and Creation. It is sometimes argued that if the Holy Spirit is confined to the church, it would make pneumatology too narrow and exclusive.[12] Such a pneumatology would indeed be too narrow if the church is conceived as a subspecies of Creation. This view, in fact, is based on a particular way of reading the Biblical narrative in which the work of Creation becomes the key to understanding all of God's subsequent work. Creation . . . fall . . . redemption, or in Yong's terms, Creation . . . re-creation . . . new creation, sums up the Biblical plot.[13] This way of reading the Biblical narrative assumes that the church is only an instrument to restore the fallen creation.[14]

But there is another way of reading the Biblical narrative and that is to see Creation as the *backdrop* for understanding God's ultimate plan for creation, namely, to build His church.[15] The work of *Creator Spiritus* must then be

---

[10] Colle, 338.

[11] One indication of the failure to implement a fully Trinitarian theology of religions is the reticence to address the issue of evangelization as part of the total Christian understanding of religions. E.g., Yong is quite clear about what false evangelizations are but is not very clear about how true evangelization could be an essential part of a theology of religions. See Yong, *The Spirit Poured Out,* 257.

[12] Yong, *Beyond the Impasse,* 118, referring to Pinnock's "An Inclusivist View," in *Four Views on Salvation in a Pluralistic World,* ed. Dennis L. Okholm and Timothy R. Phillips (Grand Rapids: Zondervan, 1995) 105.

[13] *Beyond the Impasse,* 36.

[14] For example, Jürgen Moltmann, *The Spirit of Life: A Universal Affirmation* (Minneapolis: Fortress, 1992) 230.

[15] This reading has found support from a non-supersessionist understanding of the relationship between Israel and the church. Non-supersessionism sees Israel and the

understood as primarily with reference to the church. God made the world in order to make the church, not vice versa. Human beings are born into the world in order to be reborn into the church. As Robert Jenson puts it so succinctly, "The church *is* the world's agenda. What the world is there to do is to provide the raw materials out of which God creates His church."[16] Or, if I may paraphrase Lindbeck's famous phrase, the church absorbs the creation, rather than creation the church.[17]

If the church is simply an agent of creation, then there is a need to find a way of relating Christ to the larger world outside the church. The concept of the cosmic Christ is introduced to deal with this situation. This sets up a dualism between the particular Christ and the cosmic Christ,[18] with the former being subsumed under the latter just as the church is subsumed under creation. When the church is subsumed under creation, two consequences follow. First, there is the tendency to distinguish the Spirit's work in two distinct realms. The Spirit works one way in the church and another way in creation. And if the church is merely an instrument to fulfill God's purpose for creation, then the Spirit's working in creation may well be more determinative. This means, secondly, that the finality and uniqueness of Christ will have to be redefined in terms of what the Spirit is doing within the larger creation rather than in terms of what He is doing in the church.

This is the usual strategy adopted by an inclusivist view of religion. But inclusivists will have difficulty making meaningful predication of the concept of the uniqueness of Christ. In what sense is Christ decisive and unique if the Spirit of God is in some way present in non-Christian movements? Sometimes it is taken to mean no more than both Christians and non-Christians sharing certain common values which Christians identify as signs of the kingdom of God.[19] But by

---

church as irreplaceable and therefore as ends in themselves rather than serving an instrumental purpose such as restoring creation. See Douglas Harink, *Paul Among the Postliberals* (Grand Rapids: Brazos, 2003) 151-84.

[16] Robert Jenson, "The Church's Responsibility for the World," in *The Two Cities of God: The Church's Responsibility for the Earthly City*, ed. Carl E. Braaten and Robert W. Jenson (Grand Rapids: Eerdmans, 1997) 4.

[17] George A. Lindbeck, *The Nature of Doctrine: Religion and Theology in a Postliberal Age* (Philadelphia: Westminster, 1984) 118: "It is the text . . . which absorbs the world rather than the world the text." Lindbeck here is referring to the typological interpretation of the ancient church in which "the religion instantiated in the Scripture . . . defines being, truth, goodness, and beauty, and the nonscriptural exemplifications of these realities need to be transformed into figures (or types or antitypes) of the scriptural ones." Such a hermeneutic implies an ecclesiology very similar to the one advocated here.

[18] Yong, *Beyond the Impasse*, 47-48.

[19] Yong, *The Spirit Poured Out*, 250, 256.

the same token, there is no reason why Buddhists could not regard these values present in Christianity as the presence of the "cosmic" Buddha.

But if creation is consummated in the church, then the concept of the cosmic Christ needs to be redefined. The real cosmic Christ is not some christic principle mysteriously embedded in the world (à la Panikkar)[20] but the *totus Christus*. There is, therefore, no dualism between the particular Christ and the cosmic Christ. In the continuation of the gospel story, the particular Christ who ascended to heaven sends the Holy Spirit to indwell the church, making it the *totus Christus* that transcends space and time—that *is* the cosmic Christ.

This framework for understanding the relationship between the Holy Spirit and the church is very much in line with the Pentecostal spiritual instinct. Pentecostals have always favored the concrete "old, old story" over abstract principles, even if these principles are thought to be faithful reinterpretations of the gospel story. The translation of the story into metaphysics leaves out something vital in Pentecostal spirituality—namely, the experience of the fully embodied story of the triune God, which includes the story of the baptism in the Holy Spirit to make the church the embodied Christ to the world. The countless Pentecostal testimonies always have this common thread: the reality of the persons of the Spirit and of Jesus. If anything, the danger for Pentecostals sometimes is the "over-hypostasization" of the Spirit.[21] But the abuse only shows what the correct emphasis ought to be: the distinct personhood of the Spirit. A pneumatological contribution to a theology of religions must proceed from the concrete gospel story, and this includes the story of the Spirit *as* third person in the church. Any theology that circumvents this cannot be said to be faithful to Pentecostal spirituality.

Pentecostal Spirituality as a Global Phenomenon

Pentecostal spirituality as the experience of the third person in the church implies that to be truly Pentecostal is to be open to the continuation of the gospel, and this means the development of doctrine.[22] The seed of Pentecostal spirituality planted in Azusa needs to develop and grow or it will fossilize. We go back to the past not in order to canonize one particular period of our history (the "golden age" of Pentecostalism), but to reset our trajectory, if need be, to ensure that it is in line with the narrative of the triune God.

---

[20] Raimundo Panikkar, *The Unknown Christ of Hinduism*, rev. ed. (London: Darton, Longman & Todd, 1981).

[21] E.g., David Yonggi Cho's *The Holy Spirit, My Senior Partner* (Altamonte Springs: Creation House, 1989).

[22] Simon Chan, "The Church and the Development of Doctrine," *Journal of Pentecostal Theology* 13, no. 1 (2004): 57-77.

A Pentecostal spirituality that is eschatologically open to the Spirit's continuing work in the church is a spirituality that is open to the Christian tradition. Pentecostal spirituality is not the tradition, but an essential component of it, a tributary to the river of the great tradition. Thus Pentecostal spirituality is best understood within and sustained by the church catholic (or universal), since it is the distinctive task of the third person of the Trinity to realize the church (as explained above). The church is where His distinctive identity is revealed. Perhaps the early Pentecostals grasped this truth implicitly, which accounted for their ecumenical impulse. This catholic tendency, however, is being threatened from two opposite directions. One is to subsume the Pentecostal Movement under a narrowly defined evangelicalism;[23] the other is to diffuse the Spirit into the world.[24] The first undermines the ecumenical breadth of the Pentecostal Movement; the second undermines its dogmatic specificity. Perhaps the greatest challenge for Pentecostal spirituality in the 21st century is to develop further ecumenical breath and dogmatic depth without losing one or the other.

Pentecostals themselves can be hopeful that such a challenge can be met because Pentecostalism at its best has been able to navigate between extremes and hold seemingly opposite positions in tension. Pentecostals have their feet planted in both heaven and earth simultaneously. In Grant Wacker's terms, it is a spirituality of "heaven below."[25] This ability, according to Harvey Cox, defies "schematic interpretation":

> Why . . . when worship is so spontaneous and highly emotional, do the ministers and other leaders usually appear to be so securely in control of the services? If adherents truly believe—as they often say—that we are living in the last days, then why do they save money, buy homes, and send their children to school with more regularity than other people who share their general social status? If they hold to the Biblical teaching about the man being the "head of the woman"—as they insist they do—then why

---

[23] This is the strategy that John Carpenter recommends. Carpenter would like to see Pentecostals affirm their links with only the evangelicalism growing out of the Reformed-Puritan tradition. "Genuine Pentecostal Traditioning: Rooting Pentecostalism in Its Evangelical Soil: A Reply to Simon Chan," *Asian Journal of Pentecostal Studies* 6, no. 2 (2003): 303-26. See my reply, "The Renewal of Pentecostalism: A Response to John Carpenter," *Asian Journal of Pentecostal Studies* 7, no. 2 (2004): 315-25.

[24] This is the difficulty I have with Amos Yong's pneumatological approach to other religions. The criteria for discerning the Spirit are essentially moral, while dogmatic criteria are conspicuously absent. See *The Spirit Poured Out*, 247-57.

[25] Grant Wacker, *Heaven Below: Early Pentecostals and American Culture* (Cambridge: Harvard UP, 2001). "The genius of the Pentecostal Movement lay in its ability to hold two seemingly incompatible impulses in productive tension" (p. 10).

do so many women not only join Pentecostal congregations but bring their husbands and relatives along?[26]

Unfortunately, Pentecostalism has not always operated at its best by failing to hold these opposing impulses together. Sometimes futuristic eschatology is so emphasized that one wonders if there is anything worth doing on earth besides winning souls and sending them over to the other shore. At other times the future is practically forgotten—swallowed up by an over-realized eschatology. How are Pentecostals to sustain their "heaven below" spirituality over the long haul? What must they do to maintain the Biblical eschatological tension? The future of Pentecostal spirituality will depend on how the last question is answered.

There are three emerging trends in present-day global Pentecostalism that may well provide an answer to this question. The first is the emergence of a sacramental theology. It has been observed that Pentecostal spirituality bears deep affinities with the primal religious instincts found in many non-Western societies.[27] One area of convergence is the primal concept of a sacramental universe, "the conviction that the 'physical' acts as the vehicle for 'spiritual' power."[28] Unfortunately, the historical circumstances of classical Pentecostalism in the West have prevented it from developing its sacramental side.[29] But in the non-Western world, the implicit sacramentalism finds an appropriate context to come to self-conscious expression, as seen in some indigenous Charismatic groups in Africa and in Asia.[30] In the primal religions, however, the sacramental worldview frequently includes the belief

---

[26] Harvey Cox, *Fire From Heaven: The Rise of Pentecostal Spirituality and the Reshaping of Religion in the Twenty-First Century* (Cambridge, MA: De Capo, 2001) 172-73.

[27] Harold Turner, "The Primal Religions of the World and Their Study," in *Australian Essays in World Religions* (Bedford Park: Australian Association of World Religions, 1977) 27-37. Cf. Kwame Bediako, *Jesus in Africa: The Christian Gospel in African History and Experience* (Ghana: Regnum Africa, 2000) 91-106, 210-30.

[28] Turner, "Primal Religions," 32.

[29] I am thinking primarily of Pentecostalism's emergence from the anti-sacramental Free Church context and its alignment with rationalistic fundamentalism, as evidenced in its advocacy of doctrines like the inerrancy of Scripture.

[30] E.g., J. Ade Aina, "The Church's Healing Ministry," in *A Reader in African Christian Theology,* rev. ed., ed. John Parratt (London: SPCK, 1997) 104-8. Aina defends the use of "blessed water" in the church's healing ministry. For Asia, see Myung Soo Park, "Korean Pentecostal Spirituality as Manifested in the Testimonies of Believers of the Yoido Full Gospel Church," in *David Yonggi Cho: A Close Look at His Theology and Ministry,* ed. Wonsuk Ma, William W. Menzies, and Hyeon-sung Bae (Baguio, Philippines: APTS Press, 2004) 50-51. As a pastor for some years in Singapore, Malaysia, and the Philippines, I had encountered many instances where non-Christian parents would allow their children to go to church as long as they did not get baptized. They had a better grasp of the sacramental nature of baptism: at baptism, one became a "real" Christian; it was, for them, a point of no return.

that spiritual power could be manipulated by means of physical objects, formulas and incantations. This propensity to control is designated by the term *magic*. The line separating the acknowledgment of a sacramental universe and the attempt to control it is a thin one, and Christians, no less, are sometimes tempted to exercise their own brand of magic.

We see this among the Third Wavers, who often speak of the need to understand the operating principles in the spiritual world and to discover the techniques to deal with it, such as naming territorial spirits in order to free up a locality for evangelism. One of the challenges facing Pentecostals in the coming years is how to develop a sacramental spirituality without succumbing to magic.

A second trend revolves around the primitivist impulse. It is almost a truism that Pentecostalism was, at least in its initial phase, a restorationist movement, seeking to bring back "the apostolic faith" to the church.[31] But in recent times, Third Wavers are moving beyond the faith and practices of the early apostles; they see "apostleship" as largely an issue of authority as well, more specifically the authority of *individuals*.[32] As Peter Wagner, probably the most conspicuous representative of the Third Wave, puts it, "The biggest difference between New Apostolic Christianity and traditional Christianity is the amount of spiritual authority delegated by the Holy Spirit to individuals."[33]

Wagner is right in identifying the issue of authority, but wrong in his understanding of its nature and how it is legitimated. He fails to see that any legitimate apostolic ministry will have to be established on the basis of *historical continuity* with the apostles, and this means accepting the apostolic succession of "traditional Christianity." Consequently, Wagner's kind of apostleship is simply an imitation of the real—a counterfeit!

Perhaps an illustration might help to show why historical continuity is so essential. How does one become a bona fide member of the Salvation Army? One does not belong to the Salvation Army simply by donning a uniform and marching down the streets to the tune of "Onward Christian Soldiers." To become a part of the Army, one needs to be inducted into it by people who belong to the Army. Some form of actual link must be established with that historical movement if one is to become a genuine part of it.

This is what apostolic succession is about. But despite the muddleheadedness, Third Wavers are right about some things. While they may have

---

[31] This has been widely noted by historians of Pentecostalism. See e.g., Edith L. Blumhofer, *Restoring the Faith: The Assemblies of God, Pentecostalism, and American Culture* (Urbana and Chicago: U of Illinois P, 1993).

[32] Blumhofer describes this development as having "potentially frightening implications" (*Restoring the Faith*, 3).

[33] *http://www.globalharvest.org/index.asp?action=apostref.*

corrupted sacramental theology into magic, and apostolic tradition into authoritarianism, they have raised the right questions for the future of Pentecostalism. If Pentecostal spirituality is to remain vibrant, be self-corrective and see healthy development, it needs a sound traditioning structure; and this means coming to terms with the dogma of the church, with its sacraments and authority. Elsewhere, I have suggested what a Pentecostal ecclesiology might be like[34] and what sort of ecclesial structure is necessary.[35] I hope that the emerging Pentecostal scholarship will be "led by the Spirit" to engage in further reflection on, and systematic development of, these concerns.

The two foregoing trends inevitably entail a third: An apostolic church (i.e., a church existing in historical continuity with the apostles) with a sacramental theology is sustained by a living liturgy. In the last two decades or so, some classical Pentecostals are coming to recognize the centrality of liturgical celebration of word and sacrament. They recognize that the liturgy is the primary means by which the truth of who they are is kept alive. The future of Pentecostal spirituality will be determined by the extent to which it is integrated with the Christian liturgy. This is what we are seeing in the so-called convergence movement, which "seeks to blend or merge the essential elements in the Christian faith represented historically in three major streams of thought and practice: the Charismatic, Evangelical/Reformed and Liturgical/Sacramental."[36]

> God's holy fire is now being kindled in furnaces of faith where liturgical forms, once considered lifeless, are no longer creating the fear of moving into error. Liturgies are being reintroduced into the church to bring a balance in worship among all the elements Scripture revealed as necessary for worshiping God in spirit and truth.[37]

One of the concrete expressions of the convergence movement is found in the fast-growing International Communion of the Charismatic Episcopal Church. What the ICCEC and other convergence churches have demonstrated is that being Pentecostal and liturgical are not mutually exclusive; rather, one becomes more truly Pentecostal by practicing the liturgy! Furthermore, as churches acknowledge the centrality of the Eucharist in worship, adopt a common lectionary,

---

[34] "Mother Church: Toward a Pentecostal Ecclesiology," *Pneuma: The Journal of the Society for Pentecostal Studies* 22, no. 2 (Fall 2000): 177-208.

[35] "The Church and the Development of Doctrine," 67-72.

[36] Wayne Boosahda and Randy Sly, "The Convergence Movement," in *The Complete Library of Christian Worship,* vol. 2, ed. Robert Webber (Nashville, TN: Star Song, 1994) 134-40.

[37] Boosahda and Sly, "The Convergence Movement," 138.

observe the feasts in the church calendar, and use the ancient signs and symbols, they become deeply aware of themselves as existing in solidarity with the church worldwide and throughout history: the one, holy, catholic and apostolic church. This sets the stage for true ecumenism to take place.[38] For what truly unites the people of God is not merely a set of beliefs professed, but the lived faith actualized in liturgical celebration.

Conclusion

If the Pentecostal Movement is to continue to grow as a vibrant spirituality characterized by a comprehensive vision of the church catholic and a dogmatic specificity with respect to its understanding of the Holy Spirit, Pentecostals themselves must continue to nurture these emerging trends. To do so, they must also take certain corrective measures.

First, they must assess their current practice of modeling their worship after the world of entertainment. The fundamental answer to the worship crisis is to develop a liturgical spirituality. This is not a matter of choice or "taste" but is required by our distinctive Trinitarian theology.[39]

Second, they must be open to doctrinal development, and this implies, among other things, engagement with other Christians and non-Christians. We cannot do otherwise if we believe that the Holy Spirit is the future of the divine narrative. It would be a mistake to look back nostalgically to "the good old days." Romanticism and conservatism will only stunt the church's growth. Growing up is always painful and adjustments are necessary, but in the end, the church of the Spirit will attain the full stature of Christ. This is a hope we share with all who confess belief in one, holy, catholic and apostolic church.

---

[38] Perhaps the most difficult problem for ecumenism is that of apostolic succession.

[39] See my forthcoming book *Liturgical Theology: The Church as Worshipping Community* (Downers Grove, IL: InterVarsity, 2006).

13

Pentecostal Eschatology
What Happened When the Wave Hit the West End of the Ocean

Wonsuk Ma

Introduction

As half a billion Pentecostal believers celebrate 100 years of growth, Asia has reason to be thankful to the Lord and to early Pentecostal pioneers in North America and Asia. As the spiritual eruption made waves across the Pacific Ocean, its power generated varying effects in different parts of Asia, just like the recent tsunami force destroyed areas across the Indian Ocean.

It is completely reasonable to expect continuity, as well as discontinuity, between the Azusa Street spirituality and what is found among Asian Pentecostals today. Azusa's unique spiritual tradition continues, but the temporal and spatial gaps between the extreme ends of the Pacific Ocean resulted in marked differences. These are often a creative modification of existing traditions or even the emergence of something quite new in Asia.

How much direct correlation one can trace between these two entities is another challenging question. There is no doubt the early Pentecostal Movement began

---

*Scripture references in this chapter are taken from the *New International Version* unless otherwise noted.

as a powerful missionary force, and many Pentecostal missionaries reached parts of Asia and preached the Pentecostal message. However, an increasing number of studies, primarily based on Asian evidence, have issued a challenge to the "one-fountainhead" theory of the movement, that is, the Azusa Street Mission as the mother of all Pentecostal churches.[1]

Asian Pentecostalism has come a very long way, and now it is a vanguard in its growth and development. The size of Pentecostal Christianity in Asia, around 135 million according to Barrett and others, is quite comparable to its counterparts in Africa (142 million) and Latin America (142 million).[2] However, what makes up this proportion in Asia is surprisingly distinct: (1) the astonishingly high proportion of Pentecostals to the total Christian population (43.1 percent in Asia, in comparison with 29.4 percent and 40 percent in Latin America and Africa, respectively); and (2) an equally stretching "growth-room" of Pentecostal Christianity with the total Asian population to reach 27 times that of the Pentecostal-Charismatics in Asia. This is in comparison with 3.7 times and 6.2 times in Latin America and Africa, respectively, considering their total populations.[3] This expectation may not be a distant dream, but may actually happen in the near future. For example, the robust expansion of the house church networks in China, currently estimated as 70 million, can impact the topography of Asian Christianity in the coming decades.[4]

My reflection is intentionally theological, and this focus comes from two assumptions: (1) Theological conviction directly influences behavior, and (2) theology is shaped through constant interaction between the imported (thus, foreign) message and the real-life situation where the message should be received as the Word of God to receptors. Using hindsight, many feel that Asian Pentecostal theology has been shaped not through intentional reflections, but often by default; that is, by the lack of intentional action in preserving Azusa theological traditions and in bringing these to an active dialogue with a given sociocultural context.

---

[1] E.g., Yung Hwa, "Endued With Power: The Pentecostal-Charismatic Renewal and the Asian Church in the Twenty-first Century," *Asian Journal of Pentecostal Studies* 6, no. 1 (2003): 63-82. 66.

[2] David B. Barrett, G.T. Kurian, and T.M. Johnson, eds., *World Christian Encyclopedia: A Comparative Survey of Churches and Religions in the Modern World,* 2nd ed. (Oxford: Oxford UP, 2001) 1:12, 13.

[3] For a detailed discussion on its future, see Wonsuk Ma, "Asian Pentecostalism: A Religion Whose Only Limit Is the Sky," *Journal of Beliefs and Values* 25, no. 2 (Aug. 2004): 191-204, particularly 193.

[4] A recent popular portrait of Chinese Christianity and its possible impact on China and the world is found in David Aikman, *Jesus in Beijing: How Christianity Is Transforming China and Changing the Global Balance of Powers* (Washington, D.C.: Regnery, 2003), particularly pp. 285-92 for its future impact.

This discussion focuses on one theological issue, eschatology, which shaped the Pentecostal ethos in the early days. The inquiry has four aspects:

1. How did eschatology impact early Pentecostal theology?
2. How was this transmitted to Asians (as it crossed the ocean)?
3. How does this Asian version of Pentecostal eschatology give birth to unique spiritual traditions that we see in Asia?
4. In what areas do Asian Pentecostals need to exert an intentional theological engagement for the sound future of the Asian Pentecostal Movement? In the course of discussion, the contextual elements will come into constant interaction with the "message."

This discussion also centers on Classical Pentecostals, although, due to the ambiguous nature of Asian Pentecostalism, Charismatic Pentecostalism will naturally be considered when needed. An equally important consideration for the reader is to keep in mind the complexity and diversity of Asian countries in their history, society, culture, religion, economy and political systems.

PENTECOSTAL ESCHATOLOGY: THEN, NOW AND FUTURE
One-Hundred Years Ago, Then . . .

It is not an overstatement to view an immanent eschatological expectation as the backbone of early Pentecostal spirituality. Although this may appear less unique than other cardinal Pentecostal doctrines, such as baptism in the Holy Spirit with speaking in tongues as the "initial physical evidence,"[5] the eschatological framework enhanced Pentecostal distinctives. In fact, Anderson forcefully argues that the primary message among early Pentecostals was "Jesus is coming soon."[6] This early Pentecostal eschatology had several unique expressions.

1. *Realized Eschatological Urgency.* Christianity in North America at the turn of the 20th century was a middle-class phenomenon, with the pious anticultural Holiness Movement balancing the Christian world. Interestingly, eschatological urgency was not found in either camp. It was the Keswick movement, based on John Darby's dispensationalism, that proposed a sweeping revival to usher in the eschatological climax, the return of the Lord.[7] Thus, Pentecostalism was born as an eschatological movement by interpreting the outbreak of the unprecedented

---

[5] Robert M. Anderson, *Vision of the Disinherited: The Making of American Pentecostalism* (Peabody, MA: Hendrickson, 1979) 44-45. Anderson puts it, "In short, the Pentecostal Movement was as much a departure from the Wesleyan tradition as a development from it," 43.

[6] Anderson, 79-97.

[7] E.g., Frank Macchia, "The Struggle for Global Witness: Shifting Paradigms in Pentecostal Theology," in *The Globalization of Pentecostalism: A Religion Made to Travel,* ed. Murray Dempster, Byron Klaus, and Doug Petersen (Oxford: Regnum, 1999) 8-29.

revival as the prerequisite for the imminent return of the Lord in their lifetime. The experience of the Holy Spirit among them was quickly labeled as the "latter rain," assuming that the original advent of the Holy Spirit recorded in Act 2 was the "former rain."[8]

In the premillennial framework, this also signals the last hour of the great harvest before the Tribulation. That was where the baptism in the Holy Spirit to empower believers to witness found its eschatological and missionary impetus. In fact, Acts 1:8 has become the motto for Pentecostal believers: "But you will receive power when the Holy Spirit comes on you; and you will be my witnesses in Jerusalem, and in all Judea and Samaria, and to the ends of the earth." The only other passage that has attained a similar status is Zechariah 4:6, "Not by might, nor by power, but by the Spirit, saith the Lord of hosts" (KJV). This eschatological urgency was evident in many early testimonies. The very first issue of *The Apostolic Faith* (Los Angeles) reports the following:

> The gift of languages is given with the commission, "Go ye into all the world and preach the gospel to every creature." The Lord has given languages to the unlearned Greek, Latin, Hebrew, French, German, Italian, Chinese, Japanese, Zulu and languages of Africa, Hindu and Bengali and dialects of India, Chippewa and other languages of the Indians, Esquimaux, the deaf mute language and, in fact the Holy Ghost speaks all the languages of the world through His children.[9]

This eschatological urgency led naturally to the missionary focus of the Pentecostal Movement.

2. *Other-worldly Orientation and Missionary Impetus.* Almost all authors agree that the early Pentecostal expectation of the imminent return of the Lord fueled missionary zeal. Their premillennial eschatology conditioned them to view the world as the object of God's judgment for the seven-year Tribulation, while the church would be taken to heaven to meet the Bridegroom. Because of this theological orientation, they were preoccupied with "soul winning," leaving very little room for anything else. The first issue of *The Apostolic Faith* also reports, "Hundreds of dollars have been laid down for the sending of missionaries and thousands will be laid down."[10]

This commitment to mission with eschatological urgency was expressed in

---

[8] E.g., Joel 2:23 where the "former rain" is to be moderate.
[9] *AF* 1, Sept. 1906: 1.
[10] *AF*

various ways.[11] Theological education was strictly a practical and short-term ministerial training. Unlike established divinity schools, this program was to produce pastors, evangelists and missionaries in a minimum amount of time. Their summer activities consisted primarily of evangelistic tours. The most noteworthy development was the deployment of zealous missionaries, appropriately called "missionaries with one-way tickets."[12]

They left for mission fields without any intention or expectation to return home, not only due to their commitment to mission but also because of their eschatological conviction. With the experience of the baptism in the Spirit, they were experientially and theologically convinced that they were called, empowered, and were now being sent. Eschatological urgency simply "put a pair of wings to a tiger," as Koreans would say.

3. *Revision by Default.* It is perfectly reasonable to expect that the eschatological urgency, which the Pentecostal pioneers held, would face some revisions as the second generation slowly came into leadership. Various symptoms appeared, such as "spiritual dryness and lack of God's presence" as early as the 1940s, when the Latter Rain Movement brought back much of the early Pentecostal emphases, including the "imminence of the premillennial return of Jesus Christ, preceded by an outpouring of God's Spirit."[13]

Theological revision was not unfamiliar to early Pentecostals. Parham's contention that tongues were meant to be a missionary gift that bypassed the language-learning process[14] was quickly revised.[15] By nature, Pentecostal theology has been intuitively and experientially shaped, thus, the revision of the

---

[11] By the printing of the second issue of *The Apostolic Faith,* Oct. 1906, 3, "Eight missionaries have started to the foreign field since this movement began at Los Angeles a few months ago. About thirty workers have gone out into the field."

[12] Vinson Synan, *The Spirit Said "Grow": The Astounding Worldwide Expansion of Pentecostal and Charismatic Churches* (Monrovia, CA: MARC, 1992) 39-48.

[13] R.M. Riss, "Latter Rain Movement," in *The New International Dictionary of Pentecostal and Charismatic Movements,* ed. Stanley M. Burgess, with Eduard M. van der Maas (Grand Rapids: Zondervan, 2002) 830-33 (830).

[14] *AF* 1.2, Oct. 1906: 1. This recounts Charles Parham's experience suggesting that tongues were the "language of preaching": "Instantly the Lord took his [Parham's] vocal organs, and he was preaching the Word in another language. This man has preached in different languages over the United States, and men and women of that nationality have come to the altar and sought God." Under the title "Fire Still Falling," in the same issue of *The Apostolic Faith* (p. 2), a more explicit reference is found, "Missionaries for the foreign fields, equipped with several languages, are now on their way. . ." Also under "Testimonies of Outgoing Missionaries," in the same issue (p. 6), it is plainly reported, one "received the baptism with the Holy Ghost and the gift of the Uganda language." These quick surveys prove that the notion of tongues as the missionary language was widespread.

[15] By 1909, this popular notion of tongues as a Pentecostal missionary tool was simply abandoned as "many Pentecostals were becoming skeptical." James R. Goff Jr., *Fields*

nature of tongues was accordingly revised through experiential observations. Worse yet, the revision of the Pentecostal notion of eschatological urgency took place by default, that is, without any explicit or intentional process.

The consequence of this seemingly irresponsible silence on the eschatological belief of the Pentecostal pioneers has been rather negative. It took until the '60s, but the message of the Lord's return began to disappear slowly, but steadily, from Pentecostal pulpits. This vacuum was quickly filled by the exact opposite message of this-worldly concerns such as blessing, church growth and others. This second- and third-generation phenomenon coincided with the advent of the Charismatic Movement, which by nature had more of this-worldly concern due to the established social and theological state of the mainline churches.

One-Hundred Years Later, Here . . .

It is important to note that Pentecostal Christianity in Asia began to make its presence known to its own constituents in the 1960s and onward. New Pentecostal missionaries of the second and, later, third generations from North America and Europe came with the revised version of eschatology. This is also the period when most Asian nations came out of their painful colonial past, and for some, with divided nations to begin with (such as Vietnam, China and Korea). The process of establishing their self-identity often took ideological struggles and consequent bloodshed through civil wars (e.g., Indonesia, Malaysia, Myanmar and Cambodia) and even all-out wars (Vietnam and Korea).

Asia had to face much more hardship to have this unique Christian tradition introduced than, let's say, Los Angeles, in the beginning of the 20th century. It is important to remind the reader that during the 1920s and '30s, when the wave of the Azusa missionaries hit this continent, most Asian countries were still under colonial rules, the majority by Christian colonizers, but some (particularly East Asia) by non-, often anti-, Christian colonial forces. For the former cases, already established Christian traditions (e.g., Reformed Christianity in Indonesia, or East Indies) posed a challenge to Pentecostal pioneers. For the latter, such as Korea and in some sense China, the challenge was more severe as Christianity in general was viewed as an anti-Japanese force, thus a threat against the colonial authorities.

1. *Revised Version of Pentecostal Eschatology.* Until the 1950s, Pentecostal

---

White Unto Harvest: Charles F. Parham and the Missionary Origins of Pentecostalism (Fayetteville: U of Arkansas P, 1988) 16.

missionaries had a strong eschatological orientation.[16] For example, some Filipino *balikbayan*[17] missionaries from North America returned to the Philippines in the 1940s to preach their newfound Pentecostal message to their own people. They gave up their American dream and returned to their own provinces in the Philippines to propagate the Pentecostal faith. It was their new experience with the Holy Spirit that gave them new zeal and commitment, and it was the eschatological urgency of the imminent return of the Lord that caused them to return to the Philippines.[18]

The waning eschatological expectation among Western Pentecostals and the arrival of the message of hope "for here and now" through the Charismatic Movement from the 1960s quickly affected the theological orientation of many Pentecostal churches in Asia. Unlike the first half of the 20th century, the second half witnessed the influx of Western (often North American) evangelists holding mass evangelistic crusades, crowding radio, and later TV channels, with their messages. The speed with which the "charismatic" version of the Pentecostal message spread heavily influenced Asian Pentecostal churches whose theological foundations were not yet solid. For example, for several decades, "Christ Is the Answer" was the most popular theme song among Pentecostals. Many churches were named after this title. Currently the song reads:

> Christ is the answer to all my longing.
> Christ is the answer to all my needs,
> Savior, Baptizer, the Great Physician,
> Oh, hallelujah, He's all I need.

However, the last line, as some still remember, originally read: "He is coming soon." If this popular contention is correct, then all the experiences with Christ, such as salvation, the Spirit baptism and healing, originally were to be understood with the end time in view. However, with this revision, the same experiences are perceived to mean for life here and now. Today, Asian Pentecostal theology, in many places, is more accurately "charismatic" with a good dose of influence from the prosperity gospel and the faith movement. The animistic orientation of Asian minds is an extremely fertile ground for such "good news," with welcome supernatural help.

---

[16] In the 1960s and the early '70s, eschatological expectation was widespread in my own Christian experience in Korea.

[17] Returning Filipinos from overseas residency.

[18] Trinidad E. Seleky, "The Organization of the Philippines Assemblies of God and the Role of Early Missionaries," *Asian Journal of Pentecostal Studies* 8, no. 2 (2005): 271-82 (273): "They anticipated the early return of Christ and were constrained to spread the gospel to every tribe."

2. *This-Worldly Attention.* This revised version of Pentecostal eschatology, with the consequential lack of major eschatological components, began to direct the attention of Christian life from the "other world" to this world. In a sense, the eschatological immediacy was replaced by the immediacy of God's action in daily life.

As briefly observed above, this "here and now" relevancy of the Pentecostal message found an opportune audience in Asia, as daily suffering was the primary context. In addition to the political struggles Asian nations faced in the latter part of the 20th century, simple daily survival was the greatest challenge Asia has faced. Regardless of the sources of poverty in different parts of Asia, economic hardship was compounded by a rising population to the point that, for example, China imposed the one-child policy per family.

Depleted natural resources by the colonial powers, deeply rooted structural corruption, social unrest, and an inefficient socialist or communist system in some parts of Asia have driven many Asian societies to the extreme edge for survival. The preaching of the Pentecostal message, by this time fully revised through Charismatic influences, was indeed "good news for modern men (and women)."

For instance, David Yonggi Cho, who grew up under the harsh Japanese colonial rule and the devastation of the Korean War, received a Christian message that was much different from the one that was being preached in existing churches.[19] This gospel introduced him to the God who heals and performs miracles "here and now," and this God is good, not only after death, but also now. Although he was nurtured under Classical Pentecostal missionaries, theological influences also came from Charismatic sources. His Yoido era (1973-present) saw pulpit guests such as Robert Schuller, Oral Roberts and other popular Charismatic preachers. His *Fourth Dimension*,[20] a million-seller throughout the world, proves that his theology has a strong Charismatic character.

The high expectation of God's supernatural intervention in human life is the main message of Cho, often punctuated with testimonies of healing and miracles. His message can easily be summed up as a theology of blessing through the supernatural intervention of God. This explains why 3 John 2 has been the most popular passage in his church: "Dear friend, I pray that you may enjoy good health and that all may go well with you, even as your soul is getting along well."

---

[19] E.g., Young-hoon Lee, "Life and Ministry of David Yonggi Cho," in *David Yonggi Cho: A Close Look at His Theology and Ministry,* ed. Wonsuk Ma, Hyeon-sung Bae, and William W. Menzies (Baguio, Philippines: APTS Press; Goonpo, Korea: Hansei UP, 2005) 3-23 (3-4).

[20] *The Fourth Dimension,* vols. 1-2 (South Plainfield, NJ: Bridge, 1979, 1983).

However, it is unfair to give all the credit for Cho's theological shaping to Charismatic influences. His theology also bears the distinct mark that Christian (in this case, Pentecostal-Charismatic) theology has wrestled with the context of suffering. If we borrow Cox's theory, deprivation in human life and eschatological hope have been the main context and cause for the growth of Pentecostal churches throughout the world.[21]

Like Latin America, Asia's Pentecostal growth can, in part, be attributed to the sheer challenge of life. The very fact that the majority of Pentecostal believers in Asia come from the lower social strata proves this point. It is only recently that Pentecostal congregations have begun to attain respectability in some Asian societies, thus, attracting the more educated and established in social and economic aspects.

This revised version of eschatology also came with some surprising positive contributions. Attention given to social issues and environmental concerns among some Asian Pentecostals has been possible because of this worldly orientation. The growing awareness of the potential of socio-political influence was clearly brought about during the 2004 presidential election in the Philippines. Not only was a Charismatic minister among the presidential candidates,[22] but also the 9-million strong Catholic Charismatic group publicly endorsed a candidate.

The recent Indonesian election also witnessed many Pentecostal ministers running for public posts. Aside from the question of whether these decisions were right or not, both incidents indicate Pentecostal-Charismatic believers' awareness of the potential of their socio-political influence, as well as their determination to exercise it. The Korean Pentecostals included their prayer for the environment beginning in the 1980s. During the World Assemblies of God Conference in Seoul, Korea (1994), the published prayer for the gathering listed environmental concerns among the first four prayer topics.[23] Another

---

[21] Harvey Cox, *First From Heaven: The Rise of Pentecostal Spirituality and the Reshaping of Religion in the Twenty-First Century* (Reading, MA: Addison-Wesley, 1995), e.g., 58 for the Azusa Street Mission.

[22] "Brother" Eddie Villanueva, the founder (1978) of the Jesus Is Lord, the "biggest born-again Christian group" with its claim of 5 million members, was the presidential candidate. He recently held a prayer rally for the nation, attracting not only 1 million participants (according to the organizer) but also Catholic bishops, religious leaders, and many politicians; Leslie Ann Aquino and Raymund Antonio, "Thousands Join JIL Anniversary Rites, Prayer Rally at Rizal Park," *Manila Bulletin,* Oct. 3, 2005: 1, 6.

[23] See also Walter J. Hollenweger, "The Contribution of Asian Pentecostalism to Ecumenical Christianity: Hopes and Questions of a Barthian Theologian," in *Asian and Pentecostal: The Charismatic Face of Christianity in Asia,* ed. Allan Anderson and Edmond Tang (Oxford: Regnum; Baguio, Philippines: APTS, 2005) 15-25 (20-21), criticizes the handicap of Western Christianity to

surprising development is the social service area. Malaysian Pentecostal-Charismatic churches, for example, have pioneered social service programs for the neglected. Homes for orphans, single mothers, the elderly and drug addicts have become a regular feature of many Pentecostal churches. This began as a creative evangelistic strategy because Muslim law prohibits public evangelistic activities to Muslim Malays. Also, we have seen the formation of a growing number of nongovernmental organizations (NGOs) among Asian Pentecostal churches. Equally unexpected is the ecumenical initiatives of some Asian Pentecostal leaders and churches. Evidently, the exponential growth of Pentecostal churches has increased their influence among Christian communities. They not only cooperate in local and national ecumenical initiatives, but also have started to lead ecumenical movements. The Korean Assemblies of God, which joined the Korean National Council of Churches (KNCC) in 1996, had one of their Pentecostal ministers to become the general secretary of the ecumenical body. He in fact set a goal to merge the KNCC with its Evangelical counterpart in Korea. Malaysia is another case in point. Early Pentecostal churches had traditionally kept inter-church activities at arm's length, sometimes by choice but more often by external forces. Malaysian Pentecostal leaders, on the other hand, have actively cooperated with other Evangelical churches to the point that more than half of the current executive members of the National Evangelical Christian Fellowship Malaysia are Pentecostal-Charismatic.[24] Also, the chairman of the board of the Philippine Council of Evangelical Churches is a Pentecostal minister, yet, it is important to note that these encouraging signs are still far from being widespread.

3. *Theological Challenges.* This radical shift of attention from other-worldly to this-worldly concerns has become an enormous challenge to Christianity in Asia. Asia has birthed many of the world's religions as well as plenty of animistic religious beliefs. Traditional gods have been used, even exploited, for the worshiper's benefit. Spiritual power without an eschatological goal and moral commitment can easily fall into a religious utilitarianism, which is exactly what animism and shamanism are all about. It should be noted also that church growth seems to have replaced (cross-cultural) mission as the ultimate goal of the church.

---

deal with this issue adequately while he expresses hope in Asian Christians. However, the question remains: Do Pentecostals have any distinct theological contribution to make, or are we simply raising awareness of this concern with other Christians? One clue suggested by Hollenweger, although in an interreligious context, is that the *Creator Spiritus* (in the Old Testament) is to be identified with the *Spiritus Sanctus* (of the New Testament) 23.

[24] Yeu Chuen Lim, "Malaysian Evangelical Fellowship" (email message to the author, *limyc@tm.net.my*, Oct. 3, 2005). More information about the organization is available at *http://www.necf.org.my* (checked: Oct. 3, 2005).

It is true that church growth has been a positive influence in making the presence of Christianity known in predominantly non- or often anti-Christian societies. Nonetheless, the church growth movement has evolved into a shape that represents the this-worldly orientation of Pentecostal Christianity.

More seriously, this attention to the growth of local churches may have taken place at the expense of global mission, an important theological tradition of Pentecostalism. Recently a serious reflection on the mega-church movement has taken place, and alternative approaches are suggested.[25]

A careful examination of the record of Pentecostal expansion seems to suggest that, unlike the common notion that Pentecostalism is predominantly a missionary movement, the movement has an equal, if not stronger renewal potential among existing churches. One can easily point to the advent of the Charismatic Movement, which literally "renewed" existing churches as proof. Perhaps even more important is an observation that Pentecostalism seems to flourish more in already Christianized areas than in "virgin" territories.[26]

If the primary missionary character of the movement is to be proven, there must be growing Pentecostal churches in places where there is little Christian witness. However, that is rarely the case.[27] Latin America and some parts of Africa are good examples. This has caused the debate of proselytism from existing churches.[28] The only exception known to the author may be China. It is true that the majority of the house-church networks in China are characteristically Pentecostal in belief and worship;[29] yet, this phenomenon is more "indigenous" in nature and origin than the result of Pentecostal missionary efforts.

---

[25] E.g., David Lim, "A Missiological Evaluation of David Yonggi Cho's Church Growth," *David Yonggi Cho: A Close Look at His Theology and Ministry*, ed. Wonsuk Ma, William W. Menzies, and Hyeon-sung Bae (Baguio, Philippines: APTS, 2004) 181-207, strongly advocates church multiplication.

[26] This observation was made by Alan Johnson, a Pentecostal missionary to Thailand, in February 2005 in Baguio, Philippines. In his follow-up, he argues, "My gut impression is that you are hard-pressed to find a place where Pentecostals went that was a resistant hard-to-reach group and they either (a) were the first ones there or (b) had a breakthrough. Instead, what you tend to see is that where the church among every stripe has grown greatly, Pentecostals have grown greatly. Where the church is small, Pentecostals are small," Alan Johnson, "On Chapel Service" (email message to the author, *alan.johnson@agmd.org*, Oct. 6, 2005).

[27] This does not mean that in "difficult" areas such as Thailand and Japan, there are no large Pentecostal-Charismatic churches, but their overall impact to the larger church world and to the society has not been felt.

[28] The latest joint statement of the fourth phase of the international Catholic-Pentecostal dialogue (1990-1997) was titled, "Evangelization, Proselytism and Common Witness." For the full text, see *Asian Journal of Pentecostal Studies* 2, no. 1 (1999): 105-51.

[29] Recently see Wesley Luke, *The Church in China: Persecuted, Pentecostal, and Powerful* (Baguio, Philippines: AJPS, 2005) esp. 35-67.

This calls for a recovery of the early Pentecostal commitment to soul-winning, especially the cross-cultural variety. The history of the Western Pentecostal Movement has already demonstrated that the expansion of the missionary work is not solely fueled by eschatological urgency. Even by second- and third-generation Pentecostals, the missionary movement continues to flourish. For example, in U.S. Assemblies of God (2,729,000 adherents), only 5.2 percent of the world Assemblies of God family (52,811,000) has sent 33 percent (or 2,590) of the global Assemblies of God missionary force (7,796).[30]

Pentecostal mission has been known, however, to be triumphalistic in its attitude, due in part to its success, but also due to its "power missiology." Their aggressive approach to "convert" even believers, under the pretext that they are nominal, has been viewed as a sign of spiritual arrogance. As the centenary of the Edinburgh conference draws near, the Western church calls for the new shaping of Christian mission in humility and hope.[31] Pentecostal mission, as a movement of the poor fired up by the Holy Spirit,[32] needs to recover not only its trademark of power mission, but also, more importantly, its humble attitude.

There is more reason to be mindful of the triumphalistic attitude of Pentecostal mission. The reality of human suffering cannot be ignored with simple faith statements. Asians, including Pentecostal believers, are living in constant struggle for survival. It is simply impossible to list all the factors contributing to suffering. The magnitude of natural and "(hu)man-made" disasters claim thousands of lives, as seen in the tsunami incident in the Indian Ocean in December 2004, and the recent earthquake in Pakistan.

Many of the terrorist attacks have been staged in Asia, be it in Iraq, southern Philippines or Bali, Indonesia. Turning to the Christian scene, for about three years since 1996, 275 Christian churches were closed, vandalized, destroyed or burned by Muslims in Indonesia. Close to one-half (121 churches) of them were Pentecostal churches, and next on the list are Catholic churches (18).[33] In

---

[30] Assemblies of God World Missions, "Current Facts and Highlights: As of December 31, 2004" (Springfield, MO: Assemblies of God World Mission, 2005).

[31] "Edinburgh 2010—Mission in Humility and Hope," *www.towards2010.org.uk*, 2005 (checked: Oct. 15, 2005).

[32] E.g., Wonsuk Ma, " 'When the Poor Are Fired Up': The Role of Pneumatology in Pentecostal-Charismatic Mission," paper presented at the Conference on World Mission and Evangelism, Athens, Greece, May 2005.

[33] Paul Tahalele, *The Church and Human Rights in Indonesia* (Surabaya, Indonesia: Indonesia Christian Communication Forum, 1998) 7-20. Gani Wiyono, "Pentecostalism in Indonesia," in *Asian and Pentecostal: The Charismatic Face of Christianity in Asia*, ed. Allan Anderson and Edmond Tang (Oxford: Regnum Books; Baguio, Philippines: APTS Books, 2005) 307-28 (320). This points out the aggressive evangelistic activities as the main cause, thus, in a sense, self-invited.

many countries, gathering for Christian worship is still illegal, thus, subject to state punishment including death. An average first-generation Christian in Asia has to overcome much marginalization and even persecution from family and society.[34] Perhaps a good, if not the highest, proportion of modern martyrdom takes place in Asia, partly due to the extremely volatile religious context. A triumphalistic pronouncement of miracles and healings will not resolve this very real challenge. It will take far more than a Band Aid treatment, and this is where a proper understanding of Christian life from a balanced eschatological perspective becomes critical.[35]

Equally urgent is a right understanding of blessing. Due to the dire situation, God's blessing, be it supernatural, economic or social, will continue to be a main focus of Asian Christianity. In order for Asian Pentecostals to avoid the grave theological mistakes of the prosperity gospel, it is urgent to refine the popular theology blessing with the theological and eschatological understanding of Christian life in mind.

It is argued contextually and Biblically that the Spirit of God is the source of life, sustenance, rejuvenation and restoration of it.[36] Thus, it is legitimate to expect the Holy Spirit to "bless" lives for their material, physical, emotional, social and spiritual daily needs.[37] Here I stress the "needs" (versus "desires"), as God's blessing is interpreted as God's gracious means for human sustenance. This may be called "theology of blessing" in comparison with a "prosperity gospel." What is more critical is the proper theological purpose of blessing. One valid Pentecostal interpretation is to view blessings as part of God's empowerment for witness (Acts 1:8).

Unlike the common supernatural perception of empowerment among Pentecostals, the "power" which the Holy Spirit endows can be understood

---

[34] One less drastic and yet common example is found in Wonsuk Ma and Julie C. Ma, "Jesus Christ in Asia: Our Journey With Him as Pentecostal Believers," paper presented at the Asian Consultation, Global Christian Forum, May 2004, Hong Kong, to be published in *International Review of Mission* (forthcoming).

[35] Recently, David Yonggi Cho, at a monthly prayer meeting of the Korean Evangelical Fellowship on April 8, 2005, publicly repented of his preaching of [God's] "cheap grace" which more accurately refers to [physical and material] "blessing," while ignoring human suffering. Keun-young Kim, "Korean Church Leaders Repent" [in Korean], *Christianity Today*, Apr. 9, 2005, *http://www.chtoday.co.kr/news/rs_6269.htm* (checked: Oct. 7, 2005).

[36] For a contextual argument, see Wonsuk Ma, "Asian (Classical) Pentecostal Theology in Context," in *Asian and Pentecostal: The Charismatic Face of Christianity in Asia*, ed. Allan Anderson and Edmond Tang (Oxford: Regnum Books; Baguio, Philippines: APTS Books, 2005) 59-91, esp. 65-66.

[37] This is based on the creation spirit tradition of the Old Testament, e.g., as found in Isaiah 32:14ff. Wonsuk Ma, *Until the Spirit Comes: The Spirit of God in the Book of Isaiah* (Sheffield: Sheffield Academic Press, 1999) 25-32.

broadly, and elements seemingly less than supernatural, such as circumstances, should also be viewed as part of the Spirit's empowerment. The record in the Book of Acts, such as the missionary journeys of Paul, seems to suggest this point repeatedly. If we follow this interpretation, then the "blessing" attains its new missionary purpose, and thus, an eschatological significance.[38] This would safely keep the theology of blessing from the dangerous utilitarian trap.

Ultimately, the formulation of a sound Pentecostal mission theology will be the goal of Pentecostal theological inquiries. It is fascinating that Pentecostal mission did not decline along with its early eschatological urgency. This perhaps explains that eschatology was not the sole, or even main, driving force for Pentecostal mission. It is argued that by the time Pentecostalism reached the Asian shores, "the 'power' came, but 'mission' was not in the boat." It is true that much of the emphasis of early Pentecostal preaching was on the power of God. The relative silence of mission can be explained in two ways: (1) Western Pentecostal missionaries were already doing mission,[39] and (2) given the "pagan" state of Asian nations, evangelism (versus "foreign" mission) was a more urgent task. However, even after substantial growth of Pentecostal Christianity in many Asian countries, there is little evidence that the powerful missionary theology of Pentecostalism distinguished itself from the rest of the churches in crossing cultural barriers to be witnesses. For example, in Korea, in spite of its robust growth, the rate of cross-cultural missionary growth is not the highest among denominations.

The issue boils down to the theological foundation of how faithfully the missionary nature of Pentecostal theology was transmitted to Asians by Western missionaries. It is, therefore, surprisingly encouraging to see the steady and sometimes explosive growth of missionary forces among Asian Pentecostals.[40] However, the question still remains: What distinguishes the Asian Pentecostal missionary from the rest in their conviction and practices? There is no doubt that a healthy eschatology with the Pentecostal theology of empowerment will equip them to be a significant missionary force in the coming decades.

---

[38] For an elaborate treatment of this point, see Wonsuk Ma, "Yonggi Cho's Theology of Blessing: New Theological Basis and Direction," paper presented at Youngsan International Theological Symposium, May 2003, Hansei University, Goonpo, Korea.

[39] It is also plausible that the early Western Pentecostal missionaries, like their colleagues, may not have had the "full-circle mission" understanding as advocated by C. Peter Wagner, *On the Crest of the Wave: Becoming a World Christian* (Ventura, CA: Regal Books, 1983) ch. 9. For a Pentecostal reflection and possibility, see Wonsuk Ma, "Full Circle Mission: A Possibility of Pentecostal Missiology," *Asian Journal of Pentecostal Studies* 8, no. 1 (2005): 5-27.

[40] The new "Back to Jerusalem" missionary movement of the Chinese house church networks is an example. Aikman, *Jesus in Beijing,* 103-205. Also Paul Hattaway, *Back to Jerusalem: Three Chinese House Church Leaders Share Their Vision to Complete the Great Commission* (Waynesboro, GA: Authentic Media, 2003).

4. *Toward Tomorrow.* My suggestions here are restricted to the revision of Pentecostal eschatology, particularly in Asia. As Western Pentecostal scholarship continues its quest for revision,[41] Asians need to participate in this global journey by keeping in mind that every generation needs to hear the same message but often in a revised or "re-cased" form, and such collaborative work will benefit everyone.

Eschatology has at least two dimensions: the time of the Lord's return and the nature of the church and Christian life. Eschatological expectation involves the specific time of His return, as we have seen in early Pentecostal thought. Although no one knows when, the Lord's return is to be "soon." This can be explained through the journey of the church in history, as sandwiched between the Lord's ascension and the Second Coming. The end has begun, and history is moving toward the end of the end time. However, this does not always generate the kind of eschatological urgency that would in turn create a "crisis mode" of life. In order for eschatology to be more relevant, it has to relate on a personal level. Casual life experiences attest amply that we will see Him rather soon, and sometimes unexpectedly soon. Thus, either the Lord returns, or we go to Him, both soon. Even though the Lord's return may not take place in our own generation, this should not keep us from maintaining the eschatological urgency. Life's uncertainty and unpredictability, and the certainty of the closure itself, are signs of our eschatological life.

The more important aspect of eschatology is the nature of Christian life. We are *in* the world but not *of* the world. Asian Christians, including Pentecostal believers, are keenly aware that Christians bring "foreignness" to their context, not because of its Western outlook, but because of its radically "other" kingdom character. This pilgrim identity should be brought into the main focus of Pentecostal Christianity, which in turn will put the powerful experiential Christian life in right perspective with eternity in sight. From the same eschatological perspective, miracles and healing can be interpreted, not as the manifestation of the "Kingdom now," but as the sign of the token "invasion" of the kingdom of God that was inaugurated by Christ and in the anticipation of its fulfillment in the unknown near future. Thus, any supernatural manifestation is to be taken as a reminder or "sign" of God's reign that has begun and yet, not fully recognized. Donald Gee may have been theologically sound when he

---

[41] E.g., Frank Macchia, "The Struggle for Global Witness," 23, urges Pentecostals to "rediscover the original eschatological fervor that allowed them in the early years of the movement to swim against the stream of the spirit of the age and to advocate female participation in the ministry and interracial fellowship."

argued that the gift of healing has its true value when it occurs with evangelism as the ultimate goal.[42]

The good news for Asian Pentecostals is that this is not the first revision of eschatology; in fact, church history attests well that every generation has struggled with this challenge, and there are sufficient examples from which we can learn.

Conclusion

Going back to the beginning of this reflection, it is not true that eschatology has been the only determinant in the shaping of Asian Pentecostal thinking and ethos to its present form. Yet, the major shift in Pentecostal eschatology in the West has had an undeniable impact on Asian Pentecostalism.

The group that began as an anti-intellectual movement has come a long way as it crossed the Pacific Ocean in the past 100 years. Now Asia boasts more than two dozen graduate-level Pentecostal institutions with at least four offering doctoral-level programs.[43] The appearance of three international[44] and at least three vernacular Pentecostal journals in Asia attests to the rising interest in higher learning.

The revision of Pentecostal eschatology is inevitable. With the explosive growth on one hand, and the ever-changing social situations on the other, Asian Pentecostals are called to engage in the constant process of theological reflection. This is the only way the powerful spiritual tradition can have the same appeal to ever-changing generations in this diverse continent. Proactive and intentional theological undertaking is the key to the future of healthy Pentecostalism. With much history behind us, Asian Pentecostals need to demonstrate that we have learned an important lesson. Instead of blaming Western Pentecostal missionaries who unintentionally brought a revised eschatology to this most populated continent, it is our turn to evaluate whether we made conscientious choices with proper evaluation of what was introduced to us. This may be the only way to renew this renewal movement and to keep Asian Pentecostalism from falling into the trap of a modernist pop religion or an extremely self-centered utilitarian religion.

---

[42] Donald Gee, *Spiritual Gifts in the Work of Ministry Today* (Springfield, MO: Gospel Publishing House, 1963) 72, 73.

[43] A recent survey includes six schools in Korea, one in Japan, three in the Philippines, three in Indonesia, three in Singapore, two in Malaysia, one in Hong Kong, and at least five in India. If Oceania is included, at least two more schools are added.

[44] *Asian Journal of Pentecostal Studies* (Philippines), *The Spirit and Church* (Korea) and *Australasian Pentecostal Studies* (Australia).

14

The Church of God in Christ and the Azusa Street Revival

Frederick L. Ware

Introduction

The Azusa Street Revival, led by William J. Seymour, figures preeminently in the history and doctrine of the Church of God in Christ (COGIC). In the spring of 1907, COGIC leaders, namely Charles H. Mason, John A. Jeter and D.J. Young attended the Azusa Street Revival. While there, Mason and Young had a "Pentecostal" experience of baptism in the Holy Spirit accompanied by tongue-speaking. Their pilgrimage to the Azusa Street Revival set in motion a series of events that resulted in COGIC's transformation from a Holiness to a Pentecostal denomination. As these leaders were changed, so were the denomination's teachings and practices.

This article examines five distinctives of the Azusa Street Revival that COGIC has retained. It begins with a brief historical overview of COGIC's transformation from a Holiness to a Pentecostal denomination, emphasizing Mason's pilgrimage to the Azusa Street Revival. Next, the article describes these five distinctives:

1. Interracial, ecumenical, egalitarian fellowship
2. Ecstatic worship
3. Tongues as the Biblical sign of baptism in the Holy Spirit
4. Divine healing
5. Premillennialism

Mason's personal and collegial relationship with Seymour, along with Mason's role and authority as "chief apostle" and "senior bishop" of COGIC,

*Scripture references in this chapter are taken from the King James Version.

were crucial in COGIC's retention of beliefs and practices characteristic of the Azusa Street Revival. The article ends with reflection on challenges today facing COGIC, including its maintenance of contiguity with the Pentecostal tradition initiated by the Azusa Street Revival.

COGIC's Transformation Into a Pentecostal Denomination

C.H. Mason's Trip to the Azusa Street Revival

In March 1907, Charles H. Mason, as a seeker, traveled to the Azusa Street Revival in Los Angeles, California. He was accompanied by John A. Jeter of Little Rock, Arkansas, an overseer of COGIC in the state of Arkansas, and D.J. Young, a COGIC pastor from Pine Bluff, Arkansas. Mason pastored churches in Lexington, Mississippi, and Memphis, Tennessee. Mason was the COGIC overseer of the state of Tennessee. Jeter and Young also went as seekers.

Mason was eager to attend the revival because he had already preached about Pentecost, the possibility of experiencing a baptism in the Holy Spirit similar to the spiritual experiences mentioned in the Book of Acts, and the members of his church were hungry for this baptism in the Holy Spirit.[1] Mason was already quite successful in ministry.[2] However, he was hungry for a deeper relationship with God. Prior to his trip to Azusa, Mason had been struggling to understand tongues-speaking. Though he had never spoken in tongues, he had a mystical experience of hearing languages and sounds that he could not understand.[3] Mason experienced a miraculous healing when he was about the age of 14. While in his church meetings there were testimonies of healing, in other churches there were no such testimonies. From childhood into adulthood, he was troubled by dreams and visions he did not understand.[4]

Mason's baptism in the Spirit was an experience of resolution. He was freed from years of confusion and lack of certainty. He was able to reconcile himself to something that subconsciously was a part of his religious life. The Baptism

---

[1] C.H. Mason, "Tennessee Evangelist Witness," *The Apostolic Faith*, May 1907; reprinted in *Azusa Street: The True Believers: Part 2*, ed. Larry Martin (Joplin, MO: Christian Life Books, 1999): 28.

[2] Mason, *History and Life Work of Elder C.H. Mason, Chief Apostle, and His Co-Laborers*, recompiled in 1924 by Mary Mason (Memphis: Howe, 1920; repr. Memphis: Church of God in Christ, 1987) 25.

[3] Ithiel C. Clemmons, *Bishop C.H. Mason and the Roots of the Church of God in Christ* (Bakersfield, CA: Pneuma Life, 1996) 62.

[4] Mason, *History and Life Work of Elder C.H. Mason*, 19.

healed his psyche and made him whole. He was empowered to do greater work in ministry. He felt himself to be "full of the power."[5] For Mason, tongues-speaking not only signified his baptism in the Spirit but was a spiritual gift. In addition to the gift of tongues, he reports of having received other gifts, such as the interpretation of tongues, sounds and mysterious writings in the Spirit, divine healing, and the working of miracles.[6] In COGIC lore, Mason was also known to have the power of exorcism (casting out demons, evil spirits and even death).

C.H. Mason's Relationship With W.J. Seymour

Mason was not a casual attendee of the Azusa Street Revival. Mason had met Seymour about two years earlier when Seymour visited Jackson, Mississippi, in 1905.[7] When Mason went to Los Angeles for the revival in 1907, he stayed for an extended period of time. He stayed in Los Angeles for five weeks in order to learn about the operations of the Holy Spirit in the meetings over which Seymour presided.[8]

After returning to Memphis, Mason remained in contact with Seymour. The two men became personal friends and partners in ministry and evangelism. In 1908, when Seymour was contemplating marriage to Jennie Moore, he wrote asking Mason for advice.[9] Mason gave his blessings on their marriage. In the minutes of COGIC's Holy Convocation in 1919, there is record of Seymour's being present.[10] The minutes of the meeting attest to the longstanding relationship between Mason and Seymour and the COGIC assembly's recognition of Seymour as a founder of the Pentecostal Movement.

The Split Between Mason and Jones

Charles P. Jones considered Mason's insistence on the validity of tongues-speaking (and other manifestations of the Holy Spirit that Mason witnessed at the Azusa Street Revival and sought to perpetuate among the denomination's membership) to be a delusion and distraction from holiness. Jones' rejection of Pentecostalism is ironic, given the fact that he actually encouraged Mason to

---

[5] Mason, 30.

[6] Mason, 30-31.

[7] Clemmons, *Bishop C.H. Mason,* 26.

[8] Mason, *History and Life Work of Elder C.H. Mason,* 30.

[9] Clemmons, *Bishop C.H. Mason,* 49.

[10] Lucille J. Cornelius, *The Pioneer: History of the Church of God in Christ* (Memphis: Church of God in Christ, 1975) 10.

attend the revival. Jones feared that he and others within their denomination might not have the baptism in the Holy Spirit, as described in the Bible.[11]

Mason, Jeter and Young were appointed to investigate the revival. Mason said that all three of them went seeking the blessing of baptism in the Spirit; however, Jeter became skeptical of the revival services.[12] Mason and Young returned, proclaiming a new experience of divine encounter and empowerment for ministry. In August 1907, at COGIC's meeting in Jackson, Mississippi, fellowship was withdrawn from Mason and all others who preached the doctrine of Spirit baptism with tongues.

After expulsion from the denomination, Mason led a faction headquartered in Memphis. Both factions, for a while, used the same name. Mason continued to use the name "Church of God in Christ" for his group. The Jones group used the name "Church of God in Christ" until about 1915 when it renamed itself "Church of Christ (Holiness) USA." Later, factions separating from the Jones group would name themselves, in 1917, "Church of Christ (Holiness), Inc." and, in 1920, "Church of God Holiness."

Mason's Election as "Chief Apostle" of the Church of God in Christ

In September 1907, Mason called a conference in Memphis and reestablished COGIC as a Pentecostal denomination. A small gathering of ministers from 10 congregations formed the first Pentecostal General Assembly of COGIC. Mason was elected as the general overseer and chief apostle of the denomination. As chief apostle (later designated as senior bishop), Mason was given complete authority to appoint bishops, create ecclesiastical jurisdictions, organize departments and auxiliaries, represent the denomination in religious and civic matters, and establish its doctrine. In the 1926 Constitution of COGIC, Mason was declared to have exercise of this authority until his death, whereupon a board of bishops was to be elected and empowered to oversee the denomination.[13]

Mason died in 1961 at the age of 95. His tenure and absolute authority of 64 years are unparalleled in American denominational history. Still, decades after Mason's death, oral and written histories of his life, experiences, and teachings are crucial for interpreting COGIC theology and doctrine. These histories recount

---

[11] Mason, *History and Life Work of Elder C.H. Mason,* 26.

[12] Mason, 27.

[13] Church of God in Christ, *Manual of the Church of God in Christ* (Memphis, TN: Church of God in Christ); hereafter as *Manual of the Church of God in Christ* (1940), *Official Manual of the Church of God in Christ* (1973) 47, 58.

his personal spiritual pilgrimage (i.e., how he was converted, sanctified, baptized in the Holy Spirit); his being healed from life-threatening illnesses; and his charisma, piety, humility, moral integrity, evangelism, and organizational and administrative skill. Mason's longevity and unchallenged leadership, along with his successors' commitment to preserving his legacy, ensured the continuity of COGIC's beliefs and practices, forging for the denomination a genuine sense of tradition.

Azusa Street Revival Distinctives Perpetuated by COGIC

Distinctives of the Azusa Street Revival that are at the center of COGIC's sense of Pentecostal tradition include the following:
1. Interracial, ecumenical, egalitarian fellowship
2. Ecstatic worship
3. Tongues as the Biblical sign of baptism in the Holy Spirit
4. Divine healing
5. Premillennialism

Interracial, Ecumenical, Egalitarian Fellowship

COGIC's vision of the church is influenced by the diversity and integration of those present at the Azusa Street Revival. It seems that, from the beginning and over the course of the revival, the core membership supporting the Apostolic Faith Mission, where the revival took place, was mostly African-American. Persons from various socioeconomic and racial and ethnic groups visited and participated in the worship services of the mission. Anyone who was a professing Christian with a "desire to go on to perfection," that is, a commitment to holiness, was allowed to join the mission.[14]

Blacks, women and the poor were involved in all levels of leadership and operation of the revival. Seymour described the mission as a "colored" congregation that invited him to be its pastor.[15] Afterward, whites began to join and seek the Pentecostal experience with the sign of tongues-speaking. His policy was to make them welcome and feel free. Eventually, a disproportionate number of whites came to hold leadership positions at the mission.[16]

---

[14] William J. Seymour, *Doctrines and Discipline of the Azusa Street Apostolic Faith Mission* (Los Angeles: Azusa Mission, 1915) 6 (preface) and 10; hereafter cited as *Doctrines and Discipline*. Courtesy of the Flower Pentecostal Heritage Center, Springfield, MO, USA.

[15] Seymour, *Doctrines and Discipline*, 12.

[16] Cecil M. Robeck, "Azusa Street Revival," in *Dictionary of Pentecostal and Charismatic Movements*, ed. Stanley M. Burgess and Gary B. McGee, with Patrick H. Alexander, assoc. ed. (Grand Rapids: Zondervan, 1988) 34.

Seymour later found it necessary to impose restrictions because of the ensuing fanaticism and apostasy that he perceived certain persons, who happened to be white, brought to the mission.[17] He insisted that there must be love and mutual respect between blacks, whites and other peoples. In Seymour's own words, "Christ is all in all and for all. He is neither black nor white man, nor Chinaman, nor Hindoo, nor Japanese, but God. God is Spirit."[18]

Like Seymour, Mason was committed to the vision of the church as one body, unified over the boundaries of race, ethnicity, class and gender. From 1907 to 1925, COGIC was an interracial, interdenominational Pentecostal church. Immediately following his baptism in the Holy Spirit, Mason began preaching and ministering to non-African-American audiences.[19] Mason ordained ministers from various racial and ethnic groups. Because COGIC was the only legally recognized Pentecostal church, white Pentecostal ministers sought and were given credentials from COGIC. Between the years 1909 and 1914, COGIC was equally proportioned between blacks and whites.[20] The mass exodus of whites from COGIC began in 1914, when several white ministers in COGIC withdrew to establish the Assemblies of God. COGIC also operated missions among Mexican, Indian and Hispanic populations in the Southwestern, Western and Pacific states of North America. In addition to attracting persons from various other races and ethnic groups, COGIC drew into its membership persons from other Christian denominations, mostly from Baptist and Methodist churches.

Though COGIC is today a predominately African-American Christian denomination, it maintains openness toward all groups of people. COGIC accepts for membership "any and all persons regardless of race, color and national origin."[21] COGIC affirms the kinship of all humanity and equal rights for all persons as suggested by the sovereignty of God and God's moral law for the universe.[22]

For COGIC, the meaning of church is further clarified by the model of "holy convocation." At COGIC's reestablishment as a Pentecostal denomination, the first General Assembly designated November 25–December 14 of each year

---

[17] So adamant about preventing disruption of or takeover of the mission, when he incorporated the mission, he determined that only a "colored" man may lead the mission and women could not baptize other converts or participate in the ordination of ministers. See Seymour, *Doctrines and Discipline,* 50, 91.

[18] Seymour, 13.

[19] Mason, *History and Life Work of Elder C.H. Mason,* 31-32.

[20] Ithiel C. Clemmons, "Charles Harrison Mason," in *Dictionary of Pentecostal and Charismatic Movements,* ed. Stanley M. Burgess and Gary B. McGee, with Patrick H. Alexander, assoc. ed. (Grand Rapids: Zondervan, 1988) 587.

[21] *Official Manual of the Church of God in Christ* (1973), 82.

[22] *Official Manual of the Church of God in Christ,* 126, 129-30.

for the main gathering of the denomination. At present, the holy convocation lasts for 10 days, in early November of each year, with the first three days of the meeting dedicated to fasting and prayer. Holy convocation influences COGIC perceptions of what the church is and ought to be. The late Presiding Bishop J.O. Patterson Sr. often said, "The Church of God in Christ is organized from the top down." The pattern of organization established on the national scale is replicated in jurisdictions, districts and local churches.

The assembling of God's people is a call into the Spirit. For the annual holy convocation and for other meetings of the church, Mason would cite Psalm 50:5: "Gather my saints together unto me; those that have made a covenant with me by sacrifice." He believed that it was important to bring believers together in order to turn back or resist increasing evil in the world.

As the late Ithiel Clemmons described it, holy convocation is an invitation into sacred time, a reality determined by God that serves as an alternative to contingent human social systems and establishes our identity and true worth. "The sacred time charged one with life, vigor, vitality, vision and purpose sufficient for another year of service for Christ and His church. The experience of convocation reminded each participant that he was a part of something greater, grander, and mightier than what the member experienced on a day-to-day basis."[23]

Holy convocation is a call for God's people to come together for the purpose of fulfilling their sacred functions. The gathering of saints is marked by various activities, such as establishing a context for living out and holding believers accountable to God's call to holiness, teaching and training, worship and liturgy, preparation for the return of Jesus Christ, prophetic witness (modeling a lifestyle and taking action to combat sin and evil), mission and evangelism, manifestation of God's reality and power, and conducting business and collecting finances for the material support of the church's ministries. The gathering also provides persons with moments of fellowship and belonging, the affirmation of individual self-worth and sense of connectedness to each other, history, tradition and culture.

Ecstatic Worship

The enthusiastic and ecstatic worship at the Azusa Street Revival was intended to be that way. According to Seymour, the Apostolic Faith "stands for the restoration of the faith once delivered to the saints—the old-time religion of camp meetings, revivals, missions, street and mission work and Christian unity everywhere."[24]

---

[23] Clemmons, *Bishop C.H. Mason*, 77.

[24] Seymour, *Doctrines and Discipline*, 92.

Worship services at the Azusa Revival were held three times a day, seven days a week, with the largest crowds attending on weekends. Services were long and marked by a high degree of audience participation, spontaneity and improvisation. Any service could be a creative mix of hymnal singing, prayer, preaching, exhorting, testimonies, shouting, dancing, speaking and singing in tongues, altar calls, and tarrying for baptism in the Holy Spirit.

Seymour believed in and encouraged shouting and dancing, when such actions were expressive of praise to God and joy in the Holy Spirit. However, he was averse to any bodily movements that appeared to be planned, choreographed, or aimed at drawing attention to any particular individual.[25]

A great deal of the worship at the Azusa Street Revival reflected clearly African American spirituality. The brand of Pentecostalism that Mason learned from Seymour was a mixture of holiness and Pentecostal teachings, revivalism and black folk religion. Seymour's meetings, like Mason's, would later be viewed negatively by the white press.[26] The enthusiasm of the worshipers is described as being hysterical and irrational. In spite of the racial and religious bigotry of the white press, thousands of people—black, white and other ethnic groups—flocked to these Pentecostal meetings.

Mason defended emotionally expressive worship, always citing the Bible as his authority. For example, in one treatise, he asserts the validity of dancing, shouting, trembling and falling out under the power of the Spirit, and tongue-speaking in Christian worship.[27] Guiding his reasoning was this principle: If such worship corresponds to Biblical narratives, then it must be valid. Mason, as well as Seymour, gave theological perspective and justification for ecstatic and exuberant worship, a common practice of religion among African-Americans, who converted to Christianity in large numbers during the Second Great Awakening—the religious revival in the 1820s and 1830s. The camp meeting was the context through which many African-Americans became Christians. Frontier camp meetings, and later Pentecostalism, supported and encouraged religious practices that are analogous to African religions.

In COGIC, worship is central at the gathering of believers. Worship is the church's principal context for encounter with God. The worship is spontaneous,

---

[25] Seymour, 13.

[26] "Weird Babel of Tongues," *Los Angeles Daily Times,* Apr. 18, 1906; quoted by Cheryl J. Sanders, *Saints in Exile: The Holiness-Pentecostal Experience in African American Religion and Culture* (New York: Oxford UP, 1996) 29. For newspaper reports on Mason's worship services, see also David M. Tucker, *Black Pastors and Leaders: Memphis, 1819-1972* (Memphis, TN: Memphis State UP, 1975) 91-92.

[27] Mason, *History and Life Work of Elder C.H. Mason,* 54-59.

free and enthusiastic. It involves hand-clapping, foot-stomping, shouting, dancing, rousing sermons, soul-stirring music, passionate testimony, fervent prayer, call and response, tongues-speaking, prophecy, miracles, conversion, shaking, and even falling out under the power of God.

The worship engages persons on the level of emotions. But this should not be taken to mean mere emotionalism. Because the encounter with God affects all aspects of the believer's life, his or her intellect is touched by God as well. While humans are capable of and do frequently engage in conceptual thinking, most people live, act and respond daily on the level of emotion. Worship that touches the emotions reaches people where they are, in the realm of qualitative distinctions, the place at which they live out their lives. This realm or place is where people gauge their lives by the barometers of success and failure, joy and sorrow, happiness and frustration, want and need, comfort and pain.

COGIC demonstrates appreciation for order, sacramentality and intellectual discipline. There are orders for worship. The denomination's Official Manual contains instructions for administering sacraments. The order of special services for licensing, ordination, installation, dedications, and so forth, are within the Official Manual also. From international to local church settings, there are institutions and sessions for learning.

Teachings on Tongues and Baptism in the Holy Spirit

Tongues-speaking was a significant feature of the Azusa Street Revival. Tongues were regarded as (1) a sign of baptism in the Holy Spirit; (2) a sign of the promised outpour of the Holy Spirit, revival of the church, and nearness of Christ's coming; and (3) a gift given to certain believers at the discretion of the Holy Spirit. Seymour preached that tongues are a valid sign of baptism in the Holy Spirit.

Tongues-speaking is mentioned in the Bible and frequently in connection with baptism in the Spirit. Given his tendency toward restorationism, Seymour staked claim of the apostolic era (described partly in the Book of Acts) as being a part of the church age and a reality for the contemporary church. People today can have similar experiences like those believers had in the early years of Christianity.

For Seymour, baptism in the Holy Spirit is not reducible to tongues-speaking only. According to Seymour, "The baptism in the Holy Ghost and fire means to be flooded with the love of God and power for service, and a love for the truth as it is in God's Word."[28]

---

[28] Seymour, *Doctrines and Discipline,* 92.

Baptism in the Spirit is an experience much larger than any singular expression of tongues. He believed that anyone who regarded tongues as infallible proof of baptism in the Spirit or as the only evidence of such baptism would fall prey to a host of unacceptable practices, such as witchcraft, spiritualism, heathenism (animism), free lovism (uninhibited sexuality), fanaticism and idolatry.[29] For Seymour, tongues are but one among several manifestations of the Holy Spirit.[30] As a matter of focus and priority, individuals must seek Spirit baptism and not tongues-speaking as an end within itself. The greatest evidence of Spirit baptism is inward: the believer's own sense of Christ's presence in and lordship over his or her life.[31] Soundness of mind, moral virtue, service and reconciliation contribute to the believer's conviction of Christ's presence and lordship.

Mason's testimony of baptism in the Holy Spirit involved the experience of tongues-speaking. At his baptism in the Spirit, Mason believed that he had been equipped and empowered for greater ministry. He, like Seymour, focused on people seeking this baptism without a fixation on tongues. For Mason, "The baptism of the Holy Ghost is putting on more power and receiving the glory of God."[32] Baptism in the Holy Spirit is "power for life and service."[33] In COGIC teachings, baptism in the Spirit comes third and lastly after the experiences of conversion and sanctification.[34]

COGIC's focus has been on baptism in the Spirit as a consequence of righteous living and an event that happens within a framework established by Biblical narrative rather than individuals merely acquiring an ability to make mysterious sounds. Early in COGIC history, it was thought that some may have the Spirit but not speak in tongues.[35] However, at that time, COGIC asserted that a full, complete, total encounter with God resulted in tongues-speaking. COGIC members reasoned that if God is essentially Spirit, then baptism (an immersion) in the Holy Spirit represents humanity's greatest opportunity for and deepest encounter with God. After baptism in the Spirit, not all Christians are obligated to possess tongues as a spiritual gift. COGIC gives deference to the Holy Spirit's determination of which gifts any individual will have.

---

[29] Seymour, 6, 8, 12, 91.

[30] Seymour, 91.

[31] Seymour, 93.

[32] Mason, *History and Life Work of Elder C.H. Mason,* 49-50.

[33] Clemmons, *Bishop C.H. Mason,* 68.

[34] Church of God in Christ, *Manual of the Church of God in Christ* (Memphis: Church of God in Christ, 1940) 18; hereafter referred to as *Manual of the Church of God in Christ* (1940); *Official Manual* (1973) 47, 58.

[35] *Manual of the Church of God in Christ* (1940) 18.

Divine Healing

At the Azusa Street Revival, individuals testified and, after leaving the meeting, sent letters about their being healed. Seymour affirmed God's power to heal, an act not too hard for God to perform.[36] In addition to belief in God's power to heal, Seymour believed also that the miracles described in the Gospels and the Book of Acts were possible occurrences for present-day believers.

Immediately following Mason's experience at the Azusa Revival, upon his return to Memphis, he began conducting Pentecostal meetings. At these meetings, participants claimed to be healed from various ailments—from minor to severe—such as broken bones, toothaches, tumors, hemorrhages, physical disability and blindness.[37] After being healed, they would leave their leg and arm braces, crutches and wheelchairs at the places of meeting for a witness to others of their deliverance.

COGIC continues to affirm God's capacity to perform miracles. COGIC does not define miracles as violations of God's laws of the physical universe. Rather, miracles demonstrate which laws are basic to the universe. Miracles are extraordinary with respect to defying the pattern, cycles, power and hold of natural evil and sin (moral evil) in the world. Healing and acts of deliverance from sin, trouble and ruin are miracles, but sometimes they are discussed separately for special emphasis. Miracles prove that evil and sin are not the supreme power in the universe—God is. Fundamental to the universe is life, not death; good, not evil. Miracles are samples or displays of God's power to overcome natural and moral evil and thereby "save" (rescue) human beings from peril and summon them to obedience and faith.[38]

Divine healing is regarded as a possibility for the body and the soul. By the exercise of faith, a person may be delivered from evil and sin and healed of sickness. This faith healing is performed through various means—such as prayer, fasting, physical touching (laying of hands), anointing with oil, use of symbols of faith, reading or quoting the Bible, and exorcism. The sick individual may be healed by the exercise of his own faith or through the exercise of another Spirit-filled believer's faith. COGIC recommends that its members' first response to illness be to exercise faith and follow the pastoral advice of James 5:14, 15, which reads: "Is any sick among you? let him call for the elders of the church; and let them pray over him, anointing him with oil in the name

---

[36] Seymour, *Doctrines and Discipline*, 93.

[37] Mason, *History and Life Work of Elder C.H. Mason*, 31.

[38] *Official Manual of the Church of God in Christ* (1973) 74-75.

of the Lord: and the prayer of faith shall save the sick, and the Lord shall raise him up; and if he have committed sins, they shall be forgiven him."[39]

Believing that illness is attributable to the devil and that it is not anything to which we must acquiesce, individuals may, during the act of prayer, "rebuke," "bind" or "cast out" the devil. If the illness is thought to be the result of the person's having sinned, prayer may be offered for God's forgiveness or mercy. Prayer is thought to be further efficacious through fasting. In cases where the illness is believed to be nonphysical—for example, in sin-sickness, worry or torment of the soul—similar faith practices used for physical healing are employed for the person to be made whole.

Premillennialism

At the Azusa Street Revival, Seymour proclaimed the nearness of the end. His appeal to eschatology was associated with exhorting the people to act quickly, morally and religiously. Christ was soon to return, therefore, everyone had to be ready. Eschatology was a way of making real the sense of urgency of coming into the fullness of God (i.e., receive the baptism in the Holy Spirit) and becoming involved in the church's mission of spreading the gospel to those who need to hear about God's plan of salvation. Without the gospel and baptism in the Spirit, everyone was doomed. This terror was expressed emphatically: "Get the baptism of the Spirit now so you will be ready for Christ's return and be spared the horrors of the Tribulation."[40]

Mason's teaching, as well as the position of COGIC, is premillennialist. The denomination does not specify which form of premillennialism it adheres to. COGIC's eschatology (and Seymour's also) falls under the category of historic premillennialism. Historic premillennialism does not presuppose the scheme of salvation history unique to dispensational theology.

Dispensationalism and Pentecostalism are two separate movements. Like other Pentecostals, some COGIC members have adopted dispensational (futurist) millennialism. There are several points of similarity between historic premillennialism and dispensational premillennialism. Places of divergence between them include these concerns:

1. God's plan of salvation (Is there one plan of redemption through the church, or are there two plans, one for the church and the other for the nation of Israel?)

---

[39] *Manual of the Church of God in Christ* (1940) 20, 73, 124.

[40] Douglas Jacobsen, *Thinking in the Spirit: Theologies of the Early Pentecostal Movement* (Bloomington, IN: U of Indiana P, 2003) 82.

2. The use of meta-narrative (i.e., postulating a series of dispensations) for interpretation of the Bible
3. Events preceding the coming of Christ (e.g., the rapture of the church).

In historic premillennialism, it is believed that Christ will return before the inauguration of His 1,000-year reign on earth and that prior to His return, the world will be afflicted with terrible tribulation and evil. God has one plan of salvation only, which comes through the church, the genuine Israel. COGIC proclaims the nearness of the end and perceives its role to be that of evangelism; that is, preparing people to meet the coming Christ. COGIC affirms eschatology as "a powerful factor in shaping conduct, quickening conscience and enforcing the obligations of service for God and man."[41] The exact moment of Christ's return is not known. COGIC discourages making predictions about the return of Christ and debating forms of millennialism.[42] Rather than speculate about the end, COGIC devotes its energies to spiritual and moral preparation for the end. The believer must live in a constant state of readiness. A life of holiness, sealed by baptism in the Spirit, is the best state of preparedness for which one may hope.

The Future of COGIC

COGIC's current leadership faces many complex tasks. These tasks include the following:
1. Ministering to more affluent and educated members and fostering a sense of solidarity with the less privileged
2. Maintaining headquarters and national operations comparable to those of other major mainline Christian denominations in the United States
3. Interpreting the Holiness/Pentecostal message for the present generation
4. Speaking out with clarity and conviction and leading with action on the controversial issues of our times
5. Addressing problems faced by its members who are living in U.S. inner cities and Third World countries
6. Engaging Christians and people of other faiths in dialogue and cooperation
7. Developing uniform educational and training standards for clergy
8. Inclusion of women in the ordained ministry
9. Development of uniform, equitable and enforceable policy and procedure on pastoral and other leadership appointments.

---

[41] *Official Manual of the Church of God in Christ* (1973) 61.

[42] *Official Manual of the Church of God in Christ*, 63.

The vision of Seymour and Mason was a fellowship in the Spirit, a unity of humanity that transcends the boundaries of race, ethnicity, class and gender. The Pentecostal Movement, for various reasons, splintered along the same lines that divide human beings, placing us at odds and conflict with each other. COGIC today is predominately African-American. The ending of legalized racial segregation was followed by the tremendous growth and expansion of the African-American middle class. Inequality still exists in the United States; however, several African-Americans have made substantial economic and political gains.

COGIC members represent this transformation well among African-Americans. Within one generation or so, many rose from poor and working-class occupations to middle- and upper-middle-class positions. Historically, the black church has been an advocate for the poor and oppressed. Whether COGIC perceives itself as primarily "Pentecostal" or as "black," COGIC leaders must address the question of whether African-American Christianity has the potential, in light of the economic prosperity and political power that has come to an increasing number of African-Americans, to transform American institutional structures and maintain an alternative set of values centered on social justice and the dignity and worth of human life.

The vision of unity of early Pentecostals is further compromised by several practices. For example, COGIC's egalitarian tendency conflicts with its policy on prohibiting women from being ordained. Women's only avenue for ministry is through the Women's Department. COGIC has dual tracks for women and men. The track for women, no matter how gifted for ministry and leadership, never leads to ordination, formal recognition as a pastor, or appointment as a superintendent or a bishop. Once a male minister is ordained, theoretically, he enters a system whereby he may rise to the highest position of leadership in the church—a bishop.

Most ministers become pastors by starting their own congregations. After the founder dies, an appointment must be made. Appointment and promotion within COGIC is influenced by familial relations, charisma, financial contributions, and relations with authority figures. While COGIC's hierarchical structure functions poorly at times in the accomplishment of very important tasks, it most always succeeds in concentrating power, money and esteem in the hands of a few—usually those who are close to the top. The development of patriarchy in COGIC is oppressive to women and those men who are not fully integrated in the male network.

Another example is COGIC's relation to communities of those who have different lifestyles. COGIC has made a courageous stand in challenging the notion that homosexual preference is a right. However, COGIC's position that homosexuality and same-sex marriage are inconsistent with Christian living distracts the denomination's attention from the valid claims of gays and lesbians to civil and human rights in employment, housing, education, and protection from harassment and physical harm. Maintenance of basic respect for everyone is crucial, not only for the development of fellowship among believers, but also for peace and the promotion of goodwill in society.

The Azusa vision of unity summons COGIC from its isolationism. While COGIC participates in the Pentecostal and Charismatic Churches of North America and Congress of National Black Churches, it has yet to engage in larger, more inclusive, ecumenical partnerships such as the World Council of Churches and National Council of the Churches of Christ in the U.S.A. The world is characterized by a high degree of diversity and pluralism. In response, COGIC must actively pursue coalition-building with secular and non-Christian institutions. No single denomination can achieve its goals without cooperation and support from other institutions and organizations.

In this climate of diversity, COGIC must come into its own voice. From Azusa, Pentecostalism became a global movement. The power of personal and social transformation declared and spread from Azusa has been experienced by many individuals drawn into the membership and reach of COGIC. However, there remain even more in need of this radical change that occurs when the human meets the divine in the Spirit. COGIC must foster, encourage and support theological reflection on its own history and distinctive beliefs and practices.

COGIC has preserved several distinctives of Pentecostalism that originated from the Azusa Street Revival. African-American Pentecostals are noted more for their contribution to worship and public representation of Pentecostalism than for their development of institutions and construction of theology. Now, as the largest Pentecostal denomination and, by some estimates, the largest African-American denomination in the United States, COGIC has a new calling—to address and be heard on matters affecting people throughout the world. COGIC must do this passionately and theologically, and then only after undergoing extensive reform. Already within COGIC, a substantial number of theologically trained people are acquiring the acumen to communicate in traditional theological categories the convictions and practices of COGIC.

15

The Blessings of Azusa Street and Doornfontein Revivals and Pentecost's Blind Spot

Frank Chikane

Introduction

Our generation is fortunate to have an opportunity to celebrate, as well as reflect on, the 100 years of the Modern Pentecostal Movement. With the benefit of hindsight and available researched and published material, we are able to understand better the nature of this movement, its impact on the church and on the complex global village which has been its theatre. Our forebearers have left us with valuable experiences and traditions which, like all established traditions, must be open to critique to enable us to correct the wrongs of the past, sharpen our tools of trade and build the movement further into the future, as we tarry for the coming of the Lord.

The challenge we face as Pentecostals, or Pentecostal theologians, is our averse attitude to criticism, especially "critical thinking," mainly because we work within a worldview of "absolutes" that are God-ordained and final. Here, a critique of the world in narrow "spiritual terms" is allowed, but a critique of the world in general to understand how it impacts our "spirituality,"[1] in broader

---

[1] The traditional understanding of the word *spirituality* is set within a narrow religious context which limits it to say "devotion to spiritual things" and exclude the material life or what would be considered as "worldly." In contrast to this, African "spirituality"

terms, is like engaging in "worldly things." Furthermore, the internal belief systems within which the movement functions are proscribed.

I am therefore going to take the risk of critically looking at this experience of a century and identifying weaknesses that have militated against the credibility of our witness and mission as a Pentecostal family. Our thesis here, which we invite the reader to test, is that the Pentecostal tradition, in general, responds effectively to the manifestation of sin in the personal lives of people but fails, in the main, to address the complex societal challenges that confront humanity.

Secondly, Pentecostals are good at critiquing the theories and philosophical issues that arise out of humanity's efforts to deal with such challenges rather than engage in such an exercise. This is what I would like to call "Pentecost's Blind Spot," which could be rephrased as "Pentecostals' Blind Spot" for those who are sensitive about the preserve and sanctity of the word *Pentecost*.

To establish the thesis, I will review the blessed experiences of the Azusa Street Revival and the related experience at Doornfontein in Johannesburg, which (for the Apostolic Faith Mission) is considered "the Azusa of South Africa." We will celebrate the experiences and blessings, learn lessons anew from these experiences, as well as relive the blessing. We will do this with the hope of being revived again and reempowered to press on with the mission of reaching out to the world and saturating it with the gospel.

As we are celebrating history, we will be constrained to use the narrative method. I shall tell the story, which can then be celebrated and analyzed. Where the information is now common knowledge, I shall not burden the reader with unnecessary references. This notwithstanding, I will try to acknowledge the specific contributions of others where it is due. Although I will refer to other Pentecostal churches and organizations in South Africa, the Apostolic Faith Mission (AFM) will be our primary case study because the author is a member of the AFM and understands it better and because it is the largest Pentecostal church in South Africa.[2]

The Impact of the Azusa Street Revival in South Africa

Ninety-eight years ago, two American Pentecostal missionaries, John Graham Lake and Thomas Hezmalhalch, arrived in South Africa to bring the message of the gospel, the ministry of healing and the "new" Pentecostal experience.[3] Both

---

integrates the narrow concept of "spirituality" with the "material life," that is, life in its totality. In this integrated holistic approach to "spirituality," there is no dichotomy between the spiritual and the material, sacred and secular.

[2] See 1996 South African Government Census.

[3] Although this experience looked "new" for this generation of Evangelicals and the Holiness Movement, the special phenomenon has occurred at various times "during

Lake and Hezmalhalch had ties with John Alexander Dowie of the Zion Catholic Apostolic Church in the United States who was known for his successful healing ministry. Both visited Azusa Street following the outpouring of the Holy Spirit there and worshiped in William Seymour's church. Reports are that both were highly inspired by the revival.[4] Lake is recorded to have said this about Seymour:

> "It was not what he said in words; it was what he said from his spirit to my heart that showed me he had more of God in his life than any man I had ever met up to that time." [5]

Lake and Hezmalhalch started their ministry in May 1908, in a black church in Doornfontein, Johannesburg. A great revival ensued, making Doornfontein the Azusa of South Africa.[6] It was like a "spiritual cyclone had struck Doornfontein."[7] Many people were saved, many were baptized with the Holy Spirit, and still many more were healed of all kinds of sicknesses. Although the services started from a black church, many whites visited the services after hearing about what was happening. Racism was strong in South Africa, but the power of the racial spirit in Johannesburg could not prevail against the power of the Holy Spirit. Burton reports that although, as a rule, the white population would scorn to sit in the same place of worship as the natives . . .

> "Now, however, there was a great wave of conviction, and hunger after God, so that in the little Doornfontein Chapel all shades of colour and degrees of the social scale mingled freely in their hunger after God."[8]

Here, as in Azusa, through the blood of the Lord Jesus Christ and the outpouring of the Holy Spirit, the walls of race and color were erased: "Before long, the black Africans found themselves standing around watching their employers being blessed."[9]

When the small Doornfontein church could not contain the numbers, they

---

periods of spiritual revival and enthusiasm." See Donald Gee, *The Pentecostal Movement* (Luton, Beds: Assemblies of God Publishing House, 1949) 8. What is special about Azusa is that the experience was not that of "showers" but of the "outpouring" of the Spirit resembling that of the "Jerusalem experience."

[4] J.G. Lake, *Adventures in God* (Tulsa: Harrison, 1881).

[5] Isak Burger, *Geloofs Geskiedenis van die Apostoliese Geloofsending van Siud Africa, 1908-1958* (Braamfonrein, South Africa: Evangelie Uitgewers, 1987) 131-32.

[6] For the Apostolic Faith Mission, the Doornfontein Revival was like a repeat of Azusa Street Revival.

[7] Gordon Lindsay, *John G. Lake: Apostle to Africa* (Dallas: Christ for the Nations, 1981) 25.

[8] W.F.P. Burton, *When God Makes a Pastor* (London: Victoria, 1934) 32.

[9] B. Slosser, *A Man Called Mr. Pentecost* (Plainfield, NJ: Logos International, 1977) 106.

moved to the Central Tabernacle in Bree Street. Through their ministry, one of the largest Pentecostal churches in South Africa, The Apostolic Faith Mission of South Africa (AFM) was born. By 1996, the AFM had more than a million members (Government Census). Through its mission work, the AFM is now established in 16 countries on the African continent, in Asia (India and Pakistan), Europe (Belgium and the United Kingdom), South America (Brazil) and North America (Dallas). The work in Europe and the United States signifies a new trend of what missiologists call "reverse mission," that is, mission from the developing to the developed countries or "mission from the underside."[10] The AFM developed as an independent indigenous church without any links to any international movement or structure, as both Lake and Hezmalhalch had all returned to the United States by 1913 and never maintained any structural or institutional relationship. The church was registered in 1913 before Lake left South Africa.

Between 1909 and 1914, two other major Pentecostal churches, the Full Gospel Church (FGC) and Assemblies of God (AOG), were born in South Africa through missionaries who were influenced or inspired by the Azusa Street Revival. Charles Chawner from Canada and Henry Michael Turney from the United States arrived in South Africa and started a mission work that gave birth to the Assemblies of God. George Bowie, from the Bethel Pentecostal Assembly in the United States came to South Africa in 1909 as a missionary and started a Pentecostal Mission that became the Full Gospel Church.

We can tell of many more Pentecostal experiences and Pentecostal churches in South Africa that derived their inspiration from, and have a claim in one form or another to, a historical lineage to the Azusa Street Revival. Although there were earlier showers of the Holy Spirit in many places around the world, including South Africa, the Azusa Street Revival indeed gave birth to the modern Pentecostal Movement, and Doornfontein was its mirror image in South Africa.[11]

Return to "Original Christianity"

The impact of Azusa Street to the people of South Africa was not only the Pentecostal message or the new "blessing" of the baptism with the Holy Spirit, as some called it in the early days. Azusa was a call for us to return to the glory of *the early church* or the "primitive church," which included the baptism with

---

[10] Roswith Gerloff, "The Significance of the African Christian Diaspora in Europe With Special Reference to Britain," in *African Christian Outreach*, vol. 1: *The African Initiated Churches*, ed. Marthinus L. Daneel (Menlo Park: Southern African Missiological Society, 2001) 166-67.

[11] See note 4 above.

the Holy Spirit. Azusa Street and Doornfontein call on us to return to the *apostolic faith* with its power of Pentecost and emphasis on the charismatic gifts, especially supernatural healing.[12] It was a restoration of the church to its former New Testament glory, the "original Christianity."[13] Donald Gee states this in a more succinct manner:

> The distinctive testimony of the Pentecostal Movement within the church is to the abiding possibility and importance of the supernatural element in Christian life and service, particularly as contained in the manifestation of the Holy Spirit.[14]

The return to "original Christianity" by the Pentecostal Movement built on the Holiness Movement tradition and its emphasis on *holy living*. It focused more on a "new birth," a "new lifestyle," a "clean life," and what was called "Christian Perfectionism." For instance, a number of the followers of Wesley[15] became important exponents of what they call the "higher Christian life." The Methodists, who spread rapidly across the American frontier, went beyond the conversion experience common to all Evangelicals, to emphasize a post-conversion crisis that Wesley and his followers called variously "entire sanctification," "perfect love," the "second blessing," or "Christian perfectionism."[16]

One may not agree with some of the primitive theological formulations of the time. The point one would like to make here, though, is that Pentecostalism built on the foundation of the Holiness Movement. But its significance is that it went beyond the "second blessing" of the Holiness Movement and stressed the critical importance of the gifts of the Spirit (the charismata)—especially "healing"—and emphasized the baptism in the Holy Spirit with the evidence of speaking in tongues. In a sense, what happened at Azusa and Doornfontein brought together the Biblically sound Wesleyan holiness theological elements with those of Pentecost (baptism in the Holy Spirit) to develop what we regard today as Pentecostal theology. This theology has given us the heritage of our soteriology (doctrine of salvation) and pneumatology (doctrine of the Holy Spirit), which

---

[12] N. Bloch-Hoell, *The Pentecostal Movement* (London: Allen and Unwin, 1964) 4; and G.C. Oosthuizen, *Pentecostal Penetration Into the Indian Community in the Metropolitan Durban, South Africa* (Pretoria: Human Sciences Research Council, 1975) 66.

[13] Bloch-Hoell, *Pentecostal Movement*, 4.

[14] Gee, *Pentecostal Movement;* Bloch-Hoell, *Pentecostal Movement*, 8.

[15] These included D.L. Moody, William E. Boardman, Charles Cullis, Hannah Whittall Smith, Robert Pearsall Smith, George Muller, William Arthur, A.B. Simpson, S.D. Gordon, Andrew Murray, and R.A. Torrey. See the *Dictionary of Pentecostal and Charismatic Movements,* ed. Stanley M. Burgess and Gary B. McGee, with Patrick H. Alexander, assoc. ed. (Grand Rapids: Zondervan, 1988) 280.

[16] *Dictionary of Pentecostal and Charismatic Movements*, 282.

covers in a systematic way the areas of repentance, reconciliation, justification, regeneration, sanctification, baptism with the Holy Spirit and the gifts of the Holy Spirit. The contribution of Pentecostals, therefore, is a new understanding of the Baptism and gifts of the Holy Spirit and a "missiological ecclesiology," which we now turn to.

Missiological Ecclesiology

Spirit Baptism brought about a "pneumatological revision of ecclesiology that made it inherently missiological."[17] Peter Watt and Willem Saayman elaborate on this view as follows:

> It is our opinion that at the very heart (or centre) of Pentecostalism lies a complex of distinctives that imbue it with an all-consuming sense of mission and witness inspired by a personal experience of baptism in the Spirit.[18]

As at the Azusa Street Revival and Doornfontein, once people had heard the Word, witnessed the healing power of the Lord and experienced the Baptism of the Holy Spirit, they left the scene and replicated the experience wherever they went in the tradition of the New Testament witnesses. As the Pentecostal Movement grew from Azusa Street to the rest of the world, so did the message of Doornfontein move from town to town as well as beyond the borders of South Africa. Ordinary (lay) people: workers, merchants, traders, mineworkers, unemployed, peasants, black and white, men and women, old and young, educated and those with no formal education—collectively and individually—heard the message and carried it to the far-flung areas of South Africa and beyond. For instance, the AFM, planted initially in the Southern African region, was mainly through miners who worked in South Africa. They heard the gospel and the experience of Pentecost, and returned home as "missionaries to their own people." Angola, Mozambique, Zambia and Zimbabwe are classical examples in this regard. Organized missions from South Africa and Germany followed after this initial outreach by individual lay persons.[19]

---

[17] Peter Watt and Willem Saayman, "South African Pentecostalism in Context: Symptoms and Crisis," *Missionalia* 31, no. 2 (Aug. 2003): The South African Missionary Society, 327.

[18] Watt and Saayman. See also A. Tizon, "Mission as Wonder: A Pentecostal Theology of Mission for an Age of Postmodernism, in Dialogue with David Bosch," *Missionalia* 29, no. 3 (2001) 405-22.

[19] The AFM International is engaged in a study of the histories of the AFM churches worldwide, and this phenomenon has already presented itself as a general trend, particularly in Southern Africa. AFM International Headquarters, Centurion, South Africa.

When our forebearers, both in the United States and in South Africa picked the name, Apostolic Faith Mission, they wanted to keep the concept of mission in the name. P.L. le Roux, the first president of the AFM after John G. Lake, said at an ordination service in 1916:

> We call ourselves the Apostolic Faith Mission; we expect the same power to rest upon us that rested on the early church, and we expect to do the same work.[20]

For them, this would indicate that there can be no church without mission as its core business. In the Pentecostal Movement, every member is a witness, a missionary, a preacher, a counselor. Specific gifts may endow one or the other with more abilities in the particular areas of work, but all are "workers" in God's vineyard. J.L. Langerman, one of the general secretaries of the AFM says:

> The first members of the AFM held a dim view of all professional church leaders. The result of this attitude was that ministerial leadership in the newly formed Pentecostal church was organized along the New Testament concept of voluntary ministry of the whole body of Christ. [21]

Those volunteers who measured up to certain standards and were actively witnessing and working for the Lord on a part-time basis were called "workers." That is why the AFM used the expression: "Workers' Council" for the meeting of all the workers in the church that included pastors, evangelists, preachers, deacons and elders.

Watt and Saayman focused extensively on this unique phenomenon which is similar to the tradition and practice of the early church of the Apostles and Disciples of the "New Way." They say:

> The pneumatological revision of ecclesiology placed the Reformation doctrine of the priesthood of believers in a new light, giving it new meaning and practical application in the liturgical structure of a Pentecostal meeting. . . . Spirit baptism is both an intensely personal experience as well as a shared experience. . . . The experience of the Spirit is also a shared experience in the liturgical structure of a congregational gathering. It is this shared experience of the Spirit in the Pentecostal liturgy that makes an enormous soteriological impact on the participants.

---

[20] *Comforter,* June 1916: 6.

[21] Jan L. Langerman, "The Apostolic Faith Mission of South Africa: A Revitalization of the Theological Concept of Church Ministry" (D.Min. diss., Fuller Theological Seminary, Pasadena, CA, 1983) 83.

It is at this point that the idea of "power"—the enabling power of the Spirit—is important. The liberating (soteriological) effect of this belief among those whose lives have been shaped by powerlessness cannot be overemphasized. The presence of the Holy Spirit empowers the individual to "be" (a somebody) and "do" (something of value) within the fellowship of the believing community.[22]

Watt and Saayman continue:

In other words, the Pentecostal believer is enabled by gifts of the Spirit to become an active participant contributing spontaneously and meaningfully to the unfolding development of the liturgical content of a particular Pentecostal meeting. *A participatory ecclesiology is therefore the genius of the Pentecostal meeting* which becomes a liberating, ennobling and salvic experience[23] (my own emphasis).

G.C. Oosthuizen comes to the same matter from a completely different perspective. He says that *Pentecostalism* is "a reaction against social and ecclesiastical paternalism." It does so by "democratizing society," he says. The point Oosthuizen is making, although in an exaggerated manner,[24] is clear. He continues to say that the Pentecostal Movement is one where "the adherents express their freedom and emphasize the functional aspects of Christianity."[25] For Allan Anderson, this is the "democratization of Christianity." Henceforth, for him, "the mystery of the gospel would no longer be reserved for a select, privileged and educated few, but would be revealed to whoever was willing to receive it and pass it on."[26]

To sum up this point, I submit that the Pentecostal Movement is distinctively missionary, and its ecclesiology must be a "missionary ecclesiology."[27] Once it ceases to be "missionary," it loses its Pentecostal character and reduces itself to the old static institution the Holiness Movement reacted against.

---

[22] Watt and Saayman, "South African Pentecostalism," 327-28.

[23] Watt and Saayman, 328 (my own emphasis). See also A. Anderson, "Pentecostal Movements in East Asia: Indigenous Oriental Christianity?" *STM: Swedish Missiological Themes/Svensk Missions Tidskrift* 87, no. 3 (Spring 2000) 319-40.

[24] Democratizing "society" for me seems exaggerated. I would say that the democratization process within the Pentecostal service and mission should be a pointer to the democratization of society. The reality is that the Pentecostal Movement democratizes the life, form, and practice of the Pentecostal community.

[25] Oosthuizen, *Pentecostal Penetration,* 67.

[26] Allan Anderson, "The Mission Initiative of African Pentecostals in Continental Perspective," in *African Christian Outreach,* vol. 1: *The African Initiated Churches,* ed. Marthinus L. Daneel (Menlo Park: Southern African Missiological Society, 2001) 93.

[27] Watt and Saayman, "South African Pentecostalism," 327.

The three matters we have discussed above have been mainly a major focus of the Pentecostal Movement. Some lapses have occurred sometimes and within specific institutions and organizations that claim to be Pentecostal. Even if there could be blind spots in these areas, there are always multiple mirrors which assist us to shed light on those spots. This is worthy to be celebrated. There are, though, new worrying trends of a return to the Episcopal way of life for some emerging Pentecostal and Charismatic churches in recent times. This trend is also encroaching into the century-old classical Pentecostal churches. Should it gain root, the democratization of the services, the participation, the freedom in worship forms, the priesthood of the believers and the missiological dimensions of the Pentecostal Movement may be lost, resulting in the loss of the "missiological" dimension, which is the hallmark of Pentecostalism.

The Demon of Racism—The Blind Spot of Pentecostalism

The real blind spot of Pentecostals for me has been the readiness of the Movement to settle with the demon of racism rather than exorcise it. Many Pentecostal historians are content to record the experiences of racism throughout the history of Pentecostalism without lifting a finger to reverse its tide or eradicate it. In most of the literature, it is considered as unfortunate or unacceptable. Many would even agree that it is unchristian and not Biblical. But few would take the risk to challenge the phenomenon in a programmatic way. In fact, any attempt to challenge it and the related structures and institutions of power through which it is expressed is normally considered as unChristian and a violation of the Biblical injunction to respect those in authority. The infamous Romans 13 here becomes very handy.

Azusa and Doornfontein demonstrated beyond any doubt that when the Spirit came down, the historical demon of racism gave way. In both experiences, whites and blacks worshiped together against the natural dictates of a long history of racism occasioned by about 500 years of slavery; about three centuries of colonization and subjugation of peoples of Africa, Asia, the Middle-East and South America; many years of the subjugation and even extermination of the aborigines in the Americas, Australia and other places; many years of exploitation of the resources of the colonized regions around the world; many years of neo-colonial exploitation; many years of segregationist laws and the institutionalized system of apartheid in South Africa; and many years of unfair and unequal terms of trade between developing and the developed countries. Against all this, the racial harmony in these services must have been a miracle in itself.

About this miracle, Frank Bartleman is reported to have said: "The color line was washed away in the blood."[28] Other historians refer to the Pentecostal Movement as an intercultural agent throwing a bridge across the troubled waters between two cultures which otherwise may never meet."[29] We have already dealt with similar experiences in Doornfontein in presenting the South African experience of Pentecost. In fact, Azusa and Doornfontein were a radical critique of the racist societies that prevailed at the beginning of the 20th century. Azusa and Doornfontein presented an alternative model of societal relations where color, class or sex did not matter. What mattered was that all were created in the image of God, and all had need for salvation, healing and the baptism in the Holy Spirit.

About Azusa, Japie Lapoorta says this:

> The Azusa Mission . . . was not only a prophetic word addressed to the existing structures of society, but it was a word to the mainline churches that failed to address the issue of racism, but rather conformed to those structures. In doing that, they neglected fundamental imperatives of the gospel such as love for the neighbour and the unity of the church of Jesus Christ. Azusa therefore is a sign of judgment of the existing churches on the one hand, because they failed to be what God intended them to be. On the other hand, Azusa serves as a sign of hope to both the church and society.[30]

But this moment of glory at Azusa and Doornfontein did not last long. The details of this experience are documented in many historical texts. It should suffice to say that in Azusa there were three major splits within a period of five years involving Charles Fox Parham, Florence Crawford and Clara Lum, and William Durham—mainly on racial lines.

In Doornfontein,[31] within four months the first Executive Committee met without any blacks represented. Clearly, a decision must have been made to exclude them in line with the societal practice of the time. This "all-white" committee decided to separate places of worship between blacks and whites. In less than six months, they decided to sequence the baptism of the "natives" and whites, starting with whites. In eight months' time, a racially based concept of mission was instituted where the superintendent of the "Native work" must be white. Fourteen

---

[28] Frank Bartleman, *Azusa Street* (Plainfield, NJ: Logos International, 1980 [1925]) 54.

[29] Iain MacRobert, *The Black Roots of White Racism of Early Pentecostalism in the USA* (London: MacMillan, 1988) xiv.

[30] Japie J. Lapoorta, *Unity or Division? The Unity Struggles of the Black Churches Within the Apostolic Faith Mission of South Africa* (Kuils Revier: J.J. Lapoorta, 1997) 37.

[31] All the decisions on the matters which follow are in the minutes of the Executive Committee of the AFM.

months later, the separation was complete with a decision to separate the baptism of whites from that of blacks. By July 1917, about 11 years after the blessed revival of Doornfontein, the final nail on nonracialism in the AFM was in place.

In a historical but contradictory resolution the Executive Committee agreed that . . .

> We do not teach or encourage social equality between Whites and Natives. We recognize that God is no respecter of persons, but that in every nation he that feareth Him and worketh righteousness is acceptable to Him. We, therefore, preach the gospel equally to all peoples, making no distinctions. We wish it to be generally known that our white, Coloured and Native people have their separate places of worship, where the Sacraments are administered to them.[32]

The Council continued to deal with the reservation of seats in the Central Tabernacle "for coloured persons who may attend there." They also decided that for certain "worthy colored" families the matter would be left in the hands of the Spiritual Committee. No Scriptures were used to justify their position.[33] The opening statement of the resolution is in fact an antithesis of the later part, as Christiaan Rudolph De Wet observes.[34]

The tragedy about this matter is that even John G. Lake, who initially resisted the sin of racism, gave in and became a president of a racially exclusive white AFM by November 1910, a mere two years and eight months after the blessing of Doornfontein and his refusal to throw out blacks from the revival services in Braamfontein. He came to South Africa as a missionary to all South Africans, but he ended up in a white church and presided on the process of exclusion and marginalization of blacks.

In effect, the color line was redrawn within months after Azusa and Doornfontein.[35] In both instances, it was like the demon (unclean spirit) that returned after it was cast out. But when it returned, it did not come alone, but brought along seven other spirits more evil than itself, and the last state was worse than the first (see Matthew 2:43-45; Luke 11:24-26). The breakdown between Seymour and Parham in Azusa demonstrates this. In South Africa,

---

[32] Minutes of the Executive Council, July 7, 1917.

[33] Christiaan Rudolph De Wet, "The Apostolic Faith Mission in Africa: 1908–1980: A Case Study in Church Growth in a Segregated Society" (Ph.D. thesis, University of Cape Town, 1989) 166.

[34] De Wet, 65-166.

[35] See Robert Mapes Anderson, *Vision of the Disinherited: The Making of American Pentecostalism* (New York: Oxford UP, 1979) 188; and Vinson Synan, *The Holiness-Pentecostal Movement in the United States* (Grand Rapids: Eerdmans, 1971) 180.

resolution after resolution was taken to formalize racist policies within the church. This resulted in four racially divided churches of the AFM (White, Colored, Indian, and African) which only united 88 years later in 1996.

Similar stories can be told about the Assemblies of God (AOG) and the Full Gospel Church (FGC) in South Africa and many other Pentecostal groups.

The questions that need to be asked are: Why did the Pentecostal Movement fail to resist this trend that caused enormous pain among brothers and sisters who were created in the same image of God, washed by the same blood of Christ and baptized by the same Spirit? Why did our white brothers choose to conform to the racist culture of the world, rather than resist it as evil and a sin before God? How is it possible for Pentecostals to preach the gospel of love and reconciliation and still harbor racist sentiments and attitudes and participate in a discriminatory system against their own brothers and sisters in the Lord? How is it possible for a deacon of the AFM to supervise the torture of his brother in the Lord and still go and worship God in tongues? How possible is it for Pentecostals who are filled with the Spirit to allow discriminatory relationships with their own brothers and sisters in the Lord?

These are questions many black Pentecostals and outsiders are asking. The Pentecostal family, especially Pentecostal theologians, still need to answer these questions. This is urgent because the credibility of the Pentecostal message and experience is at stake. South African Evangelicals and Pentecostals were forced by the brutality of the apartheid system and its heretical theological justification thereof, to participate in a series of initiatives to protest against and critique the racist practices within and outside the church during the 1980s. They started with the Kairos Document[36] at an ecumenical level, followed by the Evangelical Witness[37] and then Relevant Pentecostal Witness.[38]

Nico Horn discusses this protest movement with its documents in his paper on "The Experience of the Spirit in Apartheid: The Possibilities of the Rediscovery of the Black Roots of Pentecostalism for South African Theology."[39] Leonard Lovett ventures into the most difficult area of the Holy Spirit and racism. He says that "no man can genuinely experience the fullness of the Spirit and

---

[36] *The Kairos Document: Challenge to the Church* (Johannesburg: Skotaville, 1986).

[37] *The Evangelical Witness in South Africa: Evangelicals Critique Their Own Theology and Practice* (Soweto: Concerned Evangelicals, 1986).

[38] *A Relevant Pentecostal Witness* (Durban: The Relevant Pentecostals, 1988).

[39] See J. Nico Horn, "The Experience of the Spirit in Apartheid: The Possibilities of the Rediscovery of the Black Roots of Pentecostalism for South African Theology," in *Experiences of the Spirit: Conference on Pentecostal and Charismatic Research in Europe at Utrecht University, 1989,* ed. Jan A.B. Jongeneel, Studies in the Intercultural History of Christianity 68 (Frankfurt am Main; New York: Peter Lang, 1991) 118-20.

remain a bona fide racist."[40] This is a tough and uncompromising statement that needs further evaluation. Unfortunately, it cannot be done in this paper because of constrains of space.

Turning Pentecostal Theology Upside-Down

The blind spot of Pentecostalism on the matter of racism is occasioned by the fact that those who were served by racism were the ones who had to interpret the rightness and wrongness of the positions they took and the lives they lived. The voices of the victims or targets of racism were suppressed to ensure that the interests of the privileged and powerful were not adversely affected. The slaves and colonized and the oppressed and exploited were treated like nonpersons, without identity or history and without views and opinions.

On the matter of history, the classic text on the history of the Apostolic Faith Mission of South Africa covering the period 1908-1958[41] is very illuminating. The text presents itself as *Die Geskiedenes van die Apolstoliese Geloofsendingvan Suid Afrika* (AGS) without any qualification indicating that this was the history of the white section of the church. Black "workers" (as per our earlier definition) are referred to only when they are encountered by the white church or when the mission work of the white church was discussed. In fact, the last chapter of this text (ch. 16) is the only direct reference to some history of the black churches (African, Colored, and Indian). Even here, they are discussed as "departments of the AGS," that is, the white AFM.

In his book, *The Colonizer and the Colonized,*[42] Albert Memmi makes a case about the usefulness of denying the colonized any history or identity to affect the project of the colonizer. He says:

> The colonized seems condemned to lose his memory. . . . The memory which is assigned to him is certainly not that of his people. The history which is taught . . . is not his own. He knows who Colbert or Cromwell was, but he learns nothing about Khaznadar; he knows about Joan of Arc, but not about El Kahena. Everything seems to have taken place out of his country.[43]

In dealing with the blind spot of Pentecostalism, we need to start from the

---

[40] Leonard Lovett, "Black Origins of the Pentecostal Movement," in *Aspects of Pentecostal-Charismatic Origins,* ed. Vinson Synan (Plainfield, NJ: Logos International, 1975) 140.

[41] Burger, *Geloofs Geskiedenis;* Lovett, "Black Origins," 140.

[42] Albert Memmi, *The Colonizer and the Colonized* (Boston: Beacon, 1965) 102-5.

[43] Memmi, 102-5

point that all of us work within a particular ideological framework of interpretation defined by our worldview, our perspectives of reality, the way we have been brought-up and socialized, our strata in the society, and our collective and individual interests. The sociology of knowledge shows that we always think out of a definite context of relations and action, out of a given praxis. In this regard, there is no such a thing as "neutral knowledge."[44]

Accordingly, it is necessary for any person with integrity to criticize one's own praxis from within in order to re-project it in a deeper, more significant, and more effective way.[45] Jose Miguel Bonino elaborates as follows on this matter:

> Such criticism must be done from within in a double sense. On the one hand, it must be done in the context of active engagement, in relation to the real questions which are posed in the praxis itself. On the other hand, it should deepen and push further the theory which is incorporated in such praxis.[46]

Bonino continues to say that this means:

> Theology cannot claim to have some "pure kerygmatic truths or events," unengaged, or uncompromised in a concrete historical praxis, from where we can judge the concrete Christian obedience of a person or community.[47]

What was missing in the praxis of the Pentecostal Movement for the century was criticism of its praxis of racial practices and prejudice from where we can judge it against its Christian obedience. Anyone who engages in such criticism would realize that the probability of knowing the truth about a particular praxis or experience is higher when looked at from the perspective of the victim or from the underside. Robert McAfee Brown refers to Hugo Assmann's startling expression, "the epistemological privilege of the poor." Assmann uses this expression:

> To underline the fact that the way the poor view the world is closer to the reality of the world than the way the rich view it. Their "epistemology," i.e., their way of knowing, is accurate to the degree that is impossible for those who see the world only from the vantage point of privileges they want to retain.[48]

---

[44] Jose Miguez Bonino, *Doing Theology in a Revolutionary Situation* (Philadelphia: Fortress, 1975) 90.

[45] Bonino, 99.

[46] Bonino.

[47] Bonino.

[48] Robert McAfee Brown, *Theology in a New Key: Responding to Liberation Themes* (Philadelphia: Westminster, 1978) 61.

In his *Letters and Papers from Prison,* Dietrich Bonhoeffer deals with this matter from the experience of Hitler's genocide against the Jews. He says:

> There remains an experience of incomparable value. We have for once learnt to see the great events of world history from below, from the perspective of the outcast, the suspects, the maltreated, the powerless, the oppressed, the reviled—in short, from the perspective of those who suffer.[49]

The choice of the Lord for location and context of the origins of the modern Pentecostal experience was not an accident or a mistake. God seems to always choose humble circumstances to communicate with us. God chose a manger as the birth place of the Lord, and a black church in both Azusa and Doornfontein to hold the revival services. God chose William Seymour, a black person and the son of a slave, to be the symbol and father of the new Pentecostal Movement. Even in the case of whites in South Africa, it was the Afrikaners who welcomed the Pentecostal message and experience. After the Anglo-Boer War (now called the South African War) many white families, particularly Afrikaners, lived in conditions almost similar to those of black South Africans, notwithstanding legislation favoring them.[50] Unfortunately, the tsunami of racism and apartheid overwhelmed them.

The struggle to end racial structures and practices within the AFM and the push for unity came mainly from the black AFM churches than from the white division of the church. When the black churches hit a white brick wall, they went ahead with the unity of the black churches in 1993, which they called "Composite Division." Unity with the white division only came in 1996.

It is clear from these experiences that the sins related to positions of power and dominance are not easily discernible by the strata of society that benefits out of the advantage occasioned by such a position of power.[51] That is why the sin of racism eluded white Pentecostals, despite their baptism in the Holy Spirit. The white ruling classes of the time did so in their favor, thereby, guaranteeing their interests.

Paul is instructive in this regard. He writes in 1 Corinthians 1:26-29:

> Consider your own call, brothers and sisters: not many of you were wise by human standards, not many were powerful, not many were of noble birth.

---

[49] Dietrich Bonhoeffer, *Letters and Papers From Prison,* enlarged ed., 17.

[50] See Burger, *Geloofs Geskiedenis,* 117-23; and Watt and Saayman, "South African Pentecostalism," 319-22.

[51] See a letter by Frank Chikane titled "Till kyrkorna och de kristna I Europa," *Svensk Missionstidskrift* 75:3 (1987) 23-27.

> But God chose what is foolish in the world to shame the wise; God chose what is weak in the world to shame the strong; God chose what is low and despised in the world, things that are not, to reduce to nothing things that are, so that no one might boast in the presence of God (*NRSV*).

If the powerful, rich and privileged were given the honor to host this blessed moment of the return to Pentecost, they would most probably have appropriated the blessing for themselves and kept Seymour outside the church like at Topeka, to listen to the lessons through an open door.

In South Africa, where the missionaries happened to be white Americans who were partnered by white South Africans, it was easier to snap the blessings from the small black Doornfontein church, exclude blacks from leadership, relegate them to the margins of the church and deprive them of full membership for almost 75 years. Even Letwaba, who was relatively well educated, was excluded from the leadership. They separated water baptism and Communion services and treated blacks as dependents who had no capacity of their own. Until a decade ago, as a result of the AFM, South Africa was racially divided for 88 years. One shudders to think what would have happened to the Pentecostal message if God had chosen the rich and powerful of the time to be carriers of this message.

It is instructive to recall that at the time of the Azusa Street Revival and Doornfontein, major decisions had been taken already on the questions of the "rights of man." The American Declaration of Independence of American colonies from Great Britain was adopted in 1776; the preamble of the French Constitution of 1789 contained the Declaration of the Rights of Man, and the Emancipation Proclamation in the United States was made in 1863. In all of these, notwithstanding, the rights of black people were still grossly violated in various colonies and occupied territories worldwide. The only way in which one could explain this is that black people were not considered to be human beings. At best, they were considered as subhuman.

We need to open our eyes, and engage in self-criticism (self-introspection) and criticism of our praxis through the eyes of those who paid the price for us to maintain our lifestyles, so that we can see what many prophets and kings could not see (Luke 10:23, 24).

Grappling With the Broader Issues in Society

The last matter we need to deal with is the complexity of the world, which is the theatre of our mission and service. I would like to submit that Evangelicals and Pentecostals tend to marginalize themselves and limit their scope of witness to serious but peripheral issues, which in many instances are products of the major discourse they have chosen not to engage in. Most of the theological issues the Evangelicals and Pentecostals deal with arise out of specific historical events (praxis) that generate new debates and theories that become subjects of concern for us.

The period of the 18th and 19th centuries presented humanity with a complex combination of new challenges that called for a similarly complex combination of responses from the governments of the day and the church of the time. These challenges included the period of Enlightenment *(Aufklarung)*, which emphasized rationalism, intellectual freedom and freedom from prejudice and superstition in social and political activity. This allowed for critical thinking, which became a challenge to the orthodox church and the forms of governance of the time. This period was preceded by that of *humanism,* which is still a challenge to many Pentecostal theologians. Ironically, it is this thought system that gave rise to the great revival of art and learning called the *Renaissance.*

The second challenges arose from the *Industrial Revolution,* which resulted in great changes in the lives and work of people. For some, these were changes for the better, creating enormous wealth for them. For others it meant harsh working conditions, poverty and social dislocation. Class formations intensified, resulting in the *Capitalist/Socialist* conflicts of the 20th century and the threat of self-annihilation of humanity through weapons of mass destruction (WMD). Various churches responded in different ways, including the "Social Gospel Movement," which is a subject of serious critique by Pentecostals. Some responded by entering into the ideological war of *capitalism and communism* and others just had no response, except to live through it.

The third challenge was the period of *colonization* and *neo-colonization,* as well as the *post-colonial* period, which were preceded by the brutal age of slavery and the never dying resilient sin of racism. In these instances—perhaps because of direct state involvement—the church (particularly the evangelical and Pentecostal traditions) chose to conform.

All these events brought new theological questions that Christians and people of other faiths had to grapple with. The period of slave trade, colonialism and neo-colonialism confronted us with the challenge of a systematized ideology of racism; the period of Enlightenment raised questions of critical thinking and new Hermeneutical and Epistemological challenges that worry Evangelicals and Pentecostals alike. The question of humanism, capitalism, socialism, communism, Marxism, and so forth arose in the same manner.

Our blind spot in all this is that we do not think that getting involved with society to deal with the new challenges that flow out of the Enlightenment, Industrial Revolution, Colonialism and now Biotechnology and Information

Technology is part of our calling. What we do is watch the world change as in a movie, avoid dealing with the consequences of the changes and then engage only at a theoretical level on matters that arise out of it. By this time, we have missed the context, we have missed the questions people were grappling with, and the actual concrete experiences (praxis).

When we arrive, we unload our ideological baggage, carry our preconceived ideas into the scene and prescribe predetermined solutions for those who are engaged in the dialogue. This is what is called an "ahistorical approach to reality" which has no respect for the context from which these challenges arise.

If the Pentecostal Movement is going to make a difference in the future, it must be ready to get involved with the challenges that confront the society at large while retaining the distinctive features of the early church, particularly the Pentecostal experience.

16

A Journey Toward Racial Reconciliation

Race Mixing in the Church of God of Prophecy

Harold D. Hunter

The faith community that came to be known (in 1952) as the Church of God of Prophecy (CGP) has been captive to the spiritual journey of founder A.J. Tomlinson, an Indiana Quaker. Nowhere is this more evident than the distinction that CGP defied the axiom that most North American Pentecostal groups failed at interracialism within a decade of the fabled 1906 Azusa Street Revival.

David Harrell judged CGP to be the "largest racially mixed church in the South from 1945 until the mid-1960s. Unlike the larger Pentecostal sects, the CGP never separated its black members into a satellite organization. While local churches have generally been either black or white, the state assemblies, international assemblies, and church institutions have been integrated throughout the history of the sect."[1]

The account here will view the prehistory of this body in the narrative of its founder. Some attention will be given to the fusion of an ecclesiology linked to June 13, 1903, with a resolve to work toward racial reconciliation.

---

[1] David E. Harrell Jr., *White Sects and Black Men in the Recent South* (Kingsport, TN: Vanderbilt UP, 1971) 95.

The Westfield Years

Ambrose Jessup Tomlinson was born on September 22, 1865, near Westfield, Indiana, to Milton and Delilah Tomlinson. Grandparents Robert and Lydia Tomlinson joined the Antislavery Friends and participated in the underground railroad. Having studied at the prestigious Westfield Academy and reared in a moderately well-to-do entrepreneurial family in Westfield, Indiana, provided the young A.J. Tomlinson with forays into the business and political arenas.

The gospel call came to overshadow the serene life one would envision in this large, rural Quaker community. A.J. would alter the course as a result of encounters with Holiness Friends. This group was epitomized in the person of A.J.'s boyhood neighbor Seth Rees, the "Indiana Earthquaker," who scorned mediocrity by proclaiming "Win or die!" Holiness evangelists owed much to 19th-century Quakers when they dismissed creeds and rituals, spurned ecclesiastical hierarchy, or acknowledged Holy Spirit inspiration from both male and female, clergy and laity. Meanwhile, the significant African American community in Westfield meant that among the closest neighbors of the Tomlinsons were two black families. Freed blacks and slaves who escaped through the Underground Railroad participated in "colored" camp meetings held each summer in Westfield, which attracted whites.[2]

J.B. Mitchell, a graduate of Oberlin, introduced A.J. to the famous revivalist Charles G. Finney. Founded in 1833, Oberlin College was the first institute of higher education in the United States to conduct the "joint education of the sexes." By 1835, race was no longer a barrier to Oberlin admission, either. In 1894, Mitchell and Tomlinson founded the Book and Tract Company. During this time, Tomlinson corresponded with Martin Wells Knapp and did colporteur work on short-term trips to Appalachia.

Tomlinson was also exposed to D.S. Warner, who wrote a hymn titled "The Evening Light," and his followers were often known as the "Evening Light Saints." Warner centered his work in and around Indianapolis, eventually ending up in Anderson, Indiana. When Tomlinson started a paper for the Church of God (Cleveland) in 1910, the first name was *The Evening Light and Church of God Evangel.*

---

[2] For a full treatment of the early life of A.J. Tomlinson, see Roger G. Robins, "Plainfolk Modernist: The Radical Holiness World of A.J. Tomlinson" (Ph.D. diss., Duke University, 1999); cf. Roger Robins, "A.J. Tomlinson: Plainfolk Modernist," in *Portraits of a Generation*, ed. James R. Goff Jr. and Grant Wacker (Fayetteville: U of Arkansas P, 2002) 347-68. There are gaps in this earliest period inasmuch as the first set of Tomlinson's diaries have been lost. Voy Bullen, Homer Tomlinson's successor, showed them to me in 1980 but refused to allow them to be photocopied.

When Martin Wells Knapp's God's Bible School opened in 1900, the student body included Evening Light Saints. Some of the students at God's Bible School became colporteurs and sold Knapp's periodical known as *God's Revivalist*.[3] Since Tomlinson was doing this kind of work at the time, and copies of *God's Revivalist* were left in his personal collection, it heightens the possibility that he could have stayed for a 12-week course in Cincinnati, perhaps in 1903. That this school and Warner's group were integrated is highlighted by the fact that W.J. Seymour became part of the Evening Light Saints after moving to Indianapolis in 1895, then a student at God's Bible School in Cincinnati in 1900.[4]

This colporteur work led to short-term trips to Appalachia and exposure to more radical holiness figures like Frank Sandford, who published the *Tongues of Fire* (1894). Stays at Sandford's "Holy Ghost and Us Bible School" in Shiloh, Maine, account for two water baptisms there, one at the hands of Sandford himself when A.J. wrote in his diary on October 1, 1901: "I was baptized by Mr. Sandford in the Androscoggin River into the 'church of the living God,' for the evangelization of the world, gathering of Israel, new order of things at the close of the Gentile age."[5]

Appalachia Beckons

The exposure to the Acts 2 commune as practiced by Shiloh, and some awareness of John Alexander Dowie's Zion City in Illinois, would provide models A.J.'s family sought to imitate in Culberson, North Carolina. The family move was complete in 1899 and ultimately accounts for the unexpected interaction with B.H. Irwin's Fire-Baptized Holiness Association (FBHA). Some of Irwin's staunch supporters planted what amounted to an emerging national headquarters in a Bradley County, Tennessee hamlet named Beniah.[6]

Tomlinson launched an eight-page serial, *Samson's Foxes,* while simultaneously publishing reports of living on the faith lines like George Mueller in the *Pentecostal Herald, God's Revivalist,* and the *Evangelical Visitor.* Tomlinson

---

[3] Cecil M. Robeck Jr., *The Azusa Street Mission and Revival: The Birth of the Global Pentecostal Movement* (Nashville: Thomas Nelson, 2006) ch. 1.

[4] Robins, "Plainfolk Modernist," 263 n. 154, speculates that Tomlinson may have met Seymour around this time in either Indianapolis or Cincinnati.

[5] A.J. Tomlinson, diary, vol. 1, Oct. 1, 1901, Manuscripts Division, Library of Congress, Washington, D.C. See Frank S. Murray, *The Sublimity of Faith* (Amherst: Kingdom Press, n.d.) 288-89, 166 et al.; Shirley Nelson, *Fair, Clear, and Terrible: The Story of Shiloh* (Latham: British American Publishing, 1989) 162.

[6] See Harold D. Hunter, "Beniah at the Apostolic Crossroads: Parham, Tomlinson, Sandford, Irwin," *Cyberjournal for Pentecostal-Charismatic Research* 1, www.pctii.org/cyberj/cyber1.html (Apr. 24, 2003).

projected his Mount Zion Mission Home that opened with an industrial school and orphanage to be a virtual "garden of Eden."[7]

Shades of the FBHA were seen in Tomlinson's rejection of "tobacco, opium, pork, tea and coffee."[8] Yet another like source would be a group of evangelists —Milton McNabb, Joe Tipton, William Hamby and William Martin—who preached the noteworthy 1896 Shearer Schoolhouse Revival in Cherokee County, North Carolina.[9] Some of these evangelists and others either living in, or associated with, Beniah eventually carried the FBHA message to W.F. Bryant's home at Camp Creek, North Carolina.[10]

Various issues of the FBHA's *Live Coals of Fire* (1899-1900) reported on common efforts of William M. Martin, R. Frank Porter and Stewart T. Irwin, the son of B.H. Irwin. This same magazine showcased the interracial character of the group mostly in the person of Ruling Elder W.E. Fuller, an African-American pioneer who planted 50 churches in 10 years. Fuller would rise to the level of assistant general overseer of the FBHA when the group was led by J.H. King, an imposing figure in IPHC history.

Bryant's small group witnessed crosscurrents of various spiritualities, like fellowship with R.G. Spurling. Spurling's roots lay in Landmark Baptists, but his identity was captured in the independent Christian Unions he started. Spurling's first such effort was the short-lived Christian Union at Barney Creek, Monroe County, North Carolina in 1886.[11] The ideals that defined

---

[7] A.J. Tomlinson, diary, vol. 1, Apr. 14, 1902, Manuscripts Division, Library of Congress, Washington, D.C.

[8] A.J. Tomlinson, diary, vol. 1, Jan. 30, 1906, Manuscripts Division, Library of Congress, Washington, D.C.; *Samson's Foxes* 1, no. 1 (Jan. 1901): 4. B.H. Irwin had himself coroneted as General Overseer "for life" in the 1898 national organization of the FBHA. Homer Tomlinson captured this period of A.J.'s life in an article titled "The Fanatic," in *The Faithful Standard* 2:2, Oct. 1923: 20-23, where commandments on a tree read: (1) no hog meat; (2) no violin-playing; (3) no neckties; (4) plain dress for women; (5) no chewing tobacco; (6) no smoking or drinking; (7) no work on Sunday; (8) pay tithes; (9) no chewing gum; (10) no riding on Sunday.

[9] A.J. Tomlinson, *The Last Great Conflict* (Cleveland, TN: Walter E. Rogers, 1913) 189. After the initial revival, it was reported that approximately 100 persons spoke in tongues during later meetings. See Harold D. Hunter, "Spirit-Baptism and the 1896 Revival in Cherokee County, North Carolina," *Pneuma: The Journal of the Society for Pentecostal Studies* 5, no. 2 (Fall 1983) 1-17.

[10] See: Daniel Woods, "Daniel Awrey, the Fire-Baptized Movement, and the Origins of the Church: Toward a Chronology of Confluence and Influence," paper presented to 2nd annual meeting of the Church of God Movements Historical Society, Cleveland, TN, May 24, 2003.

[11] During a 1949 interview by H.L. Chesser, W.F. Bryant said that Spurling's 1886 church "went dead." See Deborah Vansau McCauley, *Appalachian Mountain Religion: A History* (Chicago: U of Chicago P, 1995) 280, 283, 292, 295. McCauley cites Joe Abbott, *The Forgotten*

Spurling were compiled in his *The Lost Link,* published in 1920, but drafted years earlier.

Another player in the ferment was R. Frank Porter, recently Ruling Elder for the FBHA in Tennessee. The seminal organization of the Holiness Church at Camp Creek on May 15, 1902, was carried out by both Spurling and Porter. Spurling was chosen pastor, while Porter soon thereafter married Alice Cooke of Cleveland, Tennessee, and entered the University of Chattanooga at Athens (1905). Although May 15, 1902, is integral to the identity of the Church of God (Cleveland, TN),[12] only one of the first group of leaders, including M.S. Lemons, would remain with the Church of God (Cleveland, TN). This is William F. Bryant, whose service as a state overseer ended in 1918.

June 13, 1903

The circle of those associated on various levels with the Holiness Church at Camp Creek included A.J. Tomlinson, who was destined to transform this group. A diary entry dated June 13, 1903, simply said, "I was ordained as minister of the gospel of the Holiness Church at Camp Creek, N.C."[13] Tomlinson had arrived at Bryant's house the previous evening and prayed on the mountain the next morning before continuing their discussions.

An expanded version of this event can be found in a significant book published by A.J. Tomlinson in 1913, while serving as general overseer of the Church of God (Cleveland, TN). Titled *The Last Great Conflict,* we are told a "more careful study of the New Testament order" resulted in the work being "revived and taking on a new impetus."[14] Although the Church of God (Cleveland, TN) later revoked Spurling's license, at this point he cast a long shadow over the group.

Tomlinson had sometimes been received as something of a foreigner, so acknowledging Spurling's 1886 contribution in *The Last Great Conflict* would help keep the coalition together. That 1903 was the decisive turning point for A.J. Tomlinson manifests itself in a diary now consumed with merciless details of

---

Church (n.p., 1962) 38, to say a glut of Holiness churches look back to Spurling's 1886 declaration as their origin. Abbott's work is often based on third-generation oral tradition from independent Holiness Pentecostals.

[12] M.S. Lemons, "History of the Church of God" (unpublished manuscript, ca. 1937) 4, 5, 10. See also Chesser interview of Lemons, 17-18, and Bryant, 18. In a 1924 deposition with the Murray and McCalla law firm in Chattanooga, Tomlinson was asked who organized the Holiness Church of Camp Creek, and he replied: "R.G. Spurling and Frank Porter, Ministers." This draws attention to the absence of Porter in Tomlinson's *The Last Great Conflict.*

[13] A.J. Tomlinson, diary, vol. 1, June 13, 1903, Manuscripts Division, Library of Congress, Washington, D.C.

[14] A.J. Tomlinson, *The Last Great Conflict,* 192.

organization in motion. Tomlinson was immediately chosen pastor of the Camp Creek congregation, and within a year he was pastor of three of the four related local groups. He edited, with M.S. Lemons, a periodical titled *The Way*, which ran an article by R. Frank Porter.

Tomlinson's rescue and expansion of this loose association helps explain, in part, his 1904 move from Appalachia to Cleveland, Tennessee, and its well-connected train station. Without this intervention, the original cluster, which lasted no more than 10 years, would have surely followed the fate of the independent nondenominational churches that populate the Appalachian mountain regions, some of which count Spurling as their founder.[15] Writing in 1939, Homer A. Tomlinson mentioned: ". . . they called themselves an Association, [they] had not yet called themselves the Church of God."[16] A.J. Tomlinson's first account of the January 26-27 conference—which is counted as the first General Assembly of the Church of God (Cleveland, TN)—may be found in a diary entry dated January 30, 1906: "I arrived home about midnight last night from Camp Creek, N.C. We held a church assembly there, I acted as the Ruling Elder and made the minutes of the proceedings."[17]

It was not until January 11, 1907, the second such conference, that the group took on the name Church of God. Depicting this action as dropping the name Holiness Church, Tomlinson claimed he and others referred to Camp Creek as "The New Testament Church, or The Church of God."[18] Despite his restorationist impulse, Tomlinson would have known that the name Church of God was first used by John Winebrenner's Church of God, having done so as far back as 1830. D.S. Warner had also identified with this "Bible name" in Indiana by 1880, and Frank Sandford by 1897. Writing in *The Last Great Conflict,* Tomlinson continues: "This, however, was not meant to debar the use of the other Scriptural names, such as: 'The Church,' 'Churches in Christ,' 'Church in God Our Father and the Lord Jesus Christ,' etc."[19]

---

[15] See McCauley, *Appalachian Mountain Religion,* 276-90. See also A.J. Tomlinson court testimony in Dec. 1924, 8:1717f.

[16] Homer A. Tomlinson, *The Great Vision of the Church of God* (Queens Village, NY: published by the author, 1939) 6. In court testimony given in Dec. 1924, A.J. Tomlinson (8:1714) stressed that the early assembly had no authority over the local churches.

[17] A.J. Tomlinson, diary, vol. 1, Jan. 30, 1906, Manuscripts Division, Library of Congress, Washington, D.C.

[18] A.J. Tomlinson court testimony in Dec. 1924, 8:1749. Tomlinson says the other churches consistently used the name Church of God before it was accomplished with Camp Creek.

[19] A.J. Tomlinson, *The Last Great Conflict,* 193. McCauley, *Appalachian Mountain Religion,* 290, suggests the name Church of God was used in the mountains by the mid-1880s. However, for the propriety of Tomlinson in this sequence, see Robins, "Plainfolk Modernist," 460.

In 1914, this same group would make final their selection of A.J. Tomlinson as general overseer, or as he put it in his diary dated November, 15, 1914, "until Jesus comes or calls."[20] Amid a charismatic outbreak during this business session, M.S. Lemons took Tomlinson by the arm and led him to the front. Some said the position was for life, and when M.S. Lemons said, "I think you can all see that God's approval is on this selection, and I don't see any use of ever saying anything more about a change," then the minutes added "This remark met a unanimous approval."[21]

Pentecost Linked To Reconciliation

Looking back, Tomlinson would say he became "more fully awakened" in January, 1907, about the fledgling Pentecostal Movement. *The Last Great Conflict* praised "Dr. Seamore"—actually W.J. Seymour, pastor of the legendary 1906 Azusa Street Mission in Los Angeles—whose message of Pentecost that washed away the "color line" spread around the world.[22] The priority of the Azusa Street Revival was obvious when A.J. Tomlinson started *The Evening Light and Church of God Evangel* and later ran a series on Pentecostal history in *The Faithful Standard*.[23] Tomlinson preached on "The baptism with the Holy Ghost and Fire" at the 1907 assembly, but his own personal Pentecost did not come for one full year.

Tomlinson invited G.B. Cashwell to preach in Cleveland at the conclusion of the third assembly in 1908. A minister with the [Pentecostal] Holiness

---

[20] A.J. Tomlinson, diary, vol. 3, Nov. 15, 1914, Manuscripts Division, Library of Congress, Washington, D.C.

[21] *Echoes From the Tenth Annual Assembly of the Churches of God Held at Cleveland, Tennessee, November 2-8, 1914*, 24; A.J. Tomlinson court testimony in Dec. 1924, 8:1759f.

[22] A.J. Tomlinson, *The Last Great Conflict*, 137. No source is specified, but these likely included the papers by W.J. Seymour and J.M. Pike that influenced other Holiness leaders in the South. Cashwell wrote about the Dunn Revival in *AF*, and Pike attended the revival while running reports in the *Way of Faith*. Another possible source is M.W. Knapp's *God's Revivalist*, which wrote negative reviews of the Azusa Revival. Homer Tomlinson conceded the priority of Azusa Street in his 1939 *Great Vision of the Church of God*, 3, 5. This was certainly the case in his uncluttered *Amazing Fulfillments of Prophecy* (Cleveland, TN: White Wing Publishing House, 1934) 125-26. The same can be said of an important document titled *The Book of Doctrines* (Cleveland, TN: Church of God Publishing House, 1922), 46ff., which gave clear evidence of Homer's fingerprints. Cf. Homer A. Tomlinson, *Mountain of the Lord's House* (New York: Churches of God of Greater New York, Inc., 1941) 10.

[23] See *The Evening Light and Church of God Evangel*, Mar. 1 and Mar. 15, 1910; "History of Pentecost," *The Faithful Standard* 1:5, Aug. 1922; *Historical Annual Addresses: A.J. Tomlinson*, vols. 1-3, compiled by Perry Gillum (Cleveland, TN: White Wing Publishing House, 1970, 1971) 1:109.

Church of North Carolina, Cashwell traveled to Los Angeles to experience the Pentecostal outpouring firsthand. Cashwell's latent racism[24] resisted the message of racial reconciliation that was part and parcel of Seymour's Azusa Street Mission. However, after five days of praying for deliverance, Cashwell consented to have blacks lay hands on him, whereupon he received a fiery baptism in the Holy Spirit with the sign of speaking in tongues.

When Cashwell preached in Cleveland on Sunday morning, January 12, 1908, Tomlinson would pen one of the most celebrated accounts of transportation in the Spirit that carried him into countries with 10 different languages.[25] Finally, the flame was lit for Tomlinson himself that would forever change the destiny of many related in one way or another to the Pentecostal branch of the Church of God movement.

Illustrating the power of Seymour's message, Tomlinson arrived in Memphis, Tennessee, on November 12, 1908, in order to participate in a "Pentecostal convention" led by Charles H. Mason, head of the Church of God in Christ.[26] Tomlinson personally carried the flame to many locations, but none more important than the Pleasant Grove camp meeting in Florida. His diary dated May 22, 1909, announces the first of several visits by Tomlinson to this venue.

Among those who received the Pentecostal message here were Edmond and Rebecca Barr. On May 31, 1909, Tomlinson would grant evangelist licenses to both of them. By November of that year, the Barrs took the same message to their native Bahamas. It was February 1911, when Tomlinson held his first international campaign in Nassau. Writing in his diary about the campaign in the Bahamas, he noted, "Blacks and whites all come to meeting together."[27]

Later in 1911, New Mexico added to its numbers a congregation of Mexican Americans in Raton. In his diary, dated February 27, 1912, Tomlinson reports on a convention he attended in Raton that required the use of a Spanish-speaking interpreter. Minutes of the 1913 assembly counted three Spanish-speaking

---

[24] Outsiders criticized the interracial character of some of A.B. Crumpler's revivals in North Carolina, and in 1903, Cashwell reported preaching at "the colored" church near Goldsboro in a meeting also attended by whites.

[25] A.J. Tomlinson, diary, vol. 2, Jan. 13, 1908, Manuscripts Division, Library of Congress, Washington, D.C.

[26] A.J. Tomlinson, diary, vol. 2, Nov. 26, 1908, Manuscripts Division, Library of Congress, Washington, D.C. Homer Tomlinson reproduced this part of A.J.'s diary in *Diary of A.J. Tomlinson: 1901 to 1923* (Queens Village, NY: Church of God, World Headquarters, 1949) 1:75ff. Homer relates that, in 1948, he was invited by the Church of God in Christ to celebrate this event on behalf of his deceased father.

[27] A.J. Tomlinson, diary, vol. 2, Feb. 15-16, 1911, Manuscripts Division, Library of Congress, Washington, D.C.

congregations in New Mexico. Juan B. Padilla, who first assisted T.F. Chávez, white pastor of the original congregation in Raton, was ordained a bishop in 1913, and became pastor of Corrumpa, New Mexico.[28] Padilla, who did not speak English, served a term (1921-1922) on the Council of Seventy. On July 3, 1936, A.J. Tomlinson would grant Church of God of Prophecy ministerial licenses to this same Juan Padilla.[29] J.O. Sandoval, an evangelist in Colorado, wrote A.J. Tomlinson late in 1923, pledging his support. Sandoval's printed stationary read: "Iglesia de Dios, Oficina Principal en Cleveland, Tenn. A.J. Tomlinson, Sobreveedor." On August 13, 1923, Tomlinson wrote to Sandoval saying he would like for him to come to Cleveland to "help me circulate Spanish literature."

When giving an account of the ordination of "the colored brother" Edmond Barr, Tomlinson wrote in his diary on June 4, 1912: "Held a conference meeting yesterday to consider the question of ordaining Edmond Barr (colored) and setting the colored people off to work among themselves on account of the race prejudice in the South."[30]

At the 1915 assembly, Edmond Barr began a two-year term as overseer of the "colored" work in Florida.[31] Then Tomlinson appointed C.F. Bright overseer of Pennsylvania in 1919, followed by New Jersey in 1920.[32] There was

---

[28] H.C. Ball published a report in *The Pentecostal Evangel* 312 and 313, Nov. 1, 1919: 22-23, under the title "Report on the Pentecostal Mexican Work in Texas, New Mexico, Colorado, Arizona and Old Mexico." Ball casts Padilla as pastor for the Assemblies of God in Corrumpa. Ball says of Padilla that he "lives twenty miles from a railroad, has 14 children, works during the week and preaching on Sundays and in the week as much as he can." Gastón Espinosa, "Borderland Religion: Los Angeles and the Origins of the Latino Pentecostal Movement in the U.S., Mexico, and Puerto Rico, 1900-1945" (Ph.D. diss., University of California, Santa Barbara, 1999) 162-63, seems unaware of the Church of God presence in New Mexico at this time.

[29] Juan B. Padilla, Ministers' Records, Church of God of Prophecy Archives. Padilla was originally from Trinidad.

[30] A.J. Tomlinson, diary, vol. 2, June 4, 1912, Manuscripts Division, Library of Congress, Washington, D.C. This entry is missing from the diaries as edited by Homer Tomlinson.

[31] Ministerial records at the Church of God (Cleveland, TN) headquarters dispel the notion that racial prejudice removed Barr from office. Barr, who was ordained in 1914, reported on his work to the General Assembly in 1915. See *Minutes of the Eleventh Annual Assembly of the Churches of God Held at Cleveland, Tennessee, November 1-7, 1915,* 18.

[32] *Church of God Evangel* 11, no. 35 (Aug. 28, 1920): 4, gives names and addresses of the current state overseers, including "16 Pennsylvania, Col. C.F. Bright." When black ministers were first listed in the January 7-12, 1913 minutes, there was no indication of race. This changed the next assembly later that year but then was repeated in 1921. No satisfactory explanation exists of these changes. Bright left his position in 1920 to join the Church of God in Christ. He returned to the Church of God in 1924 and became a prominent leader. Perhaps one dynamic for African-Caribbeans who initially left the Church of God (Cleveland, TN) was that the Church of God in Christ is predominantly African-American.

one white church in Pennsylvania at this time, but Bright, perhaps an African-American,[33] would likely have had jurisdiction over only "colored" churches. Bright preached at the 1919 assembly, and W.R. Franks and T.J. Richardson preached at the 1920 assembly.

Tomlinson seemed agitated that prior to 1919, blacks were only called on extemporaneously during the assemblies. Tomlinson propelled this cause forward in his annual address by applying the apostle Paul's "one blood" to affirm a universal humanity. Tomlinson added, "Our dark-skinned brothers and sisters have received the Holy Ghost as well as we, and we have long ago learned that God is no respecter of persons."[34]

At the 1917 assembly, an unnamed person suggested that the *Church of God Evangel* should also be published in Spanish for "Mexicans and other Spanish speaking people." A Native American from Oklahoma addressed the same assembly.[35] When Ree, North Dakota was organized in 1920, it may have been the first Native American Pentecostal congregation in North Dakota.[36] In a section of his 1920 annual address titled "The Spanish-Speaking People," Tomlinson advocated translating the *Church of God Evangel,* books and tracts into Spanish.[37]

African-American T.J. Richardson, two or more African-Caribbeans and one Hispanic were part of the Council of Seventy and various assembly committees starting in 1921. The number of blacks present during these assemblies is unknown, but it is known they were relegated to segregated seating.[38] However, perhaps blacks on the Council of Seventy were not segregated during the 1922 assembly business sessions when the Council of Elders sat on the platform, and the Council of Seventy sat in front of the platform.[39]

---

[33] Trudy D. Pratt says that her grandfather, C.F. Bright, was "of (western) African descent" and he had "some Indian blood" (email dated Oct. 8, 2003). It is unknown if the latter reference in any way connects Bright to Trinidad.

[34] *Historical Annual Addresses: A.J. Tomlinson,* 1:109.

[35] *Minutes of the Thirteenth Annual Assembly of the Churches of God Held at Harriman, Tennessee, November, 1-6, 1917,* 26, 30.

[36] Darrin J. Rodgers, *Northern Harvest: Pentecostalism in North Dakota* (Bismarck, NC: North Dakota District Council of the Assemblies of God, 2003) 38-39, 241-42. Although the majority of Church of God congregations in North Dakota cast their lot with Tomlinson in 1923, through the intervention of Paul H. Walker, Ree remained with Church of God (Cleveland, TN).

[37] *Historical Annual Addresses: A.J. Tomlinson,* 1:144-46.

[38] *Minutes of the Fifteenth Annual Assembly of the Church of God Held at Cleveland, Tennessee, November 3-9, 1920,* 54: "Bishop Tomlinson gave an invitation for the people to seek the Lord. The colored people were given space in their part of the building for an altar service."

[39] In A.J. Tomlinson's 1924 deposition with the Murray and McCalla law firm in Chattanooga, Tomlinson says that J.B. Ellis made this proposal, and the ushers immediately reconfigured the

In this same General Assembly, A.J. Tomlinson pointed out that "on account of conditions that seem unalterable, a number of them are going away from us each year." This appears to be a suggestive statement about limitations on blacks, not only in American society, but also inside the church.[40] A loss of 1,744 members was reported in 1921, with perhaps most of the blacks going to The Church of God in Christ. Tomlinson lamented that "South of the Mason and Dixon line it is difficult to show them all the courtesy that we would like to" and exclaimed, "I do not like any separations between nationalities and races."[41] However, at the 1922 assembly, Tomlinson appointed T.J. Richardson as overseer of the Church of God "Colored Work" [in Florida and other states].

The Church of Destiny

A.J. Tomlinson's diary is silent from September 2, 1921 until February 28, 1924 when he writes: "Much has happened since my last writing, and my time has been so taken that I have not had time."[42] This is a considerable understatement with details of the tumultuous era chronicled in the *Church of God Evangel, White Wing Messenger,* newspapers, and assorted court documents. Tomlinson was now general overseer of an alternative faith community that, in 1952, courts would mandate it be known as The Church of God of Prophecy. Both A.J. Tomlinson and W.F. Bryant gave court testimony in 1924 that relegated 1886 to the margins.[43] In Tomlinson's 1929 General Assembly annual address, he served notice of a fresh look at Church of God origins. Looking back to June 13, 1903, he said only "later on it became clear . . ." what this event would mean to CGP.

---

seating arrangements. See also Tomlinson's testimony in Dec. 1924, 8:1931f., 1940. Not only was this the first time business was handled by the "official assembly," but some controversial items, like an amendment by J.S. Llewellyn, were approved only by this group, prompting Tomlinson to say (8:1949) he was not sure there was a "general assembly" in 1922. Compounding the misery (8:1937f.), Llewellyn changed some of the wording before printing the minutes without—for the first time—a review by Tomlinson.

[40] See H. Paul Thompson Jr., "'On Account of Conditions That Seem Unalterable': A Proposal About Race Relations in the Church of God (Cleveland, TN) 1909-1929," *Pneuma: The Journal of the Society for Pentecostal Studies* 25, no. 2 (Fall 2003): 240-64.

[41] *Historical Annual Addresses: A.J. Tomlinson,* 1:197.

[42] A.J. Tomlinson, diary, vol. 4, Sept. 2, 1921, Manuscripts Division, Library of Congress, Washington, D.C.

[43] In a deposition given December 1, 1924, A.J. Tomlinson gave testimony filed by the court clerk, James M. Stuart, January 20, 1925 (8:1707) to the effect that there were a few others on the "same line" as the 1902 Holiness Church at Camp Creek, but they were called "The Christian Union." "This church was organized by a minister of the Christian Union Church, and thus in that way, it might have been connected but not especially; and yet afterwards they were associated together." See also the deposition of W.F. Bryant filed by James M. Stuart, Aug. 21, 1924 (5:1327).

One can witness some of the ferment by looking at the minutes of the 1923 CGP General Assembly. We are immediately told black musicians with "faces aglow" joined in with zest. Those who preached included J.R. Smith, T.J. Richardson and Mrs. Mamie E. Richardson. Stanley Ferguson was active in the business sessions and the worship services. In his annual address, Tomlinson defended himself against the notion that he was a thief and condemned the constitution as fatal to theocracy. Chiding those who sought class warfare based on formal education, Tomlinson also declared that he sided with the "common people." When the subject of divorce and remarriage was tackled, Ferguson was among those who uttered a message in tongues in this business session.[44]

The 1923 impeachment by Church of God (Cleveland, TN) supreme judges was, to Tomlinson, a battlefield over whether general assemblies were to be judicial rather than legislative or executive. Tomlinson drafted this language that was affirmed by many of the early assemblies and repeated in his annual addresses. The earliest practice, that is continued even today by the CGP, is that votes were not taken, but all male[45] members in attendance discussed given subjects until consensus was achieved. Considerable emphasis was placed on praying about each business item and being open to charismatic outbreaks during these sessions. Tomlinson argued that a representative government is like a republic, whereas a theocracy is judicial only.[46]

T.J. Richardson, the most prominent African-American at the time, cast his lot with Tomlinson, although the majority of black constituents in the United States—especially outside North Carolina—did not follow his lead. Working out of his home and not having access to the *Church of God Evangel,* helps

---

[44] *Minutes of the Eighteenth Annual Assembly of the Church of God Held at Cleveland, Tennessee, November 22-27, 1923,* 1, 6, 11, 13, 16-18, 20, 29. A resolution was also passed authorizing the need of "making and preserving" a history of the group.

[45] Since the 1906 assembly called for an annual meeting for "elders, and chosen men and the women from each church" to come as members and not as representatives, it raises the question of whether women originally participated in the business meetings. See Tomlinson's testimony given Dec. 1924, 8:1709f. Notice the 1908 assembly affirmed female deacons, but this was reversed the next year, and the 1910 assembly decided that women could not be ordained. In the 1912 assembly, M.S. Lemons spoke against women participating in business sessions. Yet when Tomlinson introduced the idea of cell groups to the 1915 assembly, he depicted the group as a "vast body of thoughtful men and women." *Historical Annual Addresses: A.J. Tomlinson,* 1:71.

[46] A.J. Tomlinson described in detail this process in his testimony given in December 1924, 8:1740-1742, 1789. Tomlinson noted that on occasion nonmembers talked during the business sessions. His intention was to distinguish the 1922 "official assembly" from the general assemblies. In this regard, he asked if in fact there was a general assembly in 1922 (8:1949). He further argued that the Council of Elders was not originally designed as a representative body (8:1790). The CGP continues the original practice of having local churches ratify the business acts of the general assemblies (see 8:1862).

explain that neither did the majority of whites identify with Tomlinson, but the Bahamas was a different story. Richardson, W.V. Eneas (Bahamas) and William R. Franks (Bahamas) were on the Council of Seventy, but perhaps only Richardson was present during the June 12-21, 1923 council meeting.[47] However, the following names were given on a petition submitted by C.T. Anderson against J.S. Llewelleyn, J.B. Ellis, and M.S. Lemons at this elders' council: T.J. Richardson, J.H. Curry, J.D. Williams, David LaFleur, J.R. Smith, R. Williams, Fred Beneby and C.C. Sapp.

The Anderson petition has this typed note from Richardson at the end of the list of names: "As overseer of the Colored Churches in the State of Florida and other states, I am free to say that all of the men are one voice with this petition. Amen." Did those named on this list actually sign a petition? Yes, according to various letters from C.T. Anderson to A.J. Tomlinson.[48]

When Anderson was confronted by Florida State Overseer John L. Stephens in July 1923, Stephen charged Anderson had "only had a few names on the paper as signatures, and most of them were negroes."[49] Anderson's letter of July 29, 1923, clearly marks blacks who signed the petition, as well as overseers and those on the Council of Seventy. Anderson's resolute stand with Tomlinson accounts for his having been arrested in July and put in prison. However, he was exonerated in a jury trial. This would have had an unsettling affect on other ministers in Florida.[50]

When newly selected Church of God (Cleveland, TN) General Overseer F.J. Lee revoked Richardson's license and appointed LaFleur[51] in his place, blacks

---

[47] A.J. Tomlinson, *The Church of God Marches On: History of the Battles and Victories of the Church of God From 1903 to 1939* (n.p., n.d.) 10, says "eighty or more ministers were called together." It is known that not all of the 70 came to Cleveland, and that other persons were on hand in addition to the 12 elders.

[48] It is also true, however, that although Anderson put himself in position for this kind of project by his own initiative after the 1922 General Assembly, A.J. Tomlinson wrote early drafts of part of the petition and gave names to Anderson for him to get their signatures. Tomlinson would consider this a just response to the "deceitful" tactics of Llewellyn and Lemons who, he says on May 12, 1923, even got to "our dear Brother Lee." The primary person in view is J.S. Llewellyn, who was dismissed by the Church of God (Cleveland, TN) four years later.

[49] Anderson to Tomlinson from Williston, Florida, on July 9, 1923.

[50] C.T. Anderson to Tomlinson dated July 19, 1923: "No doubt but you have noticed that certain ones have tried to silence me from the ministry. I have never had the semblance of a trial, neither is there any foundation for their charges. Not satisfied with this, our State Overseer had me arrested and thrown in jail 3 days and then tried in the common courts, and I was freed without ever putting a witness on the stand or having any one to plead for me. They hired a lawyer. Luke 21:15. It is only a [game?] with them to wreck the Church of God."

[51] Tomlinson told Richardson about a letter he received from LaFleur, but I have not been able to locate this letter. Such a letter might clarify the deciding issue for those in Florida.

on the "west coast" of Florida went with CGP, while those on the "east coast" of Florida stayed with the Church of God (Cleveland, TN). This may witness to varying reactions to events as reported in *The Church of God Evangel,* where editor J.S. Llewellyn exercised much editorial freedom as he had also done with the minutes of the 1922 General Assembly and like projects. Possible differences over church government may have become pronounced and perhaps tension between African-Americans and African-Caribbeans. African-Americans and African-Caribbeans in both Church of God (Cleveland, TN) and CGP at times found themselves at odds in the 1920s. A solution to this tension remains elusive in CGP to this day.

On September 27, 1923, nine black ministers from southern Florida wrote General Overseer Lee, declaring their intent to "take a stand for the Church of God proper" and saying that their congregations were also "perfectly settled with our decision."[52] In his report on the "Colored Work" at the November assembly that year, Bishop J.H. Curry announced that "We have had our conflicts along with the other brethren, but we have come out more than conquerors and are sticking to the church."[53]

A.J. Tomlinson cast the ordeal as "twenty years of labor" being "swept away" with only a few ministers remaining loyal.[54] Tomlinson reported that it took 10 years to restore the number of adherents recorded in 1922. Homer Tomlinson wrote in 1939 that perhaps 20 ministers out of 800 "stood with" his father. Then, he emphasized the role played by the Bahamas:

> From November 1922 until February 1923, he endeavored[55] to bear up. Then the path for him to walk was opened before him. It was in the Bahamas, the land of his first foreign missionary effort, that the way was opened. The late beloved Stanley Ferguson, overseer of that work, stood with him, encouraging him to start again. When the way was opened in this manner, he was recreated in a day.

The ministerial file of T.J. Richardson illuminates various aspects of the debate. Richardson writes Tomlinson, July 9, 1923, expressing a desire to hold a campaign in Cleveland. In his reply, dated July 20, 1923, Tomlinson speculates on whether "some white people"—meaning the "Lee/Llewellyn" faction—would "ruin the meeting." Tomlinson goes on to note that a "number of colored

---

[52] "The Colored Work—Church of God Proper," *Church of God Evangel,* Oct. 13, 1923: 2.

[53] *Minutes of the Eighteenth Annual Assembly of the Church of God (1923)* 7.

[54] Tomlinson, *The Church of God Marches On,* 11.

[55] H.A. Tomlinson, *Great Vision of the Church of God,* 15.

here are standing with me." Until the Church of God of Christ opened a small work in Cleveland around the year 2000, CGP had the only black, Pentecostal congregation in town.

Richardson participated in the August 8-10, 1923, "Call Council," where Tomlinson responded to the charge of impeachment. An early printed report failed to name Richardson as a participant. Tomlinson wrote on September 20, 1923, that this was an "oversight." Tomlinson said he was embarrassed because Richardson's name would have given "it more prestige." Richardson wondered if he had been deliberately left off the list, to which Tomlinson responded that he wanted him on the list "because you are (colored)." During this Call Council, T.J. Richardson was chosen for the CGP Council of Elders.[56] Following the earlier formula of the general overseer selecting two elders and these three selecting the remaining 10, Richardson was chosen by Tomlinson, and the two original elders Geo. T. Brouayer and S.O. Gillaspie who joined CGP. This evokes the question of whether these three would have earlier supported integrating the all-white Church of God (Cleveland, TN) council of 12 elders.

The 1923 CGP records reveal a black constituency in at least Florida, North Carolina, Georgia, Alabama, Kentucky, New York and Tennessee.[57] There was an Hispanic presence in Colorado and maybe New Mexico and likely Native Americans in South Dakota or North Dakota, but I have not been able to search all the pertinent records.

From this point on, blacks were present on all General Assembly programs, not only as singers, but preachers, leaders, and members of important committees. T.J. Richardson, who served on the Bible Government committee, led a delegation during the state marches at the 1924 Assembly which counted 21 compared to, for example, 115 for Tennessee, 3 for Alabama, 4 for South Carolina, 23 for Georgia, 23 for North Carolina and 75 for Virginia. A photograph of the Assembly in session seems to show that not all blacks sat in a reserved section. This same Assembly passed a resolution against the Ku Klux Klan.[58]

---

[56] Amid exuberant charismatic manifestations and at the recommendation of Tomlinson, CGP did away with the 12 elders and council of 70 during the 1923 assembly.

[57] T.J. Richardson, "Stick to the Church of God," *White Wing Messenger* 1:9, Jan. 12, 1924: 1, 4; A.J. Tomlinson letter to T.J. Richardson, Sept. 24, 1923. Tomlinson's letter notes Florida, North Carolina, Alabama and Kentucky, and suggests other locations not yet clearly identified in the transition. Possible locations would include Pennsylvania, New Jersey and Delaware. Richardson relates Ferguson's visit to Richardson's church in Miami after the assembly and also names Liberty, Pastor J.R Smith, Coconut Grove and Homestead, Pastor Randolf Williams, Hallandale, Pastor Fred Beneby, Dania, "some holding on," and West Palm Beach with Sister Mamie E. Richardson. Richardson also mentions a district conference in Littletown, N.C.

[58] *Minutes of Our Nineteenth Annual Assembly of the Church Over Which A.J. Tomlinson Is General Overseer Held at The Central Avenue Tabernacle, Cleveland,*

Many CGP overseers outside the United States were national leaders like Stanley Ferguson, who, when he died in 1934, A.J. Tomlinson ordered flags lowered to half-mast, and the church observed three days of mourning. These overseers had authority like state overseers and had their own budgets. Even if there were white missionaries present—very rare in the Caribbean—these whites did not have control over any of the money.

In a diary entry dated April 14, 1926, Tomlinson noted that during an Alabama convention, "I was told I gave a short message in the Chocktaw language."[59] Tomlinson claimed 10 languages with his initial xenolalic Spirit baptism, and on occasion made references to various xenolalic outbursts. This particular case might in someway relate to his commitment to Native Americans.

During the 1926 General Assembly, A.J. Tomlinson took up the question of blacks having their own sub-organization within the larger organization. Tomlinson said this approach had been imposed by the 1921 constitution and resulted in keeping the races apart. Since this constitution had been dismissed by CGP in 1923 with support from Ferguson and Richardson, the segregated structure would be discontinued. It is unknown to what degree this change reflected tension between African-American Richardson over against the African-Caribbean majority in Florida.

The exchange of letters between Richardson and Tomlinson in the wake of these events leave some questions unanswered. Richardson, who had worked with authority like a state overseer, writes on October 21, 1926, that he should be reinstated. Richardson explains what happened to Wilkerson, the state overseer of Florida: "The Dear Brother Wilkerson was arrested four days after he preached here in the city and is not allowed to preach among the colored people, and that will happen with every other white man in the Southern States . . . " Writing on October 26, 1926, Tomlinson said he lacked the authority to recreate a position removed by the General Assembly but offered to appoint Richardson

---

Tennessee, September 10-16, 1924, 42. It is possible that CGP numbered no more than 3,000 persons at this time. Grady R. Kent, *Flogged by the Ku Klux Klan* (Cleveland, TN: White Wing Publishing House, 1942) 5: "On November 25, 1941, I was called before the Governor of Georgia, Eugene Talmadge, by the Assistant Attorney for the purpose of opposing the Order of the Ku Klux Klan, because of the cruelty and injustice that were shown by them to the citizens of America, and religious freedom of which I stand this day as one of their victims. I suffered cruel persecutions and bore many stripes from this secret organization because they did not agree with my way of worship and praising and glorying God as in the days of old. . . . That day I stood with Bishop A.J. Tomlinson, General Overseer of the Church of God, and a great number of other ministers, Methodists, Baptists, Holiness, and other denominations to uphold the law and religious rights."

[59] A.J. Tomlinson, diary, vol. 4, Apr. 14, 1926, Manuscripts Division, Library of Congress, Washington, D.C.

over Barbados. Dissatisfaction with this decision drove the Richardsons away from CGP for 12 years.

What role did race riots of 1919 and Jim Crow laws play as over against prejudice among white members? What about the 1896 ruling known as Plessy v. Ferguson that demanded "separate but equal" rights in the South that defined segregation? If CGP in 1926 is an example of integration, it came at the expense of African-American power in the United States. Clearly, A.J. Tomlinson was paternalistic and even advocated separate schools and churches for the races.

Writing to the state overseers before the 1932 General Assembly, Tomlinson said of the state marches that no one other than the overseer speak " . . . except in states where there are colored representatives or Indians or other races."[60] During this Assembly, Tomlinson would affirm that "The middle wall of partition is broken down between the races . . . when they get into the Church of God"[61] He appropriated Jeremiah's "Speckled Bird" to exhort the union of " . . . the whites, the colored, the browns, the Indians called the red men, the yellow race—and all under one government, one rule, one faith or doctrine—all one." This language may sound offensive to 21st-century ears, but it was a vehicle used to espouse a ministry of reconciliation.

That same Assembly featured sermons by Stanley Ferguson, J.R. Smith and Olive B. Smith, while Francisco Olazábal and Pattie K. Scotton led the annual healing service. Olazábal has been compared favorably to Oral Roberts and Benny Hinn.[62] Dubbed El Azteca, Olazábal joined the CGP on September 10, 1936, before a spell-bound General Assembly, thus adding to the rolls a reported body of 50,000 Spanish-speaking adherents.[63] This union was never realized because Olazábal died tragically in a 1937 automobile accident. This consolidation failed to hold together despite the courting of Frank Olazábal in New York by Homer Tomlinson and A.J. Tomlinson's appearances before

---

[60] Lillie Duggar, *A.J. Tomlinson* (Cleveland, TN: White Wing Publishing House, 1964) 793.

[61] *Historical Annual Addresses: A.J. Tomlinson,* 2:170.

[62] See "Hundreds Pray All Night at Unique Healing Service," *Cleveland Daily Banner,* Sept. 12, 1936: 1. The report claimed healings of "cripples, blind, deaf and sick."

[63] See Espinosa, "Borderland Religion." Also see his article that first appeared in *JAAR,* "Francisco Olazábal: Charisma, Power, and Faith Healing in the Borderlands," later in *Portraits of a Generation,* ed. James R. Goff Jr. and Grant Wacker (Fayetteville: U of Arkansas P, 2002) 177-98. Espinosa gets it wrong both when he says that Olazábal was caught off guard about joining CGP and that the CGP general assemblies and Homer's church in New York were strictly "Anglo." Homer attracted a wide range of nationalities and had a black group by 1925. He was CGP Foreign Language Secretary and claimed to handle several (about 14?) languages. Homer could speak publicly in Spanish and translate letters written in Spanish. The 1936 assembly ceremony was so well known that it was run on the cover of the *White Wing Messenger,* August 29, 1936, in advance of the event.

the Council of Latin American Churches which was unable to hold Olazábal's coalition together. In 1938, A.J. Tomlinson was joined by his son, Homer, who spoke to this convention in Spanish. L.A. Moxley, a European American leader, preached on all races being joined in one body.[64]

In the final years before his death in 1935, R.G. Spurling was credentialed by A.J. Tomlinson. Spurling was present for the 1933 General Assembly during the general overseer's annual address. During that same year, Tomlinson reflected on the 30th anniversary of June 13, 1903. Having said in *The Last Great Conflict* that church "government" was not adopted until May 15, 1902,[65] Tomlinson now writes that this was when the group had been "definitely organized." He continues:

> Then I ventured to ask if they would be willing to receive me into the church with the understanding that it is the Church of God of the Bible. They were willing, and soon proceeded in regular order. I took the obligation with deep sincerity and extreme sacredness never to be forgotten (Jeremiah 50:5).[66]

In 1934, the White Wing Publishing House published a manuscript by Homer A. Tomlinson under the title *Amazing Fulfillments of Prophecy*. Here, one finds the pregnant observation that the first successful flight in 1903 by the Wright brothers was in North Carolina. The text goes on to point out that at the same time, in the same state, there was a group " . . . searching the Scriptures for the mysteries of the Bible Church." Looking back at Jesus' prayer in John 17, Homer announces: "The great vision that was born there was that God's people will be one." [67]

Middle Wall of Partition

At the general assembly in 1935, A.J. Tomlinson spoke of the middle wall of partition "that had been broken down by the cross" and spoke of the tragedy of the limited increase of black membership. Mississippi, an example he cited, had 1,022,009 blacks, and yet CGP had only one small black church.[68] The

---

[64] A.J. Tomlinson, diary, vol. 5, Oct. 31, 1938, Manuscripts Division, Library of Congress, Washington, D.C.

[65] A.J. Tomlinson, *The Last Great Conflict*, 193.

[66] A.J. Tomlinson, "I Took the Obligation Thirty Years Ago the Thirteenth Day of This June 1933," *White Wing Messenger* 10:12, June 17, 1933: 1.

[67] Homer A. Tomlinson, *Amazing Fulfillments of Prophecy* (Cleveland, TN: White Wing Publishing House, 1934) 125-26.

[68] *Historical Annual Addresses: A.J. Tomlinson*, 2:250.

General Assembly in 1936 said an orphanage must be opened for children of color because the church is "for all races." At the next General Assembly, W.M. Lowman and L.A. Moxley, European American leaders, preached sermons on reaching all races. Others who spoke that year were Dorothy Deadrick, J.R. Smith, and R.C. Smith. In 1938, C.H. Holley preached an Assembly sermon on bringing in all races, including Cubans. A.J. Tomlinson established churches in Puerto Rico in 1926 that were lost, but a successful campaign was completed there by 1940.

Tomlinson suffered a stroke in 1937 and soon thereafter turned his diaries over to elder son Homer to write a history. In 1939, A.J. Tomlinson began to purchase land that evolved into a 216-acre Biblical theme park located in Cherokee County, North Carolina. The erection of makeshift markers was recorded in Tomlinson's diary on November 15, 1940. One marker at the newly named Fields of the Wood was "Prayed and Prevailed," and another proclaimed "Arise shine, for thy light is come, June 13, 1903."

Similar efforts culminated in a grand celebration held September 7, 1941, when Tomlinson recounted in detail the proceedings on June 13, 1903. When the group reached the steepest part of the mountain, they were greeted by a dramatic demonstration of the "Great Speckled Bird," which emphasized the inclusion of all races. The group then sang the old country anthem by the same name as it had been revised by Homer A. Tomlinson and Sarah Dillon.

After Richardson, Tomlinson never appointed an African-American state overseer. John W. Wood carried a letter from Tomlinson saying he would be appointed over the work if he could get something going in Washington, D.C. Wood organized a church, but was listed by 1941 as "representative" rather than state overseer.[69] However, when overseers were called together in 1943 to select a successor to A.J. Tomlinson, Wood was part of that historic meeting.

Tomlinson's annual address during the 1941 General Assembly returned to the theme of breaking down the "middle wall of partition."[70] That same Assembly reported on a work among Native Americans in South Dakota and featured a sermon by Ralph C. Scotton on "All Races in One Mighty Church with Christ the Head for All." Scotton, who attended the inaugural session of

---

[69] *Minutes of the World-Wide 36th Annual Assembly of the Church of God Over Which A.J. Tomlinson Is General Overseer, October 15-21, 1941,* 13, records that Wood led a group during the annual "call of states and provinces." The same is reported in *Minutes of the 39th World-Wide Annual Assembly of the Church of God Over Which M.A. Tomlinson Is General Overseer,* held at the World-Wide Annual Assembly Tabernacle, Cleveland, Tennessee, U.S.A., September 13-19, 1944, 14. The same minutes, p. 151, list Wood as a Male Evangelist, not a Bishop.

[70] *Historical Annual Addresses: A.J. Tomlinson,* 3:209.

Bible Training Camp two months earlier, was appointed Field Secretary No. 2 at this assembly.

The 1942 General Assembly heard sermons from Dorothy Deadrick, Pattie K. Scotton and Ralph Scotton on "Work Done by Colored People." The 1943 General Assembly heard again from Dorothy Deadrick, Alvin Moss and another Ralph Scotton sermon about black progress. A.J. Tomlinson passed away less than one month after this General Assembly, just as many Hispanics joined CGP in California.[71]

Epilogue

In some states, the CGP may have been the first church to defy Jim Crow laws in their worship services. African-Caribbeans, African-Americans, and Latin Americans have been charged with the leadership of states, some of which include European-Americans as the majority. This unprecedented approach distinguishes the CGP, not only among Classical Pentecostals, but many denominations in the United States. Yet the egalitarian vision espoused by CGP has never been fully put in practice and is always at risk.

---

[71] C.T. Davidson, *Upon This Rock* (Cleveland, TN: White Wing Publishing House, 1976) 3:186.

17

The "Place" of Women in Pentecostal/Charismatic Ministry Since the Azusa Street Revival

Pamela Holmes

Introduction

Although the Pentecostal and Charismatic Movements have arisen in various contexts and in a variety of ways throughout the last century, many members of the modern day Pentecostal Movement trace their origins back to the Azusa Street Revival,[1] the label given to events that started in 1906 centered around the Apostolic Faith Mission located at 312 Azusa Street in Los Angeles, California, established by the son of ex-slaves, William J. Seymour.[2] As one of several reactions to modernity[3] and with roots in the Wesleyan, Anglo-Catholic,

---

[1] Azusa Street has been directly credited with the establishment of various black, white, and ethnic congregations throughout the United States and the world. Today, the majority of Pentecostal congregations are in the "Two-Third World" with many of them led by women. Harvey Cox, *Fire from Heaven: The Rise of Pentecostal Spirituality and the Reshaping of Religion in the Twenty-First Century* (New York: Addison-Wesley, 1995) 137-38.

[2] H.V. Synan, "Seymour, William Joseph," in *Dictionary of Pentecostal and Charismatic Movements*, ed. Stanley M. Burgess and Gary B. McGee, with Patrick H. Alexander, assoc. ed. (Grand Rapids: Zondervan, 1988): 778-81.

[3] I would argue that fundamentalism and liberal Protestantism were two other such reactions to modernity. However, I do not position Pentecostalism as a subset

*Scripture references in this chapter are taken from the King James Version.

holiness movement as well as the African American slave experience,[4] Azusa Street functions as a sort of "corporate mythology" for many Pentecostals and Charismatics. As such, the themes and visions of Azusa Street exert a paradigmatic influence for many Pentecostals and Charismatics as examples of both the problems and potentialities of the ongoing Spirit-focused movements.

In stark contrast to many of the mainstream churches of the time that tended to reflect the cultural norms that included racial segregation, the subordination of women and class consciousness,[5] Azusa Street was a small group of poor people from various ethnic groups.[6] Leadership included people of color and Caucasians, men and women[7] who together took responsibility for proclaiming the "full gospel."[8] Working alongside of men who not only made a "place"

---

of fundamentalism as is often historically done. Christian Fundamentalism officially opposed Pentecostalism in 1928, a fact which many historians seem to overlook. Fundamentalists (among whom are found some of my closest friends—this is an explanation, not a judgement) tend to be rational and text-oriented. Pentecostals tend to be mystical and Spirit-oriented.

[4] For a discussion of the Anglo-Catholic influences in Wesleyanism, see Walter Hollenweger's "The Catholic Root," in *Pentecostalism: Origins and Developments Worldwide* (Peabody, MA: Hendrickson, 1997): 144ff. For a discussion on the black, oral roots of Pentecostalism, see the same work, 18ff.

[5] Carl Brumback, in describing "Azusa Street," claims that the word *Azusa* is a misspelling of the third-person singular of the Spanish verb, *azuzar* meaning "to provoke, to irritate, to stimulate, to incite, to stir up, to put one against another, to cause conflict." He then goes on to explain that, misspelled or not, the word is significant because the Pentecostal Movement since Azusa Street has "provoked, irritated, stimulated, incited, stirred up, put one against another, and caused conflict." "Azusa (or Azuza) sparked a 20th-century-reformation against formalized religion." Carl Brumback, *A Sound from Heaven: The Dramatic Beginning of the 20th Century Pentecostal Revival* (Springfield, MO: Gospel Publishing House, 1961, 1977) 39-40.

[6] Edith L. Blumhofer, *Restoring the Faith: The Assemblies of God, Pentecostalism and American Culture* (Urbana and Chicago: U of Illinois P, 1993) 56. The press typically described Azusa Street as a "'colored' congregation that met in a 'tumble-down shack' and made the night 'hideous' through the 'howlings of the worshippers.'" The congregation itself, consisting of "whites, blacks, Hispanics, Asians and others" considered the "color-line" virtually nonexistent. See C.M. Robeck Jr., "Azusa Street Revival," in *Dictionary of Pentecostal and Charismatic Movements,* ed. Stanley M. Burgess and Gary B. McGee, with Patrick H. Alexander, assoc. ed. (Grand Rapids: Zondervan, 1988): 36.

[7] Robeck, "Azusa Street Revival," 34, mentions that William Seymour, the pastor, Richard Asberry and James Alexander, two trustees, were black. Louis Osterberg, a trustee, George E. Berg, the secretary, Glenn Cook, the business manager, and R.J. Scott, the camp meeting organizer, were white. Jennie Evans Moore, Lucy Farrow, and Ophelia Wiley, all black, shared public leadership roles with Clara E. Lum and Florence Crawford, both white. Brumback, 50, has a picture of the "leaders of the Azusa Street Mission, Los Angeles, 1907" which shows seven women and one girl, a daughter of one of the seven women, among the thirteen leaders. Together they led worship, published the mission's newspapers, visited, evangelized and exhorted the congregation. See Brumback, *A Sound from Heaven.*

[8] In fact, women's involvement as ordained ministers in the early years of the Pentecostal movement and in the earlier Holiness movement was so great that, even

for them but also learned from and depended upon them, ministering women, whether ordained or not, functioned as pastors, evangelists, educators, Bible teachers, theologians, missionaries, church planters, publishers and editors of periodicals and books and founders of congregations and denominations.[9]

Today, throughout the world, whether in the United States, Latin America, Europe or Asia, when the "pentecostal fire breaks through" and "the Spirit's gender impartiality" is not undercut, "women shine" as they take their "place" alongside of men and participate fully as teachers and preachers, prophets and healers, pastors and "principal bearers of the Pentecostal gospel to the four corners of the earth."[10]

The "Canadian Azusa"

Many Pentecostals within Canada point to Azusa Street as an egalitarian story of beginnings.[11] According to Gloria Kulbeck, who wrote one of the first histories of the Pentecostal Assemblies of Canada (PAOC), the "Pentecostal revival of 1906" as a new "non-Conformist sect" was designed to illustrate once more that God is no respector of persons."[12]

However, Canada also had its own version of Azusa Street in the form of the East End or Hebden Mission. Opening on May 20, 1906, at 651 Queen Street East in Toronto, this "faith" style mission was led by Ellen Hebden, a British born immigrant who was supported by her contractor husband, James.[13]

---

though their numbers declined significantly after 1920, in 1995, more than 50 percent of all women from all denominations who had ever been ordained came from these two groups. Barbara Brown Zikmundk, "Women and Ordination," in *In Our Own Voices: Four Centuries of American Women's Religious Writing,* ed. Rosemary Radford Ruether and Rosemary Skinner Keller (San Francisco: Harper & Row, 1995): 299.

[9] Men such as Charles Parham, Thomas Barratt, Frank Bartleman, and William Seymour himself depended upon, affirmed, and supported many of these women as colaborers establishing the Pentecostal movement. See Barbara Cavaness, "How First-Generation Pentecostal Leaders Viewed Women in Ministry," Society for Pentecostal Studies 2005 Annual Papers (Virginia Beach: Society for Pentecostal Studies, 2005).

[10] Cox, *Fire from Heaven,* 125.

[11] Within Canada, Gloria Kulbeck credits "the first signs of the renewal of Pentecost in North America" to "a little coloured lady from Los Angeles" who was visiting Houston, Texas" where "Elder W.J. Seymour," a "Spirit-filled man," was ministering. This woman invited Seymour to Los Angeles, which he did in 1906. Gloria Grace Kulbeck, B.A., *What God Hath Wrought: A History of The Pentecostal Assemblies of Canada,* ed. Rev. Walter E. McAlister and Rev. George R. Upton (Toronto: The Pentecostal Assemblies of Canada, 1958) 25.

[12] Kulbeck, *What God Hath Wrought,* 27.

[13] Ellen Hebden, "How Pentecost Came to Toronto," *The Promise,* no. 1, May 1907: 1-3, 1. See also Thomas William Miller, "The Canadian 'Azusa': The Hebden Mission in Toronto," *Pneuma: The Journal of the Society for Pentecostal Studies* 8, no. 1 (Spring 1986): 5-29, 6.

At first the work was slow going. However, seemingly without any knowledge of the Azusa Street Revival, Ellen Hebden was baptized in the Holy Ghost with the evidence of speaking in tongues on November 17, 1906, an experience which she reported in both her own periodical, *The Promise*, and in Seymour's *Apostolic Faith* once she became aware of its existence at the end of 1906.[14] After that, all "heaven" broke out.

Many prominent "gospel workers" were involved in the Hebden Mission including several eventual leaders and founders of the Pentecostal Assemblies of Canada.[15] *Gospel Workers*, the term Hebden preferred for ministering peoples, was common in Ontario at the time, so much so that a "Gospel Workers Church in Canada" was established in 1902 with one-third of its leaders Spirit-led women.[16] Women establishing "faith" missions was also common. One such mission was located in Trenton, Ontario, the small city from which I am writing, founded and led by Mary Gainforth.[17]

Canadian Ministering Women Since Azusa Street

Nevertheless, similar to the situation in other parts of the world, women were active within the early years of the Pentecostal Movement within Canada. While Ellen K. Hebden ministered tirelessly to establish Pentecostalism on a firm footing in Toronto, Ontario, Alice Belle Garrigus[18] and two sisters, Carro and Susan Davis,[19] did likewise in Newfoundland and New Brunswick, Nova Scotia, and Prince Edward Island respectively.

Aimee Semple McPherson, a remarkably talented and flamboyant Canadian

---

[14] Hebden, See also *The Apostolic Faith* 1:6, Feb.–Mar. 1907: 4. Miller, "Canadian 'Azusa,'" 6-7.

[15] Thomas W. Miller, *Canadian Pentecostals: A History of the Pentecostal Assemblies of Canada* (Mississauga, ON: Full Gospel Publishing House, 1994) 44.

[16] Helen G. Hobbs, " 'What She Could': Women in the Gospel Workers Church, 1902-1955," *Changing Roles of Women within the Christian Church in Canada*, ed. Elizabeth Gillan Muir and Marilyn Färdig Whiteley (Toronto, Buffalo, London: U of Toronto P, 1995): 201-18, 202, 206.

[17] Gainforth has published her account of some of her Trenton-based Faith Mission's exploits in her small book: *Mrs. Mary Gainforth, The Life and Healing of Mrs. Mary Gainforth* (Trenton, ON: Jarrett Printing and Publishing, n.d.).

[18] Burton K. Janes, *The Lady Who Stayed: The Biography of Alice Belle Garrigus, Newfoundland's First Pentecostal Pioneer*, vol. 2 (St. Johns, Newfoundland: Good Tidings Press, 1983).

[19] Fred H. Parlee, "Carro and Susie Davis," *The Pentecostal Testimony*, Dec. 1987: 16-17. *Canadian Pentecostal Testimony* no. 9, Oct. 1921: 1.

farm girl from Southwestern Ontario,[20] "put Pentecostalism on the map" with her Ziegfeld-like productions at Angelus Temple in Los Angeles[21] while Zelma Argue, a musician, evangelist and preacher from Winnipeg, Manitoba, spread the Pentecostal version of the gospel throughout Canada and parts of the United States.[22] The list of ministering could go on and on.

On the surface, at least, it appeared that women performed the same functions as men without any interference or objection by the men. So much so that many Evangelicals criticized the Pentecostal Movement within Canada as unscriptural due to the fact that "many of the outstanding evangelists, missionaries, teachers and pastors . . . have been women."[23]

However, while many women were involved in all areas of ministry during these early years, giving at least the appearance of an egalitarian ethos, the reality was much more complex. As Kulbeck explained in response to the criticism by Evangelicals, the PAOC position was similar to that of the Assemblies of God as understood by Carl Brumback whom she quotes, "Perhaps the present-day Pentecostal Movement has been somewhat lenient in its enforcement of 1 Corinthians 14:34, 38." She continues citing Brumback:

> This leniency may be due to a reaction against the extremely legal attitude of other groups; or it may be that we have been influenced by the 20th century idea about "women's rights" or it may be that we have emphasized the Scriptural exception rather than the rule. Nevertheless, we do feel that the spirit of the rule is in effect in our midst. On the whole, women are not given undue prominence in the movement; they represent a very small percentage of the ministry; and they are virtually silent with respect to doctrinal and governmental questions . . . in some instances, women may speak in the church without violating their subjection to men.[24]

However, both between the Brumback quotes and after them, Kulbeck highlights women's active involvement! A certain ambiguity is obvious. Although women were actively involved in ministry before and during the early years of

---

[20] Edith L. Blumhofer, *Aimee Semple McPherson: Everybody's Sister* (Grand Rapids: Eerdmans, 1993) 3.

[21] Cox, *Fire from Heaven,* 124.

[22] *Canadian Pentecostal Testimony* no. 1, Dec. 1920, 1; no. 4, Mar. 1921: 1, 4; no. 8, Sept. 1921: 4.

[23] Kulbeck, *What God Hath Wrought,* 13.

[24] Kulbeck, 14, referring to Carl Brumback, *What Meaneth This?* (London: Elim Publishing, 1946) 314-15.

the Pentecostal Assemblies of Canada's formation, their participation in ministry was accepted but limited, affirmed but restricted. A "place" may have been created for women in public ministry, but women's involvements seemed to require a defense or an explanation.

Women's "place" was explicitly limited when the PAOC institutionalized in 1919.[25] The PAOC was to be an organization controlled and led by male elders and male pastors. The "place" created for women was limited to that of evangelist, missionary or deaconess.[26] The numbers of ministering women diminished seriously after that. So much so that in 1970, a committee was mandated to study the situation.[27]

ANALYSIS OF WOMEN'S INVOLVEMENT
The American Situation

The involvement of ministering women in the early years of American Pentecostalism followed by the subsequent decline in their numbers has been explained in various ways. Michele Jacques Early, who focuses on the involvement of African American women in early Pentecostalism, offers two explanations for the pattern. First, it was an attempt on the part of these women to preserve African influences within their religious expressions. Pentecostalism included these influences. Second, many women may have made an intentional decision to take advantage of the possibilities of attaining prestigious and powerful positions for themselves.[28]

Cheryl Sanders mentions some of the African influences more specifically, particularly prophetic preaching and a holistic worldview which included a pervasive presence of religion and spirituality. The way in which Azusa Street prophetically proclaimed various Christian and nonChristian themes and impulses

---

[25] See the first page of the *Charter Issued to the Pentecostal Assemblies of Canada*, May 17, 1919.

[26] Miller, *Canadian Pentecostals*, 360, citing the *Combined Minutes of the Pentecostal Assemblies of Canada, Ltd., District Council of the General Council, Assemblies of God, U.S.A., 1919-1922*, 3.

[27] Handwritten Minutes of Ministry of Women Committee Meeting held in Toronto on Jan. 17, 1974, found in the PAOC Archives.

[28] Such a decision may be viewed as self-interested, practical, or simply the way it should be. Michele Jacques Early, " 'Into the World, But Not of It': The Socio-theological Framework of Womanhood in the Church of God in Christ" (Ph.D. diss., Emory University, 2003), 50, quoting Felton O. Best, "Breaking the Gender Barrier," in *Black Religious Leadership From the Slave Community to the Million Man March Flames of Fire*, ed. Felton O. Best, Black Studies 3 (Lewiston, NY: Edwin Mellen, 1998): 153.

as the "full gospel" may have resonated with African-American women, thus encouraging their active participation.[29]

Similarly, Walter Hollenweger points to the oral liturgy, narrative theologizing and testifying along with the acceptance of dreams and visions,[30] all of which held the potential for anyone to be involved in worship, a potential upon which many ministering women capitalized through their creative and empowering use of call narratives. However, Pentecostalism's involvement with Evangelicalism with its assumption of male supremacy worked against this potential,[31] creating an ambiguous and conflicted place for women.

Edith Blumhofer attributes Pentecostalism's nature as a loosely organized lay movement that considered ordination unimportant, economic factors whereby poorly paid women often served where men would not,[32] and the pragmatic emphasis upon evangelism that insisted that every means possible be utilized to achieve the goal of winning the world as explanations for the extensive involvement of women within the early years.[33] Reading Scripture with a restorationist motif in mind and in a literal, fundamentalist fashion, encouraged the limiting of women's sphere of ministry.[34]

Harvey Cox points to Pentecostalism's emphasis on Acts 2 and Joel 2 coupled with belief in direct-in-God and personal calls as reasons for women's early ministering. Unfortunately, "theological alliances with fundamentalists" with their "flame-extinguishing literalist theology" often quenched the experiential flame of the Spirit.[35]

Charles H. Barfoot and Gerald T. Sheppard suggest that the shift from an

---

[29] Cheryl J. Sanders, ed., introduction to *Living the Intersection: Womanism and Afrocentrism in Theology*, by Kelly Brown Douglas and Cheryl J. Sanders (Minneapolis: Fortress, 1995) 11. Additionally, interlocking systems of religious marginalization, racism, classism, and sexism experienced by African-American women complicated the choice between African or Western styles of worship. This conflict was particularly noticeable within Black Methodist and Baptist churches which eventually adopted the more formal and liturgical Western approach. Black Pentecostalism, including Azusa Street, with its retention and affirmation of African ways of worshipping, at least in part appears to have been a response to this tendency to adopt Western ways. 59-64.

[30] Walter J. Hollenweger, *Pentecostalism: Origins and Developments* (Peabody, MA: Hendrickson, 1997) 18.

[31] Hollenweger, 267-68.

[32] For example, Edith Blumhofer, *The Assemblies of God: A Chapter in the Story of American Pentecostalism*, vol. 1: *To 1941* (Springfield, MO: Gospel Publishing House, 1989) 15, 356-61.

[33] Edith Blumhofer, *Restoring the Faith: The Assemblies of God, Pentecostalism, and American Culture* (Urbana and Chicago: U of Illinois P, 1993) 164-65.

[34] Blumhofer

[35] Cox, *Fire from Heaven*, 131.

early, itinerant, evangelistic, prophetic ministry where women were able to exercise a fair amount of independence to a congregationally based, priestly ministry as the movement organized[36] made women's place more difficult.

David G. Roebuck emphasizes the limited nature of Spirit-filled women's authority as "vessels" that the Spirit uses coupled with the anti-culturalism of Pentecostalism for the decline in the number of ministering women after the early years.[37]

The Canadian Situation

Canadian scholar Randall Holm echoes many of the explanations from the American scene in his work dealing with the ordination of women within the Pentecostal Assemblies of Canada. Holm mentions the lack of bureaucracy, a theology centered in experience, a theology which "favors the optimism of grace (New Testament) over the pessimism of nature (Old Testament)," a "laissez faire attitude" to ordination, the "burgeoning movement for women's rights," an apocalyptic eschatology which stressed the need for all to be involved in evangelizing the world before the Lord's imminent return, the stress on listening to the Spirit, the example of Methodist women, the need for laborers, women's willingness to go and do without remuneration and pragmatism as reasons for a "place" being created for ministering women within the early years of Canadian Pentecostalism. Later on, once the PAOC institutionalized, the necessity for order, limited finances now under the control of the institution, a professional understanding of ordination along with formal requirements for education and ministry experience, the availability of more men and the re-emphasizing of a "separate sphere" ideology for men and women restricted women's options.[38] Some of these factors will be explained later.

Feminist Analysis

While all of these explanations seek to explain the reasons why a place was made for women during the early years of the Pentecostal Movement followed by the subsequent restrictions, none of them attempt to analyze why it was necessary to make a place for women at all. All assume that it was unusual for women

---

[36] Charles H. Barfoot and Gerald T. Sheppard, "Prophetic vs. Priestly Religion: The Changing Role of Women Clergy in Classical Pentecostal Churches," *Review of Religious Research* 22, no. 1 (Sept. 1980): 2-17, 3-4.

[37] Barfoot and Shepphard.

[38] Randall Holm, chapter 7, "Ordination of Women," in *A Paradigmatic Analysis of Authority Within Pentecostalism* (Ph.D. diss., Laval University, 1995): 1-7.

to be in a leadership position within the churches and society. This assumption has been highlighted and analyzed extensively by various types of feminists.[39]

Within theological contexts, Christian feminists assert that women are people of God. They critique any authorities, structural systems, doctrines or assumptions (conscious or unconscious) that deny women their full flourishing as human beings. While both men and women are affected by patriarchy,[40] andocentrism,[41] sexism,[42] and misogyny,[43] women have been particularly victimized due to the monopoly of public power and control of ideology by elite ruling men. Women have been economically subjected to men and have had their very being, their reality as women, (including their spiritual reality) defined by men. As Susan Hyatt explains,

> The Church's traditional theology of womanhood is unequivocally patriarchal, ascribing to women an inferior condition, a secondary importance,

---

[39] While many Pentecostal women shy away from a frank discussion of patriarchy or the use of feminist insights, perhaps partly out of fear of being labeled a "feminist," I am convinced that Pentecostals can do so with confidence and credibility. For example, Janet Everts Powers, in her insightful chapter entitled "'Your Daughters Shall Prophesy': Pentecostal Hermeneutics and the Empowerment of Women," *The Globalization of Pentecostalism: A Religion Made to Travel*, ed. Murray W. Dempster, Byron D. Klaus, and Douglas Petersen (Oxford, CA: Regnum Books, 1991): 313-37, argues for a Pentecostal exploration of women in ministry based on a Pentecostal appropriation of Scriptures, rather than a "secular or feminist grid which ends up misunderstanding or distorting the tradition."

[40] *Patriarchy* is the term that refers to the ideology and social system of the "rule of fathers" in a "clan or family" or the rule of men over women, and husbands over wives and children. Patriarchy has resulted in women and children being understood as the property of husbands and fathers, which is why even today we still hear of women being "given" and "taken" in marriage. Patriarchy is the virtually universal pattern of social organization in our world. Patriarchy both stems from and feeds the pervasive privileging of males and male reality. Patriarchal societal structures are organized so that women and children bear the names of husbands and fathers and take much of their identity from the male. A fundamental feature of patriarchy is a conviction about the naturalness of hierarchical social ordering. Patriarchy functions on the assumption that social order is dependent on there being a hierarchy of relationships—the ruler and the ruled, with elite men at the top of the hierarchical heap.

[41] *Andocentrism* means male-centeredness, indicating the obsession with the masculine at the expense of the feminine. While *patriarchy* describes a socio-cultural pattern, *andocentrism* describes a worldview—the worldview in which the male is the normal and the female the "other." Within the Christian churches and tradition, andocentrism has been rampant.

[42] *Sexism* is the attitudinal and behavioral consequences of andocentrism and patriarchy, that is, the conviction, and its consequences in every sphere of life, that men are superior to women simply because they are male. Sexism is expressed in various ways through discrimination, marginalization, exclusion, oppression, and abuse of women and their dependents.

[43] *Misogyny* is the fear and hatred of women.

and a subordinate status. Consequently, under authoritative male headship, covering and control, women have, at the best of times, been "honored" as second-class citizens. They have been dominated, marginalized and occasionally patronized, while men have been elevated.[44]

And the struggle for women does not end there. As womanists,[45] mujuristas,[46] and others have pointed out, the interlocking systems of sexism, racism, classism, colonialism and other oppressions including spiritual, political, cultural, emotional and psychological facets make women's place a site of ongoing struggle.[47] Feminist, Biblical theologian, Elisabeth Schüssler Fiorenza, uses the label kyriarchy or "rule of the lord" to refer to these multiple, interlocking layers of oppression.[48]

Patriarchal Pentecostalism

That American and Canadian Pentecostalism was patriarchal from the beginning even with its egalitarian impulse is clearly demonstrated in its treatment of women and their ministries. At Azusa Street, even though many women influenced and ministered with him and his wife, when Jenny Moore eventually took over, William Seymour bequeathed his ministry to a "man of color." William Seymour was, and still is, credited with being the mission's

---

[44] Susan Hyatt, "A Biblical Theology of Womanhood for Spirit-Oriented Believers: A Course Designed for Pentecostal/Charismatic Training Contexts" (D.Min. diss.: Virginia Beach, VA, May 2000) 9.

[45] The word *womanist* builds on Alice Walker's term found in her work *In Search of Our Mothers' Gardens*. In this work, the word *womanish* meaning the opposite of *girlish* is changed to *womanist* to stress the love that Black women have for their own culture and history. Alice Walker, *In Search of Our Mothers' Gardens: Womanist Prose* (New York: Harcourt Brace Jovanovich, 1983) xi-xii. As Delores S. Williams explains it, womanists are not concerned about women alone. Rather, womanists are concerned also about Black men and children whom they struggle alongside of for "the liberation, survival and positive quality of life" of the whole oppressed Black community." Delores S. Williams, "'Straight Talk, Plain Talk': Womanist Words about Salvation in a Social Context," in *Embracing the Spirit: Womanist Perspectives on Hope, Salvation & Transformation*, ed. Emilie M. Townes (Maryknoll, NY: Orbis, 1997): 97.

[46] A *mujerista* is someone who makes a preferential option for Latina women and their struggle for liberation, not as individuals but as members of a Latino community. Mujerista theology both attempts to enable Latina women and to impact mainstream theology. The sources of mujerista theology include the lived, reflected upon experiences of Latina women, the community, and feminist and liberation theologies.

[47] Sanders, *Living the Intersection*, 9-10.

[48] Elisabeth Schüssler Fiorenza, *But She Said: Feminist Practices of Biblical Interpretation* (Boston: Beacon, 1992) 8.

designated leader.⁴⁹ Azusa Street's legacy regarding the place of ministering women is ambiguous.

Within Canada, the legacy of Ellen K. Hebden and her Toronto-based East End Mission has been both disparaged and coopted. Even though Hebden reported in her publication, *The Promise,* that she had received the baptism of the Holy Spirit on November 17, 1906, possibly making her the first Canadian to have spoken in tongues,⁵⁰ the leading male figure behind the establishment of the PAOC, R.E. McAlister, was given that honor.⁵¹ When the Trinitarian Hebdens, along with many other early Pentecostals, were against organization of any kind,⁵² Ellen Hebden's prophetic ministry came under public scrutiny and was condemned.⁵³ R.E. McAlister's oneness position was handled much more discreetly as the PAOC adopted Trinitarian theology!⁵⁴

That Canadian Pentecostalism remains patriarchal can be just as easily

---

⁴⁹ H.V. Synan, "Seymour, William Joseph," in *Dictionary of Pentecostal and Charismatic Movements,* ed. Stanley M. Burgess and Gary B. McGee, with Patrick H. Alexander, assoc. ed. (Grand Rapids: Zondervan, 1988): 778-81, 781.

⁵⁰ Hebden, "How Pentecost Came to Toronto," 1-3. See also William Seymour, ed., *The Apostolic Faith* 1:6, Feb.–Mar. 1907: 4. Ellen Hebden is *possibly* the first person because there is one other account in the December 1906 edition of *The Apostolic Faith* (1:4) of a man named John Loney of Snowflake, Manitoba, who had received the baptism of the Spirit evidenced by tongues even earlier. However, it is not clear whether he actually lived in Canada or the United States.

⁵¹ Kulbeck, *What God Hath Wrought,* 29, n. 23.

⁵² Letter to Douglas Rudd from H.H. Barber, PAOC Archives. See also Miller, *Canadian Pentecostals,* 44.

⁵³ For instance, G.A. Chambers, one of the early leaders of the PAOC, explained that the early Pentecostals believed that "God was forever through with organization." *Pentecostal Testimony,* Nov. 1934: 7. Along with Hebden, he had openly spoken against early attempts at organization. See Miller, *Canadian Pentecostals,* 105-7, 113; and Gordon Francis Atter, *"The Third Force": A Pentecostal Answer to the Question So Often Asked by Both Our Own Young People and by Members of Other Churches: "Who Are the Pentecostals?"* (Peterborough, ON: College Press, 1962) 95, 107.

⁵⁴ Miller, *Canadian Pentecostals,* 65. As late as 1994, with knowledge of Hebden and the East End Mission having become more widespread, this ministry has been coopted as part of "several religious events in Canada that played a significant role in the formation of the Fellowship," that is, the PAOC. While being acknowledged as having been influential, Hebden is described as a "pastor of a small, downtown Mission in Toronto" who "placed an undue emphasis on prophetic utterances" and "vigorously opposed" organization but was, "[n]evertheless," remembered respectfully by many first-generation Pentecostals. In contrast, R.E. McAlister, described as a "zealous evangelist pastor" and "founding member of the PAOC" renowned "for his biblical expertise" and "photographic memory" is credited with being the "first *man* in Canada to receive the Baptism." No mention was made that Hebden, as a *woman,* had previously spoken in tongues. And no mention was made of McAlister's earlier oneness position. Dr. Thomas Miller, " 'Firsts' for the Fellowship," *The Pentecostal Testimony,* Sept. 1994: 24-26, 24-25.

demonstrated. It wasn't until 1984, and then only after decades of infighting, that the PAOC finally decided to allow the ordination of women.[55] Nevertheless, male headship was still protected in that restrictions were placed on women that prevented them from exercising leadership at the district or national level.[56] A radical reorganization of institutional policy was required at the national level in 1998[57] before women's involvement in these areas was opened up and a place was made for lay delegate Dr. Lillian Douglas on the general executive in 2000.[58] However, no woman has yet held the position of general superintendent of the Pentecostal Assemblies of Canada.[59]

Not only is Canadian Pentecostalism patriarchal, there are those who believe it is appropriate, even divinely ordained, though others have credibly refuted that belief. Sometimes this belief is based on particular interpretations of Scriptures. Sometimes it is based on ideology.

Regarding the Scriptural basis, two papers written in response to a request by the PAOC's "National Committee on the Role of Women in the Church" in 1975 are typical of the dilemma posed by particular interpretations. Based on her review of Scripture, Grace Brown concluded that men and women were equal before God. Therefore, women who were in charge of music, Christian education or youth work within a local congregation deserved to be called "pastors" like their male counterparts.[60] Based on his review of Scripture, G.R. Ewald concluded that, although he had voted for the ordination of women because they were doing the job anyhow, he thought that women should remain

---

[55] *Minutes of the 34th Biennial General Conference of the Pentecostal Assemblies of Canada,* 1984, 10-20, and photocopied note overlaid on page 20.

[56] Ordained women were not eligible to serve at the district or national leadership level. The Executive Officers and Members of the General Executive were to continue to be filled by "men of mature experience and ability . . . ordained," which was made clear at the next General Conference when the "Chairman" responded in relation to a question regarding the election of "Members at Large to the General Executive" that "a man meant a male." *Minutes of the 35th Biennial General Conference of the Pentecostal Assemblies of Canada,* 1986, 5, 29. See also the *PAOC General Constitution,* By-law 3, election of officers, Section 1, Qualifications a) Executive officers, By-law 14, District Conference, Section 9, Elections, (a) Qualifications, 3, PAOC Archives.

[57] *Minutes of the 1998th Biennial General Conference of the Pentecostal Assemblies of Canada,* 1998, 3-4.

[58] "Proposed Amendments" appended to the *Minutes of the 44th General Conference of the Pentecostal Assemblies of Canada,* 2000, 7.

[59] Which is not unusual. Within Canada, only one woman has ever been Prime Minister and then only for a short term. However, women non-Anglos have been appointed as Governor-General, the Queen's representative in Canada.

[60] Grace Brown, *Women in Ministry: Prepared by Grace Brown for the PAOC as part of a study on the position of women in the church as ministers,* June 6, 1975, PAOC Archives.

in supportive roles. In his understanding, even though Reverend was not a Scriptural term, women should only be granted the title "deaconess."[61]

Regarding ideology, Holm's analysis serves as an illustration of its influence. Even though he does not define his approach as feminist, Holm credits "prophetic pragmatism"[62] for women's active involvement in the early years of the PAOC and "accomodationist pragmatism" to a "patriarchal" society when the PAOC institutionalized for the restrictions placed on such.[63] The early "prophetic pragmatism" allowed Scriptures to be interpreted in such a manner that a "latter rain" emphasis preempted patriarchal "social norms and freed *men and women* to actualize their potential"[64]

The diminishment of the earlier "counter-cultural zeal," coupled with an accommodation to "conservative Christianity" with its "Victorian gender roles" and "separate spheres ideology," limited the involvement of ministering women as it insisted that "preaching, teaching and pastoring were best suited for men."[65] This separate sphere of ideology held such sway that, even when a woman felt called to ministry, her obligations to home and family, coupled with the need to be in submission to men often mitigated against that call.[66]

An article in a 1955 *Pentecostal Testimony* explains the reasoning for men teaching as "the great influence they can wield in their community—particularly to men" and "they are best able to reach the boys of our generation who are the potential church leaders of tomorrow . . ."[67] In short, because society is patriarchal and men are patriarchal, the PAOC should be patriarchal in order to "maximize their numerical results."[68] Pragmatic, yes, but also patriarchal.

While women's ministries were necessary and useful to the institution, the

---

[61] G.R. Eward, *An Examination of the Scripture on the Role of Women in the Church: As Requested by the National Committee on the Role of Women in the Church,* May 1975, PAOC Archives.

[62] Holm, "A Paradigmatic Analysis," 5.

[63] Holm, 5-6.

[64] Holm, 5.

[65] Holm, 1-3.

[66] For instance, a 1947 article in the *Pentecostal Testimony* ridicules the call to preach of a "young married woman." "Her main qualification was ability to sing a few hymns to accompaniment of a guitar. Her knowledge of the Bible was negligible, but she could exhort a little. Her husband felt no leadings in that direction, and their only child had to be neglected if she were to go. In considering the matter, one could not help but feel that the woman was ambitious for public life. She was willing to neglect the training of her son so that she could go out holding meetings." C.B. Smith, "From the Editor's Chair," *Pentecostal Testimony* 28:8, June 1, 1947: 1, 17.

[67] Holm, "A Paradigmatic Analysis," 5-6, quoting G.R. Upton, "Why Men Should Teach" *Pentecostal Testimony,* Sept. 1955.

[68] Holm, 6.

openly accommodated patriarchal ideology demanded that such ministry at least appear to be under the headship of men. Therefore, a two tier practice of ministry was adopted. Men were ordained men with rights and benefits as full voting members, and women became either missionaries of deaconesses. Later, in 1935, a third tier was added in the form of a "Ministerial Licence for Women," which, until 1950, did not include the right to vote or the right to perform rites of marriage.[69] This came about seemingly in recognition of those rare women who were pastoring churches when a man was not available.[70] If a man was available, women pastors were required to defer to them when it came to presiding over the "ordinances" of baptism and the Lord's Supper.[71]

Despite the efforts of Pentecostal women[72] to demonstrate that Scriptures can be interpreted in an egalitarian manner, many Pentecostal churches still refer to their own patriarchal interpretations in order to legitimize patriarchal assumptions, practices and teaching. To continue to choose a male headship and female submission model demonstrates the pervasiveness and power of patriarchy even within a Spirit-empowered church.

Kyriarchal Pentecostalism

That American and Canadian Pentecostalism is kyriarchal can be easily demonstrated as well.

Within the United States, while the influence of Azusa Street and William J. Seymour continued to be felt, not only within Pentecostalism, but also within the black community and American society as a whole,[73] the American culture within which Pentecostalism emerged in the early years of the 20th century was racist, class conscious and patriarchal. Much of the Pentecostal Movement within the United States soon became likewise. Significantly betraying its beginnings, Pentecostalism split into predominately male-dominated, African American, and Caucasian groups. Caucasian Pentecostalism, as embodied by the Assemblies of God, has acknowledged its racism in the Memphis Dialogue of October 17-19, 1994. Time will tell if anything substantial results from such

---

[69] Holm, 6.

[70] Holm, 3.

[71] D.N. Buntain, "Should Women Preach and Teach," *Pentecostal Testimony,* Mar. 1, 1939: 3.

[72] Such as Susan Hyatt and Janet Everts Powers.

[73] As Gayraud S. Wilmore points out, "concentric waves spread out from [Seymour's] Azusa Street Revival to carry Martin Luther King Jr. to the Mason Temple Church of God in Christ in 1968 and to the garbage workers' strike in Memphis, where most of the strikers were members of that Pentecostal denomination." Gayraud S. Wilmore, *Pragmatic Spirituality: The Christian Faith through an Africentric Lens* (New York and London: New York UP, 2004) 40.

acknowledgment. Time will also reveal whether or not Bishop Barbara Amos' forceful criticism, as the *only* female among the 200 participants, of the sexism inherent within that "dialogue" and I would add, the Pentecostal Movement, will be acknowledged.[74]

Within Canada, the issues of race and colonialism are noticeable within the ongoing tensions between the Anglo and French-Canadian segments of the country. Interestingly enough, when it comes to ministering women within the PAOC, the traditional hegemony of the Roman Catholic Church within the province of Quebec, where the largest French population is found, may be working in favor of these women. As Holm explains, Pentecostal people often rebel against the power and authority the Catholic church still exercises within Quebec—including its "paternal authority," thereby opening up a "place" of ministry for women that traditionally has been banned. Added to this rebellion is the pragmatic considerations of a relatively younger movement with smaller churches which require the services of all to survive, and attitudes toward women in leadership are relatively inclusive.[75]

However, outside of Quebec, even while Canada is "officially"[76] a multicultural mosaic, the question remains open as to the acceptance of French Canadian, ordained women serving as pastors within a predominately Anglo congregation. Conversely the acceptance of Anglo women clergy within a predominately French Canadian congregation also remains unanswered as there are still relatively few women in ministry within the PAOC.

The Prophetic[77] "Place" of Women

Pentecostal women have prophetically challenged, with little lasting results, the restrictions placed upon them by patriarchal and kyriarchal ideology and practices. In many cases, they have struggled somewhat successfully to over-

---

[74] Frank D. Macchia, "From Azusa to Memphis: Evaluating the Racial Reconciliation Dialogue Among Pentecostals," *Pneuma: The Journal of the Society for Pentecostal Studies* 17, no. 2 (Fall 1995): 203-18, 213. See also Barbara M. Amos, "Race, Gender, and Justice," *Pneuma: The Journal of the Society for Pentecostal Studies* 18, no. 1 (Spring 1996): 132-35.

[75] Holm, "A Paradigmatic Analysis," 2.

[76] As compared to "in practice." Racism is alive and well in Canada. As the words of a recent television commercial stated, "We're just more polite about it."

[77] For a sense of how I am using the word *prophetic,* see for example, Roger Stronstad's article "Affirming Diversity: God's People as a Community of Prophets," *Pneuma: The Journal of the Society for Pentecostal Studies* 17, no. 2 (Fall 1995): 145-57. For a discussion of the prophetic vs. institutional stance and its affect on women within Pentecostalism, see Margaret M. Poloma, "Charisma, Institutionalization and Social Change," *Pneuma: The Journal of the Society for Pentecostal Studies* 17, no. 2 (Fall 1991): 245-52, 252.

come any lack of confidence in their ability to discover and own God- and self-generated identities. However, such a struggle is oftentimes personally costly.

Aimee Semple McPherson is a well-known example of one woman's approach to overcoming kyriarchal limitations which transcends the American-Canadian border. McPherson was committed to a "place" for women in ministry. As she argued, "Women must preach to fulfill the Scriptures," as a legitimate sign of the end times.[78] As McPherson stated, "When God anoints you to preach, here are your credentials and authority, students (sic), whether male or female. When people say a woman should not preach in church, remember thus saith the Scripture, 'Your sons and your daughters shall prophesy.' "[79]

McPherson was also deeply committed to the understanding that the Spirit transcended the humanly-created color line by bringing together the races.[80] Perhaps it was McPherson's proximity to one of the end points of the historical Underground Railroad in Southwestern Ontario. Perhaps it was her experiences at Hebden's Toronto-based Mission where she and her first husband, Robert Semple, had been exposed to the large Chinese population.[81] Perhaps it was her experiences in the Deep South of the United States where she witnessed people of all shades praying together in the Spirit as she ministered. Whatever the reasons, as Cox has pointed out, McPherson's name for the denomination she founded and led, The International Church of the Four Square Gospel, not only referenced the "foursquare" teaching of Jesus as Savior, Sanctifier, Healer and Coming King. It also was an allusion to the hope for a new and just city, the New Jerusalem, which "lies foursquare" according to Revelation 21:16 (KJV).[82]

Nevertheless, in the end, McPherson not only left her home in Canada in order to find her "place" in Los Angeles, she also suffered widowhood, divorce, family feuds and died young.[83] This was not unusual.[84] Unfortunately humanity has always preferred a patriarchal and kyriarchal ordering, a "kingship," to a Spirit-birthed and empowered "theocracy." Prophetically challenging, the kingdom can be costly.

---

[78] Edith L. Blumhofer, *Aimee Semple McPherson: Everybody's Sister* (Grand Rapids: Eerdmans, 1993) 195.

[79] Barfoot and Sheppard, quoting Aimee Semple McPherson, "Class notes on the Book of Acts at Life Bible College (Los Angeles), 9.

[80] Cox, *Fire from Heaven,* 125-26.

[81] Blumhofer, *Aimee Semple McPherson,* 84.

[82] Blumhofer, 128.

[83] See Blumhofer's *Aimee Semple McPherson,* for the story of her life.

[84] For the story of two other women, Mary Magdalena Tate and Ida Robinson, as well as McPherson's, see Estrelda Y. Alexander, "Gender and Leadership in the Theology and Practice of Three Pentecostal Women Pioneers," (Ph.D. diss., The Catholic University of America, 2003).

Signs of Hope

The Pentecostal Assemblies has changed. It has opened up a place for women both in policy and in practice. Soon after the 1984 decision to allow for a "place" for women in ordered ministry, several women were ordained.[85] Nevertheless, 10 years later, in 1994, only a few single women were ministering on their own in senior pastoral positions. Married women were in team ministry with their husbands.[86]

However, also in 1994, a delegate at the General Conference "expressed her concerns regarding the fact that the ordination of women had been approved in 1984, but since that time, there had "been no enabling legislation to allow women to be candidates for certain elected offices."[87] Her concerns were eventually heard.

In 1998, as part of a significant "International Office Redesign," representation on the General Executive was opened up to women. How this came about was significant. Resolution #1 in the minutes of that year's General Conference used inclusive language such as "ordained credential holders" and "lay persons" when referring to officers of the corporation. No longer could anyone point to particular, exclusive language such as "men" as an excuse to bar women from the executive as had occurred earlier in years. A motion to reconsider the resolution by secret ballot was defeated and "the preconference nomination procedure for four executive officer positions" which would have proceeding under the "male only" basis was "disregarded."[88] The male executive leaders were advocating on the behalf of their female coworkers!

Eighty-one years after its inception, and after almost three decades of fighting throughout the '70s, '80s, and '90s, the Pentecostal Assemblies of Canada finally opened up a "place" for their ministering women at the district and

---

[85] See "Women Ordained to the Ministry," *The Pentecostal Testimony*, Feb. 1985: 27.

[86] Charles P. Holman, *Organization Blues: The Struggle of One Pentecostal Denomination With the Bugbear of Institutionalism* (Unpublished paper, 1994) 22, n. 54.

[87] *Minutes of the 41st Biennial General Conference of the Pentecostal Assemblies of Canada*, 1994, 41.

[88] *Minutes of the 1998th Biennial General Conference of the Pentecostal Assemblies of Canada*, 1998, 3-4. At stake was Resolution #7 of the appended "Resolutions Agenda" which were "Updated to August 13, 1998" and "Subject to Review and Presentation by the General Conference Resolutions Committee," which could have limited women once again as it continued to list the qualifications of "Executive Officers" and "Members of the General Executive" as "men of mature experience." Rather than bring this resolution forward, the minutes noted that this resolution, along with several others, were included in the "redesign which has now been approved, and therefore would not need to be dealt with individually." "36 Resolutions," appended to the *Minutes of the 1998th Biennial General Conference of the Pentecostal Assemblies of Canada*, 1998, 4-5, as compared with the *Minutes of the 1998th Biennial General Conference of the Pentecostal Assemblies of Canada*, 1998, 5, 7.

national level. Now not only was an exceptionally gifted woman of color a member of the executive, but by 2004, of the 852 women in ministry, 20 occupied senior pastoral positions.[89]

While this is encouraging, there is still a long way to go. It is important to remember that, at least once before, Pentecostal women were active in all areas of ministry in large numbers only to have their freedom in the Spirit limited and their "place" restricted to those areas that fit more appropriately with patriarchal and kyriarchal ideologies and practices. Patriarchy and kyriarchy are well-entrenched within human cultures and society. Until they are no more, the presence and "place" of women will remain prophetic and ambiguous. The fact that the place of women is still a topic of discussion 100 years after Azusa Street is evidence enough of the ongoing power of patriarchal and kyriarchal ideology.

Conclusion

Both Azusa Street and the Hebden Mission were founded and led by marginalized members of society, that is, women and people of color. Both were a beginning for many strong leaders. Neither survived long.

Within the United States, a large African American Pentecostal community emerged where women continue to struggle for recognition as ministers.[90] In the predominately Caucasian Assemblies of God (AG), the presence of ministering women resulted in access to ordination for women by 1935,[91] and the racism inherent in its beginnings has been acknowledged.[92] William J. Seymour and Azusa Street have been remembered and honored, despite efforts to replace him with a Caucasian father figure in the form of Charles Parham.

Within Canada, Ellen Hebden and her mission were eclipsed by the fame of the founding father of the Pentecostal Assemblies of Canada, R.E. McAlister. Access to ordination was denied women until 1984.[93] Time will tell whether or not Hebden will be remembered and significantly honored for the role she played.

Pentecostalism owes its ministering women an apology for the ambiguous

---

[89] "PAOC Credential Men and Women in Ministry," *Vital Statistics: Pentecostal of Canada Fellowship Data for 2004*, PAOC Web site, Aug. 2005.

[90] See for example, Early, "'Into the World.'"

[91] Edith Blumhofer, "Assembles of God," in *Dictionary of Pentecostal and Charismatic Movements,* ed. Stanley M. Burgess and Gary B. McGee, with Patrick H. Alexander, assoc. ed. (Grand Rapids: Zondervan, 1988): 23-28, 26.

[92] For examples, see Cecil M. Robeck Jr., "Historical Roots of Racial Unity and Division in American Pentecostalism," at *www.pctii.org/cyberj/cyberj14/Robeck.pdf.*

[93] *Minutes of the 34th Biennial General Conference of the Pentecostal Assemblies of Canada,* 1984, pp.10-20, and photocopied note overlaid on page 20.

"place" it continues to place them in. For women of color, recognition of and apology for the ongoing racism and sexism within Pentecostalism is long overdue. The struggle of African-American women as they oppositionally form their sense of identity by dialectically resisting and engaging both Eurocentric and Afrocentric definitions of womanhood while attempting to deal with religious subjugation within Pentecostalism's marginalized context as a protest and reform movement which, nevertheless, further oppresses its women and, white Pentecostalism, doubly so, is untenable. Black women's situation is as complex as the previous sentence.[94]

Since Azusa Street, women remain caught in a personally and communally costly "place" between their Pentecostal empowerment and a patriarchal and kyriarchal Pentecostal culture that oftentimes uses Scriptures to reinforce its ideology. While a Spirit-empowered Theocracy continues to struggle to emerge among the Pentecostal people of God, many of the people still cry out for a king. It's time this human preoccupation for kings and kingdoms was named for what it is—human, patriarchal and kyriarchal ideology—even though such naming will be met with firm resistance particularly from those who have the most to lose, that is, the "kings" and those around them (including women) who benefit from their reign.

If it weren't for the women, Pentecostalism probably would not have been established in many of the countries throughout the world. The role of those of African descent with its emphasis on oral liturgy and narrative theology and witness cannot be underestimated.

Ministering women have always had and continue to have a vital and essential place in ministry—with or without the blessings of ruling men and their institutions—but always with the anointing of the Spirit and the blessing of God.

Come, Holy Spirit, we *need* you.

---

[94] Early, "Into the World," 93.

18

After Azusa Street

Identity and Function of Pentecostlisms in the Processes of Social Change

Bernardo Campos Morante

Introduction

This chapter presents five sociological hypotheses concerning the identity and function of Pentecostalisms in social processes. Space and style limitations do not permit me an evaluation in detail of these hypotheses. These are presented with the sole purpose of initiating dialogue.

THE SOCIOLOGICAL CONTEXT OF THE PRESENT DISCUSSION
The Religious Answer to Social Problems

The theme of a possible relationship between religion and society constitutes one of the fundamental problems for social sciences, political science and for the science of religion. Starting from this main point of relationships, it is possible to locate tendencies and schools of interpretation. The unfolding of various methods and theoretical frames of reference that explain the multiple and complex religious practices may also be seen. Among them *Pentecostalisms* are found.

In a topic that is as wide and complex as this one is, the question of how religion, in particular, popular or grassroots religion, contributes to social change is of particular interest.

In any given religion or particular way of doing religion, and in addition to responding to the demands or religious interests of the population as is natural, this has to do with the "symbolic benefits of salvation." It can also contribute to the effective response to the social needs and interests of the same population. This has to do with, for example, the "very real" necessities of the grassroots sectors of society.

This does not have to do only with verifying the forms, directions, and ambiguities of the religious answer to determined social problems such as facilitating or impeding social change. It has to do with explaining that along with the external conditions, there are *in* the religious system in question, in its doctrines, in its practices, in its organization or ethical standards, elements that may permit its orientation during a determined social moment in a specific direction. It may also permit one to discern *when* and *under what* religious-cultural conditions the popular religion has to exercise its function as a witness, or one to contest or protest (Desroche). This may not be randomly successful because of its *ambiguity* or the lack of definition in the sociopolitical field as all religion is recognized traditionally.[1]

The religious answer to social problems probably has to be of a different order and of a different grade of efficiency. That depends on three basic factors: (1) the external social conditions that favor it; (2) the identity and function that the religious community assumes in the complex spectrum of the religious field of which it is an integral part;[2] and (3) the position and capacity of leading that it occupies, in the actual state of a hegemonic configuration (Gramasci) as is promoted by Roman Catholicism in Peru and Latin America.

The Complexity of the Peruvian Religious Field

The configuration of the Peruvian Religious Field (PRF) can be illustrative in order to determine at what point it is possible for Pentecostalisms to be

---

[1] Paul Tillich (philosopher and Protestant theologian) has treated precisely and positively the ambiguity of religion. A formulation of its consequences for the transformation of culture can be seen in his *Teología sistemática III: La vida y el Espíritu; La historia y el reino de Dios* (Salamanca, Spain: Sígueme, 1984) 216.

[2] In its theoretic aspect, the *religious field* is understood as "the space in which a group of actors and religious institutions *produce, reproduce and distribute* symbolic benefits of salvation." The dynamic of the religious field is due to the *objective demand* of the dispossessed by the clergy, from the production and control of those benefits: the laity. In this sense, the demand and the *correspondent offer* always respond to the interests of the class of the laity, interests that express themselves in the religious area by demands of *legitimacy* of *compensation* and of symbolic *protest* (Brandao).

seen as part of popular religion. In order to do that, it is necessary to locate the diverse social actors that conform to the Peruvian Religious Field.

The PRF is constituted, *grosso modo,* by the following actors:

1. **Roman Catholicism** in its three currents: the Catholicism of Christianity (traditional and cultural), Catholicism of New Christianity (modernizing current and of Social Promotion) and the popular or grassroots Catholicism.
2. **Historic Protestantism**, weakly linked, in Peru, with the official Protestant reform of the 16th century in Europe.
3. **Denominational or Mission Protestantism**, in direct organizational and ideological relation to mission agencies of the pietistic tradition that is fundamentally of North American origin.
4. **Pentecostalism** with four basic tendencies: (1) the *Pentecostalism of expansion* international, with strong influence from North American fundamentalism; (2) Pentecostalism with an intermixture of national roots, in open differentiation from American fundamentalism; (3) *Neo-Pentecostalism,* closer to Catholicism than Evangelical Protestantism; and (4) the movements of divine healing, which I will call *Iso-Pentecosalisms* for being responsive to the social or interpersonal nature of Pentecostalism, but which appears to be of another nature.
5. **So-Called New Religious Movements (NRMS)**, among which we can distinguish basically:
   a. *Medium religions,* such as Spiritism, and certain magical-religious practices related to aboriginal shamanism
   b. *Messianic religions,* among which one needs to discern between those with a religious face and those with a political face (such as the subversive groups)
   c. *Esoteric religions,* with the scholastic and philosophical stamp of Oriental or Occidental origin
   d. *Aboriginal Religions*

In the space of Peruvian social formation, one must ask among other things: Who are the *laity* in the complex Peruvian Religious Field? In concrete terms, what are the figures of the offer and demand of the symbolic benefits of salvation, and in what political direction are the laity situated with respect to the social processes? All of these are questions that underline the analysis of the identity and the function of popular religion.

The Importance of Locating the Pentecostalisms in the Complex Picture of the Laity

In the complex and conflictive PRF, the study of Pentecostalisms occupies an important place for the following reasons: First, in its actual state, it constitutes "a religious instance in process of change" and, as such, it reflects very well the processes of social change of those to whom we wish to make reference. In the case of Peru, Pentecostalism has a trajectory of 86 years (to 2005) and that makes possible, at least, a deductive analysis in relation to the Protestant presence in Peru of some 153 years of existence, and in the face of Catholicism, which has more than 474 years in the country.[3]

Second, in various countries in Latin America, Pentecostalism has been converted into a socioreligious alternative, in light of the breaking up of the established religious and politic order. Pentecostalism has meant the possible construction of a popular identity by means of religion.

In many cases, through its lay constituency, Pentecostalism has been the means of legitimization, compensation and symbolic protest of the popular subjectivity.

In this sense, it would be profitable to establish a comparison between Pentecostal religion and Protestant and Catholic religion in regard to its functions and vocations, in a country that, in spite of new economic initiatives, is still marked by social injustice and by the lack of articulation of diverse social subjects in a national project that integrates the diversity of interests and is representative of the totality of its population.

Third, it is necessary to contribute to the knowledge of the complex PRF, since we do not have scientific studies about the diversity of the religious groups that until now have been classified provisionally as "sects" or religious "dissidents" because of lack of other categories for referring to them with propriety.

The few studies on the "messianisms" as a factor of change in society (as it is in the Peruvian case) are still in the descriptive or exploratory stage. Therefore, it would be premature to formulate sociological explanations about specific contributions of the messianic predisposition of Pentecostalism to social change. The few, but concrete, studies that have been made of Pentecostalism in Argentina, Brazil, Chile and Central America permit, at least, some theoretical and deductive approaches.

A presentation of the principal interpretive hypotheses of Pentecostalism will put us on the road to examine the possibilities of Pentecostalism functioning as the "organic intellect" of the popular organizations in process of change.

---

[3] Officially it counts its establishment in Peru from the First *Concilio Limense* (1531); cf. M. Marzal, *La transformación religiosa peruana* (no city: PUCP, 1983) 57ff.

On the other hand, it will help us maintain dialog with those who try to be intermediaries of a movement that wants to be something more than a simple social phenomenon, an object of scientific observation, or a pastoral menace to other religious communities.

Principal Interpretative Hypotheses of the Relationship Between Pentecostalism and Society
Complexity of the Fundamental Sociological Question

The fundamental problem that guides the sociological search is this: Given the sociohistoric conditions of the country, as a popular religion, how does Pentecostalism favor or impede the desired social change for development?

The simple formulation of the fundamental problem includes an ample range of questions that, even without being answered in detail, constitute the whole body of the subject. Given that this essay is exploratory in nature, permit me to simply formulate them.

The first, and perhaps the most important question, can be formed in these terms: Since the establishment of Pentecostalism within the country, what has been and what continues to be the function of Pentecostal religion in the process of Peruvian social formation?[4]

A first response to this question would require us to differentiate by the historic route, the function of the church already established, from the function that is generally assigned to a new religion or to a group of dissidents. Secondly, it would require that we determine if Pentecostalism, besides being in the condition of a "dissident" of official Protestantism, also implies, reflects or manifests the condition of an alternative political dissidence for social change, through the mediation of symbolic forms of self-production or by "direct" participation in national political life.

A question that is related to the general theory of religion, and all that underlies this first set of questions, ought to clarify the problem of whether Pentecostal religion, as Otto Maduro has indicated, is a *product* of social conflicts: terrain relatively autonomous of social conflicts or an active factor in social conflicts; or if these three conditions interact.[5]

---

[4] Pentecostalism was implanted in Peru in 1919 with the arrival of the Assemblies of God. Since then, the majority of Pentecostal "denominations" is at dissidence with, or is a derivative of this, or is a symbiotic product of the Pentecostalization of some reformed Protestant churches that in Peru are identified imprecisely as "historic churches."

[5] Otto Maduro, *Religión y conflicto social* (México City: Centro de Estudios Ecuménicos-Centro de Relexión Teológica, 1980).

The second order of questions proceeds from dialogue between the disciplines of theology and the social sciences: What relation exists, or ought to exist, between the religious project of salvation and the socio-historical project, on the horizon of the re-creation of old and new Utopias?

In this order of things, another series of questions arises: Who are the subjects of social change, and in what measure do the people participate in its promotion and realization? What is the model of society to be carried out and substituted for the old order? What is the condition of the actual order, their degree of certainty, and the causes that justify a radical or progressive structural change? What is the tendency of the actual political processes that favor or impede the attainment of a true and just change at the least social cost? What, if any, are the ideal models upon which it is possible to construct a country?

The common denominator of the investigations of Pentecostalism as a social phenomenon, has been that of understanding its significance and explaining its appearance, insertion, presence and phenomenal growth, in the midst of national and regional social processes in Latin America.[6]

In that search, social scientists have formulated several significant hypotheses that pastors and theologians cannot ignore. In what follows, I present some of the most thought-provoking hypotheses.

SOCIOLOGICAL HYPOTHESES

When one asks how the social scientist explains the growth and expansion of Pentecostalism in Latin America, the answers are as follows:

1. One Type of Answer for the Social Phenomenon

Latin American Pentecostalism is formed as an answer to the social situation produced by the process of migration that took place with the beginning of the industrialization of dependent Latin America.

Well-known investigators such as Emilio Willems, Christian Lalive D'Epinay, Prócoro Ferreira Camargo and Bryan Wilson,[7] among others, arrived at the

---

[6] David Stoll and David Martin have been busy in the presentation of comprehensive visions of the Pentecostal phenomenon in Europe and Latin America. For the continent, see D. Stoll, *Se vuelve América Latina Protestante? Las políticas de crecimiento evangélico,* tr. María del Camen Andrade (Ecuador: Abya-Yala, s/f); English original, 1990.

[7] Emilio Willems, *Followers of the New Faith* (Nashville, TN: Vanderbilt UP, 1967). Christian Lalive D'Epinay, *El Refugio de las masas* (Chile: Pacífico, 1968); idem, *Religion, dynamique sociale et dépendance, les mouvements protestants en Argentine et au Chile* (Paris: Nouton, 1975). C.P.F. Camargo, *Kardecismo e Umbanda* (Sao Paulo: Pioneira, 1970). Bryan Wilson, *Sociología de las sectas religiosas* (Madrid: Guadarrama, 1970).

conclusion that Pentecostalism responds to abrupt cultural and structural changes that result in migration, in the line of correcting the situation by the integration of its subjects in the urban scene. According to Willems, the expansion of Pentecostalism is similar to that of spiritism and Umbanda. It is applied in terms of its functional adaptation to a society and culture in process of change.[8]

Both Willems and Lalive start from the hypothesis that changes in the value system and in the traditional structure can create conditions favorable to the acceptance and spread of different Protestant creeds. From this point of view, the penetration of Protestantism is explained as only taking place after the weakening of the social ecclesiastical controls that, for three centuries, had been a religious monopoly in the monolithic societies of Latin America.[9]

Pentecostalism represented, then as now, an alternative for the migrant, that experiencing the anguishing effects in body and soul of the social disorganization and of the patterns of conduct that have been produced by the industrialization (social situation) looks for, by testing out, a group in which he can feel emotionally related and personally recognized.[10]

Along the same line of thinking, J. Pierre Bastian has pointed out that the great power of Pentecostalism is linked to the message of a millennial type that is proclaimed and its success lies in its capacity to create a political-religious counter-power on a local level.[11] In another sense, one can also affirm that popular traditional Catholicism acted in some capacity as a circumstantial ally in the face of the irruption and promotion of the spirit of modernism on the part of historic Protestantism and the neo-Catholic Christianity that was equally modernizing.[12]

In such an order, Pentecostalism appears as a sacred and functional alternative that is important in the process of social change, where it competes equally with spiritism, in spite of their doctrinal differences, fulfilling the role of integration and of adaptation to the urban scene.

Lalive has also pointed out that Pentecostalism represents a continuity and a discontinuity of the traditional societies of a manorial type, in which the style of the *hacienda* is reproduced.[13]

---

[8] Willems, *Followers of the New Faith,* 208. Lalive, *El Refugio,* 275.

[9] Willems, *Followers of the New Faith,* 180-81.

[10] Willems.

[11] J. Pierre Bastian, *Breve historia del protestantismo en América Latina* (México: CUPSA, 1986).

[12] José Miguez Bonino, "Historia y Misión," in *Raíces de la teología latinoamericana* (Costa Rica: DEI, 1985).

[13] Lalive, *Religión dynamique,* 1973.

It presents to the popular masses the faith in a God of love, the certainty of salvation, the security of the community, and the participation in common responsibilities to perform. As such, it offers the humanity that society has denied them.

If the people assume Pentecostalism, it is because, in its quality as an ideology, it is an answer to their problems and immediate needs. This is because the forms of expression of the Pentecostal creed, as well as its organization and institutions, are inspired and in direct proportion to the sociocultural plans proposed by the global society. By achieving the translation of its ideology and cultural system that accompanies it to the social and cultural language of the people, Pentecostalism has succeeded in converting itself into an essential element in society, a *refuge of the masses*.

The axiological differences in the interpretations of Lalive and Willems appear when we ask, "In what does Pentecostalism happen to be *effective* for the masses?" We can diagram the answers in this way:

Pentecostalism Is . . .

According to LALIVE	According to WILLEMS
Substitute society with social participation	Compensatory society with social and economic benefits not received
It makes possible: 1. It articulates its radical negation of the world (social strike in the religious community which substitutes the civic society). 2. It becomes an actual paralyzer of the proletariat masses looking for liberation.	It makes possible: 1. To be affirmed as a subject, as a person (participatory society) in compensation for the benefits not received. 2. It is a potential agent of history.
Therefore, Pentecostalism . . . 3. Needs a transformation of its *conscience* in order to transform its *transcendental apocalypticism* in revolutionary action and that, as we know, is only possible with change from outside, from the same social practices.	Therefore, Pentecostalism . . . 3. Ought to wait for changes in the liberal-democratic sense that would favor its participation in the society, that is, if Pentecostalism gets to be recognized as *a social actor* in a society in transition.

2. "The Religion of the Oppressed Classes"

Pentecostalism that is the religion of the band of the poor of society, of the oppressed classes, is explained in the dynamic of social relations in the manner of capitalist production that imprints its seal of its condition as a class and an ideology.

Francisco Cartaxo Rolim[14] has shown that while Pentecostalism, principally of the Protestant form, is concerned about the sacred, it is not politically neutral, and it is not immune to the forces of the relations between classes.

As a sub-alternate class, Pentecostalism is the product of the influence of the ideology of the dominant class. As a religion of the poor, it moves between accommodation and submission, and between questioning and protest, and has active participation in social mobilization (although this last is not always present permanently, in contrast with the religious practices that it maintains).

According to Rolim, religion is determined by social class relations. This does not have to do with determinism, given that the "Pentecostal religion" is relatively autonomous. In his opinion, the question is to understand at what point the social conditions diminish or annul the religious specificity of Pentecostalism, given the fact that "to point out an absolute autonomy is to create a greater problem than that which points to relative autonomy."[15]

At the same time and in a dialectic manner, an explanation of Pentecostalism that does not pay attention to the role of class and the role of religious agents is theoretically impossible. According to Max Weber, Rolim points out that the "acceptance of a salvation creed—as does Pentecostalism—stems, not from the beliefs in themselves, but rather from the concrete social conditions in which its followers are found." From that point of view, the basis of Pentecostal growth lies in its *adequateness* to the religious proposal, to the interests of the interlocutors and not the reverse. "Without *response* to the announced, however true it may be, no creed can germinate and grow."[16] Rolim says precisely: "The determination of the Pentecostal religion does not come from its internal religious center, but rather from the social conditioner, in relation to its root, base, foundation of the religious interests, but that it not only *exists* in our society. It is part of it, inserted as one of its components",[17] and as such is conditioned by it.

---

[14] Francisco Cartaxo Rolim, *Pentecostais no Brasil: Una interpretacao Sócio-Religiosa* (Petrópolis: Vozes, 1985).

[15] Rolim, 11.

[16] Rolim, 12.

[17] Rolim.

In light of this, it is easy to understand how the condition of "poor bands" and "popular hordes" of the Pentecostals arises specifically from the type of social relationships one finds in the manner of capitalist production by those that form a part of it, but only as workers without salary and that do not produce.

According to Rolim, this is the way to understand it, because in capitalist production the only productive worker is the one who directly produces profit. In the great majority of "those who accept Pentecostalism, if on the one hand belong to the working world, and in this live in dependence as employees, on the other hand, they do not register in the fundamental sector,"[18] but rather, view themselves as part of the unproductive sub-alternate classes.

In the ideological aspect, Pentecostalism forms part of the dynamic that imposes itself in the dominant/dominated type of relationship. The social relationships of production assign basically and fundamentally to the Pentecostals the title of a *dominated class*.

Now that they are registered in reciprocal relationships in the class system, it is not possible to understand them apart from reference to the *dominant,* in other words, in reference to the relationship between domination/subordination.

This situation of dominance appears in the ideology under two aspects. The first is in the affirmation of the dominant class and its imposition of its dominion over the sub-alternative classes. With that, several distinct mechanisms, including those of a religious nature, invade a vision of the lay and secular society in such a manner as to obtain assent and conformity to the rest of the classes. In this vision, the dominant class imposes its interests, not frontally nor directly, but as representing the interests of the totality of society.

In such a way, the reference to the sacred—once it is concretized in words, rites, gestures and attitudes—is mediated by the relationship of domination, inscribed in cultural and ideological levels. The Pentecostal ideology is taken as a space where it is surprising to see the amount of submission to the dominant as well as confrontation of the same.

The consequence is clear. When the Pentecostals exalt the power of God, presenting Him as the remedy for the present immediately felt evils, and receives an avalanche of initiates, it transfers for the transsocial and for the ahistoric as an aspiration for liberation latent in the poor masses, covering for them the possibility that they might become autonomous by social practices. On the contrary, when the dominated, whether they be individual believers or groups, begin to perceive that scarcities, poverty, the present evils that come from the social order that creates privileges and inequality, it puts them without a doubt, in confrontation with the dominant lay and secular ideology.

---

[18] Rolim, 172.

For this reason, and definitely according to this interpretation, it is the social practices that are the road that leads to a reformulation of the religious ideology of the dominated. Only thus can the power of God not eliminate the autonomy nor the initiative of social practices, but rather demand an active presence in history as a transformer of the society.

Rolim contends that from his sociological investigation of Brazilian Pentecostalism, Pentecostal protest in Brazil is not only symbolic; it is also effective and real in a variety of ways, including political.[19] On the other hand, he is convinced that to explain Pentecostalism, starting with the process of urbanization and migration and even from the concept of social disorder, is to see Pentecostalism from outside in, and to leave in silence the religious production and religious interests, pointed out by Weber. That would be "to speak in an arbitrary way and without theoretic justifications, in accommodation to the system and in legitimatizing the social order."

3. "A Response to the Affliction and Suffering of Society"

Pentecostalism, like Umbanda in Brazil, is a response to the afflictions and sufferings of society, and its application to it represents a means for political and economic strategies to be related to the social experiences previously different of those members that are affiliated. Peter Henry Fry and Gary Nigel Howe[20] try to go a bit further than the approximations of Willems, Lalive, Camargo and others. They think to state that Pentecostalism responds to the classic dichotomies of relationships—such as folk/urban, order/social disorder, marginalization/integration—is not sufficient nor does it explain why the masses *elect* indistinctly some Pentecostalism and other Umbanda.

> We prefer to see the affiliation of persons to religious associations, they say, as a *social strategy* that some people adopt for specific reasons that still have not been revealed. Our argument is that urbanization and industrialization affect the way in which whichever individual, be he migrant or not, relates to society and vice versa. The changes brought by industrialization and urbanization are principally changes in the form and content of the social network of an individual.[21]

All the migrants do not arrive necessarily poorly equipped to confront

---

[19] Rolim, 13.

[20] Peter Henry Fry and Gary Nigel Howe, "Duas Respostas á afiliacao: Umbanda e pentecostalismo," *Debate e Critica,* nro. 6 (Julho 1975): 75-94.

[21] Fry and Howe, 85.

the way of urban living. Besides, rural immigrants are not totally ignorant with respect to the problems of the city when they arrive. They easily follow *networks of kinship.*

Thus, certainly, "Pentecostalism provides an ideological and organizational structure that is more conducive to the generation of confidence between coreligionists. In this way, (if) Pentecostalism is not, it at least provides an institutional base for the exercise of power and authority that are denied in the wider society"[22] and at the same time it serves the role of an *extended family* for those who need one.

In Weberian terms, Fry and Howe point out that Pentecostalism is close to being more like typical ideal "bureaucratic rational," while Umbanda is closer to the typical "Charismatic" ideal.[23] In this sense "the Pentecostal churches could be more attractive, in terms of *ideas,* for those who might have had some 'bureaucratic,' impersonal social relationships, and that might find the way to order their social life satisfactorily and conveniently. As well, Umbanda could be more attractive for those whose daily life is structured on the basis of experience of the 'bureaucratic' way of ordering social relationships and that find that system inconvenient."[24]

Now, neither global society nor religious societies are homogeneous. Therefore, they offer a complex field of possibilities (offers) for such a complex group, who are oriented socially in diverse forms (demands).

This fact makes it impossible to predict the orientations of the people in a given religious association. But "in a time in which the man in the street is denied whatever political expression, this results in the major importance of the fact that such persons are attracted to associations with religious ideology" (Gramsci).

It is certain that the election of one or another religious association depends even more on the *effectiveness of the symbols of the group* as much as the political and economic recompenses that the followers hope to derive from their energies; but, we ought not to forget, Fry and Howe point out that there are socioeconomic aspects that enter into play in the religious affiliation. The fact is, to become a member of a group, whichever it may be, "involves certain losses in terms of other opportunities, but also there are certain benefits *(bendiciones)* offered in the form of relationship and social interchange with other members. There is *progressive dialectics* between what is perceived as

---

[22] Fry and Hower, 87.

[23] Fry and Howe, 88.

[24] Fry and Howe, 91.

pleasing to God and to the spirits, and what is felt as being immediately of advantage for the man."[25]

For Fry and Howe, in each one of these cases, Pentecostalism or Umbanda, the socioeconomic aspects are equally those that determine, in general, one or another religious affiliation. Therefore, they believe that we ought to ask both congregations what are the benefits received by its members, what is the cost of enjoying those benefits, and finally, what kind of person would feel attracted by this particular social contract.

One appropriate answer to the question planted by Fry and Howe would undoubtedly rest in a theological re-conceptualization of the concept "economy" in terms of offer and demand and in anthropological differentiation of its followers of whatever religion once these have been acquired. But this suggestion must be verified so that it does not fall into the economic reductionism of the relationship between the individuals and the religions and that it is always the economic motivations that produce conversions and followers.

4. "The Construction of a Popular Subjectivity: Social Self-Production"

Considering beliefs, discourses and religious practices as constituting a "religious world" and as a type of product in the world of culture which supposes a process and determined relationship of production in that religious world, Pentecostalism is interpreted as a form in which important sectors of the popular classes (urban subproletariat, rural farmers who are or are not proletariat, and the Indian sections) recuperate for themselves or appropriate for themselves the means of production of the "religious world," repel, and at the same time, assume the sociocultural, liberal mediation of bourgeois origin.

This is the interpretation that Juan Sepúlveda, a Pentecostal, uses to sum up the situation for Chile.[26] He begins with the theoretical proposals of Otto Maduro, Burdieu and Lalive D'Epinay, with reference to a type of homegrown Pentecostalism that is the product of the recreation of Methodism in the same religious field in Chile. Such a homegrown Pentecostalism is different from the strain of Pentecostalism of foreign "mission" origin that arrived later in Chile.

In contrast with popular Catholicism and in direct relation to a kind of *mastery* as an official process of "religious cultivation," Pentecostalism appears as though it were produced directly and legitimately from a valid discourse

---

[25] Fry and Howe, 84.

[26] Juan Sepúlveda, "Pentecostalismo y Religiosidad Popular," *Pastoral Popular* 32, no. 1 (1981): 16-25.

and religious practice and establishes a clear element of *rupture* in the middle of existing religious *continuity*.

Pentecostalism, in the space of the Chilean society, operates as a kind of socialization or polarization of *mastery* and of the means of production of the "religious world." Sepúlveda, and in this he distances himself from various sociological type interpretations, points out that "this capacity of Pentecostalism has its origin not so much in external factors of a social nature, nor in theology, but in the specific religious *structure* of Pentecostalism," that is to say, in the capacity or religious *interest* to produce its own religious world.

Distinguishing with F.C. Rolim[27] two planes of actions and religious rites in Pentecostalism, some constitute *formal rites,* such as Baptism and Communion, and the other by public *services,* private services of prayer, preaching on public squares, and healing services in which normally the clear social division of religious work takes place between the *qualified agents* who produce the rite (the pastors) and the simple *consumers* of the rite (the laymen, the people), Sepúlveda concludes:

> The Pentecostal religious structure has this characteristic trait: the believer is a direct *producer* of the benefits of his religious world marked by the belief and the force of the Spirit. The important thing is not to be a presbyter, pastor or deacon, but to be the direct producer of the Pentecostal religious world.

In this sense Sepúlveda emphasizes:
1. Believers are, at the religious structural level, the direct producers of the religious world—that is what defines them as Pentecostals.
2. The position they occupy in this structure is characterized by the relationship of property and possession of the means of religious production (beliefs, sentiments, words, gestures).
3. There is no more social division of religious work, as a result.
4. There is no more social division between manual and intellectual work, that is, the difference between those who plan and those who execute the preaching, the prayers and the positions. Thus the dichotomy between specialized agents and simple believers, between the ignorant and the learned, between those who exercise power and those who are governed, between the planners and the executors disappears.

---

[27] F.C. Rolim, "Petecostisme et Societé au Brásil," *Social Compass* 26, nos. 2-3 (1979): 345-72, quoted by Juan Sepúlveda, "Pentecostalismo y Religiosidad Popular," 19.

This interpretation has been taken and explained recently by Samuel Palma and Hugo Villela, also Chileans, in the frame of reference of an investigation on "Popular subjectivity, the religion of popular sectors: the Pentecostal field" until 1987.[28]

Both interpretations explain the Chilean social process as a progressive one, closing off the possibilities of ascension and social mobility of the people; a process that places it in a situation of "popular frustration," of psycho-social deterioration where the loss of assertiveness is an expression of impotence, of the deteriorization of identities and of the loss of affective references.

In such a context, the "religious setting" [sic] is viewed as a viable road, even if it does not lead to social ascension, but permits, at least, the recuperation of identities and affection.

In the midst of that "crisis of subjectivity" of the "common people," Catholicism shows itself deficient before the demand for a religious setting. This is . . .

- Because Catholicism has been associated historically with the political power
- Due to the erudite character of Catholic religious personnel (priests, nuns, lay agents) that are placed at a distance in respect to the way of living the sacred on the part of sectors of the population such as rural farmer and urban dwellers
- Because of the formality of the structures that house the Catholic churches in the way they constitute a community.

The Catholic Church appears, thus, as a religion imposed and as a proposal of religion that is foreign to popular interests.

Facing this kind of vacancy of effective support of the identity of the people, Pentecostalism offers two exits:

1. The "exit to the world" in order to construct another world that is not a mere "refuge" as Lalive wanted to see, or
2. The exit from one sacred area (the Catholic) in order to produce another sacred space, Pentecostalism.

In this way, Pentecostalism offers to the popular sectors the possibility of constructing the world.

But this "world" is not a "refuge" in the sense that Lalive said "as a place for

---

[28] Samuel Palma and Hugo Villela, "El pentecostalismo: La religión popular del protestantismo latinoamericano: Algunos elementos para entender la dinámica de las iglesias pentecostales en América Latina" (Santiago, Chile: Mimeo, 1989) 15. Cf. Manuel Canales, Samuel Palma, y Hugo Villela, *En tierra extraña II: Para una sociología de la religiosidad popular protestante* (Chile: Amerindia, 1991).

idealized reconstruction of an order of extinction" (the traditional society in the scheme of the hacienda). On the contrary, it is the "support in the form of possible social identity in a world of precarious identities." And it represents, through a process of transformation that begins with new social practices, a possibility of returning to the daily world of the poor, a kind of reencounter with one's own identity in the same experience as the street preacher, for example.

In other words, Pentecostalism also represents the change of level of the symbolic universe of the sacred. It is the *change* from the "Catholic sacred" to the "Pentecostal sacred" that tells of the search for a direct relationship with the sacred, eliminating, removing and displacing the erudite mediation (priest) or competitive (the saints), for an affirmation of a "classist mediation" (the grassroots pastor). (This means that on the one side, the creative invention of his own religious universe with the elements of a "given religion.") This then, has to do with a bricolage of the re-creation of the traditional religion into a new religion.

This difficult and creative process explains, at least in part, the difficulty of Pentecostalism to reach an important level of "organicity" in time. Thus it has a tendency to fragment and to produce schisms.

Such facts and processes belong to the people, even though they do not enjoy in its totality the levels worthy of employment. They are in the midst of the process of cultural production and work that affirms the popular identity, the road to constructing a new society.

5. A Religious Satisfaction After the Shock of the Conquest

In the same way that first Catholicism, then the Protestantisms, then socialist ideas and populisms, among others, have gone, Pentecostalisms form a search for religious satisfaction produced in the Amerindian people after the bitter root of the violation of its mythical-symbolic substratus during the Conquest and Spanish colonization and later on by colonialisms.[29]

The Indian people of Indoamerica were raped during the Conquest and military-missionary colonization in the most fundamental of its social-cultural structure, that is to say, in its mythical-religious substratus, given that the center of its social and economic organization rested in its religious structure. The religious structure was the basis for the social organization.

---

[29] See my article, "Religión y Liberación del pueblo" (Lima: CEPS, 1969) 19.

In the moment of being violated and raped socially, culturally, economically, politically and religiously with the instruments of the sacred, there were Latin American people who testified of the type of aggression to which they were forced to submit earlier. Then in general, the victims of a violation changed, but kept in their subconscious, the traumatic memory of the aggression. Their frustrations, their complexes, their deformed conduct, their mania, their fears, and so on, are none other than a reflection of the subconscious to the critical point in which they were affected. On the social level, many festivity days which are Andean rituals are nothing but grotesque reproductions of aggressions, shocks, tragedies, violations and former sufferings to which they were forced to submit, even though these are remote and relatively distant.

In this way, the process of the colonizer and the Hispanic Christianizer gradually favored the formation of these traces of collective subconscious and this would take preferably a religious form, translating in a *pathos* of intensified religious life the context from which the people would ...

- Reproduce by means of folklore, the original action of the Conquest and the colonization
- Maintain in its ancestral mythical tales the figure of a white man who would come from the sea, of a king who would return (vision of the defeated)
- Dramatize ritually its protest with regional symbolic actions even though they were not always well expressed politically (liturgical fatalism)
- Tend to deflect the attention from its real needs (alienation).

Thus, the atrophy of the social, starting with the violence suffered in the religious symbolic substratus of the Amerindio people[30] by the Spanish Conquerors, had created the conditions and the psychosocial conditioning for the future generations as a kind of *collective religious anxiety.*

In such conditions, the Amerindio people had remained, as was determined by their social personality and religious condition. For this reason, this people tried out, permanently and in different directions, situations that would permit them to calm their anxiety and religious needs.

One of these ways was, in turn, the same Catholicism of Christianity, the Protestantism, the Populisms, the socialistic ideas, and also the Pentecostalisms and other new and old religious movements. They represent for the people alternatives for religious satisfaction, more than alternatives for change, interchange or expression of its own frustrated historical-social projects.

---

[30] Name used to designate the Indian people of South America.

For that reason the actual "rapture with" or intensification of popular religious experiences, closer to the religious dissidents of symbolic protest (such as the political messianisms) than to the Catholic of the new Christianity, would not be more than a sign of the popular experience, an alternative among others, of the search of roads for liberation of its condition as an oppressed people."[31]

---

[31] In order to continue the discussion of the "post-Pentecostalism," see my article "The Post-Pentecostalism: Renovation of the Leadership and Hermeneutic of the Spirit," *Cyberjournal for Pentecostal Charismatic Research*, http://www.pctii.org/cyberj/cyberj13/bernado.html.

19

Pentecostalism and Social Transformation

Donald E. Miller

The thesis of this chapter is that Pentecostals are increasingly engaged in community-based social ministries. Throughout the history of Pentecostalism, there have been examples of compassionate social service, so this is not a new phenomenon. But I believe we are witnessing an emergent movement within Pentecostal churches worldwide that embraces a holistic understanding of the Christian gospel.

Unlike the social gospel tradition of the mainline churches, this movement seeks a balanced approach to evangelism and social action that is modeled after Jesus' example of not only preaching about the coming kingdom of God, but also ministering to the physical needs of the people He encountered. This movement reflects the increasing maturation of Pentecostalism as it develops from being an otherworldly sect to a dominant force in reshaping global Christianity.[1]

---

[1] Dozens of books have been written recently on the subject of global Pentecostalism. See, for example, R. Andrew Chesnut, *Competitive Spirits: Latin America's New Religious Economy* (Oxford: Oxford UP, 2003). Andre Corten and Ruth Marshall-Fratani, eds., *Between Babel and Pentecost: Transnational Pentecostalism in Africa and Latin America* (Bloomington: Indiana UP, 2001). Paul Gifford, *Ghana's New Christianity: Pentecostalism in a Globalizing African Economy* (Bloomington: Indiana UP, 2004).

My exposure to this emergent expression of Pentecostalism occurred when Tetsunao Yamamori and I began a research proposal in which we set out to study congregations that had the following characteristics:

1. They were fast-growing.
2. They were located in the developing world.
3. They had active social programs addressing needs in their communities.
4. They were indigenous movements that were self-supporting and not dependent on outside contributions.

We solicited nominations for congregations to study by writing to 400 different mission experts, denominational executives and informed individuals. To our astonishment, nearly 90 percent of the churches suggested for the study were Pentecostal or Charismatic. Very quickly we decided to focus our attention exclusively on these congregations, ignoring mainline Protestant churches. For the next four years we spent two months each spring visiting Pentecostal and Charismatic congregations that matched our criteria in Africa, Asia, Latin America and several CIS countries. We explicitly excluded churches in Europe and the United States from our research, since the study was already unwieldy in scope.[2]

Contextualizing Progressive Pentecostalism

Given the fact that Pentecostalism is a multifaceted phenomenon with many different branches and expressions, it is important to clarify that we studied a particular element within this vast and complex movement of some 500 million Christians. Pentecostalism is not a monolithic phenomenon. There are churches associated with the historic Pentecostal denominations such as the Assemblies of God (AG), but even these are not uniform. Some AG churches are extremely traditional and legalistic, while other AG churches are quite contemporary and progressive in their worship and social outlook. Another major strain of Pentecostalism is "prosperity-gospel" churches that emphasize health and wealth.[3] Many of these churches are indigenous to countries in the developing world and have formed substantial networks that cross national boundaries, although there

---

David Martin, *Pentecostalism: The World Their Parish* (Oxford: Blackwell, 2002). Alan Anderson, *An Introduction to Pentecostalism: Global Charismatic Christianity* (Cambridge: Cambridge UP, 2004). Philip Jenkins, *The Next Christendom: The Coming of Global Christianity* (Oxford: Oxford UP, 2002).

[2] The research by Donald E. Miller and Tetsunao Yamamori will be published by the University of California Press in 2006. The tentative title of the book is *Pentecostalism and Social Transformation: A Global Analysis.*

[3] See, for example, Simon Coleman, *The Globalisation of Charismatic Christianity: Spreading the Gospel of Prosperity* (Cambridge: Cambridge UP, 2000).

is some influence from U.S.-based movements, especially through the media. In addition, there is a growing number of independent Neo-Pentecostal churches that are distinguished by their innovative worship, decentralized organizational structures and embrace of modern technology. Many of these Neo-Pentecostal churches have spawned clusters of daughter churches, but they have not routinized into a formal denomination. Indeed, these churches typically want to distinguish themselves from what they perceive to be the limitations of denominational structures.

Cutting across these various expressions of Pentecostalism is a new breed of churches that emphasize what theologians sometimes call the "integral" gospel.[4] These churches see no contradiction between a strong emphasis on evangelism and ministering to the social needs of people in their community. Indeed, they see social ministry as being at the heart of the Christian gospel. Tetsunao Yamamori and I have struggled with what to call this new emphasis we have studied, but finally have settled on the label *Progressive Pentecostalism*. By employing the adjective *progressive*, we do not mean to link Pentecostalism to any particular political movement, such as the Progressive Era in America (1890-1920). Rather, we wish to acknowledge by this term that Pentecostalism has often been otherworldly, emphasizing personal salvation to the exclusion of any attempt to transform social reality. The movement we are describing continues to affirm the apocalyptic return of Christ but also believes that Christians are called to be good neighbors, addressing the social needs of people in their community.

Stated somewhat abstractly, we define *Progressive Pentecostals* as "Christians who, inspired by the Holy Spirit and the life of Jesus, seek to address holistically the spiritual, physical, and social needs of people in their community." It is impossible to quantify this emergent movement, but our guess is that the label applies to less than 10 percent of all Pentecostal churches if one is referring to churches that explicitly articulate a commitment to social ministry. Excluded from our definition are congregations that may, on occasion, provide informal services to poor members of their congregations. Instead, we are applying the term *Progressive Pentecostalism* to churches that are programmatic in their emphasis, developing ministries for people with AIDS, establishing community-based medical clinics, building schools and providing other educational programs for children in the community, promoting economic self-sufficiency through micro-loans and other community development projects, and so on. Another important element

---

[4] See, for example, Tetsunao Yamamori and C. Rene Padilla, eds., *The Local Church, Agent of Transformation: An Ecclesiology for Integral Mission* (Buenos Aires: Kairos, 2004).

of our definition of Progressive Pentecostals is that their social ministries are available to everyone in the community as an expression of God's unconditional love and, therefore, they are not simply incentives for people to convert or join their church, although this may be a by-product of the church's commitment to addressing the needs of people in their community.

Although Progressive Pentecostals may be found in varying degrees in all the previously mentioned categories of the Pentecostal Movement, our feeling is that they are less likely to occur within the legalistic branches of the classical denominations as well as within prosperity-gospel churches that are focused on health and wealth. In our experience, Progressive Pentecostalism typically occurs more frequently within the non-legalistic elements of denominations, such as the Assemblies of God and in independent Neo-Pentecostal churches. In addition, there are a growing number of independent Charismatic churches, some of which are very large, that do not explicitly identify themselves as Pentecostal but are very engaged in social ministry. We are claiming them also as part of this emergent movement of Progressive Pentecostalism.

Types of Social Ministries

In the course of our research, we encountered numerous different expressions of social ministries. A partial listing includes the following: efforts to feed, clothe and shelter people; drug rehabilitation programs; HIV/AIDS interventions; micro-enterprise loans intended to help people—especially women—start their own businesses; visitation of people in prison, as well as support systems for their families; attempts at family reunification, including divorce intervention and bridging programs between teenagers and their parents; pregnancy counseling; ministries to prostitutes and sex workers; medical and dental services; services to the elderly, handicapped and single parents; schools and educational assistance and programs for children; residential programs for street children and orphans; efforts to counteract racial prejudice and other forms of discrimination; and the list continues. Some churches that we studied had only one or two of these social programs, while other churches had a comprehensive menu of social projects.

This rather dizzying array of programs can be ordered under the following eight types of services, programs or ministries:

1. Mercy ministries (e.g., food, clothing, shelter)
2. Emergency services (e.g., floods, famine, earthquakes)
3. Education (e.g., day care, schools, tuition assistance)
4. Counseling services (e.g., addiction, divorce, depression)

5. Medical assistance (e.g., health clinics, dental clinics, psychological services)
6. Economic development (e.g., micro-enterprise, job training, affordable housing)
7. Appreciation and enjoyment of the arts (e.g., music, dance, drama)
8. Policy change (e.g., government corruption, community organizing, etc.).

There is clearly some overlapping among categories within this typology, but analytically it helps to distinguish activities that are primarily *humanitarian* in nature (such as feeding and clothing people) from programs that are intended to serve people in moments of *personal crisis* (such as divorce, addiction and depression), and those that are attempting to promote *community development* and *social transformation* through education, economic development or policy change. Based on our experience, many Pentecostal churches are involved in the first two categories of response, while community development and structural change are emergent responses that should be encouraged.

The key variable in analyzing a church's social ministries is whether it is internally focused—that is, serving primarily members of the church community—or whether these activities are available to the broader community as well. As previously mentioned, to fit our definition of Progressive Pentecostalism, there needs to be some intentionality that these services are for the community, not just for members of the church. In addition, it is important that social ministry not be viewed in purely instrumental terms—that is, as a means of attracting new converts. A key Scriptural reference for many of the people we interviewed was Jesus' parable in Matthew 25 regarding the sheep and the goats and who enters the kingdom of heaven. The clear implication of this parable is that one encounters God by addressing the physical needs of the most disenfranchised people in society, regardless of their spiritual qualifications.

The range and depth of social ministries within Progressive Pentecostal churches depends on a number of factors. An important variable is the size of the congregation. Most small congregations simply do not have the capacity to launch comprehensive programs. However, if they are intentional in encouraging their members to participate in community-based programs, they fit our definition of Progressive Pentecostalism. On the other end of the size spectrum, some large congregations are able to fund numerous social ministries from their own resources. And other churches are partnering with various faith-based NGOs, such as World Vision, in projects that address social needs in their community.[5]

---

[5] We encountered resistance by some congregations to the lingering legacy of colonialism. They were very hesitant to become too dependent on outside funding, arguing that this not only creates dependency but potentially distorts their mission.

In fact, sometimes even relatively small Pentecostal congregations can play a powerful role in the community when they join forces with other churches (e.g., Catholic, Seventh-day Adventist, Methodists, Anglicans, etc.) in partnerships that are facilitated by international NGOs.

In our four years of research, we only encountered a few instances of Pentecostal congregations taking direct political action.[6] The more likely scenario was for them to create *alternative institutions* rather than butt heads with corrupt government officials.[7] In this regard, Progressive Pentecostals differ substantially from organizing efforts inspired by liberation theology where the goal is to create systemic change. Liberation theology is inspired by Marxist theories related to power, conflict and exploitation. Progressive Pentecostals, in contrast, tend to embrace an ethic of nonviolence and even nonconfrontation with civil authorities. Their operative strategy is to "grow" a new crop of civic, business and educational leaders from the ground up with the hope that they will infiltrate these institutions and inspire a higher level of moral engagement.

Examples of Progressive Pentecostalism

A few examples from our research will illustrate some of the categories discussed above. In Johannesburg, South Africa, we spent considerable time at Highway Assemblies of God Church, which is a midsize congregation of several hundred people. Located in a fairly affluent white neighborhood, the leadership of the church realized that if the church were to close, no one would really miss them because they were not making a real impact on their community. The response, under the leadership of a remarkable lay member, Colleen Walters, and her pastor, was to address the racial divide in South African society by establishing a training program for women in the townships who wanted to open day-care centers for young children. This project met a real need because preschool children were being minded by grannies and other caretakers who forced them to sit on a mat the entire day while their parents worked. They were receiving virtually no stimulation and certainly were not becoming prepared for primary school.

In response to this situation, Colleen established a model nursery school at her Assemblies of God church that was half white (children from the church) and half

---

[6] For a discussion of this issue, see Paul Freston, *Evangelicals and Politics in Asia, Africa and Latin America* (Cambridge: Cambridge UP, 2001).

[7] See Douglas Petersen's fine discussion of Latin America ChildCare as an example of creating alternative social institutions that reflect Pentecostal values: *Not by Might Nor by Power: A Pentecostal Theology of Social Concern in Latin America* (Irvine, CA: Regnum Books, 1996).

black (the children of housekeepers who were living in the homes of the church members). This nursery school became the training ground for women from the townships who wanted to start a child-care business in their community. For several months these women train at the Highway Assemblies of God Church observing how a first-class child-care center operates, and then they launch their own program—overseen by Colleen—who visits them regularly.

From Johannesburg, we travel northward to Uganda and Kampala Pentecostal Church. Meeting in a former theater, this congregation literally pulsates on Sunday morning. In fact, our first introduction to the church was at a youth concert with full band and a 100-member choir that sent our hair flying. A centerpiece of this church's social ministry is a network of villages that are headed by widows who bring their own children into the household but, in addition, adopt another five or six children who have been orphaned because of AIDS.

The church builds homes for these families, assists them in cooperative buying of food, digs community wells, and provides the children with medical care and a good education. Furthermore, recognizing that these kids need a male father figure in their lives, each household has a male volunteer from the church that visits the children regularly, serving as a surrogate father for the household. In both Johannesburg and Kampala, church leaders have worked with civil authorities in establishing their programs, but they really function as alternative institutions to any of the government-funded programs that are available.

From the continent of Africa, we jump to Latin America and the city of Sao Paulo in Brazil. Our introduction to this city was attending the annual "March for Jesus," which had over 1 million participants. For several miles people lined the street as they walked and danced beside dozens of semitrucks and trailers that had huge loud speakers and live bands. This event was orchestrated, in part, by Renacer Church, which balances its dynamic worship each Sunday by sending a dozen buses out every weeknight with volunteers who feed people on skid row and offer them blankets and words of encouragement. This feeding program is but one of a number of social programs for the community.

Further north in Caracas, Venezuela, we attended an all-night prayer meeting in a small home in a barrio on the side of a hill where several dozen teens and young adults gather regularly to testify, sing and support each other in their effort to resist drugs and postpone sexual intimacy until they are ready to start a family. This ministry was started by a member of a Pentecostal church who lost her son to gang violence, and it illustrates the point that not every expression of Progressive Pentecostalism has to be supported through large church budgets.

From Venezuela, we cross the ocean to Hong Kong, where Jackie Pullinger has established a network of drug-treatment facilities for heroin addicts. Our initial encounter with St. Stephen's Society was to attend a meeting of addicts and ex-addicts who had gathered for Bible study. In the room were people who had only recently injected themselves with heroin for what they hoped was the last time. They were there because a friend told them this was the way to get off drugs permanently. Little did they know that they would be speaking in tongues before the evening was over.

Following this initial meeting, addicts spend the next year or even longer in one of the residential programs run by St. Stephens. In this setting, they were loved unconditionally; if they fell off the wagon, they were welcomed back without incrimination. They were learning what life was like in a family that didn't abuse you.

These examples could be multiplied. In the Republic of Armenia, we visited a growing Pentecostal church—the largest Protestant church in the country—filled with young adults who were addressing the problem of poverty in their country by building houses and assisting people who were unemployed. In Thailand, we witnessed the remarkable ministry of a wealthy woman whom God called off her exercise bike to start a home for babies whose HIV mothers had abandoned them. In Cairo, we went into the homes of people who make their living by sorting garbage. Mama Maggie, an Egyptian version of Mother Teresa, has created a network of nursery schools and programs to intervene in the lives of children and youth who otherwise have little hope of a life different from the squalor in which they were raised.

Countering Misconceptions

When we first started this research project, I shared the same set of misconceptions of most people whose knowledge is based on stereotypical images of Pentecostals seen in Hollywood movies. While there is a grain of truth to each of the following three perceptions, the reality is much more complex.

First, while Pentecostals believe in the Holy Spirit, worship services are not always populated with people being slain in the Spirit, speaking in tongues, prophesying, or having their crutches thrown away by faith healers. These things happen in some churches, but they do not happen on a weekly basis in all Pentecostal churches, and sometimes these activities, when they occur, are relegated to small-group meetings or special occasions. In fact, in many Progressive Pentecostal churches the music may be lively, and people may raise their hands in praise and dance to contemporary gospel choruses, but they are seldom rolling in the aisles or practicing shamanistic forms of healing.

A second stereotype about Pentecostals is that they are lower-class, marginalized people for whom religion is an opiate. As is the case with the first stereotype, there is some evidence for this image. But it is not the whole story. True, Pentecostalism was born among lower-class people. Also, much of its amazing initial growth was because it connected with impoverished people, including those with animistic religious backgrounds. But over the last few decades, Pentecostalism has attracted a new class of more affluent and educated people. With this education has come greater sophistication in responding to social problems in the community.

The third stereotype is that Pentecostals are "so heavenly-minded they are no earthly good." Historically, it is true that Pentecostals were very otherworldly, with many of their members evangelizing their neighbors as they waited expectantly for the imminent return of Christ. This otherworldly characteristic of Pentecostalism, however, is changing. There is an emergent group of Pentecostals who are pursuing the integral or holistic gospel in response to what they see as the example of Jesus, who ministered both to people's physical needs, as well as preached about the coming kingdom of God.

In many ways these stereotypes about Pentecostalism make life easy for social scientists who can explain the growth of this movement in terms of economic deprivation, anxiety about death, or the need for security in an unstable world. Karl Marx viewed religion as an "opiate" that took the edge off the pain of life;[8] Sigmund Freud thought religion was a fantasy-escape mechanism, employed by weak people in search of security;[9] Emile Durkheim believed that religious ritual, especially for "primitive" people, was a way of maintaining collective order.[10]

All of these theories are rooted in deprivation theories of one sort or another, and, indeed, they are helpful in explaining some aspects of the growth of Pentecostalism. The question is whether viewing religion from a purely functional perspective is adequate, or whether it is important to add another variable to one's tool kit—namely, the role of the Spirit.

In my view, there is a place for functional theories of religion, but they should be balanced by frameworks that take into account the internal experiences of people. For example, while religion may sometimes serve as an "opiate" for converts from impoverished backgrounds, an alternative metaphor is that Pentecostal worship serves as a "stimulant" that propels people into productive behavior. In many instances, Pentecostals experience upward social

---

[8] See, for example, David McLellan, *Karl Marx: Selected Writings* (Oxford: Oxford UP, 2000).

[9] See, for example, Sigmund Freud, *Future of an Illusion* (New York: Norton, 1961).

[10] For his interpretation of the role of ritual, see Emile Durkheim, *The Elementary Forms of the Religious Life* (Oxford: Oxford UP, 2001).

mobility after conversion. They quit drinking, gambling and womanizing, and the result is that they have surplus capital to invest in their small-scale businesses, their children's education, and health care for their family. Even if they are very poor, their Christian lifestyle gives them a competitive advantage over their neighbors. But unlike Max Weber's description of the Protestant ethic,[11] which seems duty-bound and joyless, Pentecostals are empowered through ecstatic worship and joyful celebration. It is this combination of a disciplined lifestyle and joyous worship that may be one reason why Pentecostalism is growing so rapidly worldwide.

The Emergence of Progressive Pentecostalism

If our perception is correct that Progressive Pentecostalism is a movement that emerged primarily in the last decade or so, one might ask, "Why now?" Why was it not more evident in the early years of the Pentecostal Movement? Obviously this is a complex question, but I think the answer may have something to do with the emergence of a more educated and affluent middle class within Pentecostalism.

Renewal movements like Pentecostalism typically attract people who are marginalized from the dominant cultural institutions, and this was certainly true of the Azusa Street Revival and the global audience Pentecostalism attracted in the early years of the movement—which was primarily poor people, many of whom were from animistic backgrounds, especially in the developing world.[12] Pentecostalism prospered because it offered people hope for a better life in the next world; it provided mechanisms for casting out destructive demons that were distracting people from leading productive lives; it gave people a means of addressing their physical problems through the hope of supernatural healing; it provided women a social role and a sense of dignity they often lacked, as well as a means to reform their husband's abusive and irresponsible tendencies; and ecstatic worship opened up a bit of heaven here on earth. Hence, it is not surprising that Pentecostalism was attractive to the lower classes.

What happened, of course, is that commitment to the Pentecostal ethic tended to produce upward social mobility. Not everywhere and every time—it depended on whether the social context allowed for this to occur—but many

---

[11] See Max Weber, *The Protestant Ethic and the "Spirit" of Capitalism* (New York: Penguin, 2002).

[12] Cecil M. Robeck Jr., *The Azusa Street Mission and Revival: The Birth of the Global Pentecostal Movement* (Nashville: TN: Thomas Nelson, 2006). See also Grant Wacker, *Heaven Below: Early Pentecostals and American Culture* (Cambridge: Harvard UP, 2001).

Pentecostals ended up having a competitive advantage over their neighbors who tended to spend too much of their money on gambling, alcohol and other indulgences. So long as Pentecostals were poor, it made sense to have legalistic rules that proscribed what one could not otherwise afford. But wearing clothes that are intended to distinguish members from the rest of the world does not go down well with middle-class women who see nothing wrong with lipstick, jewelry and pants. Furthermore, hip Neo-Pentecostal churches began to attract increasing numbers of middle- and even upper-middle-class people.

Sectarian methods also don't make much sense when one is no longer a minority struggling for identity. In fact, in some places around the world, Pentecostals are becoming the majority population, or at least they have significant representation within society. When this occurs, the hope for transforming society, as opposed to fleeing from a corrupt and sinful world, becomes viable. Given this change in social status, middle-class Pentecostals began reading their Bibles in a more inclusive manner. Rather than simply focusing on the coming kingdom of God, the responsible Christian is one who binds up the wounds of those who are suffering, but also seeks to transform society.

In addition, educated Pentecostals started thinking in more complex ways, realizing that the mere application of Band-Aids to social problems may not be an adequate solution. For example, we did extensive interviews in a large Assemblies of God Church in Calcutta, India, very close to Mother Teresa's home for the dying. The church had an extensive noon-time feeding program that served several thousand people daily, but the leadership within the church increasingly realized they had created dependency that was not healthy for the long-term survival of people living on the street. Indeed, in a number of places we encountered Pentecostals who were rethinking their approach to humanitarian service.

For example, in Addis Ababa, Ethiopia, we did considerable interviewing in an extremely poor community where a Christian medical doctor with public health training had decided that she could treat symptoms of bad hygiene forever. So establishing a clinic was not the answer. Instead, she mobilized a group of "health evangelists" who regularly visited their neighbors and taught them proper hygiene. As a result, the incidence of infections and stomach disorders had dropped remarkably within a one-year period.

We found a similar perspective in nearby Nairobi. A well-meaning pastor had taken several abandoned street children into his own home, but then realized that it was much better to keep them in the community and teach them skills to survive on their own rather than put them into a hothouse environment that protected them from developing these coping skills. Hence, I fully expect Pentecostals to become increasingly sophisticated in their response to social issues as they become more aware of the underlying etiology of disease and poverty.

If Progressive Pentecostals were residing in first-world countries, they might simply pressure their government to care for the disenfranchised of society. Unfortunately, in many of the countries where we did our research, there simply are not adequate government resources to deal with the educational, medical and social welfare needs of people. Hence, rather than reform schools with 100 children per classroom, Pentecostal churches are establishing their own schools where they can maintain standards conducive to education. The formation of alternative institutions by Pentecostals is not simply a sectarian response; it is rooted in a recognition that this may be the best way to grow a new generation of people who can reform society.

The Future of Progressive Pentecostalism

A cynical interpretation of Progressive Pentecostalism is that it is simply a tool of capitalist ideology. Namely, it helps create sober, hardworking, honest employees who are pawns within a capitalist system. In countries where there are huge disparities between classes and castes, this may be an apt criticism. For example, we spent a considerable amount of time with Father Xavier in India who had been involved with the Charismatic Movement of Catholicism, but decided that it was ineffectual in helping low-caste people who politically are disenfranchised. His strategy currently is to organize poor and landless people to demand their rights, forcing the government to acknowledge their humanity. For him, liberation theology has much more to offer than does Pentecostalism, which he tends to see as escapist. As we shared dinner with him one evening and he made his case for a radical, if not revolutionary, political agenda, he was very compelling—especially as we were served a simple meal by his cook who appeared to have leprosy and yet was living in the same house with Father Xavier.

While Pentecostalism currently seems to lack a radical edge, it is conceivable that this might develop in the future. For example, while churches advocating the prosperity gospel seem subject to Marx's critique of religion being an opiate for the masses, it is also true that these churches are promoting this-worldly success, and once expectations have been raised regarding the possibility of a better life, it may be difficult to pacify them with off-the-shelf religious drugs. When their child is not healed, or they continue to live in grinding poverty after contributing financially beyond their means to the church, they may turn to political means to alleviate their suffering. The peasant class remains pacified only so long as its members have no hope. But what happens when their expectations are raised? It is possible that the growth of "health and wealth" churches may have an unintended social consequence that Marxist analysts would never have predicted.

Furthermore, some Pentecostal churches are laying a foundation for revolutionary action simply by teaching that everyone is made in the image of God. For example, we visited a Pentecostal congregation of indigenous people (Indians) in Guatemala where the pastor repeatedly stressed that people have political rights because they are all equal in God's sight. Once you are treated as "somebody," you begin to demand respect; you become less fearful; you are empowered to think about your circumstances in a different way. Hence, there may be revolutionary potential present in Pentecostalism, even though it is currently seldom expressed in overt political ways.

Concluding Reflections

In one of our interviews with a Latin American theologian, he quipped, "Liberation theology opted for the poor, and the poor opted for Pentecostalism." If this is the case, one has to raise the question of whether Pentecostalism is up to the task of dealing with the massive suffering that characterizes our world, especially in the Southern hemisphere. Will Pentecostal churches be able to move beyond moralizing to confront the AIDS crisis that exists, not only in their community, but within their own congregations? Who is going to house the increasing number of orphans and street children who are filling many urban centers in the developing world? Will Pentecostals have anything to say about the growing inequity that is occurring because of globalization? And what about the broad range of ecological crises that exist, especially in developing countries? Will Pentecostals simply pin their hopes on being transported to a heavenly kingdom, or will they become actors on the world stage by addressing issues that confront all of humanity?[13]

Pentecostalism has a number of assets that it can utilize in confronting these issues. First, it has a substantial population base from which to operate. The liability of this base, of course, is that it is deeply fractured along denominational and various theological, as well as personality, lines. Nevertheless, there seems to be an emerging body of theological writing that is sketching the basis for a Pentecostal social ethic.[14]

---

[13] For an excellent introduction to sophisticated Pentecostal theology, see Amos Yong, *The Spirit Poured Out on All Flesh: Pentecostalism and the Possibility of Global Theology* (Grand Rapids: Baker Academic, 2005).

[14] See Section III of Murray W. Dempster, Byron D. Klaus, and Douglas Petersen, eds., *The Globalization of Pentecostalism: A Religion Made to Travel* (Oxford: Regnum, 1999).

Secondly, Pentecostals have no shortage of vision. They believe God can do the impossible. From our observation, the major resource of Pentecostals is their life-transforming worship. Week by week and often day by day, individuals are renewed in worship by connecting with a transcendent source.

And, thirdly, Pentecostals are a remarkably creative group of people. If they can apply the same cutting-edge innovation to social ministry that they do to worship—especially the way it is done in many of the Neo-Pentecostal churches—then they have the potential to make a substantial contribution to ameliorating the social problems confronting our world.

My major worry, however, is that Pentecostals will formulate their social ministries around individualistic models that do not confront issues at a systemic or structural level. It is relatively easy to give someone a cup of cold water or to feed them a meal. It is more difficult to help them be self-sufficient, or tackle the causes of malnutrition or the spread of AIDS.

For answers to these issues, Pentecostals need to flip backwards in their Bibles to the teachings of the Hebrew prophets regarding justice and fairness. If one is going to pursue the whole gospel, then one needs to embrace the whole Bible. Love needs to be understood within the context of justice. And justice will inevitably involve confronting the issue of political and economic power.

20

The Azusa Street Revival and the Historic Churches

Thomas P. Rausch, S.J.

In the spring of 1967, Roman Catholics in the United States were startled to see reports of a number of instances in which their coreligionists had begun speaking in tongues and praising God like Pentecostal Christians. American Catholics, not generally known for affective expressions of their religious feelings, were breaking out in tongues, tears and cries of "Praise the Lord!" What was happening?

The Azusa Street Revival and the Pentecostal Renewal that flowed from it have undoubtedly had an impact on the so-called historic churches, both positive and at times controversial.[1] If it has changed the ways that many in those churches pray, it has also led to tensions that in some countries have yet to be fully resolved. Most importantly, it has brought both traditions into a somewhat tentative conversation with each other. Even these small steps will not be without lasting effects on the Pentecostal Movement itself.

---

[1] D.B. Barrett and T.M. Johnson break down the renewal into three waves: Pentecostal (mostly Classical Pentecostal), Charismatic (many in historic churches), and neo-Charismatic (many in new churches such as the African Instituted Churches); see "Global Statistics," in *The New International Dictionary of Pentecostal and Charismatic Movements,* ed. Stanley M. Burgess, with Eduard M. van der Maas (Grand Rapids: Zondervan, 2002) 284-302.

I'd like to address these questions from my own Roman Catholic perspective. We will consider first the impact of Pentecostalism on the Roman Catholic Church and other churches through the Charismatic Renewal. Second, we will examine some of the tensions between the two traditions. And finally, we will look at some of the challenges for the church's future coming out of the Catholic-Pentecostal Dialogue.

The Charismatic Renewal

What was to become the Charismatic Renewal in the United States and elsewhere first appeared in some mainline Protestant churches in the early '60s. The rector of St. Mark's Episcopal Church in Van Nuys, California, announced in April 1960, that he had experienced the transforming power of the Spirit and spoke in tongues.[2] In 1962, in Great Britain, a number of Church of England clergy and laypeople received the baptism in the Spirit. This neo-Pentecostal movement continued to grow, aided by the work of David du Plessis and the Full Gospel Business Men's Fellowship, spreading to Northern Ireland, New Zealand, Australia and South Africa by the end of the decade.[3] While some denominations were initially suspicious, most came to welcome charismatics in their midst (though the Missouri Synod Lutherans remained an exception).[4]

Gastón Espinosa traces the Catholic charismatic renewal movement back to a number of sources. One was the U.S.-based Catholic Charismatic Renewal, which began at Duquesne University in 1967. Another was a charismatic prayer group in Bogotá, Columbia, in 1967, and a third was the U.S.-based Charisma in Missions Catholic Evangelization Society, formed in 1972 in Los Angeles by two former Assemblies of God missionaries to Columbia, Glenn and Marilynn Kramer. Finally, he mentions various Latin American Roman Catholics who became Pentecostals and later returned to Catholicism.[5]

The most influential moment in the development of the Catholic Charismatic Renewal began in the autumn of 1966, when a number of lay faculty members at Duquesne University in Pittsburgh started meeting to discuss and pray over

---

[2] See Mary Jo Neitz, *Charisma and Community: A Study of Religious Commitment Within the Charismatic Renewal* (New Brunswick and Oxford [U.K.]: Transaction Books, 1987) 211.

[3] See Richard Quebedeaux, *The New Charismatics II* (San Francisco: Harper & Row, 1983) 67-72; also Kevin and Dorothy Ranaghan, eds., *As the Spirit Leads Us* (Paramus, NJ: Paulist, 1971).

[4] Neitz, *Charisma and Community,* 4, also 212-13; see also James Connelly, "Neo-Pentecostalism" (diss., University of Chicago, 1983).

[5] See Gastón Espinosa, "The Impact of Pluralism on Trends in Latin American and U.S. Latino Religions and Society," *Perspectivas*/Occasional Papers (Fall 2003) 16-18.

their lives as Christians. They read several books describing the Pentecostal experience, among them David Wilkerson's *The Cross and the Switchblade*,[6] and were attracted by the testimony to the Spirit's power among those in the Pentecostal Movement.

Knowing little about Pentecostalism, they decided to seek help from some friends, among them an Episcopal priest and a Presbyterian lay woman. Joining the woman's prayer group at the second meeting, two of them asked the others to pray over them for the baptism in the Holy Spirit. Almost immediately Ralph Keifer, an instructor in theology, began to pray in tongues. Two more received the gift a week later. In February, these faculty members joined a group of about 30 students on a retreat. During this "Duquesne Weekend," they experienced an outpouring of the Spirit that included the gift of tongues.

The movement spread rapidly. Keifer had already told some friends in South Bend, Indiana, about his interest in Pentecostalism. Two of them, Kevin and Dorothy Ranaghan, were initially skeptical. But after receiving a phone call from Kiefer after the Duquesne weekend, they were baptized in the Spirit while at a University of Notre Dame prayer group. A week later, they joined a group from the Pentecostal Full Gospel Businessmen's Fellowship, and a number of others received the gift of tongues.[7]

Shortly after this, the Notre Dame group joined a student group at Michigan State University, East Lansing, with similar results. These Catholic Pentecostals, or "Charismatics" as they were soon called, began holding a weekly prayer meeting at Notre Dame. As Catholics from across the country—priests, nuns, religious brothers, and lay religious educators—came to the university for its summer session, many of them became involved in the renewal and brought it back with them to their own churches and communities.

In the following years, Charismatic prayer groups sprang up across the country. The most common model was the weekly prayer meeting, often two hours or more in duration, with various manifestations of the charismatic gifts. There would be readings from Scripture, prophecies and testimonies, praying and singing in tongues, lengthy teachings, and prayer with the laying on of hands for healing or the baptism in the Spirit. In the '70s, many of the larger communities began organizing "covenant communities," groups that were committed to join together in "households" or living groups.

---

[6] David Wilkerson, *The Cross and the Switchblade* (Westwood, NJ: Spire, 1964).

[7] For a personal account, see Patti Gallagher, "Are You Ready?" 4-10; and Paul and Mary Ann Gray, "God Breaks In," 11-20, in *The Spirit and the Church: A Personal and Documentary Record of the Charismatic Renewal, and the Ways It Is Bursting to Life in the Catholic Church,* compiled by Ralph Martin (New York: Paulist, 1976).

In France, two signs of hope for the renewal of the Catholic Church are built on the Charismatic Renewal that flourished there in the '70s. One is the Alpha program, while the other is a communitarian movement (*les communautés nouvelles*) focused on evangelization, the praise of God, the Eucharist, and service of the disadvantaged.[8] At least five of these communities trace their roots to the Charismatic Renewal. Emmanuel (1972) and Chemin Neuf (1973) are urban communities now spread worldwide whose members gather regularly with a much larger group of associate members for prayer, teaching, and evangelization. Emmanuel has over 150 priests, two of whom are now bishops. Chemin Neuf is involved in ecumenism, retreats for couples, and ecumenical formation of the young.

The Communauté Beatitudes (1976, originally called Lion de Juda) and Verbe de Vie (1976) are mixed communities of families, priests, seminarians and other brothers and sisters consecrated to chastity. Beatitudes, with lay and religious members living together, now has 86 houses in five continents, including 37 in France. Fondacio (1974) is heavily involved in evangelization and training lay leaders. While stable in France, it continues to grow abroad—especially in Asia—and is in the process of receiving canonical recognition from the Vatican. Besides their ministries to the disadvantaged, these communities represent a strong force for evangelization in France and are a source of many of the vocations to the priesthood today. There are also many French Protestant Pentecostals who are effective evangelists; there were none before 1930; now there are some 200,000.[9]

It did not take long for the Charismatic Renewal to find official recognition within the Roman Catholic Church. The American Catholic bishops accepted it cautiously in 1969, but suggested that it should develop under the guidance of priests. Cardinal Leon-Joseph Suenens, one of the leading reformers at the Second Vatican Council, was among the first to embrace it. His work on behalf of the Renewal and ecumenism merited him the Templeton Prize in 1976, and he continued his work for the Renewal until his death in 1996. Pope Paul VI spoke to the International Conference on the Catholic Charismatic Renewal on May 19, 1975, encouraging their renewal efforts, and Pope John Paul II reaffirmed the importance of the Renewal in an address to a group of its international leaders on December 11, 1979.

Though often overlooked by scholars, the Catholic Charismatic Movement

---

[8] See Frédéric Lenoir, *Les Communautés Nouvelles: Interviews des Fondateurs* (Fayard, 1988).

[9] Agnieszka Tennant, "The French Reconnection: Europe's Most Secular Country Rediscovers Its Christian Roots," *Christianity Today*, Mar. 2005.

is one of the largest and fastest growing grass roots movements in both Latin America and the United States.[10] It is estimated that today more than 100 million Catholics participate in the renewal, and there are hundreds of Catholic charismatic communities around the world. Not a single unified movement, the Charismatic Renewal is a diverse collection of groups and activities that exists on diocesan, national or international levels. Some are officially recognized as private association of Christian faithful. Many are ecumenical communities, for the Charismatic Renewal is also present in other historic churches. For example, influenced by Charismatic Episcopalians and Catholics, the Charismatic Renewal had touched at least a million Lutherans by 1975. Though no longer a recognizable movement within American Lutheranism as it was in the '70s, many who continue to be active in the church were transformed by it. Something similar could be said for the millions of Catholics involved in the Renewal in the '70s but no longer part of the movement. The International Catholic Charismatic Renewal Services (ICCRS) is the principal coordinating organization for the Renewal and is under the Vatican's Pontifical Council on the Laity.

The Catholic Charismatic Renewal is a clear example of how Catholic piety and devotion has been not just enriched by its contact with Pentecostal Christianity; in many ways it has also been transformed. For example, in Latin America, many more traditional churches, "at first hostile to the movement, have gradually assimilated the liveliness of Pentecostal services."[11] In the words of one researcher, "other Christian churches have had to 'Pentecostalize' to survive the fierce competition of the new religious marketplace in Brazil."[12]

In the United States and elsewhere, many Catholics have learned a more demonstrative style of prayer from contact with Pentecostalism or through the Charismatic Renewal. They have learned to pray spontaneously, not just in their hearts but also aloud; to raise their hands, to use a more personal language in prayer and a more Biblical idiom, to pray over each other, to hold hands or embrace, and for some, to pray in tongues. For many it was a liberating experience.

Unresolved Tensions

In his book, *The New Christendom,* Philip Jenkins has referred to amazing

---

[10] Espinosa, "Impact of Pluralism," 15, 19.

[11] Guillermo Cook, "Protestant Mission and Evangelization," in *New Face of the Church in Latin America: Between Tradition and Change,* ed. Guillermo Cook (Maryknoll, NY: Orbis, 1994) 47; see also Espinosa, "Impact of Pluralism," 26, 43.

[12] R. Andrew Chesnut, *Born Again in Brazil: The Pentecostal Book and the Pathogens of Poverty* (New Brunswick: Rutgers UP, 1997) 3.

expansion of Pentecostal communities across the Southern hemisphere as a "new reformation."[13] Pentecostal Christians grew from 74 million in 1970, to an estimated 497 million by 1997, an increase of 670 percent.[14] In Latin America, Pentecostals constitute about 75 percent of non-Roman Catholic Christians. In Brazil, according to scholars such as Harvey Cox, there are more Pentecostals at church on any given Sunday morning than there are Catholics at Mass.[15] David Stoll estimates that by 2010, Protestants—mostly Pentecostals—will have surpassed 50 percent of the total population in countries such as Guatemala, Puerto Rico, El Salvador, Brazil, and Honduras.[16]

But Pentecostal growth, largely at the expense of the Catholic Church, has led to considerable tension between the two communities. They include differences about evangelization, the nature of the Church, the very diversity of the Pentecostal Movement in Latin America that embraces some anti-Catholic elements, and Catholic privilege.

One point of tension is the question of where evangelization ends and proselytism begins. It is estimated that some 8,000 to 10,000 Catholics leave their church each day to join Pentecostal churches.[17] Many Pentecostals aggressively seek converts from those Catholics they regard as nominal Christians who do not honor their baptism. At the same time, the Catholic Church in Latin America counts as Catholics the total number of persons baptized. The statistics suggest serious problems. While 85 percent of the continent's inhabitants call themselves Catholics, only 70 percent are baptized and only about 15 percent attend Sunday worship.[18]

One factor effecting Catholic losses is that the Catholic Church in Latin America, long secure in its cultural monopoly, until recently has not had a tradition of evangelization. Instead, it generally has waited "for nominal Catholics to come to them for assistance or spiritual support rather than actively recruiting

---

[13] Philip Jenkins, *The New Christendom: The Coming of Global Christianity* (Oxford: UP, 2002) 7.

[14] See Robert J. Schreiter, "The World Church and Its Mission: A Theological Perspective," *Proceedings of the Canon Law Society of America* 59 (1997): 49-50; also *World Christian Encyclopedia: A Comparative Survey of Churches and Religions in the Modern World*, ed. David B. Barrett, George T. Kurian, and Todd M. Johnson (Oxford/New York: Oxford UP, 2001).

[15] See Harvey Cox, *Fire From Heaven: The Rise of Pentecostal Spirituality and the Reshaping of Religion in the Twenty-first Century* (Reading, MA: Addison-Wesley, 1995) 168.

[16] David Stoll, *Is Latin America Turning Protestant? The Politics of Evangelical Growth* (Berkeley: U of California P, 1990) 8-9.

[17] See Brian H. Smith, *Religious Politics in Latin America: Pentecostal vs. Catholic* (Notre Dame, IN: U of Notre Dame P, 1998) 2.

[18] Renato Poblete, "The Catholic Church and Latin America's Pentecostals," *Origins* 27, no. 43 (1998): 718.

new members to their ranks."[19] Thus, David Martin contrasts an established, but no longer vital, Catholicism with Pentecostalism, along with Evangelical Christianity, which from a certain perspective "represents a first incursion of Christianity understood as a Biblically based and personally appropriated faith, propagated by a distinct body of committed believers."[20]

Renate Poblete, a Chilean Jesuit, notes that the 1988 meeting of the Latin American bishops at Santo Domingo acknowledged the superficiality of the Latin American Catholic Church's mode of evangelization. He attributes the effectiveness of the Pentecostals to their emphasis on a subjective experience of God, something long lost sight of in Western theology.[21]

Catholicism has responded in various ways to the changing conditions in Latin America, emphasizing a more engaged Catholicism through Catholic Action, the Charismatic Renewal, new types of popular music, liberation theology, and a new emphasis on evangelization. David Martin notes that liberation theology has not been as successful a competitor as might be expected, for in spite of its idealism, it retains a middle-class and foreign accent, particularly in terms of its leadership.[22] In the words of the national leader of the Baptists of Brazil, "The Catholic Church opted for the poor, but the poor opted for the Pentecostal churches."[23] The Charismatic Renewal has been very successful; "research indicates that there are actually more Latino Catholic Charismatics than Protestant Pentecostals in Latin America and in the U.S."[24]

Some Pentecostals remain suspicious about the Catholic understanding of evangelization. While both traditions "agree on the essential core of the gospel, namely that "in Christ God was reconciling the world to Himself" (see 2 Corinthians 5:19), on occasion they differ in practice and language concerning the emphasis they give to certain aspects of evangelization."[25] Pentecostals emphasize personal evangelism and a "crisis-type" of conversion; Catholics

---

[19] Smith, *Religious Politics in Latin America*, 76.

[20] David Martin, *Tongues of Fire: The Explosion of Protestantism in Latin America* (Oxford and Cambridge, MA: Blackwell, 1990) 289.

[21] Poblete, "The Church and Latin America's Pentecostals," 719-20.

[22] Martin, *Tongues of Fire*, 290. Guillermo Cook comments that liberation theology, once a movement with considerable promise, "is in danger of becoming a monument to aging theologians," in his *New Face of the Church in Latin America*, 270.

[23] Cited by Poblete, "Catholic Church and Latin America's Pentecostals," 720.

[24] Espinosa, "Impact of Pluralism," 16.

[25] See "Evangelization, Proselytism and Common Witness: The Report From the Fourth Phase of the International Dialogue 1990-1997 Between the Roman Catholic Church and Some Classical Pentecostal Churches and Leaders" (no. 15), in the Pontifical Council for Promoting Christian Unity's *Information Service* 97 (1998/I-II) 38-56.

also stress the need to evangelize cultures.[26] Furthermore, Catholics do not deny that the Spirit may be at work in other religions and that even those who don't know Christ but who seek God and with grace, strive to do God's will can be saved, while Pentecostals tend to be more pessimistic, seeing demonic elements in other religions.[27]

Different understandings of the nature of the church also contribute to tensions between the two communities. Catholics see the church as a visible, historical community with an unbroken succession in faith, sacraments, church order and authority. Pentecostals generally follow a restorationist ecclesiology that sees the church as having fallen under Constantine and later restored on the basis of the New Testament. In Kärkkäinen's words, they "have claimed continuity with the church in the New Testament by arguing for discontinuity with much of the historical church."[28] The real church is invisible, its unity spiritual rather than institutionally expressed.

In Latin American, many Pentecostals are reluctant to recognize Catholics as Christians, while some Catholics still have doubts about the ecclesial nature of the Pentecostal communities. The Vatican on occasion, and many Latin America bishops tend to refer to them as sects. Pope John Paul II caused considerable offense when in his remarks at the Fourth General Conference of Latin American Bishops (CELAM), held at Santo Domingo in 1992, he implicitly included the Pentecostals among the "sects" which he characterized as acting like "rapacious wolves," devouring Latin American Catholics and "causing division and discord" in Catholic communities.[29]

The very diversity of the Pentecostal Movement in Latin America often exacerbates tensions. Juan Sepúlveda acknowledges the "atomistic tendency" evidenced by Latin American Pentecostalism: "In virtually every country, numerous schisms have fractured the Pentecostal Movement. The causes of most of these divisions are to be found in the fragile nature of their ecclesial institutions, in internal power struggles, not to mention the divisions that have been engendered by doctrinal and ideological conflicts."[30]

---

[26] See Veli-Matti Kärkkäinen, "'Culture, Contextualization, and Conversion': Missiological Reflections From the Catholic-Pentecostal Dialogue (1990-1997)," *Journal of Asian Mission* 2, no. 2 (2000): 266.

[27] "Evangelization, Proselytism and Common Witness," nos. 20-21.

[28] Veli-Matti Kärkkäinen, "The Apostolicity of Free Churches: A Contradiction in Terms or an Ecumenical Breakthrough?" *Pro Ecclesia* 10, no. 4 (2001): 483.

[29] Edward L. Cleary, "Report From Santo Domingo—II: John Paul Cries 'Wolf': Misreading the Pentecostals," *Commonweal*, Nov. 20, 1992: 7.

[30] Juan Sepúlveda, "The Pentecostal Movement in Latin America," in Cook, *New Face of the Church in Latin America*, 70.

Some expressions of Pentecostalism are clearly anti-Catholic. For example, the "Universal Church of the Kingdom of God" (*La Ingreja Universal do Reino de Deus*—IURD), the largest denomination in Brazil after the Assemblies of God, caused enormous anger on the part of Catholics when one of its bishops in an attack on "idolatry" kicked and desecrated a statue of Our Lady of Aparecida, Brazil's patron, on Brazilian TV in 1995.

The IURD was founded in 1977 by Edir Macedo in Brazil. By the early '90s, it claimed over a million Brazilian members in some 1,000 churches and is now present in Europe, Southern Africa and the United States. Though generally considered as Pentecostal, some scholars classify it as Neo-Pentecostal because of its mix of classic and modern Pentecostal beliefs and practices, its emphasis on dramatic miracles and collective exorcisms (*libertação*), and its integration of elements of both sacred and secular culture.[31] It stresses being born again, baptism in the Spirit, miraculous healings, and praying in tongues. Heavily invested in radio and television stations, it preaches a radical prosperity gospel, while there is great pressure on its members to tithe. Its leaders, including Macedo, have been the objects of controversy; they have been accused of laundering money and pilfering church funds.

The IURD is not the only Pentecostal church that aggressively proselytizes Catholics and rebaptizes them. While this is not true of all Pentecostal denominations, it is too often the case, particularly in poorer countries. While finishing this essay, I heard complaints at an international meeting of Jesuit ecumenists in Ireland and during a seminar in the Philippines for pastoral workers from all over Asia about representatives of Pentecostal churches. A Jesuit colleague working in Guyana close to the border with Brazil said Pentecostals typically invite Catholic parishioners to common prayer services, only to attack their faith, using abusive rhetoric (all Catholics are going to hell, the pope is the anti-Christ) and "all sorts of inducements," including money and other gifts such as bicycles, to encourage conversion. Priests and pastoral workers from a number of Asian countries told similar stories.

Responsible Pentecostal spokesmen argue that the Catholic Church should not confuse mainstream Pentecostal communities with more extreme expressions, such as the IURD, that do correspond to sects. But the autonomous character of the Pentecostal Movement and its lack of a recognizable hierarchy or teaching office that might challenge or critique aberrant expressions or behavior, means that such sectarian movements remain under the Pentecostal umbrella. Because of this, it becomes much more difficult to convince many

---

[31] See Chesnut, *Born Again in Brazil*, 45-47.

Catholic Bishops in Latin America to regard more responsible Pentecostals as members of ecclesial communities.

At the same time, the strong state support for Catholicism in many Latin America countries, privileging the Roman Catholic Church at the expense of Pentecostal and other Protestant churches, is another source of tension. Catholic institutions or schools are often subsidized (Paraguay) or granted tax exempt status, while Protestant institutions are taxed (Nicaragua.) Public schools teach Catholic doctrine and morals (the Dominican Republic) or offer Catholic religion classes (Columbia and Chile), and national constitutions mention the special place of Catholicism (Bolivia). In Argentina and Chile, Catholic bishops have sought to have the state require legal registration requirements on all non-Catholic churches because of the growth of Pentecostal churches. A 1992 initiative to amend the constitution in Bolivia to separate church and state and recognize all denominations as equal before the law was opposed by the official newspaper of the Archdiocese of La Paz.[32] But the increasing religious pluralism in Latin America is leading to more calls for the separation of church and state and contributing to the disestablishment of Catholicism.[33]

The Beginnings of a Dialogue

If there have been tensions between the Catholic Church and Pentecostal communities, addressing them has not always been easy, especially from the Pentecostal side. And yet, what became the Roman Catholic-Pentecostal Dialogue was the initiative, not of the Catholic Church, but certain courageous and visionary Pentecostals, some of who have paid a heavy price for their efforts.

Particular credit goes to David du Plessis, a South African/American Pentecostal minister, who had long urged Pentecostals to include in their ecclesiastical associations those in the historic churches.[34] Originally a member of the Assemblies of God, he was an invited guest at the third session of Vatican II (1964) and attended the six assemblies of the WCC held during his lifetime, from Amsterdam (1948) to Vancouver (1983). In 1964, he was defrocked by his denomination because of his ecumenical activities (though he was restored in 1980).

---

[32] See Smith, *Religious Politics in Latin America* [1998] 60-63; also Espinosa, "Impact of Pluralism," 41-42.

[33] Espinosa, "Impact of Pluralism," 41-42.

[34] Jerry L. Sandidge, *Roman Catholic Pentecostal Dialogue [1977-1982]: A Study in Developing Ecumenism* (Frankfurt am Main: Peter Lang, 1987) 23; see also Cecil M. Robeck Jr., "Dialogue, Roman Catholic and Classical Pentecostal," in *The New International Dictionary of Pentecostal and Charismatic Movements,* ed. Stanley M. Burgess, with Eduard M. van der Maas (Grand Rapids: Zondervan, 2002) 575-82.

Jerry Sandidge, an Assemblies of God pastor, was another early member of the Dialogue who suffered for his involvement. Finding himself in Belgium, where he had been sent as a missionary in 1972, Sandidge decided to do a doctorate in theology at the Catholic University of Louvain. He was forced to choose between the Dialogue and his missionary appointment, deciding ultimately to leave Belgium. These are not the only examples of distinguished Pentecostals who have suffered from personal attacks by their coreligionists.

International Roman Catholic-Pentecostal Dialogue

The roots of the Catholic-Pentecostal Dialogue go back to a meeting of du Plessis with Cardinal Augustin Bea, prefect of the Vatican's Secretariat (now Pontifical Council) for Promoting Christian Unity in 1961. Bea invited him to the council's third session. In 1970, de Plessis wrote Bea's successor, Cardinal Willebrands, about beginning a dialogue. Some preliminary conversations established that the Dialogue was not to "concern itself with the problems of imminent structural union but with unity in prayer and common witness."[35]

In 1972, Willebrands authorized the first round of what would be known as the International Roman Catholic-Pentecostal Dialogue, with du Plessis and Kilian McDonnell, OSB, a Benedictine monk, as the cochairs.

So far, the Dialogue has gone through five, five-year sessions (each called a *quinquennium*).[36] It has addressed the following topics: fullness of life in the relation of baptism in the Holy Spirit to Christian initiation, the role of the charismatic gifts in the mystical tradition, the charismatic dimensions and structures of sacramental and ecclesial life, prayer and worship (1972-1976); speaking in tongues, faith and experience, hermeneutics, healing, tradition, the church as communion, ministry, and Mary (1977-1982); the church as koinonia, including the communion of saints, the Holy Spirit, church and sacrament, and baptism (1985-1989); evangelization, proselytism, and common witness (1990-1997); and conversion and Christian Initiation in the early church (1998-2002).

The 1997 statement, *Evangelization, Proselytism, and Common Witness*, points to the Reverend Billy Graham as a model whose evangelizing activity respects the ecclesial affiliation of those who take part in his campaigns (no. 96). Unethical proselytizing includes promoting one's own faith community in ways that are intellectually dishonest, idealizing one's own community at the expense of another; culpable ignorance of another Christian tradition; misrepresenting

---

[35] "Vatican Enters Dialogue on Pentecostalism," *New Covenant* 7, no. 1 (1972): 6-7.

[36] See Robeck, "Dialogue, Roman Catholic and Classical Pentecostal," 577-80; Sandidge, *Roman Catholic Pentecostal Dialogue [1977-1982]*.

their beliefs and practices; "Every form of force, coercion, compulsion, mockery or intimidation of a personal, psychological, physical, moral, social, economic, religious or political nature"; cajolery or manipulation, including exaggeration of Biblical promises; abuse of the mass media, and unwarranted judgments or acts that raise suspicions about the sincerity of others.[37]

Evaluation

The Roman Catholic-Pentecostal Dialogue is now over 30 years old. Its significance should not be underestimated. If the various forms of Pentecostalism are taken together with Roman Catholicism, the total number of adherents represent close to three-fourths of world Christianity today.[38] While many challenges remain between the two communities, much has been accomplished.

1. Dialogue between Pentecostals and other Christian communities shows that the Pentecostal Movement is playing an increasingly important role among Christian churches and traditions. In addition to the Roman Catholic-Pentecostal Dialogue, a dialogue between some Pentecostal leaders and the World Alliance of Reformed Churches (WARC) was established in 1995. Several Pentecostal denominations are full members of the World Council of Churches, and in 2000, a Joint Consultative Group was established with the WCC and Pentecostal representatives from nonmember churches.

2. Though the Catholic Church has supported the Dialogue with Pentecostals from the beginning, support from Pentecostal denominational leadership has generally been lacking. Unable to elicit any institutional support from the classical Pentecostal Movement, du Plessis appealed to Pentecostal friends and other Protestants involved in the charismatic renewal to make up the Pentecostal team for the first quinquinnum.[39] After the first session, a decision was made to invite only classical Pentecostals.

Some Pentecostal groups have supported the Dialogue (the Apostolic Faith Mission of South Africa, the International Evangelical Church, the International

---

[37] "Evangelization, Proselytism and Common Witness," no. 93; see also John C. Haughey, "The Ethics of Evangelization," in *Evangelizing America,* ed. Thomas P. Rausch (New York: Paulist, 2004) 152-71.

[38] Of the world's 2.1 billion, Roman Catholics number over a billion. Cecil M. Robeck Jr. estimates that the Pentecostal Movement represents some 25 percent of the world's Christians; see his "The Challenge Pentecostalism Poses to the Quest for Ecclesial Unity," in *Kirche in ökumenischer Perspektive: Kardinal Walter Kasper zum 70. Geburtstag,* ed. Peter Walter, Klaus Krämer, and George Augustin (Freiburg: Herder, 2003) 315.

[39] See Cecil M. Robeck Jr., "Introductory Note," in *Deepening Communion: International Ecumenical Documents With Roman Catholic Participation,* ed. William G. Rusch and Jeffrey Gros (Washington, D.C.: U.S. Catholic Conference, 1998) 364.

Church of the Foursquare Gospel, the Open Bible Standard Churches, the Pentecostal Assemblies of Canada, the Church of God of Prophecy, the Mission Iglesia Pentecostal in Chile). But others who asked not to be identified with it chose to treat it "with benign neglect," or in the case of the Assemblies of God, the largest and most influential Pentecostal denomination. Some members have worked tirelessly to end it, calling for the disciplining of AG participants.[40] Some Pentecostal Dialogue participants have to come to international meetings at their own expense.

While acknowledging the extreme suspicion Pentecostals direct toward any moves toward ecumenical understanding or cooperation, Cecil M. Robeck notes that the people are frequently more ecumenical than their leaders.[41] The new friendships between representatives of the two communities have already helped defuse misunderstandings and facilitate greater cooperation, from accusations of Catholic persecution of Pentecostals to conflicts over proselytism.[42]

3. Still the tensions that remain between the two communities make clear the importance of expanding the dialogue. The Pentecostal leadership generally remains reluctant to take its place in dialogue with the historic churches. In Latin America, many Pentecostals do not recognize Catholics as Christians, while some Latin American bishops continue to view Pentecostals as belonging to sects, as we have seen, despite the fact both Cardinal Edward Cassidy and Cardinal Walter Kasper, past and present presidents of the Pontifical Council for Promoting Christian Unity, have stated publicly that they are not to be treated as sects.[43]

Despite the hostility that so often exists between Latino Protestants and Catholics in the Americas, there are some indications of small, but growing, steps toward ecumenical cooperation in Latin America, particularly in making common cause for family values and human rights and against corruption and military dictatorships. There is even more ecumenical cooperation in the United States.[44]

4. Pentecostals present a theological challenge to the historic churches.[45]

---

[40] Robeck Jr. "Roman Catholic-Pentecostal Dialogue: Some Pentecostal Assumptions," *Journal of the European Pentecostal Theological Association* 21 (2001): 22.

[41] "Pentecostals/Charismatic Churches and Ecumenism: An Interview With Cecil M. Robeck Jr.," *The Pneuma Review* 6, no. 1 (2003): 28-29.

[42] See Kilian McDonnell, "Pentecostals and Catholics on Evangelism and Sheep-Stealing," *America* 180, no. 7 (1999): 11-14.

[43] See Edward Idris Cassidy, "Prolusio," *Information Service* 84 (1993/III-IV): 122.

[44] Espinosa, "The Impact of Pluralism," 38-39.

[45] See Robeck, "The Challenge Pentecostalism Poses," 306-20.

While their generally restorationist ecclesiology appears nontraditional to the historic churches, they are vital communities, transforming lives, stressing the charismatic and missionary dynamics of the first Christian communities. The fact that the Roman Catholic Church and the World Alliance of Reformed Churches are in official dialogue with Pentecostal representatives is evidence that there is a growing level of acceptance of their ecclesial reality by the historic churches. Roman Catholicism recognizes them as "ecclesial communities," that is, as communities of Christians, disciples of Jesus, consecrated by baptism, nourished by the Word, deeply committed to His mission, living in His Spirit, and rich in spiritual gifts and graces.[46]

But it is also true that taking their rightful place among the churches means that the Pentecostal churches will be challenged to a renewal of their own ecclesial lives and structures. Will they be able to move beyond their doctrine of spiritual unity in one invisible church and seek visible communion with other churches?[47] If they are to live in communion with Roman Catholics, will they respect the validity (thus the nonrepetition) of Roman Catholic baptism, refrain from aggressive proselytizing of Catholics, and enter into dialogue on those questions that continue to remain divisive?

The Roman Catholic/Pentecostal Dialogue has only begun to address the difficult ecclesiological differences on baptism, Eucharist, ministry and church order.[48] Robeck points to the "subject of tradition and the role of a teaching magisterium as two of those places, then, where Cardinal Kasper has rightly observed that the Dialogue may serve a constructive purpose by pressing the Pentecostal Movement to develop its own formal theological position."[49] But the fact that questions like these are even being raised in some Pentecostal circles means that David du Plessis's vision of a broader association of Pentecostals with the historic churches shows some signs of being realized.

---

[46] *Lumen Gentium* 15; *Unitatis Redintegratio* 3; see *The Documents of Vatican II*, ed. Walter M. Abbott (New York: Guild, 1966).

[47] Robeck notes that the tremendous growth of the Pentecostal Movement has "put pressure upon the classical understanding of the 'oneness' of the church. Instead of the Pentecostal Movement being a single denomination, even a single ecclesial reality that could be easily and fully integrated into the life of the one church, it had developed into as many as 30,000 separate denominations" ("The Challenge Pentecostalism Poses," 315).

[48] See "Perspectives on Koinonia, 1985 to 1980," in *Growth in Agreement II: Reports and Agreed Statements of Ecumenical Conversations on a World Level, 1982-1998*, ed. Jeffrey Gros, Harding Meyer, and William G. Rusch (Geneva: WCC Publications; Grand Rapids: Eerdmans 2000) 735-52.

[49] Robeck, "The Challenge Pentecostalism Poses," 314; see Walter Kasper, "Present Situation and Future of the Ecumenical Movement," *Information Service* 109 (2002/I-II) 13.

Divine Mandates of the Azusa Street Revival

1. Every person must have the opportunity to hear the gospel of Jesus Christ so that they may be reconciled to God and experience the love and joy of knowing Him. Thus, the church must be evangelistic and missionary in its vision, going into the entire world to make disciples (Acts 1:8; Romans 10:14, 15; Matthew 28:18-20).

2. Every Christian must serve to the fullest, the living God of Abraham, Isaac and Jacob, the Father of our Lord Jesus Christ (Romans 12:1, 2).

3. Every Christian must know that serving a Holy God requires that they also seek to live a life of holiness unto the Lord (1 Thessalonians 4:3; 5:23; Romans 6:11-14; 8:9; Hebrews 12:14). There is no substitute for the fruit of the Spirit (Galatians 5:22, 23). These are manifest in a willingness to contravene the popular culture when it is crucial to Christian identity.

4. All believers must be encouraged and given opportunity to encounter God through the Holy Spirit in such a way that the Spirit starts a transformation and empowers them for a life of service. The result of such a divine encounter will be an expression of the "Bible evidence" that this has taken place, and a life lived in the fullness of the Spirit (Acts 2:4). Markings of this journey include miracles, healings, dreams and visions, and charisms ranging from

prophecy and speaking in tongues to administration. Discernment exercised by faith communities emerge as a premium spiritual discipline.

5. Every Christian must recognize and accept the diverse nature of the church, and be willing to participate fully in the church that includes all people regardless of race, color, ethnicity, gender, class, previous condition of servitude, or level of education (Galatians 3:26-29). At times this will require resolve in the face of persecution and restrictive laws.

6. All Christians must seek to discern what contribution the Holy Spirit desires to make through them to the ongoing life of the church (1 Corinthians 12:7-11).

7. Every Christian who truly follows Christ must be willing to share the gospel with those whom God places in their path (Luke 9:23, 24; Romans 1:16, 17). Yet the clarion call is so urgent that it must be taken even to those on the "highways and hedges" (Luke 14:23). The shadow of the return of the Lord Jesus is visible to those who look for His appearing (Titus 2:13; 2 Peter 3:12).

8. Every Christian is encouraged to trust God for their healing and wholeness that comes through Christ Jesus, and to minister that healing and wholeness to others as the occasion arises (Jeremiah 32:27; Exodus 15:26; Matthew 8:16, 17; Mark 16:16, 17; James 5:14).

9. Even as Jesus came to preach good news to the poor, proclaim freedom to the prisoners, recovery of sight to the blind, release to those who are oppressed, and to proclaim the year of the Lord's favor, so every Christian is to follow His example in the power of the Holy Spirit. Both the spiritual and the literal interpretations of this mandate are to be wholly embraced (Luke 4:18, 19).

10. The Azusa Street Mission and Revival declared that it stood for "Christian unity everywhere." Every Christian must seek to maintain the health and unity of the whole church (Ephesians 4:3; 1 Corinthians 1:10-13; John 17:20-23).

www.ingramcontent.com/pod-product-compliance
Lightning Source LLC
Chambersburg PA
CBHW070010010526
44117CB00011B/1500